RETHINKING **Multicultural** EDUCATION

Teaching for racial and cultural justice

EDITED BY WAYNE AU

A RETHINKING SCHOOLS PUBLICATION

Rethinking Multicultural Education: Teaching for Racial and Cultural Justice
Edited by Wayne Au

A Rethinking Schools Publication

Rethinking Schools, Ltd., is a nonprofit educational publisher of books, book-lets, and a quarterly magazine on school reform, with a focus on issues of equity and social justice. To request additional copies of this book or a catalog of other publications, or to subscribe to *Rethinking Schools* magazine, contact:
Rethinking Schools
1001 East Keefe Avenue
Milwaukee, Wisconsin 53212
800-669-4192
www.rethinkingschools.org

© 2009 Rethinking Schools, Ltd.
First edition

Cover Design: Patrick Flynn
Cover Illustration: Jordin Isip
Managing Editor: Fred McKissack
Curriculum Editor: Bill Bigelow
Book Design: Kate Hawley
Proofreading: Jennifer Morales
Business Manager: Mike Trokan

Library of Congress Cataloging-in-Publication Data
Rethinking multicultural education : teaching for racial and cultural justice / edited by Wayne Au. -- 1st ed.
     p. cm.
  ISBN 978-0-942961-42-3 (pbk.)
  1. Multicultural education--United States. 2. Discrimination in education--United States. 3. Minorities--Education--United States. 4. Social justice--United States. I. Au, Wayne, 1972-
  LC1099.3.R494 2009
  370.1170973--dc22
              2009001983

Acknowledgments

All writing is a collective process, and none more so than with Rethinking Schools. This book would have not been possible without the collective efforts of many people. First I would like to thank *Rethinking Schools* managing editor Fred McKissack and curriculum editor Bill Bigelow. Without Fred's shepherding of this project and Bill's regular guidance, this book would not have gotten done. I would also like to thank Patrick JB Flynn for his wonderful art direction, Kate Hawley for the layout, and Jennifer Morales for the proofing. These folks provided the nuts-and-bolts of making this book happen. Mike Trokan, Amalia Oulahan, and Michaele Datsko also helped out along the way. Special thanks goes to all the artists who contributed images, but especially to Jordin Isip for making such a beautiful and moving cover. As always, the *Rethinking Schools* editorial collective provided tremendous support for this project. So continued thanks goes to Terry Burant, Linda Christensen, Kelley Dawson Salas, David Levine, Stan Karp, Larry Miller, Hyung Nam, Bob Peterson, Rita Tenorio, Stephanie Walters, and Kathy Williams. I also want to thank all the contributors for doing the important work they do, and for being willing to write about it. Finally, thanks to my wife and partner, Mira Shimabukuro, for always supporting me in my work.

— Wayne Au

127104

Contents

Rethinking Multicultural Education

By Wayne Au

Rethinking Multicultural Education: Teaching for Racial and Cultural Justice has been a long time coming. Over the last twenty-plus years of its existence, Rethinking Schools has published nearly 200 articles that dealt with issues of race and culture. Even though Rethinking Schools has always kept racial and cultural justice amongst our main focal points, we have never published a book that specifically addressed race and culture in education in their own right. This book is an attempt to do just that: provide a Rethinking Schools vision of anti-racist, social justice education that is both practical for teachers and sharp in analysis.

Jordin Isip

It is my hope that the selections included in *Rethinking Multicultural Education: Teaching for Racial and Cultural Justice* offer a more robust and powerful definition of multicultural education than we see so often used. For instance, some educators and teacher educators say they teach multicultural education, but do it under the guise of "global education." This form of multiculturalism feels safer to some because it uses the veneer international cultures to avoid more serious and painful realities of issues like racism. Similarly, "diversity education" and "cultural pluralism" get used with the singular intent of promoting heroes and holidays and "celebrating" individual differences, again circumventing issues of power and privilege.

The terms 'diverse students' and 'urban students,' have devolved into meaning 'poor, African American and Latino students' or 'students who aren't white.'

The terms "diverse students" and "urban students," two more stand-ins for "multicultural" students, have devolved into meaning "poor, African American and Latino students" or "students who aren't white." This is particularly ironic in some school districts in the United States, where schools that are 98 percent Latino, as they are, for instance, in Santa Ana, California, are regularly referred to as "diverse" by professors, teachers, and politicians alike. While certainly urban, Santa Ana schools are not diverse.

The right wing has also developed its own, sometimes-contradictory definitions of multicultural education. While some conservatives have vehemently attacked multicultural education as representative of the downfall of Western Civilization, others such as E.D. Hirsch (founder of the Core Knowledge curriculum) have developed a different definition of multicultural education. As Kristen Buras, professor of education at Emory University, talks about in her book *Rightist Multiculturalism*, Hirsch's Core Knowledge curriculum has recently taken up the banner of multicultural education by defining the United States as a multicultural nation of diverse immigrants—while simultaneously covering up systematic oppression based on class, race, and nation status.

Multicultural education is also being narrowly defined as a path students can take to "higher" status literature. Teachers use Tupac's lyrics to move students to Shakespeare; students can unpack hip hop lyrics as a way to learn literary language like stanza and rhyme, but they need to study Frost and Yeats to be considered well-read. Students in regular classes can read "thug" literature, but AP classes need to read the classics. (Does anyone read Morrison as a precursor to Chaucer? She's harder than *The Canterbury Tales*). This version of multicultural education focuses on access to the canon of high-status knowledge. In doing so, such a definition not only keeps the Eurocentric canon of knowledge at the heart of "real" education, it also communicates to students the idea that the diversity of their identities, lives, and communities does not really matter when it comes to learning.

Rethinking Multicultural Education is an attempt to reclaim multicultural education as part of a larger, more serious struggle for social justice, a struggle that recognizes the need to fight against systematic racism, colonization, and cultural oppression that takes place through our schools. In the chapters included here, multicultural education:

- is grounded in the lives of our students.

- draws on the voices and perspectives of those "being studied."

- teaches through dialogue.

- critically supports students' identities.

- embraces and recognizes the value of students' home languages.

- critiques school knowledge, knowledge that has historically been Eurocentric.

- invites students to engage in real social and political issues.

- creates classroom environments where students can meaningfully engage with each other.

- is rigorous, and recognizes that academic rigor is impossible without it.

- connects to the entire curriculum.

- is rooted in an anti-racist struggle about which knowledge and experiences should be included in the curriculum.

- celebrates social movements and the fight against nativism, xenophobia, and white supremacy.

- explores how social, economic, and cultural institutions contribute to inequality.

The chapters included in the section entitled "Anti-Racist Orientations" examine the importance of recognizing the role of race and culture in education in our schools today. Here, chapters focus on general anti-racist orientations that are important for teachers to carry into the classroom, on dispositions that take

Rethinking Multicultural Education is an attempt to reclaim multicultural education as part of a larger, more serious struggle for social justice.

justice seriously and examine privileges as they exist in practice. This exploration includes understanding the relationships between teaching, culture, and privilege, as well as recognizing the more historical and institutional inequalities that we see today.

Language is central to culture, and how we understand and treat language in our classrooms speaks to issues of power both inside and outside of education. The chapters in the section entitled "Language, Culture, and Power" look at the relationship between language and culture, finding connections between the cultural politics of Black English, bilingual education, and the cultural norms for communication, as well as address the ways in which we deal with culture and language in the classroom speak specifically to student identities.

"Transnational Identities, Multicultural Classrooms," includes chapters that look at what it means to be an anti-racist, social justice educator within the context of immigration, globalization, and colonization—where our students' identities are transnational, both rooted in the United States and not rooted in the United States. This section attempts to stretch our normal categories for students, many of whom are immigrants, and many of whom, while not immigrants themselves, hail from immigrant communities. The transnational, even globalized, identities of our students sometimes make issues of cultural identity relative to the U.S. and "home" countries mixed up and even contradictory, forcing educators to recognize the dynamic nature of cultures and communities.

The final section, "Confronting Race in the Classroom," provides concrete examples of anti-racist teaching at the elementary and secondary levels, in multiple grades and across multiple subject areas. Even though other chapters in other sections are clearly grounded in classroom practice, here the focus is on how elementary and secondary teachers have critically considered issues of race and culture into their curriculum—often times experiencing both success and difficulty in raising such important and complex issues.

In these times of high-stakes testing, the standards movement, shrinking budgets, and increased workloads, teachers are continuously being pushed to leave justice and equality behind. Instead they find themselves having to focus on test scores, pacing guides, and scripted instruction. But, as W.E.B. DuBois once said, "Education must keep broad ideals before it, and never forget that it is dealing with Souls and not with Dollars." Teaching for racial and cultural justice is one of those "broad ideals" that

> *In these times of high-stakes testing, the standards movement, shrinking budgets, and increased workloads, teachers are continuously being pushed to leave justice and equality behind.*

we can't lose sight of if we are to live up to our commitments to teach all children. *Rethinking Multicultural Education* is a tool for educators to address these ideals in their classrooms, to take a stand against the dollar-ization of education and *for* the souls of our students, communities, and world.

SECTION I

Anti-Racist Orientations

CHAPTER ONE

Taking Multicultural, Anti-Racist Education Seriously:

An interview with Enid Lee

Enid Lee is the director of Enidlee Consultants Inc., a Toronto-based consultancy dedicated to anti-racist education and organizational change. She has over 35 years' experience in the classroom and is the former supervisor of race/ethnic relations for the North York Board of Education in metropolitan Toronto. Her publications include Letters to Marcia: A Teacher's Guide to Anti-racist Education, *and* Beyond Heroes and Holidays: A Practical Guide to K–12, Anti-racist, Multicultural Education and Staff Development, *which she co-edited. She is currently a Visiting Scholar with Teaching for Change in Washington, D.C., and formerly held the same position at The New Teacher Center, University of California at Santa Cruz. She was interviewed by Barbara Miner.*

Enid Lee

What do you mean by a multicultural education?

The term "multicultural education" has a lot of different meanings. The term I use most often is "anti-racist education."

Multicultural or anti-racist education is fundamentally a perspective. It's a point of view that cuts across all subject areas, and addresses the histories and experiences of people who have been left out of the curriculum. Its purpose is to help us deal equitably with all the cultural and racial differences that you find in the human family. It's also a perspective that allows us to get at explanations for why things are the way they are in terms of power relationships, in terms of equality issues.

So when I say multicultural or anti-racist education, I am talking about equipping students, parents, and teachers with the tools needed to combat racism and ethnic discrimination, and to find ways to build a society that includes all people on an equal footing.

It also has to do with how the school is run in terms of who gets to be involved with decisions. It has to do with parents and how their voices are heard or not heard. It has to do with who gets hired in the school.

If you don't take multicultural education or anti-racist education seriously, you are actually promoting a monocultural or racist education. There is no neutral ground on this issue.

If you don't take multicultural education or anti-racist education seriously, you are actually promoting a monocultural or racist education.

Why do you use the term "anti-racist education" instead of "multicultural education"?

Partly because, in Canada, multicultural education often has come to mean something that is quite superficial: the dances, the dress, the dialect, the dinners. And it does so without focusing on what those expressions of culture mean: the values, the power relationships that shape the culture.

I also use the term anti-racist education because a lot of multicultural education hasn't looked at discrimination. It has the view, "People are different and isn't that nice," as opposed to looking at how some people's differences are looked upon as deficits and disadvantages. In anti-racist education, we attempt to look at—and change—those things in school and society that prevent some differences from being valued.

Oftentimes, whatever is white is treated as normal. So when teachers choose literature that they say will deal with a universal theme or story, like childhood, all the people in the stories are of European origin; it's basically white culture and civilization. That culture is different from others, but it doesn't get named as different. It gets named as normal.

Anti-racist education helps us move that European perspective over to the side to make room for other cultural perspectives that must be included.

What are some ways your perspective might manifest itself in a kindergarten classroom, for example?

It might manifest itself in something as basic as the kinds of toys and games that you select. If all the toys and games reflect the dominant culture and race and language, then that's what I call a monocultural classroom even if you have kids of different backgrounds in the class.

I have met some teachers who think that just because they have kids from different races and backgrounds, they have a multicultural classroom. Bodies of kids are not enough.

It also gets into issues such as what kind of pictures are up on the wall? What kinds of festivals are celebrated? What are the rules and expectations in the classroom in terms of what kinds of language are acceptable? What kinds of interactions are encouraged? How are the kids grouped? These are just some of the concrete ways in which a multicultural perspective affects a classroom.

How does one implement a multicultural or anti-racist education?

It usually happens in stages. Because there's a lot of resistance to change in schools, I don't think it's reasonable to expect to move straight from a monocultural school to a multiracial school.

First there is this surface stage in which people change a few expressions of culture in the school. They make welcome signs in several languages and have a variety of foods and festivals. My problem is not that they start there. My concern is that they often stop there. Instead, what they have to do is move very quickly and steadily to transform the entire curriculum. For example, when we say classical music, whose classical music are we talking about? European? Japanese? And what items are on the tests? Whose culture do they reflect? Who is getting equal access to knowledge in the school? Whose perspective is heard; whose is ignored?

The second stage is transitional and involves creating units of study. Teachers might develop a unit on Native Americans, or Native Canadians, or people of African background. And they have a whole unit that they study from one period to the next. But it's a separate unit and what remains intact is the main curriculum, the main menu. One of the ways to assess multicultural education in your school is to look at the school organization. Look at how

I have met some teachers who think that just because they have kids from different races and backgrounds, they have a multicultural classroom. Bodies of kids are not enough.

much time you spend on which subjects. When you are in the second stage you usually have a two- or three-week unit on a group of people or an area that's been omitted in the main curriculum.

You're moving into the next stage of structural change when you have elements of that unit integrated into existing units. Ultimately, what is at the center of the curriculum gets changed in its prominence. For example, civilizations. Instead of just talking about Western civilization, you begin to draw on what we need to know about India, Africa, China. We also begin to ask different questions about why and what we are doing. Whose interest is it in that we study what we study? Why is it that certain kinds of knowledge get hidden? In mathematics, instead of studying statistics with sports and weather numbers, why not look at employment in light of ethnicity?

Then there is the social change stage, when the curriculum helps lead to changes outside of the school. We actually go out and change the nature of the community we live in. For example, kids might become involved in how the media portray people, and start a letter-writing campaign about news that is negatively biased. Kids begin to see this as a responsibility that they have to change the world.

I think about a group of elementary school kids who wrote to the manager of the store about the kinds of games and dolls that they had. That's a long way from having some dinner and dances that represent an "exotic" form of life.

In essence, in anti-racist education we use knowledge to empower people and to change their lives.

> *In anti-racist education we use knowledge to empower people and to change their lives.*

Teachers have limited money to buy new materials. How can they begin to incorporate a multicultural education even if they don't have a lot of money?

We do need money and it is a pattern to underfund anti-racist initiatives so that they fail. We must push for funding for new resources because some of the information we have is downright inaccurate. But if you have a perspective, which is really a set of questions that you ask about your life, and you have the kids ask, then you can begin to fill in the gaps.

Columbus is a good example. It turns the whole story on its head when you have the children try to find out what the people who were on this continent might have been thinking and doing and feeling when they were being "discovered," tricked, robbed, and murdered. You might not have that information on hand, because that kind of knowledge is deliberately suppressed.

But if nothing else happens, at least you shift your teaching, to recognize the native peoples as human beings, to look at things from their view.

There are other things you can do without new resources. You can include, in a sensitive way, children's backgrounds and life experiences. One way is through interviews with parents and with community people, in which they can recount their own stories, especially their interactions with institutions like schools, hospitals, and employment agencies. These are things that often don't get heard.

I've seen schools inviting grandparents who can tell stories about their own lives, and these stories get to be part of the curriculum later in the year. It allows excluded people, it allows humanity back into the schools. One of the ways that discrimination works is that it treats some people's experiences, lives, and points of view as though they don't count, as though they are less valuable than other people's.

I know we need to look at materials. But we can also take some of the existing curriculum and ask kids questions about what is missing, and whose interest is being served when things are written in the way they are. Both teachers and students must alter that material.

How can a teacher who knows little about multiculturalism be expected to teach multiculturally?

I think the teachers need to have the time and encouragement to do some reading, and to see the necessity to do so. A lot has been written about multiculturalism. It's not like there's no information. If you want to get specific, a good place to start is back issues of the *Bulletin of the Council on Interracial Books for Children*.

You also have to look around at what people of color are saying about their lives, and draw from those sources. You can't truly teach this until you reeducate yourself from a multicultural perspective. But you can begin. It's an ongoing process.

Most of all, you have to get in touch with the fact that your current education has a cultural bias, that it is an exclusionary, racist bias, and that it needs to be purged. A lot of times people say, "I just need to learn more about those other groups." And I say, "No, you need to look at how the dominant culture and biases affect your view of nondominant groups in society." You don't have to fill your head with little details about what other cultural groups eat and dance. You need to take a look at your culture, what your idea of normal is, and realize it is quite limited and is in fact

I think the teachers need to have the time and encouragement to do some reading, and to see the necessity to do so.

just reflecting a particular experience. You have to realize that what you recognize as universal is, quite often, exclusionary. To be really universal, you must begin to learn what Africans, Asians, Latin Americans, the aboriginal peoples and all silenced groups of Americans have had to say about the topic.

How can one teach multiculturally without making white children feel guilty or threatened?

Perhaps a sense of being threatened or feeling guilty will occur. But I think it is possible to have kids move beyond that.

First of all, recognize that there have always been white people who have fought against racism and social injustice. White children can proudly identify with these people and join in that tradition of fighting for social justice.

Second, it is in their interest to be opening their minds and finding out how things really are. Otherwise, they will constantly have an incomplete picture of the human family.

The other thing is, if we don't make it clear that some people benefit from racism, then we are being dishonest. What we have to do is talk about how young people can use that from which they benefit to change the order of things so that more people will benefit.

If we say that we are all equally discriminated against on the basis of racism or sexism, that's not accurate. We don't need to be caught up in the guilt of our benefit, but should use our privilege to help change things.

I remember a teacher telling me last summer that after she listened to me on the issue of racism, she felt ashamed of who she was. And I remember wondering if her sense of self was founded on a sense of superiority. Because if that's true, then she is going to feel shaken. But if her sense of self is founded on working with people of different colors to change things, then there is no need to feel guilt or shame.

What are some things to look for in choosing good literature and resources?

I encourage people to look for the voice of people who are frequently silenced, people we haven't heard from: people of color, women, poor people, working-class people, people with disabilities, and gays and lesbians.

I also think that you look for materials that invite kids to seek explanations beyond the information that is before them, materials that give back to people the ideas they have developed,

I encourage people to look for the voice of people who are frequently silenced, people we haven't heard from.

the music they have composed, and all those things which have been stolen from them and attributed to other folks. Jazz and rap music are two examples that come to mind.

I encourage teachers to select materials that reflect people who are trying and have tried to change things to bring dignity to their lives, for example Africans helping other Africans in the face of famine and war. This gives students a sense of empowerment and some strategies for making a difference in their lives. I encourage them to select materials that visually give a sense of the variety in the world.

Teachers also need to avoid materials that blame the victims of racism and other "isms."

In particular, I encourage them to look for materials that are relevant. And relevance has two points: not only where you are, but also where you want to go. In all of this we need to ask what's the purpose, what are we trying to teach, what are we trying to develop?

What can school districts do to further multicultural education?

Many teachers will not change curriculum if they have no administrative support. Sometimes, making these changes can be scary. You can have parents on your back and kids who can be resentful. You can be told you are making the curriculum too political.

What we are talking about here is pretty radical; multicultural education is about challenging the status quo and the basis of power. You need administrative support to do that.

In the final analysis, multicultural or anti-racist education is about allowing educators to do the things they have wanted to do in the name of their profession: to broaden the horizons of the young people they teach, to give them skills to change a world in which the color of a person's skin defines their opportunities, where some human beings are treated as if they are just junior children.

Maybe teachers don't have this big vision all the time. But I think those are the things that a democratic society is supposed to be about.

Multicultural education is about challenging the status quo and the basis of power.

Origins of
Multiculturalism

By Christine Sleeter and Peter McLaren

Multicultural education can be traced historically to the Civil Rights Movement. African American scholars and educators, working in conjunction with the Civil Rights Movement as a whole, provided much of the leadership of multicultural education.

The term "multiethnic education" was used to bridge racial and ethnic groups: "multicultural education" broadened the umbrella to include gender and other forms of diversity. The term "culture" rather than "racism" was adopted mainly so that audiences of white educators would listen. As a result, however, many white educators have pulled multicultural education

IStockphoto

away from social struggles and redefined it to mean the celebration of ethnic foods and festivals; the field is sometimes criticized as having turned away from its initial critique of racism in education. It is important to locate multicultural education in the civil rights struggle for freedom, political power, and economic integration.

The late 1960s and early 1970s witnessed several other movements that have connected loosely with multicultural education. The women's movement gained strength and impacted schools with passage of Title IX in 1972. Although the women's movement has had a white middle-class orientation, there has been continued effort on the part of some workers to link struggles against racism with struggles against sexism. Bilingual education was advanced in the late 1950s by Cubans fleeing Castro's revolution. This was a relatively privileged minority. Since then Mexican Americans, Puerto Ricans, and Asian Americans have advanced bilingual education legislation, theory, and practice. The history and development of bilingual education is somewhat separate from that of multicultural education, although the two have grown in a mutually reinforcing symbiosis. Also during this time, ethnic studies and women's studies departments were established on some university campuses, providing a basis for contemporary debates about multiculturalism in higher education.

Multicultural education frames inequality in terms of institutionalized oppression.

Multicultural education frames inequality in terms of institutionalized oppression and reconfigures the families, and communities of oppressed groups as sources of strength. By the early 1980s, this formulation was turned on its head in the dominant discourse about education. Discussions about education were framed mainly in terms of how to enable the United States to maintain international supremacy in the Cold War and the "trade war." The early 1980s saw a wave of educational reform reports, beginning with the National Commission on Excellence in Education's *A Nation at Risk*. In this context, students of color, those from poverty areas, and those whose first language was not English were defined as "at risk" of failure, and their homes and communities were defined as culturally deprived and morally depraved.

Nevertheless, by 1985 demographic data reports were informing educators and the general public that people of color would become the majority during the 21st century and multicultural education received renewed attention. At the K-12 level, workshops on multicultural education became "in" again, with many teachers interpreting it to mean teaching supplementary lessons about "other" cultures. Multicultural educators had made some substantive changes in curricula, however, which led to fierce battles in states such as California and New York. In higher education, lively debates about the canon were met by conservative challenges against "political correctness." The roots of Western civilization were connected with Africa and Asia, a connection that was fiercely rejected by those who feared that the loss of European supremacy would mean loss of civilization.

However, as white teachers in K-12 classrooms developed "tourist" conceptions of multicultural education and as desegregated schools demanded children of color go far more than halfway to bring about integration, many educators of color grew disillusioned with the fading promises of the Civil Rights Movement and multiculturalism. At the center of the disillusionment has been the failure of white people and institutions to grapple substantively with our own racism at personal as well as systemic levels, concomitant with the escalated transfer of economic resources and the mobility of capital away from poor communities. Native American, African American, Chicano/a, Puerto Rican, and other communities of color responded with resurgent self-determination. [Native American] tribal schools and Afrocentric schools and programs are vibrant examples of this response. These efforts argue compellingly for the need to center oneself spiritually and culturally before one can connect meaningfully across cultural borders and illustrate the failure of white-controlled, multicultural schools to advance the interests and needs of communities of color.

At the center of the disillusionment has been the failure of white people and institutions to grapple substantively with our own racism at personal as well as systemic levels.

What Do We Need To Know Now?

By Asa G. Hilliard III

The following is condensed from a speech in the spring of 1999 to a conference on Race, Research and Education, held in Chicago at an African-American symposium sponsored by the Chicago Urban League and the Spencer Foundation.

Some say that the contemporary concept of "race" is grounded in Nazi Germany. Adolph Hitler was surely aware of the "race" matter and was the person who most clearly saw its full political potential. Scholar Max Weinreich quotes Hitler as admitting to an associate that "in the scientific sense, there is no such thing as race." But Hitler goes on to note that as a politician he needs a conception *"which enables the order which has hitherto existed on [a] historic basis to be abolished and an entirely new and*

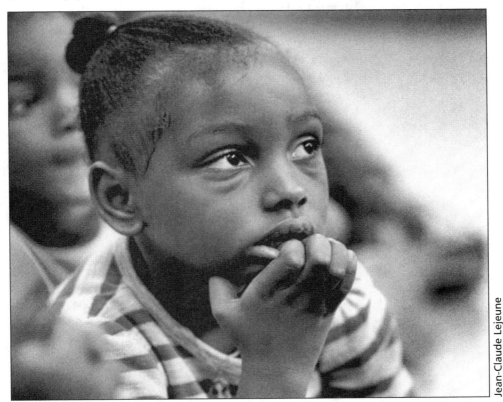

Jean-Claude Lejeune

anti-historical order enforced and given such an intellectual basis. ... With [the] conception of race, national socialism will carry its revolution abroad and recast the world." (Italics added.)

Hitler was very clear about "race" as a fabrication, as *anti-historical*, and as a tool of *political* power.

In preparing for this [speech] on race, education, and research, I found that it is premature to discuss research needs until the "race" dialogue is clarified. Otherwise, we could spin our wheels by using the same popular language, definitions, constructs, paradigms, and problem definitions that have been typical of past work.

Most important, we must tie together the issues of "race," identity, hegemony, and education. Fundamentally, the question of "race" is not a matter of skin color, anatomy, or phenotype, but a matter of the domination of one group of people by another. Any consideration of "race" is useless unless it also considers racism, white supremacy, and any other form of racial supremacy—and considers them as a hegemonic system. The real problem is hegemony, not "race!"

We must tie together the issues of 'race,' identity, hegemony, and education.

Naming Africans

During my lifetime, I have witnessed several transitions in the ethnic group name used by people of African ancestry. I was born during the time when it was popular to use "colored" when referring to African people. "Negro" was also used. During the 1960s, many people felt a major shift had been made when "black" became popular, with the predictable addition that the "b" in black be capitalized, just as the Spanish version of the word for black (negro), had gradually evolved to the status of capitalization. We even became "Black and proud," i.e. we made black a positive instead of a negative name.

These changes represented struggles within the African community to take control of our naming and self-definition from our oppressors, and to imbue our collective ethnic name with positive meaning. Yet we wrestled with the ascribed terms, "colored," "negro," and "black," as if we had no other choices.

Yet historically, "African" was often the preferred term, especially up until the early 1900s. The term was also used by some in the 1960s, following the publication of the book by Richard Moore, *The Name "Negro": Its Origin and Evil Use.* At a national conference in New Orleans led by the Rev. Jesse Jackson and Dr. Ramona Edlin Hodge, the name "African American" was advocated—followed by widespread acceptance of that designation within the African community. This happened even as many Europeans opposed the action, as if they had any right to enter dialogue about an African family matter.

In my opinion, few of us in the 1980s were prepared to deal properly with this matter of naming, because few of us were well-informed about the history of our people before our enslavement by Europeans. We did not understand our history as a whole and healthy ethnic people, as not merely a pigmented people. We did not understand how and why we were coerced by Europeans to change our ethnic names to names that caused us to become pre-occupied with aspects of our phenotype, mainly our skin color, hair texture, and facial features. The Europeans were looking for names that dehumanized and subordinated us, that contained us in our physical being, separating us from our minds, souls, and spirits. We did not understand how they, the authors of this specious system, were using their "race" construction in irrational and pseudoscientific but calculated political ways.

The names "colored," "negro," "black," "African," "African American," are more or less terms that have been accepted within the African family. My own strong preference is for African. Nationality and ethnicity are not always the same. The term "African" fits our actual historical, cultural, and even political circumstances more precisely than any other name. As Sterling Stuckey has shown, the Western experience has fused Africans from all over the diaspora into a new family that still shares the African root culture at the core, in the same way that diverse ethnic groups from Europe are tending toward a common European ethnic identity after having spent so many years believing that they had no ethnicity or that they were just Americans. The African continental name reflects that reality of a common cultural heritage and a common political need. Naturally, we recognize that the influences in the diaspora among other ethnic groups are reciprocal. We also recognize that cultural change in response to new environments will continue to happen.

Nationality and ethnicity are not always the same.

External to the African community, other terms have been used as euphemistic designators to refer primarily to people of African ancestry. Nonethnic terms, such as "minority," "the disadvantaged," "culturally deprived," "culturally disadvantaged," "inner-city," and "at-risk," are ascribed, fostering amorphous identities that detach Africans from time, space, and the flow of human history. Note that these terms emphasize numerical status, social class, and political status, e.g., how many we are, how wealthy we are, how powerful we are. But they do not denote ethnic identity;

they do not tell us who we are. In fact, these names apply easily, potentially, to any ethnic group.

Almost without exception, the group names ascribed by Europeans to Africans are adjectives, never proper nouns as names. Significantly, they are adjectives that suggest no respect for who we are or for our uniqueness as an ethnic family. In fact, they suggest nothing but something of minimal or even negative import. In the case of African people, this demeaning language was part of a strategy to commit "cultural genocide," a strategy to destroy ethnic family solidarity, a strategy to place emphasis on individual rather than family behavior, a strategy to confuse Africans about their ethnic identity, to destroy our consciousness. Why? As Dr. John Henrik Clarke has so often said, "It is impossible to continue to oppress a consciously historical people."

I do not believe that there can be a resolution of this matter of ethnic designation or group identity until the question of identity is situated in its historical, cultural, and socio-political context. We must understand how the idea of "race" emerged. We must also admit that the poison of "race" and hegemony, or white supremacy, is now a part of global ideology and structure. And our response to the problem ultimately must be to target ideology and structure, not merely everyday individual behavior.

The ideology of 'race' drives much of what happens in the world and in education.

The ideology of "race" drives much of what happens in the world and in education. It is like a computer software program that "runs in the background," invisible and inaudible. However, our silent and invisible "racial" software is not benign. It is linked to issues of power and hegemony, the domination of a given group by another. "Race" thinking has no reason for being except for the establishment of hegemony.

We must look beyond "race" as our criteria for identity. We need to ask questions such as: What was the historical nature of group identity when "race" was not in the picture? What is the normal basis for group identity in world history? What were the criteria for ethnic family identity prior to the invention of the race construct?

The History of "Race" and Hegemony

Color prejudice associated with white supremacy appears to be quite old, as old as several thousands of years ago in India, resulting in the dehumanizing caste system. However, "race" as a "scientific" construct or concept is quite recent. (By "race" I mean the allegedly scientific view that the human race can be divided into varieties distinguished by physical traits such as color, hair type, body shape, etc.) This concept of "race" is the product of Europe's colonization of Africa and other parts of the world, of its enslavement of Africans, and of the development of apartheid, segregation and the supporting ideology of white supremacy. Other ethnic groups such as Indians and Asians, indeed groups of color around the whole world, came under the umbrella of the construct of "race" and experienced the dehumanizing colonial treatment.

Hegemony was also at the root of the creation and adoption of the construct as it was applied to these other groups. Even European ethnic groups were divided into "races" and ranked, to establish domination of the "superior European race." In Germany the ultimate realization was the fabrication of the "Master Race."

It's important to realize that the concepts of race and racism are a Western idea. But it's more important to understand that, more specifically, race and racism are tools that Western civilization used to split and dominate the world. A society's racism is not defined by its degree of racial segregation or how racially prejudiced the population may be. These are manifestations of racism. The racism itself is the tendency of a society to degrade and do violence to people on the basis of race, and by whatever mediations may exist for this purpose.

Race and racism are tools that Western civilization used to split and dominate the world.

Ashley Montague, who has written extensively on the problem of the validity of the concept of "race," notes:

> The modern conception of 'race' owes its widespread diffusion to the white man. Wherever he has gone, he has carried it with him. ... This is not to say that discrimination against [personal] groups on the basis of skin color or difference did not exist in the ancient world; there is plenty of evidence that it did. But it is to say that such views never became the officially established doctrine, upon any large scale, of any ancient society. ...
>
> While the concept of race can be described as both an oversimplified theory and an outmoded methodological approach to the solution of a highly complex problem, it has become these things only for a small number of thinkers, and when the history of the concept of race finally comes to be written, it is unlikely that it will figure prominently, if at all, among the fruitful [ideas]. The probabilities are high that the concept will be afforded a status similar to that now occupied by the nonexistent substance known as "phlogiston."
>
> *Race is the phlogiston of our time.* (Montague, 1970 p. xii.)

According to Montague, phlogiston was a substance supposed to be present in all materials given off by burning. Phlogiston was advanced in the late 17th century by the chemist J. J. Beecher, and was accepted as a demonstrable reality by all intellectuals until the true nature of combustion was experimentally demonstrated by Lavoisier a hundred years later. It is an illuminating commentary on the obfuscating effect of erroneous ideas that Joseph Priestley, who stoutly defended the phlogiston theory all his life, was unable to perceive that he had discovered a new gas in 1774, which according to the (Fall) theory he thought to be "dephlogisticated air," but which Lavoisier correctly recognized and named "oxygen."

"Race" must also be situated in its global political context. As Mills notes:

> One could say that the Racial Contract creates a transnational white polity, a virtual community of people linked by their citizenship in Europe, at home and abroad (Europe Proper, the Colonial Greater Europe, and the "fragments" of Euro-America, Euro-Australia, etc.), and constituted an opposition to their indigenous subjects. ...
>
> Economic structures have been set in place, causal processes established, whose outcome is to pump wealth from one side of the globe to another, and which will continue to work largely independently of the ill will/good will, racist/anti-racist feelings of particular individuals. This globally color-coded distribution of wealth and poverty has been produced by the racial contract and in turn reinforces adherence to it in its signatories and beneficiaries.

Kotkin and Huntington make a similar point. They argue that while large parts of the world's population are becoming more diffused, a few ethnic groups rule the world, groups they refer to as "global tribes or civilizations." According to Kotkin and Huntington, these tribes or civilizations are able to dominate because they preserve a strong sense of ethnic identity. This is the basis of the trust within that permits collaboration in economic and political arenas.

Some scholars, I among them, argue that greed and/or fear are the elemental sources of the drive to dominate others. Scholars such as Hodge, Struckmann, and Trost further argue that the greedy and fearful actions lead to the creation of definitions, assumptions, and paradigms which are embedded in the belief system, which then dictates domination or hegemonic behavior. They write:

> A common Western notion, occasionally expressed, usually implied, is that Western culture is superior to

'Race' must also be situated in its global political context.

other cultures. Western culture is generally considered to be identical with 'civilization,' and the non-Western world is considered to be in varying states of development, moving toward civilization. "Primitive" and "uncivilized" are terms frequently used by Westerners to refer to people in cultures which are unlike the West.

That the people of a culture should view themselves as culturally superior is certainly common. But not so common is the feature contained in Western cultural thinking, that the superior should control the inferior. It is this kind of thinking which emphasizes the value placed on control, that produces the missionary imperialism. The notion of "white man's burden" is also derived from this type of thinking. Western control over non-Western people is thereby often considered morally defensible. (Hodge, Struckmann, and Trost, 1975, p. 3)

Changing Ethnicity to Phenotype

Prior to the 1700s, identity was fundamentally an ethnic identity based upon cultural traditions, linguistic traditions, historical traditions, and so forth. This does not mean that physical features or phenotypical diversity went unnoticed. It simply means that phenotype was not the core of ethnic identity!

"Race," or phenotypical diversity, did not become the core of ethnic identity, or more accurately, a substitute for ethnic identity, until there was a political necessity to make it so. Why? Because one of the most significant forces for the expansion of racism and white supremacy was the successful attempt by Europeans to shift the basis of group designation from its traditional cultural and ethnic base to an exclusively physiological one. They treated phenotype as if it were "race," and they treated "race" as if it were the primary explanatory factor in human social behavior.

What is the purpose of the use of this invalid construct of "race"? What are the consequences of the use of the construct? How is society structured to project and to legitimize the construct? These are the fundamental questions that we should be following with research.

Unfortunately, we have been following the detour of "race" rather than the ideology which propels it. Some of my most respected friends have made the study of "racial identity" a core of their academic work. Implicit in the study of "black racial identity" is the idea that "race" is real, that it is valid and meaningful, and that we should strive to have a "healthy 'racial' identity." Of course,

We have been following the detour of 'race' rather than the ideology which propels it.

when this work is conducted as an anti-hegemonic exercise, in other words to counter European defamation, I would be the first to defend it. I also suspect that these scholars tend to use "racial" categories as if they were ethnic categories.

However, I do not believe that the appropriate response to the use of invalid "racial categories" is to reify the categories by having the victims create a better use of the categories. I believe that the search for a "racial identity" leads us in the wrong direction. It is not a matter of research methodology, of assessment instruments, of educational theory. It is simply the wrong question! The right question is: "How do we restore a healthy ethnic identity?"

This does not mean that problems with respect to our perception of our phenotypical characteristics do not exist. The centuries of propaganda and defamation have definitely taken their toll. The continuing brisk sales of Nadinola and Porcelana skin lightening or bleaching creams in the United States and even in Africa itself tell us that something is wrong.

I believe that our goal should not be to search for "racial identity," but to decolonize our minds and purge them of images of white supremacy—and to restore the African family. This must include a move to restore our ethnic base and nurture a healthy ethnic identity. Then the question of our obvious phenotype will take care of itself.

We do not need an oppositional ethnic identity. We are not a "civil rights" people, even though we have fought to the death in heroic struggles for our rights. We do not exist merely because we are oppressed. The essence of our identity does not depend upon our oppressors. Who would we be if they did not exist? Our condition may find disproportionate numbers of us in poverty; however, our identity is not "the poor." Genuine identity is based upon collective culture and traditions, not on opposition to white supremacy, no matter how necessary that struggle is.

The essence of our identity does not depend upon our oppressors.

The Current Agenda in Education

Where does this bring us in terms of research and education? I believe that we must know the history, purposes, consequences, and structure of the racial paradigm. And we must dismantle that evil paradigm brick by brick. Then it is our obligation to go about the process of healing ourselves.

We cannot make ourselves whole merely by studying problems of "human relations," "stereotypes," "prejudice," "bigotry," and so forth. That vocabulary tends to trivialize the hegemony problem, to misdirect attention from the root problem. The real problem will never be remedied by capitalizing the word "black," making Africans the only group in the world's list of ethnic groups which is an adjective instead of a proper noun.

We need to do whatever is necessary so that our children and our people accept themselves, with all our magnificent phenotypes, as people of beauty. But to stop there is a gross mistake. To use phenotypical features as the essence of identity is literally to remove the bearer, or the bearer's ethnic family, from time and space, from the human historical and cultural process. That is the ultimate in dehumanization and cultural genocide.

Ethnicity implies history, culture, location, creativity. Color does not. To become pathologically preoccupied with phenotype, to the exclusion of an understanding of one's place in the cosmos, to an understanding of the evolution of the ethnic family, to creating stronger bonds among ethnic family members, will lead our people down the wrong path.

Ethnicity implies history, culture, location, creativity. Color does not.

After serious study and debate, the Harlem scholars led by Richard B. Moore concluded that we should be referred to as African Americans. They understood the cultural criteria for designating family membership. But it is the family that the hegemonic oppressor sought to destroy! They wanted to destroy any bond, any unity, any solidarity. It is family that the current systems of neo-white supremacy still seek to destroy. And, therefore, it is family and its preservation that is the issue, not phenotype. Family, independent and conscious, is the opposite of hegemonic victim.

The fundamental question, as I have stated elsewhere, for people of African ancestry, is: "To be African or not to be?"

In my work, I have looked at common elements in structures of domination throughout history. Specifically, dominating populations suppress the history of their victims, destroy the practice of the culture of their victims, prevent the victims from coming to understand themselves as a part of a cultural family, teach systematically the ideology of white supremacy, control the socialization process, control the accumulation of wealth, and perform segregation and apartheid.

It is very important to realize that these are matters of structure, and matters of systematic practices founded upon ideology. No attempt to remedy problems in education can occur apart from an understanding of these things. In fact, one of the reasons that we have been so unsuccessful in producing educational equity is that our understanding of the structure of hegemony was focused on a single element, that of segregation of "the races." This left the other elements largely untouched since they were not prominent in our understanding of segregation.

Race, Identity, and Hegemony in Education

Education, like "race," is situated in a context. There should be no need to go into great detail about the history of the education of Africans under slavery, colonization, apartheid, and white supremacy ideology. The record is clear. The treatment of Africans was not a matter of negligence or accident. It was not benign. Massive and strategic attempts were made to use educational structures to destroy "critical consciousness," to alienate Africans from tradition and from each other, to teach African inferiority and European superiority.

The treatment of Africans was not a matter of negligence or accident. It was not benign.

We have two major concerns. First, there is the need to access and to dismantle a tremendous array of aggressive negative beliefs, behaviors, and strategies. Second, there is the need to construct normal nurturing.

Appropriate research will contribute to our understanding of what is going on with race, hegemony, and education. Except for simple and overt factors, much of what we need to know is now "silent and invisible." Obviously, there are thousands of studies that could be done, producing interesting information, even useful information. However, I will limit myself here to examples of categories of needed research. The following brief list is suggestive only.

Abandoning the Race Construct. The continued use of the race construct is an issue. Racial comparisons, especially biological aspects, are prominent in educational research and in public policy. For example, I have pointed out to the American Psychological Association that our field of psychology is saturated with studies of racial comparisons in spite of the absence of construct validity for race. And yet there is a dearth of information on hegemony. For example, the words racism and white supremacy do not appear in the *Diagnostic and Statistical Manual of Mental Disorders* that defines mental illness, yet I believe they both belong there.

What might be the consequences if we continue to focus on "race" rather than hegemony?

Interestingly, the policy chapter in the popular *Bell Curve* book, which appears to seek to scientifically bolster the white supremacist view that the African "race" is genetically and intellectually inferior, speaks about those in the bottom 25 percent of IQ test scores as being "expendable." In the authors' own words:

What happens to the child of low intelligence who survives childhood and reaches adulthood trying to do his best to be a productive citizen? Out of the many problems we have just sketched this is the one we have chosen to italicize. All of the problems that these children experience will become worse rather than better as they grow older, for the labor market they will confront a few decades down the road is going to be much harder for them to cope with than the labor market is now. ... People in the bottom quartile of intelligence are becoming not just increasingly expendable in economic terms: they will sometime in the not-too-distant future become a net drag. In economic terms and barring a profound change in direction for our society, many people will be unable to perform that function so basic to human dignity: putting more into the world than they take out. ... For many people, there is nothing they can learn that will repay the cost of the teaching. (Murray and Herrnstein, 1994, pp. 519-520.)

Equitable Treatment. One of the most common errors in educational research is to operate on the assumption that when children fail to perform, the problem is with the child, the family, the community—in short the child or the child's nonschool environment. Furthermore, within the child's environment, we emphasize the problems of poverty, crime, gangs, and so forth. While these and other potent forces are important and may impact teaching and learning, it is also true that the school's treatment of the child is potent, and under some circumstances more potent than almost anything else. Therefore, we must have detailed and valid information about how the child is treated in school. These are intervening variables. Rarely do we control for them, especially in comparative studies involving "race."

The absence of sufficient studies on these factors within school foster the belief that African children tend to fail in school primarily because of internal and nonschool factors. This belief system is a part of the structure of domination.

Alien and/or Invalid Curriculum. African children are subjected to massive doses of misinformation and neglect in the school curriculum. Many of these messages are "silent and invisible." Studies must be done to reveal more precisely what goes on under the name of curriculum. Anthropologist Sheila Walker, for example, did a study of library holdings in the Oakland Unified School District. Her study showed vast gaps between the content offered about African people and what is true, valid, and important. We

African children are subjected to massive doses of misinformation and neglect in the school curriculum.

may also wish to do research on the beneficial effects on students when valid and affirming curriculum is offered.

Schools and African Academic Excellence Without Excuse. Few things are more important than to document that not only can all children learn, but that children are learning in many schools with ordinary teachers and no special programs. Yet most of these schools, or classes, are "silent and invisible." As a result, educators and policy makers become unsure about what we can "expect" from poor African children.

Tracking and 'special' services, in the main, label and stigmatize students, disproportionately by 'race,' with minimal to negative benefits.

The Effects of Special Treatment. The structure of services, such as special education, more often stratify students rather than benefit them. Tracking and "special" services, in the main, label and stigmatize students, disproportionately by "race," with minimal to negative benefits. We need many sophisticated studies on the alleged benefits of such services, especially when there is disproportionate impact by "race."

Culture as Context. The great error in behavioral research, now acknowledged by prestigious scholars, is that in most cases there has been a failure to take context into account. Research tends to proceed as if constructs, methods, instruments, and interpretations in culturally embedded studies are universal. Nothing could be further from the truth. Most researchers are ill-prepared to do research in a culturally plural environment or to deal with hegemony as it relates to culture.

So what needs to be done in terms of research and education? What do we need to know now?

We have an enormous task before us. We must forego our preoccupation with the false construct of "race" and focus instead on our African ethnic identity. We must support a healing process for damaged ethnic families. And we must focus the spotlight on hegemony so that we can take actions against it.

Scholarship is a double-edged sword. It can cut two ways, for good or for evil.

References and Selected Bibliography

Anderson, J.D. (1988). *The education of blacks in the South, 1860-1935.* Chapel Hill: The University of North Carolina Press.

Alba, R.D. (1990). *Ethnic identity: The transformation of white America.* New Haven: Yale University Press.

Ani, M. (1994). *Yurugu: An African centered critique of European thought and behavior.* New York: Africa World Press.

Barzun, J. (1965). *Race: A study in superstition.* New York: Harper Torchbooks.

Bell, D. (1992). *Faces at the bottom of the well: The permanence of racism.* New York: Basic Books.

Bell, D. (1973). *Race, racism and American law.* Boston: Little, Brown and Company.

Benedict, R. (1959). *Race, science and politics.* New York: Viking Press.

Ben Jochannan, Y. (1972). *Cultural genocide in the black and African studies curriculum.* New York: Alkebu-Lan.

Bernal, M. (1987). *Black Athena: The Afroasiatic roots of classical civilization: Volume I, The Fabrication of Ancient Greece 1785-1985,* Piscataway, NJ: Rutgers University Press. (See especially chapter 4, "Hostilities to Egypt in the 18th Century," pp. 189-223.)

Biddis, M.D. (1970). *Father of racist Ideology: The social and political thought of Count DeGobineau.* New York: Weybright and Talley.

Blauner, R. (1972). *Racial oppression in America.* New York: Harper and Rowe.

Carruthers, J. (1995). Science and oppression. In D. Azibo (ed.), *African psychology in historical perspective and related commentary.* Trenton, NJ: Africa World Press.

Chase, A. (1977). *The legacy of Malthus: The social costs of the new scientific racism.* New York: Alfred A. Knopf.

Crick, B. (1996). *Race: The history of an idea in the West.* Baltimore: Johns Hopkins University.

Cross, W., Parham, T., & Helms, J. (1998). Nigrescence revisited. In R. Jones (ed.). *Advances in black psychology.* Oakland, CA: Cobb and Henry.

Cruse, H. (1967). *The crisis of the Negro intellectual: From its origins to the present.* New York: Morrow.

Diop, C. A. (1955). *The African origin of civilization: Myth or reality.* Westport, CT: Lawrence-Hill and Co.

Edwards, L. (1997). *The power of ideas: The Heritage Foundation at 25 years.* Ottowa, IL: Jameson Books, Inc.

Erny, P. (1976). *Childhood and cosmos.* New York: Black Orpheus Press.

Erny, P. (1981). *The child and his environment in Black Africa.* New York: Oxford University Press.

Fairchild, H. H. (1991). Scientific racism: The cloak of objectivity. In *Journal of Social Issues,* 47(3), 101-115.

Fanon, F. (1967). *Black skin, white masks.* New York: Grove.

Felder, C.H. (1991). Race, racism and the Biblical narratives. In C.H. Felder (ed.), *Stony the road we trod: African American Biblical interpretation* (pp. 127-145). Minneapolis: Fortress Press.

Gould, S.J. (1981). *The mismeasure of man.* New York: Norton.

Greene, E. (1998). *Planet of the Apes as American myth: Race, politics, and popular culture.* Hanover: Wesleyan University Press.

Guthrie, R. (1998). *Even the rat was white.* New York: Harper and Row.

Hegel, G.W.F. (1991). *The philosophy of history.* New York: Prometheus Books.

Herrnstein, R. & Murray, C. (1994). *The bell curve: Intelligence and class structure in American life.* New York: The Free Press, 1994.

Hilliard III, A.G., Jenkins, Y., & Scott, M. (1979). *Behavioral criteria in research and the study of racism: Performing the jackal function. Technical reports I and II.* (Contract No. N00014-177-C0183). Washington, DC: Office of Naval Research.

Hilliard III, A.G. (1995). Either a paradigm shift or no mental measurement: The non-science and nonsense of *The Bell Curve*. *Psych Discourse*, 76(10), 6-20.

Hilliard III, A.G. (1990). Fabrication: The politics and sociology of knowledge in the study of ancient Kemet (Egypt) and Greek and Roman world. Paper presented at Temple University, Symposium on Martin Bernal's *Black Athena*, Department of African American Studies and Department of Classics. Philadelphia: Temple University.

Hilliard III, A.G. (1995). *The Maroon within us: Essays on African American community socialization*. Baltimore: Black Classic Press.

Hilliard III, A.G. (1998). *SBA: The reawakening of the African mind*. Gainesville, Florida: Makare Publishers.

Hilliard III, A.G. (1998). Psychology as political science and as a double-edged sword: Racism and counter-racism in psychology. *Psych Discourse*, 2(5&6).

Hilliard III, A.G. (1994). What good is this thing called intelligence and why bother to measure it? *The Journal of Black Psychology*, 20(4).

Hodge, J.L., Struckmann, D.K., & Trost, L.D. (1975). *Cultural bases of racism and group oppression: An examination of traditional "Western" concepts, values and institutional structures which support racism, sexism and elitism*. Berkeley: Two Riders Press.

Huntington, S. P. (1996). *The clash of civilizations and the remaking of world order*. New York: Simon & Schuster.

Jordan, W. (1968). *White over black: American attitudes toward the Negro, 1550-1812*. New York: W.W. Norton & Company, Inc.

Kly, Y. N. (1990). *International law and the black minority in the U.S.* Windsor, Canada: Clarity International.

Kotkin, J. (1993). *Tribes: How race, religion, and identity determine success in the new global economy*. New York: Random House.

Leary,W.E. (November 10, 1992). Exhibition examines scientists' complicity in Nazi-era atrocities." *The New York Times*. Medical Science Section, B-8.

Lewis, D. (1973). Anthropology and colonialism. *Current Anthropology*, 14(5), 581-602.

Lieberman, L., Hampton, R.E., Littlefield, A., & Hallead, G. (1992). Race in biology and anthropology: A study of college texts and professors. *Journal of Research in Science Teaching*, 29(3), 301-321.

Lutz, C. A. & Collins, J. L. (1993). *Reading national geographic*. Chicago: University of Chicago Press.

Maxwell, F.J. (1975). *Slavery and the Catholic Church: The history of Catholic teaching concerning the moral legitimacy of the institution of slavery*. Barry Rose Publishers.

Mills, C.W. (1997). *The racial contract*. Ithaca, NY: Cornell University Press.

Montague, A. (1970). *The concept of race*. London: Cathier Books.

Montague, A. (1968). *The concept of the primitive*. New York: The Free Press.

Montague, A. (1974). *Man's most dangerous myth: The fallacy of race*. New York: Oxford University Press.

Moore, R.B. (1960). *The name "Negro": Its origin and evil use*. Baltimore: Black Classic Press.

Muller-Hill, B. (1988). *Murderous science: Elimination by scientific selection of Jews, Gypsies and others, Germany 1933-1945.* New York: Oxford University Press.

Nunn, K.B. (1997). Law as a Eurocentric enterprise. *Law and Inequality Journal of Theory and Practice. IV*(2), 323-71.

Obenga, T. (1988). Who am I? In J. Carruther, H. Jacob, & L. Harris (eds.). *African world history project: The preliminary challenge* (pp. 31-46). Los Angeles: Association for the Study of Classical African Civilizations.

Osborne, N.G., & Feit, M.D. (1992). The use of race in medical research. *Journal of the American Medical Association.* 267(2), 275-279.

Patterson, W. L. (1970). *We charge genocide: The historic petition to the United Nations for relief from a crime of the United States Government against the Negro people.* New York: International Publishers.

Poliakov, L. (1974). *The Aryan myth: A history of racial and nationalistic ideas in Europe.* New York: Meridian.

Quigley, C. (1981). *The Anglo-American establishment: From Rhodes to Cliven.* New York: Books in Focus.

Schwartz, B.N. & Disch, R. (1970). *White racism: Its history, pathology and practice.* New York: Dell.

Selden, S. (1991). Selective traditions and the science curriculum: Eugenics and the biology textbook, 1914-1949. *Science Education,* 75(5), 493-512.

Spindler, G. & Spindler, L. (1998). Cultural politics of the white ethniclass in the mid-nineties." In Y. Zou & E.T. Trueba (eds.), *Ethnic identity and power: Cultural contexts of political action in school and society.* Albany: State University of New York Press.

Spivey, D. (1978). *Schooling for the new slavery: Black industrial education, 1868-1915.* Westport, CT: Greenwood.

Stuckey, S. (1987). *Slave culture: Nationalist theory and the foundations of black America.* New York: Oxford University Press.

Tatum, B.D. (1997). *"Why are all the black kids sitting together in the cafeteria?" and other conversations about race.* New York: Basic Books.

Thompson, A. (1998). Developing an African historiography in Carruthers. In H. Jacob & L. Harris (eds.), *African World History Project: The Preliminary Challenge.* Los Angeles: Association for the Study of Classical African Civilizations.

Tucker,W.H. (1994). *The science and politics of racial research.* Chicago: University of Illinois Press.

Van Dijk, T.A. (1993). *Elite discourse and racism. Sage series on race and ethnic relations* (vol. 6). London: Sage Publications.

Wa Thiong'o, N. (1987). *Decolonizing the mind: The politics of language in African literature.* London: Heinemann.

Walker, S., Spohn, C., & DeLonc, M. (1996). *The color of justice: Race, ethnicity and crime in America.* New York: Wadsworth Publishing Company.

Weinberg, M. (1977). *A chance to learn: The history of race and education in the United States.* New York: Cambridge University Press.

Weinreich, M. (1946). *Hitler's professors: The part of scholarship in Germany's crimes against the Jewish people.* New York: Yiddish Scientific Institute.

Welsing, F.C. (1991). *The Isis papers: The keys to the colors.* Chicago: Third World Press.

Willhelm, S. (1983). *Black in white America.* Cambridge: Schenkman.

Willhelm, S. (1971). *Who needs the Negro?* New York: Anchor.

Wobogo, V. (1995). *The prehistoric origins of white racism.* San Francisco: Unpublished manuscript.

Wynter, S. (1992). *Do not call us Negroes: How "multicultural" textbooks perpetuate racism.* San Francisco: Aspire.

Yee, A.H. (1983). Ethnicity and race: Psychological perspectives. *Educational Psychologist,* 18(1),14-24.

Zou, Y. & Trueba, E.T. (1998). *Ethnic identity and power: Cultural contexts of political action in school and society.* Albany: State University of New York Press.

CHAPTER FOUR

Diversity vs. White Privilege

An interview with Christine Sleeter

The following is condensed from an interview with Christine Sleeter, a professor ermerita at California State University—Monterey Bay and co-editor of Multicultural Education, Critical Pedagogy, and the Politics of Difference. *Sleeter was interviewed by Barbara Miner and Bob Peterson of* Rethinking Schools.

Q: You stress the importance of multicultural education as a struggle against white racism, rather than multiculturalism as a way to appreciate diversity. Why?

Both historically and in contemporary society, the relationships between racial and ethnic groups in this country are framed within a context of unequal power. People of European descent generally assume the power to claim the land, claim the resources,

Jean-Claude Lejeune

claim the language. They even claim the right to frame the culture and identity of who we are as Americans. That has been the case ever since Columbus landed on the North American continent.

Generally, people of European descent still claim white privileges. This is particularly true of wealthy people of European descent. I know a lot of poor people who, while they reap the benefits of looking white, are certainly disenfranchised in many ways.

I keep going back to the fact that multicultural education came out of the civil rights movement. It wasn't just about, "Let me get to know something about your food and I'll share some of my food." The primary issue was one of access to a quality education. If we're not dealing with questions of why access is continually important, and if we're not dealing with issues like why we have so much poverty amid so much wealth, we're not dealing with the core issues of multiculturalism.

I know it may sound trite, but the central issue remains one of justice.

I know it may sound trite, but the central issue remains one of justice.

Q. You talk a lot about white privilege. Why do you use that term and how do you explain it to white teachers?

If I do well at something, nobody is going to say, "You're a credit to your race." Saying that presumes that the race that the person is a member of ordinarily doesn't do very well.

Because I am white, nobody says that about me. Yet such statements frequently surround kids of color. People make assumptions about their intellectual ability, about their family support, simply on the basis of their skin color.

That's what I mean by reaping privileges of white racism, just on a personal level. At a more institutional level, I sometimes use this example.

My grandfather was a painter and wallpaper hanger who did fairly well in his life by buying property, renovating it, and then selling it. I grew up with the family story that he only had a 2nd-grade education and look how well he did. Yet he was buying property at a time in which property ownership was much easier for white people. As a part of New Deal legislation, Franklin Delano Roosevelt made a deal with southern senators that the money for low-cost federal subsidized housing loans would be made available to white families and not to families of color, because the southern senators wanted to keep African Americans working as sharecroppers.

Part of that New Deal legislation was specifically crafted so that people like my grandfather could buy property. I have inherited then, the benefits of that piece of systemic, historic white racism. Even today, I can walk into a real estate office and will more likely be shown places in "better" neighborhoods. I am also more likely to be given a better mortgage deal.

Those are examples of how white racism keeps reaping me benefits. Sometimes I am aware of it and sometimes I am not.

Q. A lot of white people resist using terms such as white racism, white supremacy, white privilege. How do you break through that defensiveness where they might argue, "I am where I am because I worked hard, not because I am white."

One tactic is to look at family stories and situate those stories in a historical context. Let's use my grandfather as an example again. My grandfather worked very hard and I can't say that he didn't. But I can't just individualize his success. I have to look at it in the historical context of who had access to what. This allows me to say that yes, my grandfather worked hard, but in a situation in which the doors were closed to people who may have worked equally hard but who were not white.

Q. A lot of teachers might respond, "That was 80 years ago. Today, we're in a colorblind society and it is illegal to discriminate on the basis of race. How can you say white privilege still exists?"

Often, I have my students go out and do mini-investigations in the community. Here's an exercise that helps. One of the investigations involves students pairing up—one white student and one student of color. Sometimes they've looked at places to rent and one will go in and then the other, and they later compare notes. I have a colleague who's done a similar exercise with the students applying for the same job. Sometimes my students will go shopping together—that seems to be a popular one—and they will compare their treatment by store clerks. With that one, inevitably they come back with biased differential treatment.

After these investigations, the students will try to interpret what happened. Students of color aren't surprised by the differing treatment, but the white students tend to be surprised. And some will say, "Well, that was just that store clerk, who was having a bad day."

If the white students are allowed to think of the differing treatment only in terms of one particular instance, they can still minimize and individualize the phenomenon. But in classes where I have been teaching about institutional racism, I'll have groups of students come in and report what they've found. If

If the white students are allowed to think of the differing treatment only in terms of one particular instance, they can still minimize and individualize the phenomenon.

eight of 10 students report incidents of racism, it becomes much harder to say that racism doesn't happen today. And when they report that data in conjunction with information I bring to class—statistical data about racism and home mortgages, and racism in educational tracking, and racism in racial profiling by police—it makes a powerful statement.

Q. Multicultural education is more than a self-help movement for racist whites. What does this have to do with schools and multicultural education?

Teachers will often frame multicultural education in terms of merely teaching about cultural differences. This is a sort of a stereotypical way that often happens. I remember talking with a kindergarten teacher who had this lesson around Thanksgiving about the Pilgrims and the Indians sitting down together at the first Thanksgiving. She wanted to use that as a tool for teaching about the cultures of indigenous people.

"But that isn't the story," I said. "From the perspective of indigenous people, the real story has been one of genocide and of taking land away. It's important for kids to understand that story. From the perspective of indigenous people today, what's important is reclaiming land, reclaiming sovereignty, rebuilding economies, reclaiming and rebuilding cultures that have been devastated. If kids today really want to understand relationships between whites and indigenous peoples, we need to understand that within an accurate historical context."

She responded, "Kids are too young for that." I disagree. I've seen teachers of young children teach a much more accurate version of history. I don't think kids are too young if you frame matters properly and in a way they can understand.

For example, I watched a combination 4th/5th-grade teacher teach a lesson about discrimination as part of a unit on immigration. She told the students that schools used to let only boys play sports, and asked the students if they thought that was fair. Of course the students said it wasn't and some of them giggled at what a silly idea that was.

Then she applied the same idea to the kind of discrimination that immigrants experienced historically. One of the ideas she taught was about the discrimination Asian immigrants experienced coming through Angel Island. Once students got the idea of what discrimination is, she then tried to help them understand that not everyone experienced the same discrimination all the time. She told me that helping students understand nuances was

Teachers will often frame multicultural education in terms of merely teaching about cultural differences.

difficult, as they tended to want to apply an idea uniformly to everyone, once they grasped it.

Q. You have written about the difference between psychological explanations of racism that focus on individual prejudice, and institutional racism that is manifested in social, economic, and political structures. Why is it important to move toward an understanding of institutional racism?

Let's look at a particular school issue such as tracking. As a teacher, if I am individualizing racism then I am going to be figuring out how to make myself a less prejudiced, more accepting person. I think it's very good for people to do that kind of work. But if that's the only thing, it can lead to a point where the person is saying, "Now I'm a good white. I've expunged myself of racism and I am accepting of all people."

But you can be a "good white" and still be in a school in which kids are being rank-ordered based on estimates of their learning ability and where lower tracks are predominantly kids of color and/or low income kids. So the tracking system becomes an example of institutional racism, a way of sorting kids on the basis of both race and social class. It's essential that multiculturalism address these institutional inequities.

Q. What if a teacher says, "I'm not sorting kids on the basis of race. I hate to say it, but some kids work harder and have more support at home.

If you go into classrooms that are taught at the different track levels, very often you will see qualitatively different kinds of instruction, and that tends to perpetuate tracking. I have seen schools which have eliminated the bottom track and the teachers have said, "My gosh, when you start expecting more out of the kids, the kids tend to rise to the level of expectation."

Let me give you a classic example.

In the city of Salinas, there were some 8th-grade kids who were not promoted to high school because they weren't achieving. The presumption was that they weren't ready to survive academically in high school.

These kids were aware that the system doesn't do a very good job of keeping track of where kids go, so they enrolled in the high school anyway. They cut back on some of the behavior that caused them to be noticed in the first place and kind of blended in. Halfway through the school year, some of their previous 8th-grade teachers asked, "Hey what happened to these kids, they're

The tracking system becomes an example of institutional racism, a way of sorting kids on the basis of both race and social class.

not still in the 8th-grade." And they discovered them in the high school, doing fine academically. The kids had the capability to learn well and they knew that if they went on to a more challenging environment, that they would do OK.

Oftentimes, we hold kids back by not expecting much out of them. I say that partly from having been a learning disabilities teacher in Seattle. I was trained to focus on what the kids couldn't do, rather than on what the kids could do. As I realized that the kids had a whole lot of capabilities that I wasn't aware of, my expectations went up markedly. My approach changed from trying to remediate what they didn't have to teaching to what they could do, which was actually quite considerable.

From that I started questioning the expectations we have for kids and how we teach to those expectations. The tracking system is built on presumptions about kids from low-income backgrounds and kids of color, that their parents don't care, that they have language deficits, that nobody is around to push them with their homework, that they lack a lot of those things. Then we build teaching around that presumption.

Q. Some white teachers say they are sensitive to students of color because they adopt a colorblind approach. They'll say, "I don't deal with this kid as a black kid, I see a kid. I treat everyone equally." How would you respond?

In a colorbind approach, there is a whole lot about a student that you are not seeing.

In a colorbind approach, there is a whole lot about a student that you are not seeing. For example, if you take a kid who is of Mexican descent and you say, "I don't see a Mexican kid, I just see a kid." you are preventing yourself from knowing something about that student's culture and community—and an important part of the student. Do you know much about where the kid's family came from? Do you know much about Mexican holidays and Mexican festivals that the kid may be participating in? Do you know much about church traditions or family celebrations that the kid is a part of? Do you know much about Mexican American literature and stories that the kid is learning at home?

If a teacher is insisting on being colorblind, then the teacher is putting herself in a position of saying, "I don't know about the kid's background, I don't believe that's really important, and I'm not going to learn about it."

Q. You have argued that one can educate white teachers to death but that in the long run it's more important to increase the number of teachers of color so that schools do not remain institutions dominated by white people. Why?

I argue this on the basis of several different things. First, if you look at research on who are the best teachers of kids of color, generally they have come from the kids' communities. The study that shows this extremely well is Gloria Ladson-Billings work, *The Dream-keepers: On Successful Teachers of African-American Kids.* That's one of my arguments.

The second piece of my argument involves my work as a teacher/educator over the last 25 years, of trying to prepare predominantly white groups of students to teach in culturally diverse schools. Even though I think there is a lot that can be done to educate white teachers, when I see where they start and where they finish by the end of their teacher training, most end up with a superficial understanding of the issues—unless they go into settings where people are continuing to extensively work with them. I do not want to populate urban schools with people who are coming in with superficial understandings of multicultural education and of progressive education.

The third thing I draw on is my experience working in multiracial groups of adults. At California State University–Monterey Bay, where I teach, half the faculty are faculty of color. The discussions we have, the issues that are brought to the table, the connections to the community, the breadth of wisdom that comes into the discussions—these are all qualitatively different than when I have worked with predominantly white groups of educators.

Q. You deal mostly with teacher education, where would-be teachers tend to have at least some support for multiculturalism. Do you have any advice for a classroom teacher concerned about anti-racist education but who knows they can't do all this by themselves—and may feel isolated in their school or district?

I tell people to join a network or organization in which there are people who will give them support. I also tell people to subscribe to *Rethinking Schools* so they won't feel like they're out there by themselves, and I give them the "Teaching for Change" catalog. I encourage them to join groups such as the National Association for Bilingual Education or the National Association for Multicultural Education. You need to also look around for local grassroots organizations, or local chapters of national groups. Feeling like you have to take on these issues all by yourself can be self-defeating.

Q. Some people argue that multicultural education is being undermined by standardized testing, which rewards

I do not want to populate urban schools with people who are coming in with superficial understandings of multicultural education and of progressive education.

superficial knowledge about conventional aspects of the curriculum. On the other hand, some community groups, particularly in communities of color, argue that we need much more accountability because obviously the schools have underserved their children. How might people committed to multicultural curriculum and academic equity balance those two perspectives?

That's a very important question. I don't advocate just simply throwing out testing. Testing that's used to guide instruction is extremely important. We need to monitor how kids are doing because kids of color and low-income white kids have been under-schooled historically. So I believe in testing to improve instruction.

With the extreme emphasis now on high-stakes testing, so much is getting lost in the process.

But I don't believe in testing to rank-order kids and schools, and to give some schools a lot of money while other schools get less. With the extreme emphasis now on high-stakes testing, so much is getting lost in the process. Teachers are telling me that due to the amount of testing, science is going by the wayside, social studies is going by the wayside—so there's a certain amount of devastation that's being done even to the traditional curriculum.

We're also defining what kids learn in ways that leave out important forms of knowledge. Just take the question of reading. In California, it's the English reading score that counts, even for kids whose first language is Spanish or any other language except English. They're not even thinking in terms of a child's reading ability, but only in terms of their ability to read in English. It's those kinds of issues that get lost in some of the discussion about raising test scores.

Q. In many urban areas, there is a lack of concern with segregation. How might that affect multicultural education, and what might be some strategies for moving forward?

School segregation is clearly linked to housing segregation. As long as housing segregation isn't actively on the agenda and we're only talking about school segregation, I don't know where you go with that. Back in the 1960s, we were addressing housing segregation. I don't hear much about that now.

There is nothing inherent in a predominantly black or pre-dominantly Latino school that makes it a bad school. The issue is access to resources. And that's clearly what is happening when you look at the resources gap between urban and suburban schools.

CHAPTER FIVE

The Forgotten History of Eugenics

By Alan Stoskopf

At the beginning of the 20th century, one of the most damaging experiments in public education began. Under the banner of educational reform, the American eugenics movement captured the hearts and minds of some of the nation's most influential educational researchers and policy makers. While the history of the eugenics movement has been virtually written out of American history textbooks, it nonetheless has had an insidious effect on the lives of students and the organization of public schools. It also has become part of an unexamined legacy that shadows today's standards and testing movement.

What was eugenics? The English mathematician Sir Francis Galton first coined the term in 1883. He wrote, "Eugenics is the

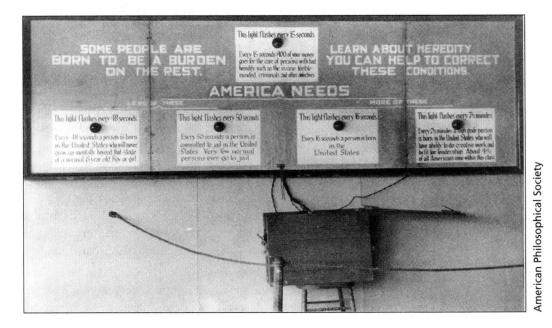

study of the agencies under social control that seek to improve or impair the racial qualities of future generations either physically or mentally."[1] What Galton saw as a new branch of scientific inquiry became a dogmatic prescription in the ranking and ordering of human worth. His ideas found their most receptive audience at the turn of the century in the United States.

Eugenics fed off of the fears of white middle- and upper-class Americans.

Eugenics fed off of the fears of white middle- and upper-class Americans. In the early 20th century, the United States was experiencing rapid social and economic change. As the nation became more industrial and urban, millions of poor immigrants from southern and eastern Europe flocked to the United States seeking a better life. Simultaneously, thousands of African Americans were beginning a great migration to northern cities from the Jim Crow South. Competition for jobs intensified existing frictions along class and racial lines.

Periodic economic recessions created further social unrest. Labor unions, civil rights groups, and the woman's suffrage movement pressed for greater equity. At the same time nativist and racist groups like the Ku Klux Klan pulled in the opposite direction. It was out of this cauldron of social upheaval that the American eugenics movement emerged. It promised prosperity and progress, not through strikes or ugly race riots, but through a new science that would combine advances in the field of genetics with the efficiency of the assembly line.

Eugenicists used a flawed and crude interpretation of Gregor Mendel's laws on heredity to argue that criminality, intelligence, and pauperism were passed down in families as simple dominant or recessive hereditary traits. Mainline eugenicists (those eugenicists who were explicitly preoccupied with issues of race), believed that some individuals and entire groups of people (such as Southern Europeans, Jews, Africans, and Latinos) were more predisposed to the "defective genes." Charles Davenport, a leader in American eugenics, argued for laws to control the spread of "inferior blood" into the general population. He told an international gathering of scholars "that the biological basis for such laws is doubtless an appreciation of the fact that negroes and other races carry traits that do not go well with our social organization."[2]

Davenport's wishes were partly realized. Eugenic advocates convinced 30 state legislatures to pass involuntary sterilization laws that targeted "defective strains" within the general population, such as the blind, deaf, epileptic, feebleminded, and paupers. On the national level, eugenic supporters played a decisive role in the congressional passage of the draconian Immigration and Restriction Act of 1924, which established blatantly racist quotas. President Calvin Coolidge embraced the eugenic assumptions behind the law when he declared, "America must be kept American. Biological laws show ... that Nordics deteriorate when mixed with other races."[3]

While those laws have been repealed, the impact of eugenics on public education was more enduring. Eugenic ideology worked its way into the educational reform movements of the 1910s and '20s, playing a key role in teacher training, curriculum development, and school organization. It also provided the guiding ideology behind the first IQ tests. Those tests were used to track students into separate and unequal education courses, establish the first gifted and talented programs, and promote the idea that educational standards could be measured through single-numbered scores. Eugenic ideas about the intellectual worth of students penetrated deeply into the fabric of American education.

Eugenics was a common feature in college curricula. Universities "offering courses in eugenics increased from 44 in 1914 to 376 in 1928."[4] An analysis of 41 high school biology textbooks used through the 1940s revealed that nearly 90 percent of them had sections on eugenics.[5] Major figures in education were attracted to eugenics and wrote books for teachers and the general public. Eugenics became a top-down model of "education reform" for these educators. A cadre of university experts trained in the latest testing methods and embracing eugenic principles believed they could make schooling a more efficient enterprise. Schools would be the place where students both learned basic eugenic principles and also were tracked into their future roles as dictated by their biological worth.

A sampling of influential textbooks used in colleges of education gives us a better sense of some of the eugenic visions of educational reform. Lewis Terman, Professor of Education at Stanford University and originator of the Stanford-Binet intelligence test, is remembered today as an early proponent of tracking. Not as well known is that his views on tracking and school organization were rooted in a eugenic conception of humanity.

Terman expressed these views in his textbook, *The Measurement of Intelligence* (1916). The book would be used for decades in teacher training. He wrote that:

> Among laboring men and servant girls there are thousands like them [feebleminded individuals]. They are the world's "hewers of wood and drawers of water." And yet, as far as intelligence is concerned, the tests have told

Eugenic ideology worked its way into the educational reform movements of the 1910s and '20s.

the truth. ... No amount of school instruction will ever make them intelligent voters or capable voters in the true sense of the word.

... The fact that one meets this type with such frequency among Indians, Mexicans, and negroes suggests quite forcibly that the whole question of racial differences in mental traits will have to be taken up anew and by experimental methods.

Children of this group should be segregated in special classes and be given instruction which is concrete and practical. They cannot master, but they can often be made efficient workers, able to look out for themselves. There is no possibility at present of convincing society that they should not be allowed to reproduce, although from a eugenic point of view they constitute a grave problem because of their unusually prolific breeding. (pp. 91-92)

Terman and other educational psychologists successively convinced many school districts to use high-stakes and culturally-biased tests to place "slow" students into special classes, rigid academic tracks, or entirely separate schools. The racist and class assumptions behind these recommendations were justified as scientifically sound because the "tests told the truth." IQ tests soon became the favorite eugenic tool for identifying "superior and inferior" students and then charting their educational destiny.

Today's gifted and talented programs had their origins in the eugenic use of IQ tests in the 1920s.

The tests were also seen as an instrument to identify students deserving special treatment. Today's gifted and talented programs had their origins in the eugenic use of IQ tests in the 1920s. Leta Hollingworth, a professor at Teachers College at Columbia University, was a founder and persuasive advocate of gifted and talented programs in schools. She and other educational leaders thought only the students from the right biological stock were capable of achieving high academic standards.

In *Gifted Children: Their Nature and Nurture* (1926), a book that is frequently cited by researchers of "gifted" programs today,[6] Hollingworth wrote:

One result recurs persistently wherever American children are tested by nationality of ancestors. American children of Italian parentage show a low average of intelligence. The selection of Italians received into this country has yielded very few gifted children. (p. 71)

[Eugenics would] ultimately reduce misery if the stupid, the criminal, and other mentally, physically, and morally deficient would refrain from reproduction. (p. 199)[7]

As with Terman, Hollingworth's ideas were not on the margins of educational thought. Eugenic themes proliferated in educational journals and textbooks from the 1910s through the 1930s. In particular, the popular belief took hold that IQ tests could label and accurately place students into academic tracks according to their inherited abilities. For example, an educational consultant for the San Jose school system recommended that the district use test scores to guide "children for their proper economic life activities in accordance with their abilities." The great majority of Mexican American school children in the district were to assume lower academic tracks because the tests supposedly revealed their inferior intellectual quality.[8]

We do not know all the ways eugenic notions affected public education. We do know that by the early 1920s, more than 2 million American school children were being tested primarily for academic tracking purposes.[9] At least some of the decisions to allocate resources and select students for academic or vocational courses were influenced by eugenic notions of student worth.

It is important to recognize that an active minority of educators, journalists, labor groups, and parents resisted these ideas. In particular, there were informed critiques by African American scholars such as W. E. B. DuBois, Horace Mann Bond, and Howard Long. They decried the use of these tests to rank racial groups. In "Intelligence Tests and Propaganda," Horace Mann Bond issued a warning about the misuse of IQ tests:

> But so long as any group of men attempts to use these tests as funds of information for the approximation of crude and inaccurate generalizations, so long must we continue to cry "Hold!" To compare the crowded millions of New York's East Side with the children of Morningside Heights [an upper-class neighborhood at the time] indeed involves a great contradiction; and to claim that the results of the tests given to such diverse groups, drawn from such varying strata of the social complex, are in any wise accurate, is to expose a fatuous sense of unfairness and lack of appreciation of the great environmental factors of modern urban life.[10]

Too few white Americans read these words. It was not until the 1960s that these early rebuttals were widely recognized as important contributions to the body of academic literature refuting racist and biologically determinist interpretations of IQ tests.

Bond's cautions also were not heeded by Richard Herrnstein and Charles Murray when they wrote the best-selling *The Bell*

It is important to recognize that an active minority of educators, journalists, labor groups, and parents resisted these ideas.

Curve in 1994. Many reviewers within the academic and lay communities have criticized the thinly veiled racism and the voluminous but misleading use of data found in the book. These tendencies were reminiscent of the eugenic advocates' interpretation of tests in the 1920s. Furthermore, Murray and Herrnstein rewrote history when they claimed that the eugenic use of tests was not used to draw any negative conclusions about immigrant groups in the country and played no role in the immigration hearings of 1924.[11] It has been this kind of denial of history that makes it all the more important to re-examine how standardized tests are being used in educational reform today.

Standardized tests can provide important diagnostic information for educators. Achieving standards of academic excellence through ongoing assessment of student work is a vital component of a young person's learning. However, too often, standards and assessment have become synonymous with top-down, externally mandated tests. Learning becomes reduced to test preparation and test taking. Test scores are often seen as proxies for intelligence or as the most important indicators of what students are learning. Quick judgments and quick fixes are the products of this kind of reform. And this phenomenon is not just a relic of the past.

Even if many supporters of high-stakes tests might recoil at the assumptions underlying the use of standardized tests earlier in the century, the consequences of this version of education reform might not be so different from the 1920s. This becomes even more apparent when performances are compared between poorer and more affluent school districts. Doing well on these tests is strongly correlated with income levels and only reconfirms the educational inequities that have characterized American education throughout the century. The academic tracking begun by "yesterday's" eugenicists is an institutional legacy we live with today. Education reform that is driven by high-stakes tests stands a good chance of entrenching that legacy.

The history of eugenics in American education needs to be examined in more depth and brought to bear on arguments supporting the use of high-stakes tests to raise academic standards in public schools. This history raises some challenging and disturbing questions for all of us today. What is the economic and political context in which the contemporary version of educational reform is being touted? What are the assumptions about student learning that fuel the current wave of testing? What are the effects of this testing on the lives of students and the educational climate

> *The academic tracking begun by 'yesterday's' eugenicists is an institutional legacy we live with today.*

of schools? How do these tests affect the equitable distribution of educational resources and opportunities between different school districts?

These questions need to be discussed with educational policy makers and representatives from diverse communities in open forums. Parents, students, and teachers have to be brought into these conversations. The eugenics movement is a reminder of what can happen when the assumptions and consequences of educational reform are not put to the test of real life experience.

For Further Reading

Selden S. (1999). *Inheriting shame: The story of eugenics in America.* New York: Teachers College Press.

Jacoby, R., & Glauberman, N. (eds.) (1995). *The Bell Curve debate: History, documents, opinions.* New York: Times Books, Random House.

Stoskopf, A., et al. (2001). Confronting the forgotten history of the American eugenics movement. Harvard/Facing History Project.

Endnotes

1. Galton, F. (1883). *Inquiries into human faculty and its development.* London: Macmillan.
2. Selden, S. (1977). Conservative ideology and curriculum. *Educational Theory*, 3, p. 218.
3. Coolidge, C. (1921). Whose country is this? *Good Housekeeping*, 72 (February), p. 14.
4. Cravens, H. (1978). *The triumph of evolution: American scientists and the heredity-environment controversy, 1900-1941.* Philadelphia: University of Pennsylvania Press. (p. 53).
5. Selden, S. (1999). *Inheriting shame: The story of eugenics in America.* New York: Teachers College Press. (p. 64).
6. ibid, p. 102.
7. ibid, p. 103.
8. Tyack, D. (1974). *The one best system: A history of American urban education.* Cambridge: Harvard University Press. (p. 213).
9. Glazer, S. (1993). Intelligence Testing. *CQ Researcher* (July 30), p. 660.
10. Bond, H.M. (1924). Intelligence tests and propaganda. *The Crisis*, 28, p. 64.
11. Herrnstein, R. & Murray, C. (1994). *The bell curve: Intelligence and class structure in American life.* New York: Free Press. (p. 5).

CHAPTER SIX

Standards and Tests Attack Multiculturalism

By Bill Bigelow

Proponents of "higher standards" and more testing promise that students will learn more and schools will finally be held "accountable." In practice, their reforms are hostile to good teaching and pose a special threat to multiculturalism.

The state where I teach, Oregon, joined the national testing craze well before No Child Left Behind became law. In the late '90s, the Oregon Department of Education gave a glimpse of the test mania to come when it field-tested its first-ever statewide social studies assessments. The tests were a multiple-choice maze that lurched about helter-skelter, seeking answers on World War I, Constitutional amendments, global climate, rivers in India, hypothetical population projections, Supreme Court decisions, and

Kathy Sloane

economic terminology. From a close reading of these tests, social studies knowledge is little more than the acquisition of disconnected facts about the world.

The version of standards pressed by "accountability" proponents threatens the development of a multicultural curriculum—one that describes and attempts to explain the world as it really exists; speaks to the diversity of our society and our students; and aims not only to teach important facts, but to develop citizens who can make the world safer and more just.

In a sense, the entire effort to create fixed standards violates the very essence of multiculturalism. Multiculturalism is a search, a "conversation among different voices," in the words of Henry Louis Gates, to discover perspectives that have been silenced in traditional scholastic narratives. Multiculturalism attempts to uncover "the histories and experiences of people who have been left out of the curriculum," as anti-racist educator Enid Lee emphasizes. Because multiculturalism is an undertaking that requires new scholarship and constant discussion, it necessarily is ongoing. Yet as researcher Harold Berlak points out, "standardization and centralization of curriculum testing is an effort to put an end to a cacophony of voices on what constitutes truth, knowledge and learning and what the young should be taught. It insists upon one set of answers." Curriculum standardization is, as Berlak indicates, a way to silence dissident voices, "a way to manufacture consent and cohesion."

Creating an official, government-approved social studies is bound to be controversial, whether at the national or state level. Thus, according to the Portland *Oregonian*, from the beginning, state education officials "tried to stake a neutral ground," in order to win approval for its version of social reality: "We have tried so hard to go right down the middle between what teachers want, what parents want and what the [Republican-dominated] Legislature wants," according to Dawn Billings, a Department of Education curriculum coordinator. Not surprisingly, this attempt to be "neutral" and inoffensive means that the standards lack a critical sensibility—an emphasis on conflict and diversity of interpretation—and tend towards a conservative "Father Knows Best" portrait of history and society. For example, one typical 10th grade benchmark calls for students to "Understand how the Constitution can be a vehicle for change and for resolving issues as well as a device for preserving values and principles of society."

Only? Is this how, say, Frederick Douglass or the Seminole leader, Osceola, would have seen the Constitution? Shouldn't

---

In a sense, the entire effort to create fixed standards violates the very essence of multiculturalism.

students also understand how the Constitution can be (and has been) a vehicle for preserving class and race stratification and for maintaining the privileges of dominant social groups? For example, in the 1857 *Dred Scott* case, the Supreme Court held that an enslaved person could not sue for his freedom because he was property, not a human being. Chief Justice Roger Taney declared that no black person in the United States had "any rights which the white man is bound to respect." The abolitionist William Lloyd Garrison called the Constitution an "agreement with Hell" for its support of slavery. And in 1896 the Supreme Court ruled in *Plessy v. Ferguson* that segregation—"separate but equal"—did not violate the 14th Amendment.

Almost 40 percent of the men who wrote the Constitution owned slaves, including George Washington and James Madison. In my U.S. history classes we look at the adoption of the Constitution from the standpoint of poor white farmers, enslaved African Americans, unemployed workers in urban areas, and other groups. Students create their own Constitution in a mock assembly, and then compare their document to the actual Constitution. They discover, for example, that the Constitution does not include the word "slave" or "enslaved person," but instead refers euphemistically to enslaved African Americans, as in Article 4, Section 2: "No person held in service or labor in one state, under the laws thereof, escaping into another, shall in consequence of any law or regulation therein, be discharged from service or labor, but shall be delivered up on claim of the party to whom such service or labor may be due." It's a vicious clause, that sits uncomfortably in the "preserving values and principles" rhetoric of Oregon's standards.

It is probably inevitable that school curricula will reflect the contradictions between a society's myths and realities. But while a critical multicultural approach attempts to examine these contradictions, standardization tends to paper them over. For example, another benchmark—"Explain how laws are developed and applied to provide order, set limits, protect basic rights, and promote the common good"—similarly fails the multicultural test. Whose order, whose basic rights, are protected by laws? Are all social groups included equally in the term "common good"? Between 1862 and 1890, laws in the United States gave 180,000,000 acres (an area the size of Texas and Oklahoma) to privately-owned railroad companies, but gave virtually no land to African Americans freed from slavery in the South. Viewing the Constitution and other U.S. laws through a multicultural lens

It is probably inevitable that school curricula will reflect the contradictions between a society's myths and realities. But while a critical multicultural approach attempts to examine these contradictions, standardization tends to paper them over.

would add texture and depth to the facile one-sidedness of Oregon's "neutral" standards.

Indeed the "R" word, racism, is not mentioned once in any of the seven Oregon 11th grade field tests nor in the social studies standards adopted by the state board of education. Even if the only yardstick were strict historical accuracy this would be a bizarre omission: the state was launched as a whites-only territory by the Oregon Donation Act and in racist wars of dispossession waged against indigenous peoples; the first constitution outlawed slavery but also forbade blacks from living in the state, a prohibition that remained on the books until 1926. Perhaps state education officials were concerned that introducing the concept of racism to students could call into question the essentially harmonious world of "change, and continuity over time" that underpins the standards project. Whatever the reason, there is no way that students can make sense of the world today without the idea of racism in their conceptual knapsack. If a key goal of multiculturalism is to account for how the past helped shape the present, and an important part of the present is social inequality, then standards and tests like those adopted in Oregon earn a failing grade.

Despite the publication of state social studies standards and benchmarks, throughout the country, teachers or parents don't really know what students are expected to learn until they see the tests. MetriTech, an out-of-state assessment corporation, developed Oregon's. As Prof. Wade W. Nelson points out in a delightfully frank *Phi Delta Kappan* article, "The Naked Truth About School Reform in Minnesota," "The content of the standards is found only in the tests used to assess them. Access to the tests themselves is carefully controlled, making it difficult to get a handle on what these standards are. It seems ironic to me that basic standards—that which every student is expected to know or be able to do—are revealed only in tests accessible only to test-makers and administrators. This design avoids much of the debate about what these standards ought to be"—a debate which is essential to the ongoing struggle for a multicultural curriculum.

It's when you look directly at the tests that their limitations and negative implications for multiculturalism become most clear. Test questions inevitably focus on discrete facts, but cannot address the deeper, multifaceted meaning of facts. For example, in the Oregon social studies field tests, one question asked which Constitutional Amendment gave women the right to vote. Students could know virtually nothing about the long struggle for women's rights and get this question right. On the other hand,

> *It's when you look directly at the tests that their limitations and negative implications for multiculturalism become most clear.*

they could know lots about the feminist movement and not recall that it was the 19th and not the 16th, 17th, or 18th Amendment (the other test choices) that gave women the right to vote.

Because there is no way to predict precisely which facts will be sought on state tests, teachers will feel pressured to turn courses into a "memory Olympics;" teachers won't be able to spend the time required to probe beneath the headlines of history. For example, in my U.S. history class at Franklin High School in Portland, students perform a role play on the 1848 Seneca Falls, N.Y., women's rights conference, the first formal U.S. gathering to demand greater equality for women. The original assembly was composed largely of middle to upper class white women. I wanted my students to appreciate the issues that these women addressed and their courage, but also to consider the limitations imposed by their race, class, and ethnicity. Thus in our simulated 1848 gathering, my students portrayed women who were not at the original conference—enslaved African Americans, Cherokee women who had been forcibly moved to Oklahoma on the Trail of Tears, Mexican women in the recently-conquered territory of New Mexico, poor white New England mill workers—as well as the white middle- and upper-class reformers like Elizabeth Cady Stanton and Lucretia Mott who were in attendance. In this more socially representative fictional assembly, students learned about the resolutions adopted at the original gathering and the conditions that motivated those, but they also saw first-hand how more privileged white women ignored other important issues such as treaty rights of Mexican women, sexual abuse of enslaved African Americans, and the workplace exploitation of poor white women, that a more diverse convention might have addressed.

The knowledge that my students acquired from this role play consisted not only of "facts"—although they learned plenty of these. They also exercised their multicultural social imaginations —listening for the voices that are often silenced in the traditional U.S. history narrative, becoming more alert to the importance of issues of race and class. However, this kind of teaching and learning takes time—time that could be ill-afforded in the fact-packing pedagogy required by multiple-choice tests. And after all their study, would my students have recalled whether it was the 16th, 17th, 18th, or 19th Amendment that gave women the right to vote? If not, they would have appeared ignorant about the struggle for women's rights.

In a demonstration of its own shaky grasp of the material on which it tests students, Oregon shows that the reverse is true as

Because there is no way to predict precisely which facts will be sought on state tests, teachers will feel pressured to turn courses into a 'memory Olympics;' teachers won't be able to spend the time required to probe beneath the headlines of history.

well: One can master isolated morsels of fact and remain ignorant about the issues that give those facts meaning. For example, in a test question repeated throughout the seven pilot tests, the state uses the term "Suffragette," an inappropriate and dismissive substitute for "Suffragist." Someone who had actually studied the movement would know this. As Sherna Gluck points out in her book, *From Parlor to Prison*, women in the suffrage movement considered this diminutive term "an insult when applied to them by most of the American press."

My Global Studies students spend the better part of a quarter reading, discussing, role-playing, and writing about the manifold consequences of European colonialism. They read excerpts from Okot p'Bitek's poignant book-length poem, *Song of Lawino* about the lingering psychological effects of colonialism in Uganda; role- play a trial on the colonial roots of the potato famine in Ireland; and examine how Asian economies were distorted to serve the needs of European ruling classes. But when confronted with Oregon's multiple-choice question that asks which continent was most thoroughly colonized in 1914, would my students answer correctly?

In a multicultural curriculum it's not so much facts as it is perspective that is important in nurturing a fuller understanding of society.

As these examples illustrate, in a multicultural curriculum it's not so much facts as it is perspective that is important in nurturing a fuller understanding of society. And sometimes considering new perspectives requires imagination as much as or more than memory of specific facts. For example, my history students read about the people Columbus encountered in 1492, the Taínos—who themselves left no written records—in excerpts from Columbus's journal and articles like José Barriero's "Taínos: Men of the Good." I ask students to write a story or diary entry from the point of view of a Taíno during the first few days or weeks of their encounter with Spaniards that draws on information in the readings, but goes further. It's necessarily a speculative undertaking, but invites students to turn the "Columbus discovers America" story on its head, encourages them to appreciate the humanity in the people usually marginalized in tales of "exploration." In response, students have written pieces of startling insight. Sure, a multiple-choice test can assess whether students know that Columbus first sailed in 1492, the names of his ships, where he landed, or the name of the people he encountered. But these tests are ill-equipped to assess what students truly *understand* about this encounter.

Necessarily, the "one best answer" approach vastly over-simplifies and misrepresents complex social processes—and entirely erases ethnicity and race as categories of analysis. One question on an Oregon social studies test reads: "In 1919, over 4.1 million Americans belonged to labor unions. By 1928, that number had dropped to 3.4 million. Which of the following best accounts for that drop?" It seems that the correct answer must be A.: "Wages increased dramatically, so workers didn't need unions." All the other answers are clearly wrong, but is this answer "correct"? Since when do workers leave unions when they win higher wages? Weren't mechanization and scientific management factors in undermining traditional craft unions? Did the post-World War I Red Scare, with systematic attacks on radical unions like the Industrial Workers of the World and deportations of foreign-born labor organizers affect union membership?

And how about the test's reductive category of "worker"? Shouldn't students be alert to how race, ethnicity, and gender were and are important factors in determining one's workplace experience, including union membership? For example, in 1919, professional strikebreakers, hired by steel corporations, were told to "stir up as much bad feeling as you possibly can between the Serbians and the Italians." And, as Howard Zinn points out in *A People's History of the United States*, more than 30,000 black workers, excluded from AFL unions, were brought in as strikebreakers. A multicultural awareness is vital if we're to arrive at a satisfactory answer to the above test question. But tests like these reward students for choosing a historical soundbite that is as shallow as it is wrong.

This leads me to an aspect of standardized tests that is especially offensive to teachers: they don't merely assess, they also instruct. The tests represent the authority of the state, implicitly telling students, "Just memorize the facts, kids. That's what social studies is all about—and if teachers do any more than that, they're wasting your time." Multiple-choice tests undermine teachers' efforts to construct a rigorous multicultural curriculum because they delegitimate that curriculum in students' eyes: If it were important it would be on the test.

At its core, multicultural teaching is an ethical, even political, enterprise. Its aim is not just to impart lots of interesting facts, to equip students to be proficient Trivial Pursuit players, but to help make the world a better place. It highlights injustice of all kinds— racial, gender, class, linguistic, ethnic, national, environmental— in order to make explanations and propose solutions. It recognizes our responsibility to fellow human beings and to the earth. It has heart and soul.

Multiple-choice tests undermine teachers' efforts to construct a rigorous multicultural curriculum because they delegitimate that curriculum in students' eyes: If it were important it would be on the test.

Compare that with the sterile fact-collecting orientation of Oregon's standards and assessments. For example, a typical 49-question high school field test includes seven questions on global climate, two on the location of rivers in India and Africa, and one on hypothetical world population projections in the year 2050. But not a single question in the test concerns the lives of people around the world, or environmental conditions—nothing about increasing poverty, the global AIDS epidemic, disappearance of the rainforests, rates of unemployment, global warming, etc., or efforts to address these crises. The test bounds aimlessly from one disjointed fact to another. In the most profound sense it's *pointless*.

Indeed the test's random amorality may reveal another of its cultural biases. Oregon's standards and assessments make no distinction between knowledge and information. The state's version of social education would appear to have no *raison d'être* beyond the acquisition of large quantities of data. But for many cultures, the aim of knowledge is not bulk, but wisdom—insight into meaningful aspects about the nature of life. Writing in the Winter 1998-99 issue of *Rethinking Schools*, Peter Kiang makes a similar point about the Massachusetts Teacher Test that calls into question the validity of enterprises such as these. He writes that:

> by constructing a test based on a sequence of isolated, decontextualized questions that have no relationship to each other, the underlying epistemology embedded in the test design has a Western-cultural bias, even if individual questions include or represent "multicultural" content. Articulating and assessing a knowledge base requires examining not only what one knows, but also how one knows.

Students "know" in different ways, and these differences are often cultural. Standardized social studies tests nonetheless subject all students to an abstract data-heavy assessment device that does not gauge what or how they have learned. As Kiang points out, test-makers address multicultural criticism by including individual questions about multicultural content—for example, by highlighting snippets of information about famous people of color like Martin Luther King Jr., Cesar Chavez, and Harriet Tubman. But these "heroes and holidays" additions cannot mask the fundamental hostility to multicultural education shown by standards and assessments like those initiated by Oregon.

Spelling out an alternative to culturally biased, superficial "accountability" plans would require another article. In brief, I want the states to abandon the effort to treat teachers as cogs in a

Students 'know' in different ways, and these differences are often cultural. Standardized social studies tests nonetheless subject all students to an abstract data-heavy assessment device that does not gauge what or how they have learned.

delivery system of approved social information. I want departments of education to support me and other teachers as we collaborate to create curriculum that deals forthrightly with social problems, that fights racism and social injustice. I want them to support teachers as we construct rigorous performance standards for students that promote deep thinking about the nature of our society. I want them to acknowledge the legitimacy of a multicultural curriculum of critical questions, complexity, multiple perspectives and social imagination. I want them to acknowledge that wisdom is more than information—that the world can't be chopped up into multiple-choice questions, and that you can't bubble-in the truth with a number two pencil.

You can't bubble-in the truth with a number two pencil.

CHAPTER
SEVEN

Race and the Achievement Gap

By Harold Berlak

That there is a race gap in educational achievement is not news. Large numbers of the nation's children leave school, with and without high school diplomas, barely able to read, write, and do simple math. But the failures of the schools are not evenly distributed. They fall disproportionately on students of color.[1]

Even when parents' income and wealth is comparable, African Americans, Native Americans, Latinos, and immigrants for whom English is not a first language lag behind English-speaking, native born, white students. The evidence for the gap has been documented repeatedly by the usual measures. These include drop-out rates, relative numbers of students who take Advanced Placement

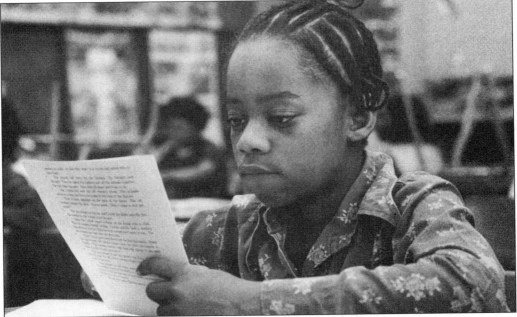

Jean-Claude Lejeune

examinations, who are enrolled in the top academic and "gifted" classes and/or admitted to higher-status secondary schools, colleges, graduate, and professional programs. And last but certainly not least, are the discrepancies in scores on standardized tests of academic achievement, on which teachers' and students' fates so heavily depend.

How is this achievement gap to be explained? This essay focuses first on the general question and then separately on the statistical gap in standardized test scores. It then discusses the crucial distinction between academic performance and academic achievement as measured by standardized tests. Though often spoken of as though they are one, they are clearly different. The failure to separate out the difference clouds and confounds educational and policy issues and misleads us in efforts to explain and eradicate the race gap in academic performance.

Explanations Over the Years

Over the years, the major reasons given for the claimed superior attainments of whites in cultural, artistic, and academic endeavors were overtly racist.

Over the years, the major reasons given for the claimed superior attainments of whites in cultural, artistic, and academic endeavors were overtly racist. It was said that the explanation lay in the superior genes of white northern European, Anglo-Americans. As the social sciences developed in the latter years of the 19th and the 20th centuries, "scientific" tracts defending white supremacy appeared with regularity. By the 1930s, the eugenics movement (which posited a biological basis for the superiority of whites) managed to gain a foothold in North American universities. And, it is relevant to add, all the leaders of this overtly racist movement were the leaders of the newly emerging field of scientific mental measurement. Many were the same men who testified before Congress in the early 1920s and lent scientific credence to the racist immigration exclusion acts which barred or greatly restricted immigration from Asia, Latin America, and southern and eastern Europe. The eugenics movement was considered a respectable academic discipline until it was discredited following the defeat of the Third Reich and the immensity of the crimes committed in the name of Nordic racial purity.[2]

In 1969, the scientific case for racism was revived by an article published in the *Harvard Educational Review* by University of California-Berkeley education professor Arthur Jensen. Based on his statistical analysis of I.Q. test scores, he concluded that African Americans were genetically inferior to whites in general intelligence. His racist thesis was widely disseminated and discussed in the popular press and in respectable academic and policy circles.

In time, Jensen's conclusions were thoroughly discredited by a spate of books and articles.[3] In 1994, once again using standardized test data, Charles Murray and Richard Herrnstein in *The Bell Curve* claimed to have proven that the inferior place of black and brown people in the social, political, and economic order was rooted in biology. The arguments for the genetic superiority of the white race were again dismembered and discredited by many geneticists and biologists.[4]

Recently a more subtle form of "scientific" racism has gained some respectability. The inferiority of the black and brown races is now said to lie not necessarily in genetics but in culture and history. This more quietly spoken academic version of the master-race ideology has also been thoroughly dismantled, yet racist explanations for the race gap persist.[5]

Once all "scientific" arguments supporting racism are dismissed, how is the ever-present gap in academic school performance to be explained? Numerous social and behavioral scientists have addressed this question.

A statistical study by Professor Samuel Meyers Jr. at the Roy Wilkins Center for Human Relations and Social Justice at the University of Minnesota sought to determine whether poverty was a primary cause of the poor performance of black students on the Minnesota Basic Standards Test.[6] Passing this test was scheduled to become a prerequisite for a high school diploma in 2000. In a 1996 trial run in Minneapolis, 75 percent of African American students failed the math test, and 79 percent failed in reading, compared to 26 percent and 42 percent respectively for whites.

The researchers found that, contrary to expectations, test scores were not statistically related to school poverty, neighborhood poverty, racial concentration, or even ranking of schools (except in the case of whites). They did find that African Americans, American Indians, and Hispanics were underrepresented in the top-ranked schools.[7] African Americans were 4.5 times as likely to be found in schools ranked low in math, and twice as likely to be found in schools ranked lowest in reading.

For both white students and students of color, success on the tests was positively correlated to how an individual had been tracked. Only 6.9 percent of students of color compared to 23 percent of white students had access to "gifted and talented" programs. This study suggests that tracking and the quality of the academic opportunities available in the school affects both the test score gap and the gap in academic performance generally. While these correlational studies are suggestive, they do not

Recently a more subtle form of 'scientific' racism has gained some respectability. The inferiority of the black and brown races is now said to lie not necessarily in genetics but in culture and history.

examine basic causes nor explain the pervasiveness and stability of the gap over prolonged periods of time.

A set of experimental studies conducted by Stanford University professor Claude Steele, an African American psychologist, sought to explain the circumstances and situations that give rise to the race gap in test scores.[8] He and colleagues gave equal numbers of African American and white Stanford sophomores a 30-minute standardized test composed of some of the more challenging items from the advanced Graduate Record Examination in literature. Steele notes all the students were highly successful students and test-takers since all Stanford students must earn SAT scores well above the national average in order to be admitted to the university.

The researchers told half the students that the test did not assess ability, but that the research was aimed at "understanding the psychological factors involved in solving verbal problems." The others were told that the test was a valid measure of academic ability and capacity. African American students who were told that the test was a true measure of ability scored significantly lower than the white students. The other African American students' scores were equal to white students'. Whites performed the same in both situations.

The explanation Steele offers is that black students know they are especially likely to be seen as having limited ability. Groups not stereotyped in this way do not experience this extra intimidation. He suggests that "it is serious intimidation, implying as it does that if they should perform badly, they may not belong in walks of life where their tested abilities are important—walks of life in which they are heavily invested." He labels this phenomenon "stereotype vulnerability."

In another study, Steele and colleagues found, to their surprise, that students most likely to do poorest on the tests were not the least able and prepared academically. To the contrary, they tended to be among the more highly motivated and academically focused.

We are left with no explanation of how 'stereotype vulnerability' is created by and also shapes everyday life in society and at school.

While Steele's research provides a plausible psychological explanation for the gap, it does not probe the historical, social, and cultural factors that have created and continue to sustain these stereotypes. We are left with no explanation of how "stereotype vulnerability" is created by and also shapes everyday life in society and at school.

The previously cited studies focus on the gap in standardized test scores. The next study cited is one of a large number of recent "qualitative" studies—observational, historical, and ethnographic studies—that illuminate relationships of culture, gender, and race to the social relations within the classroom and school.[9]

Signithia Fordham, an African American anthropologist, studied a Washington, D.C., public high school and focused on how the "hidden" and explicit curriculum shapes student aspirations and achievements, and how students of differing cultural, racial, and social backgrounds respond to the schooling experience.[10] Hers is a multifaceted, complex study, including interviews, participant observation, questionnaires, and field notes, gathered over a four-year period. She concludes that for African American students, patterns of academic success and underachievement are a reflection of processes of resistance that enable them to maintain their humanness in the face of a stigmatized racial identity. She shows that African American adolescents' profound ambivalence about the value and possibility of school success is manifest as both conformity and avoidance. Ambivalence is manifest in students' motivation and interest in schoolwork, which of course includes mastery of standardized test-taking skills. The following two quotes are taken from interviews with two African American men. The first is from a young lawyer employed in a Washington, D.C., firm who had been a National Merit finalist and whose test scores were among the top 2 percent in his state.

Commenting on why he was disappointed with his career, he observed: "I realized that no matter how smart I was [in school] or how hard I was willing to work [in the law firm] that it wasn't going to happen for me. ... Don't get me wrong, integration has been great for my life. Without it, I would be playing on a much more restrictive field, [but] there's no doubt in my mind that I would be much more successful today if I were white."

A high-performing, African American high school student offers the following view of why African Americans often underperform in school, and also expresses his doubts that his own school success will be rewarded.

"Well, we supposed to be stupid ... we perform poorly in school 'cause we all have it thought it up in our heads we're supposed to be dumb so we might as well go ahead and be dumb," he said. "And we think that most of the things we learn [at school] won't help us in life anyway. ... What good is a quadratic equation gonna do me if I'm picking up garbage cans?"

Fordham found that even the most academically talented African American high school students expressed profound

[Fordham] shows that African American adolescents' profound ambivalence about the value and possibility of school success is manifest as both conformity and avoidance.

ambivalence toward schooling and uncertainty that they will reap the rewards of school success. Virtually all African Americans she interviewed indicated that a central problem facing them at school and in larger white society is the widely held perception by whites that African Americans are less able and intelligent and their continuing need to confront and deal with this reality in everyday experience.

These three studies taken together suggest three related explanations for the race gap in academic achievement and in test scores. First, is students' perceptions of the opportunities in the wider society and the realities of "making it." Second, are the educational opportunities available in the educational system itself—within school districts, schools, and within each classroom. Third, are the cumulative psychic and emotional effects of living in a social world saturated with racist ideology, and where racist practices and structures are pervasive, and often go unnamed.

Gap in Test Scores

Most people assume that the statistical gap in scores between persons of color and whites is enormous. It is not.

There has been long-standing concern over the race gap in test scores. What is almost always overlooked is the size and educational significance of the test score gap. Most people assume that the statistical gap in scores between persons of color and whites is enormous. It is not. Depending on the test the difference varies but hovers in the range of 10 percent.[11] This difference in average scores has persisted over time, regardless of the type of test, whether it is an IQ test, norm-referenced, or proficiency test, regardless of a test's publisher, or educational level of the test-taker, be it kindergarten or graduate school.[12]

Figure 1: Percent Difference in Standardized Literacy Test Between Persons of Color and Whites

Figure 1 illustrates graphically an 8 percent difference in California's CBEST, a standardized test of basic literacy required of principals, teachers, and virtually any adult who works professionally with children in school. It is first important to note that the distributions of scores are highly overlapping. In practical terms, the difference gap amounts to a mere handful of test items. In Figure 1, the gap is an average of 3.2 multiple-choice test items on a 50-item multiple-choice test.[13] (The number will vary according to the number of items on the test.) From an educational point of view, such differences have little if any significance. Because of the way the tests are normed and cut scores set, however, minor differences in the number of correct answers on a multiple-choice test create grossly inflated failure rates for persons of color. On CBEST, for example, African American test-takers are 3.5 times more likely to fail the test than whites, Latino/Hispanics more than twice as likely, and Asian Americans more than 1.5 times as likely to fail than whites.[14]

Because of the way the tests are normed and cut scores set, however, minor differences in the number of correct answers on a multiple-choice test create grossly inflated failure rates for persons of color.

	Number Eliminated	Percent Failing
African Americans	11,200	63.0
Latinos	15,600	50.6
Asians	23,800	47.0
Whites	125,900	19.7

Figure 2: Number and Percentages of First-time Failures on CBEST 1985-95

Numerous researchers have carefully documented the highly disproportionate adverse impact on students of color of standardized achievement testing.[15] An argument might be made that these differences in test scores, while small, nevertheless represent real differences in performance, and that tests, though imperfect, eliminate those most likely to perform poorly at school or on the job. Steele's study suggests the opposite—that the more talented students are at greater risk of failure. There is no evidence to support the claim that standardized tests are valid and credible measures of academic achievement or intellectual capacity. Further, there is no demonstrable connection between observed academic performance and standardized test scores. Test scores do not predict future success in school, the university, or in the workplace. Some standardized tests, the SAT for example, do correlate statistically to future grades. But this correlation is short-lived.[16] What standardized achievement tests appear to predict best are parents' wealth and scores on other similarly constructed tests. As reported by Peter Sacks, socio-economic class accounts for approximately 50 percent of the variance in SAT test scores. He estimates that for every additional $10,000 in family income, a person on average gains 30 points on the SAT.[17] Among the more commonly heard explanations for the gap in standardized test scores is that the tests themselves are culturally and racially biased. What this has usually been taken to mean is that the bias is lodged in the content or language of individual test items. In the early years of mental measurement, the racism of the test items was often blatant. In more recent years, major test publishers have made efforts to review and eliminate items with overt cultural and racial bias. Though item bias remains, it is implausible to conclude that all the publishers in all their tests knowingly or unknowingly managed to create tests with an almost identical ratio of biased to unbiased items. The fact that scores on all commercially produced tests show the same eight to 10 percent gap suggests that the gap cannot be fully explained by racial or cultural bias lodged in individual test items. Rather, the bias is *systemic* and *structural*—that is, built into the basic assumptions and technology of standardized testing in the way the tests are constructed and administered, the way results are reported, and in the organizational structure and administrative rules of the accountability system itself.

The fact that scores on all commercially produced tests show the same eight to 10 percent gap suggests that the gap cannot be fully explained by racial or cultural bias lodged in individual test items. Rather, the bias is systemic and structural.

There is perhaps no clearer illustration of how the differences among the races are greatly exaggerated and distorted than the numerical scales used to report results. There is, as I have noted, about a 10 percent difference in scores between white and nonwhite students. On a 100-point scale, this 10 percent difference constitutes a gap of 10 points. However, California's Academic Performance Index or API (which is based entirely on students' scores on the Stanford 9 Achievement Test) creates a 200- to 1,000-point scale, and a 10 percent difference in scores morphs into a formidable 100 points. The SAT, the most commonly used test for college admissions, and also frequently used (inappropriately) to rank states' academic performance, creates a 400-1,600 scale. On this scale, a 10 percent difference is transformed to a 120-point chasm.

A major goal of social reformers of the 20th century was the elimination of legalized segregation. We still live in a society that is separate and unequal. To achieve social and economic justice, the goal for the 21st century must become the elimination of institutionalized racism in all sectors of social, economic, cultural, and political life—in business, housing, employment law enforcement, the courts, healthcare institutions, and, of course, schools. What makes institutionalized racism so pernicious and difficult to eradicate is that racist practices are often invisible because they are accepted as standard operating procedures within our institutions.

Standardized tests are a particularly invidious form of institutionalized racism because they lend the cloak of science to policies that have denied, and are continuing to deny, persons of color equal access to educational and job opportunities. An educational accountability system based on standardized testing though predicated on "standardized" measurements which are purportedly neutral, objective, and colorblind, perpetuates and strengthens institutionalized racism.

Standardized tests are a particularly invidious form of institutionalized racism because they lend the cloak of science to policies that have denied, and are continuing to deny, persons of color equal access to educational and job opportunities.

Endnotes

1. Applied Research Center (2000). *Still separate, still unequal, a research brief.* Oakland, CA: Applied Research Center. www.arc.org.
2. Selden, S. (1999). *Inheriting shame: The story of eugenics in America.* New York: Teachers College Press.
3. Gould, S.J. (1980). Jensen's last stand. *New York Review of Books*; Kamin, L.J. (1974). *The Science and Politics of IQ.* New York: Penguin; Kohl, D.M. (1976). The IQ game: Bait and switch—a review essay. *School Review* 84(4), 572-604.
4. Jacoby R. & Glauberman, N. (eds.) (1995). *The Bell Curve debate.* New York: NY Times Books/Random House.
5. Cultural supremacy arguments are dismantled in Diamond, J. (1997). *Guns, germs and steel.* New York: Norton.
6. Myers Jr., S.L., & Mandala, C. (1998). *Is poverty the cause of poor performance of black students on basic standards examination?* Roy Wilkins Center for Human Relations and Social Justice, Univ. of Minnesota. Paper presented at the American Educational Research Assoc. Annual Meeting, June 1997.
7. Schools were ranked in terms of resources, education and experience of staff, number, depth and range of academic course offerings.
8. Steele, C.M. (1997). A threat in the air: How stereotypes shape the intellectual identities. *American Psychologist*, 52(6), 613-629. Also see, Steele, C.M. (1998). Stereotyping and its threat are real. *American Psychologist*, 53(6), 680-681.
9. These include, Delpit, L. (1995) *Other people's children.* New York: The New Press; King, J.E. (1996). The purpose of schooling for African American students. In J. King, E. Hollins. & W.C. Hayman (eds.), *Preparing teachers for cultural diversity.* New York: Teachers College Press; Ladson-Billings, G. (1999). *The dreamkeepers:*

Successful teachers of African-American children. San Francisco: Josey-Bass; Berlak, A. & Moyenda, S. (2001). *Taking it personally: Racism in schools.* Philadelphia: Temple. Univ. Press.

10. Fordham, S. (1996). *Blacked out: Dilemmas of race, identity, and success at Capital High.* Chicago: University of Chicago Press.

11. Most of the data are from court records in Civil Rights challenges to standardized tests. See Haney, W., Madaus, G., & Keritzer, A. (1987). Charms talismanic: Testing teachers for the improvement of American education. *Review of Educational Research.* 14, 169-238.

12. See Linn, R. (2000). Assessments and accountability. *Educational Researcher* 29(2), 4-16. He cites data from the Florida high school competency test, given annually since 1977 to illustrate a common pattern. When first a test is introduced, scores rise markedly for several years for whites and persons of color, level off, and over time decline slightly. However, the gap in test performance between the races remains virtually constant over time.

13. In CBEST, 10 of the 50 items on the math and language section are not scored. They are used in creating items for future versions of CBEST. Eight percent of 40 items equals 3.2 items.

14. On some tests, particularly in mathematics and engineering, some Asian populations outperform whites.

15. These include: McNeil, L. (2000). *Contradictions of school reform: The educational costs of standardized testing.* New York: Routledge; Madaus, G.F. (1994). A technological and historical consideration of equity issues associated with proposals to change the nation's testing policy. *Harvard Educational Review,* 64(1), 76-95; Pullin, D.C. (1994). Learning to work: The impact of curriculum and assessment standards on educational opportunity. *Harvard Educational Review,* 64(1), 31-54.

16. Some achievement tests, the college entrance SAT for example, predict academic grades at the next level, but only in the very short run.

17. See Sacks, P. (2000). *Standardized minds.* Cambridge, MA: Perseus Books.

CHAPTER EIGHT

Once Upon a Genocide

Columbus in children's literature

By Bill Bigelow

Children's biographies of Christopher Columbus function as primers on racism and colonialism. They teach youngsters to accept the right of white people to rule over people of color, of powerful nations to dominate weaker nations. And because the Columbus myth is so pervasive—Columbus' "discovery" is probably the only historical episode with which all my students are familiar—it inhibits children from developing democratic, multicultural, and anti-racist attitudes.

Almost without exception, children's biographies of Columbus depict the journey to the New World as a "great adventure" led by "probably the greatest sailor of his time." It's a story of courage and superhuman tenacity. Columbus is depicted as brave, smart, and determined. But behind this romanticized portrayal is a gruesome reality. For Columbus, land was real estate and it didn't matter that other people were already living there; if he "discovered" it, he took it. If he needed guides or translators, he kidnapped them. If his men wanted women, he captured sex slaves. If the indigenous people resisted, he countered with vicious attack dogs, hangings, and mutilations.

On his second voyage, desperate to show his royal patrons a return on their investment, Columbus rounded up some 1,500 Taínos on the island of Hispaniola and chose 500 as slaves to be sold in Spain. Slavery did not show a profit as almost all the slaves died en route to Spain or soon after their arrival. Nonetheless, he wrote, "Let us in the name of the Holy Trinity go on sending all the slaves that can be sold."

Columbus decided to concentrate on the search for gold. He ordered every Taíno on Hispaniola 14 years and older to deliver a regular quota of gold. Those who failed had their hands chopped off. In two years of the Columbus regime, perhaps a quarter of a million people died.

This article examines eight children's biographies of Columbus, comparing the books with the historical record and analyzing how these accounts may influence young readers.

Portrait of Columbus

Why did Columbus want to sail west to get to the Indies? The answer offered to children in today's books hasn't changed much since I was in 4th grade. I remember my teacher, Mrs. O'Neill, asking our class this question. As usual, I didn't have a clue, but up went Jimmy Martin's hand. "Why do men want to go to the moon?" he said triumphantly. Mrs. O'Neill was delighted and told us all how smart Jimmy was because he answered a question with a question. In other words: just because—because he was curious, because he loved adventure, because he wanted to prove he could do it—just because. And for years I accepted this explanation (and envied Jimmy Martin).

In reality, Columbus wanted to become rich.

In reality, Columbus wanted to become rich. It was no easy task convincing Queen Isabella and King Ferdinand to finance this highly questionable journey to the Indies, partly because his terms were outrageous. Columbus demanded 10 percent of all the wealth returned to Europe along the new trade route to Asia (where Columbus thought he was headed)—that's 10 percent of the riches brought back by everyone, not just by himself. And he wanted this guaranteed forever, for him, for his children, for their children, in perpetuity. He demanded that he be granted the titles "Viceroy" and "Admiral of the Ocean Sea." He was to be governor of all new territories found; the "Admiral" title was hereditary and would give him a share in proceeds from naval booty.

As for Queen Isabella and King Ferdinand, curiosity, adventure, and "exploration" were the last things on their minds. They wanted the tremendous profits that could be secured by finding a western passage to the Indies. The books acknowledge—and even endorse—Columbus' demands and readily admit that securing "gold and spices" was an objective of the enterprise. "Of course [Columbus] wanted a lot! What was wrong with that?" James de Kay's *Meet Christopher Columbus* tells 2nd graders. But this quest for wealth is downplayed in favor of adventure. "Exploration" meant going to "strange cities" where "many wonderful things" could be seen [de Kay]. Travel was exciting: Columbus "felt the heady call of the open sea. 'I love the taste of salt spray in my face,' he told a friend, 'and the feel of a deck rising and falling under my feet.'" [Monchieri]. According to these eight biographies, a major reason Columbus wanted to sail west was because of his deep faith in God. Columbus thought "that the Lord had chosen him to sail west across the sea to find the riches of the East for himself and to carry the Christian faith to the heathens. His name was Christopher. Had not the Lord chosen his namesake, Saint Christopher, to carry the Christ Child across the dark water of a river?" [D'Aulaire]. Religion, curiosity, adventure—all those motives are given preference in the Columbus biographies. But each of these supposed motives pales before the Spanish empire's quest for wealth and power. In burying these more fundamental material forces, the Columbus books encourage students to misunderstand the roots of today's foreign policy exploits. Thus students are more likely to accept platitudes—"We're involved in the Middle East for freedom and democracy"—than to look for less altruistic explanations.

> *Religion, curiosity, adventure—all those motives are given preference in the Columbus biographies.*

The Kind and Noble Columbus

None of the biographies I evaluated—all still on the shelves of school and public libraries and widely available—disputes the ugly facts about Columbus and the Spanish conquest of the Caribbean. Yet the sad irony is that all encourage children to root for Columbus and empathize with him, using phrases such as "It was lucky that Christopher Columbus was born where he was or he might never have gone to sea," [Fritz] or "There once was a boy

Unlike the people he will later exterminate, Columbus is treated as a real human being.

who loved the salty sea" [D'Aulaire]. Some of the books, particularly those for younger readers, refer to Columbus affectionately, using his first name. Unlike the people he will later exterminate, Columbus is treated as a real human being, one with thoughts and feelings: "When Christopher Columbus was a child, he always wanted to be like Saint Christopher. He wanted to sail to faraway places and spread the word of Christianity" [Osborne].

The series title of Robert Young's *Christopher Columbus and His Voyage to the New World* sums up the stance of most biographies: "Let's Celebrate." The books cheer Columbus on toward the Indies. Each step on the road to "discovery" is told from his point of view. When Columbus is delayed, this is the "most unhappy part of his great adventure" [de Kay]. Every successful step is rewarded with exclamation marks: "Yes, [the Queen] would help Columbus!" [Osborne]. "After all these years, Columbus would get his ships!" [de Kay].

Columbus' devout Christianity is a theme in all the books—and is never questioned. The most insistent of these—and the worst of the lot in almost every respect—is Sean J. Dolan's *Christopher Columbus: The Intrepid Mariner*. By the second page in Dolan's reverent volume, we're reading about Columbus' attachment to his leather-bound Bible. Dolan is constantly dipping us into the Admiral's thoughts. Usually these meditations run deep and pious: "[He] believed that the awe-inspiring beauty that surrounded him could only be the handiwork of the one true God, and he felt secure in his Lord and Savior's protection. 'If only my crewmen shared my belief,' Columbus thought." And this is only on the third page—Dolan's narrative goes on like this for 114 more. The reader is practically strangled by Columbus' halo.

Jean Fritz's *Where Do You Think You're Going, Christopher Columbus?* is the only book somewhat skeptical about religion as a motive. Fritz tells her readers that Queen Isabella "was such an enthusiastic Christian that she insisted everyone in Spain be a Christian too. ... Indeed, she was so religious that if she even found Christians who were not sincere Christians, she had them burned at the stake. (Choir boys sang during the burnings so Isabella wouldn't have to hear the screams.)"

This is pretty strong stuff, but the implied critique would likely be lost on upper elementary students, the book's targeted readers. The close association between God and Columbus in all the books, with the possible exception of Fritz's, discourages children from criticizing Columbus. "Columbus marveled at how God had arranged everything for the best," the D'Aulaires write.

Well, if God arranged everything, who are we, the insignificant readers, to question?

No book even hints that the Indians believed in their own God or gods who also watched over and cared about them. The Columbus expedition may be the first encounter between two peoples—Us and Them—where children will learn that "God is on our side."

Evils? Blame the Workers

Columbus' journey across the Atlantic was not easy, according to most of the books, because his crew was such a wretched bunch. The sailors were stupid, superstitious, cowardly, and sometimes scheming. Columbus, on the other hand, is portrayed as brave, wise, and godly. These characterizations, repeated frequently in many of the books, protect the Columbus myth. Anything bad that happens, like murder and slavery, can always be blamed on the men. Columbus, the leader, is pure of heart. Taken together, the books' portrayals serve as a kind of anti-working class, pro-boss polemic: "Soon [Columbus] rose above his shipmates, for he was clever and capable and could make others carry out his orders" [D'Aulaire]. Evidently, ordinary seamen are not "clever and capable," and thus are good merely for carrying out the instructions of others. "Soon [Columbus] forgot that he was only the son of a humble weaver," the D'Aulaires write, as if a background as a worker were a source of shame. The books encourage children to identify with Columbus' hardships, even though his men worked and slept in horrible conditions while the future Admiral slept under a canopy bed in his private cabin. The lives of those who labored for Columbus are either ignored or held in contempt.

The lives of those who labored for Columbus are either ignored or held in contempt.

The 'Discovery'

At the core of the Columbus myth—and repeated by all eight books—is the notion that Columbus "discovered" America. Indeed, it's almost as if the same writer churned out one ever-so-slightly different version after another.

De Kay describes the scene this way in *Meet Christopher Columbus*:

> The sailors rowed Columbus to the shore. He stepped on the beach. He got on his knees and said a prayer of thanks. Columbus named the island San Salvador. He said it now belonged to Ferdinand and Isabella. He tried to talk to the people on San Salvador. But they could not understand him.

Of course he couldn't understand them, either. But de Kay attributes the inability to understand solely to the Indians. Is it these Indians' implied ignorance that justifies heavily armed men coming onto their land and claiming it in the name of a kingdom thousands of miles away? In *Christopher Columbus and His Voyage to the New World*, Robert Young doesn't even tell his young readers of the people on these islands. Young's Columbus found "lands" but no people: In illustrations we see only palm trees and empty beaches.

Why don't any of the books ask students to think about the assumptions that underpinned this land grab? Naïvely, I kept waiting for some book to insert just a trace of doubt: "Why do you think Columbus felt he could claim land for Spain when there were already people living there?" or "Columbus doesn't write in his journal why he felt entitled to steal other people's property. What do you think?"

This scene of Columbus' first encounter with the Indians—read in school by virtually every child—is a powerful metaphor about relations between different countries and races. It is a lesson not just about the world 500 years ago, but about the world today: Clothed, armed, Christian white men from a more technologically "advanced" nation arrive in a land peopled by darker-skinned, naked, unarmed, non-Christians—and take over. Because no book indicates which characteristic of either group necessitates or excuses this kind of bullying, students are left alone to puzzle it out: Might makes right. Whites should rule over people who aren't white. Christians should control non-Christians. "Advanced" nations should dominate "backward" nations. Each and every answer a student might glean from the books' text and images invariably justifies colonialism and racism.

Each and every answer a student might glean from the books' text and images invariably justifies colonialism and racism.

In Columbus' New World "adventures," the lives of the Indians are a kind of "muzak"—insignificant background noise. Only one book, *Where Do You Think You're Going, Christopher Columbus?*, tries to imagine what the Indians might have been thinking about the arrival of the Spaniards. Still, the point here seems more to gently poke fun at Columbus and crew than to seriously consider the Indians' point of view: "[I]f the Spaniards were surprised to see naked natives, the natives were even more surprised to see dressed Spaniards. All that cloth over their bodies! What were they trying to hide? Tails, perhaps?" Jean Fritz's interior monologue for the Indians makes fun of the explorers but in the process trivializes the Indians' concerns.

Not a single Columbus biography ever asks children: "What might the Indians have thought about the actions of Columbus and his men?" The silent Indians in Columbus stories have a contemporary consequence. The message is that white people in "developed" societies have consciousness and voice, but Third World people are thoughtless and voiceless objects. The books rehearse students in a way of looking at the world that begins from the assumption: *They* are not like *us*. A corollary is that *we* are more competent to determine the conditions of *their* lives: their social and economic systems, their political alliances, and so on. As shown by interventions in Iraq and Vietnam, subversion of the government headed by Salvador Allende in Chile, the invasions of Grenada and Panama, the attempted overthrow by proxy of the Nicaraguan and Angolan governments, *our* right to decide what's best for *them* is basic to the conduct of this nation's foreign policy. As most children's first exposure to "foreign policy," the Columbus myth helps condition young people to accept the unequal distribution of power in the world.

As most children's first exposure to 'foreign policy,' the Columbus myth helps condition young people to accept the unequal distribution of power in the world.

Theft, Slavery, and Murder

Columbus' genocidal policies toward the Indians were initiated during his second journey. The three books aimed at children in early elementary grades, Gleiter and Thompson's *Christopher Columbus*, de Kay's *Meet Christopher Columbus*, and Young's *Christopher Columbus and His Voyage to the New World*, all conveniently stop the story after his first journey. The Columbus myth can take root in young minds without the complications of the slavery and mass murder to come.

After his first trip, Columbus returned to a hero's welcome in Spain. He also arrived telling all kinds of lies about gold mines and spices and unlimited amounts of wealth. The admiral needed royal backing for a second trip, and had to convince his sponsors that the islands contained more than parrots and naked natives.

During his second voyage, in February of 1495, Columbus launched the slave raids against the Taínos of Hispaniola. Four of the eight books I reviewed—the ones aimed at older children— admit that Columbus took Indians as slaves [Monchieri, Fritz, Osborne, and Dolan]. Their critique, however, is muted. No account tells children what slavery meant for its victims. One of the books, Monchieri's *Christopher Columbus*, says that taking slaves was "a great failing of Columbus. ... He saw nothing wrong with enslaving the American Indians and making them work for Spanish masters. ... Missionaries protested against this policy, but they were not listened to."

Mary Pope Osborne in *Christopher Columbus: Admiral of the Ocean Sea* writes that "this terrible treatment of the Indians was Columbus' real downfall." Still, Osborne is unable to offer even this minimal critique of the admiral without at the same time justifying his actions: "Since Columbus felt despair and disappointment about not finding gold in the Indies, he decided to be like the African explorers and try to sell these Indians as slaves." Neither book ever describes the character of slave life—or slave death.

The other two biographies offer Columbus' justifications for taking slaves: "African explorers were always sending Africans back to Spanish slave markets, Columbus told himself. Besides, the natives were all heathens. It wasn't as if he were selling Christians into slavery" [Fritz]. Dolan at one point blames it all on the men: "Given the attitude of the men at large, however, [Columbus] had little choice but to give his approval to the slaving sorties."

Imagine, if you will, Nazi war crimes described in this way— nothing about the suffering of the victims, tepid criticism of the perpetrators, the horrendous crimes explained by the rationalizations of Hitler and his generals. How long would these books last in our schools?

From the beginning, locating gold was Columbus' primary objective. In one passage, not included in any of the children's books, Columbus wrote: "Gold is a wonderful thing! Whoever owns it is lord of all he wants. With gold it is even possible to open for souls the way to paradise." Two of the eight authors, Fritz and Dolan, describe Columbus' system for attempting to extract gold from the Indians. Dolan writes that Columbus instituted "a system of forced tribute: each Indian was to provide a certain amount of gold each year. Penalties for failure to comply with this rule included flogging, enslavement, or death." Nothing here about cutting people's hands off, which is what Columbus did, but still it's pretty explicit. Fritz writes simply that Indians who didn't deliver enough gold "were punished." She concludes that "between 1494 and 1496 one third of the native population of Hispaniola was killed, sold, or scared away." The passive voice in Fritz's version—"was killed, sold, or scared away"—protects the perpetrators: Exactly who caused these deaths?

More significantly, these accounts fail to recognize the Indians' humanity. The books' descriptions are clinical and factual, like those of a coroner. What kind of suffering must these people have gone through? How did it feel to have their civilization

These accounts fail to recognize the Indians' humanity.

completely destroyed in just a few years? What of the children who watched their parents butchered by the Spanish gold-seekers? These books show no passion or outrage—at Columbus or at the social and economic system he represented. This devastation happened to several hundred thousand human beings, maybe more. Why don't the writers of these books get angry?

I find the most "honest" books about Columbus' enterprise—those that admit slavery and other crimes—the most distressing. They lay out the facts, describe the deaths, and then move on to the next paragraph with no look back. These books foster a callousness toward human suffering—or is it simply a callousness toward people of color? Apparently students are supposed to value bravery, cunning, and perseverance over a people's right to life and self-determination.

Contempt for Native Resistance

Given that Columbus biographies scarcely consider Indians as human beings, it's not surprising that native resistance to the Spaniards' atrocities is either barely acknowledged or treated with hostility. Gleiter and Thompson's *Christopher Columbus* notes that in future trips Columbus "fought with the natives." In a single sentence, Lino Monchieri writes: "The Indians became rebellious because [Columbus] compelled them to hand over their gold." At least here the author credits the Indians with what might be a legitimate cause for revolt, though offers no further details. Mary Pope Osborne buries the cause of resistance in nonexplanatory, victimless prose: "But the settlers had run into trouble with the Indians, and there had been a lot of fighting."

Some writers choose to portray Indian resistance not as self-defense, but as originating from the indigenous people's inherently violent nature. In *Meet Christopher Columbus*, "unfriendly Indians" surprise the innocent Spaniards: "Suddenly more than 50 Indians jumped out from behind the trees. They had bows and arrows. They attacked the men. The men fought back." Thus, Indian resistance to the Spaniards' invasion and land grab is not termed "freedom fighting," but instead is considered "unfriendly." The violence of the Spaniards is described as self-defense. Note that in this quote, the Spaniards are "men" and the Indians are, well, just Indians. The books that bother to differentiate between groups of Indians single out the Caribs for special contempt. Caribs are presented as cannibals, even though no historical evidence exists to corroborate such a claim. The Caribs lived on islands "so wild and steep, it seemed as if the waterfalls

> *These books show no passion or outrage—at Columbus or at the social and economic system he represented.*

came tumbling out of the clouds. The Indians who lived there were wild too. They were cannibals who ate their enemies" [D'Aulaire]. In Dolan's *Christopher Columbus: The Intrepid Mariner*, Columbus sends an armed contingent to "explore" the island that today is St. Croix. Because Caribs attack the Spaniards, Dolan considers this resistance sufficient to label the Caribs as ferocious. In fact, according to the eyewitness account of Dr. Diego Alvarez Chanca, the Indians attacked only when the Spaniards trapped them in a cove. In today's parlance, the Caribs were "radicals" and "extremists"—in other words, they tenaciously defended their land and freedom.

The books condition young people to reject the right of the oppressed to rebel. We have a right to own their land, and they should not protest—at least not violently. Those who do resist will be slapped with a pejorative descriptor—cannibal, savage, communist, militant, radical, hard-liner, extremist—and subdued. The Columbus biographies implicitly lead students to have contempt for contemporary movements for social justice. Obviously, they leave children ill-prepared to respect current Indian struggles for land and fishing rights.

Columbus' Legacy

I expected each book to end with at least some reflection on the meaning of Columbus' voyages. None did. In fact, only one book, *Meet Christopher Columbus*, even suggests that today's world has anything to do with Columbus: Thanks to the Admiral, "Thousands of people crossed the ocean to America. This 'new world' became new countries: the United States, Canada, Mexico, Brazil, and many others."

Colonialism and slavery: this was the 'new world' Columbus did not so much discover as help to invent.

It's much simpler for the authors to ignore both short- and long-term consequences of Columbus' enterprise. Instead of linking the nature of Columbus' Spain to 20th century America, each book functions as a kind of secular *Book of Genesis*: In the beginning there was Columbus—he was good and so are we.

This is a grave omission. In addition to the genocide of native peoples in the Caribbean, the most immediate effect of Columbus' voyages was the initiation of the Atlantic slave trade between Africa and America.[2] Colonialism and slavery: this was the "new world" Columbus did not so much discover as help to invent. In the emerging commercial ethos of his society, human beings were commodities whose value was measured largely in monetary terms. The natural environment was likewise cherished not for its beauty but for the wealth that could be extracted.

Columbus' enterprise and the plunder that ensued contributed mightily to the growth of the nascent mercantile capitalism of Europe. His lasting contribution was to augment a social order that confronts the world in commercial terms—how much is it worth?—and which appreciates markets rather than cultures.

Asking 'Why?'

Why are Columbus biographies characterized by such bias and omission? I doubt any writers, publishers, or teachers consciously set out to poison the minds of the young. The Columbus story teaches important values, some would argue. Here was a young man who, despite tremendous adversity, maintained and finally achieved his objectives. Fear and narrowmindedness kept others from that which he finally accomplished.

But in the Columbus biographies, these decent values intermingle seamlessly with deep biases against working-class people, people of color, and Third World nations. The blindness of writers and educators to these biases is simply an indication of how pervasive they are in the broader society. The seeds of imperialism, exploitation, and racism were planted with Columbus' first transatlantic enterprise—and these seeds have taken root.

Without doubt, ours is a very different world than Spanish America in the 15th and 16th centuries, but there is a lingering inheritance: the tendency for powerful groups to value profit over humanity; racial and cultural differences used to justify exploitation and inequality; vast disparities in living conditions for different social classes; economically and militarily strong nations attempting to control the fates of weaker nations. Hence, life amidst injustice in today's United States inures many of us to the injustice of 500 years earlier. Characteristics that appear to someone as natural and inevitable in the 21st century will likely appear as natural and inevitable in the descriptions of the world five centuries ago.

The Biographies' Pedagogy

The Columbus stories encourage passive reading and never pose questions for children to think about. Did Columbus have a right to claim Indian land in the name of the Spanish crown? Were those Indians who resisted violently justified in doing so? Why does the United States commemorate a Columbus Day instead of a Genocide Day? The narratives require readers merely to listen, not to think. The text is everything, the reader nothing. Not only are young readers conditioned to accept

The Columbus stories encourage passive reading and never pose questions for children to think about.

social hierarchy—colonialism and racism—they are also rehearsed in an authoritarian mode of learning.

By implication, in this review essay I suggest the outlines of a more truthful history of Columbus and the "discovery" of America. First, the indigenous peoples of America must be accorded the status of full human beings with inalienable rights to self-determination. The tale of "discovery" needs to be told from their perspective as well as from the Europeans'. Although there is little documentation of how the Indians interpreted the Spaniards' arrival and conquest, readers could be encouraged to think about these events from the native point of view. Columbus' interior monologue should not be the only set of thoughts represented in the story. A more accurate tale of Columbus would not simply probe his personal history but would also analyze the social and economic system he represented. And children might be asked to think about how today's world was shaped by the events of 1492. Above all, young readers must be invited to think and critique, not simply required to passively absorb others' historical interpretations.

A more accurate tale of Columbus would not simply probe his personal history but would also analyze the social and economic system he represented.

Until we create humane and truthful materials, teachers may decide to boycott the entire Columbus canon. The problem with this approach is that the distortions and inadequacies characterizing this literature are also found in other children's books.

A better solution is to equip students to read critically these and other stories—inviting children to become detectives, investigating their biographies, novels, and textbooks for bias. In fact, because the Columbus books are so bad, they make perfect classroom resources to learn how to read for social as well as for literal meaning. After students have been introduced to a critical history of Columbus, they could probe materials for accuracy. Do the books lie outright? What is omitted from the accounts that would be necessary for a more complete understanding of Columbus and his encounters with native cultures? What motives are ascribed to Columbus, and how do those compare with the actual objectives of the admiral and the Spanish monarchs? Whom does the book "root" for and how is this accomplished? What role do illustrations play in shaping the view of Columbus? Why do the books tell the story as they do? Who in our society benefits and who is hurt by these presentations?

Teachers could assign children to write their own Columbus biographies—and some of these could be told from Indians' points of view. Or youngsters might take issues from their own lives suggested by the European invasion of America—

fighting, fairness, stealing, racism—and write stories drawn from these themes.

Significantly, to invite students to question the injustices embedded in text material is implicitly to invite them to question the injustices embedded in the society itself. Isn't it about time we used the Columbus myth to allow students to begin discovering the truth?

For Further Reading

Zinn, H. (1980). *A people's history of the United States*. New York: Harper and Row.

Sale, K. (1990). *The conquest of paradise: Christopher Columbus and the Columbian legacy*. New York: Knopf.

Davidson, B. (1961). *The African slave trade: Precolonial history 1450-1850*. Boston: Little, Brown.

1. Books reviewed in this article:

   Young, R. (1990). *Christopher Columbus and his voyage to the new world*. Englewood Cliffs, NJ: Silver Press.

   de Kay, J.T. (1989). *Meet Christopher Columbus*. New York: Random House.

   Gleiter, J. & Thompson, K. (1995). *Christopher Columbus*. Orlando, FL: Steck-Vaughn.

   Parin D'Aulaire, I. & Parin D'Aulaire, E. (1987). *Columbus*. New York: Doubleday.

   Fritz, J. (1997). *Where do you think you're going, Christopher Columbus?* New York: G.P. Putnam's Sons.

   Monchieri, L. (1985) *Christopher Columbus* (Mary Lee Grisanti trans.). Englewood Cliffs, NJ: Silver Burdett Press.

   Osborne, M. P. (1997). *Christopher Columbus: Admiral of the ocean sea*. Strongville, OH: Gareth Stevens Publishing.

   Dolan, S. J. (1989). *Christopher Columbus: The intrepid mariner*. New York: Fawcett Columbine.

2. For more information see Bigelow, B. & Peterson, B. (eds.) (1998). *Rethinking Columbus: The next 500 years*. Milwaukee, WI: *Rethinking Schools*.

SECTION II

Language, Culture, and Power

CHAPTER NINE

Putting Out
the Linguistic
Welcome Mat

By Linda Christensen

My friend Karen works as a relatively new principal in a
rural Oregon school where the sons and daughters of
winery owners rub elbows with the sons and daugh-
ters of their field workers. Recently, she recounted a story about
a typical day: "When I came into my office after lunch duty, three
Latino students sat waiting for me. The students told me the substitute kicked them out for speaking Spanish in class. After veri-
fying the story, I told the substitute her services would no longer
be needed at our school."

Michael Duffy

Karen is a full-time warrior for students. She battles remarkable linguistic prejudice and historical inequities to make her school a safe community for her Latino students. Before she arrived on campus, for example, school policy excluded Spanish-speaking English language learners from taking Spanish classes. Latino students had to enroll in German classes to meet their world language requirement.

At another urban school, in the Portland area, a group of teachers tallied the grammatical errors their administrator made during a faculty meeting. Their air of superiority and smugness made my teeth ache. This same smugness silences many students in our classrooms when we value how they speak more than what they say.

"Nonstandard" language speakers must negotiate this kind of language minefield whenever they enter the halls of power—schools, banks, government agencies, and employment offices. Language inequity still exists, whether it's getting kicked out of class for speaking in your home language or being found unfit for a job, a college, or a scholarship because of your lack of dexterity with Standard English.

> *As educators, we have the power to determine whether students feel included or excluded in our schools and classrooms.*

As educators, we have the power to determine whether students feel included or excluded in our schools and classrooms. By bringing students' languages from their homes into the classroom, we validate their culture and their history as topics worthy of study.

A Curriculum on Language and Power

Author Toni Morrison (1981) writes about the power of language, and Black English in particular:

> It's the thing black people love so much—the saying of words, holding them on the tongue, experimenting with them, playing with them. It's a love, a passion. Its function is like a preacher's: to make you stand up out of your seat, make you lose yourself and hear yourself. The worst of all possible things that could happen would be to lose that language. There are certain things I cannot say without recourse to my language.

These days, most of our schools and school boards fashion mission statements about "embracing diversity." Multilingual banners welcome students and visitors in Spanish, Russian, and Vietnamese in the hallways of school buildings. But in the classroom, the job of the teacher often appears to be whitewashing students of color or students who are linguistically diverse, especially when punctuation and grammar are double-weighted on the state writing test. If we hope to create positive communities in which students from diverse backgrounds can thrive academically, we need to examine how our approach to students' linguistic diversity either includes or pushes out our most vulnerable learners.

During 30 years as a language arts classroom teacher, I realized that if I wanted my students to open up in their writing, to take risks and engage in intellectually demanding work, I needed to challenge assumptions about the superiority of Standard English and the inferiority of the home language of many of my black students: African American Vernacular English, Black English, or Ebonics. When students feel attacked by the red pen or the tongue for the way they write or speak, they either make themselves small—turning in short papers—or don't turn in papers at all. To build an engaging classroom where students from different backgrounds felt safe enough to dare to be big and bold in their writing, I had to build a curricular platform for them to stand on.

I started this work by intentionally inviting students to tell their stories in their home languages. I brought in August Wilson's plays, Lois Yamanaka's stories, and Jimmy Santiago Baca's poetry to validate the use of dialect and home language. But I learned that this wasn't enough. To challenge the old world order, I needed to explore why Standard English is the standard—how it came to power and how that power makes some people feel welcome and others feel like outsiders.

To challenge the old world order, I needed to explore why Standard English is the standard.

I finally realized that I needed to create a curriculum on language and power that examined the roots of language supremacy and analyzed how schools perpetuate the myths of the inferiority of some languages. I also discovered that students needed stories of hope: stories of people's resistance to the loss of their mother tongues and stories about the growing movement to save indigenous languages from extinction.

Legitimizing the Study of Ebonics/Black English

Depending on how many pieces of the unit I include, this curriculum takes five to 10 weeks. Students watch films and read literature, nonfiction texts, and poetry. They write narratives, poetry, and a culminating essay about language. For their final exam, they create a take-it-to-the-people project that teaches an audience of their choice one aspect of our language study that they think people need to know in order to understand contemporary language issues. The curriculum includes any of the following five segments: Naming as a Practice of Power; Language and Colonization; Dialect and Power; Ebonics; and Language Restoration.

During this unit, we do discuss code-switching, or moving between home language and the language of power—Standard English—during our readings. As a teacher in a predominantly African American school where the majority of students exhibited some features of African American Vernacular English (AAVE, also called Ebonics or "Spoken Soul"), I needed to learn the rules and history of the language so I could help students move between the two language systems. In my experience, teaching black students the grammar structure and history of AAVE evoked pride in their language, but also curiosity. All students—not just African Americans—benefited from learning that African American language has a highly structured grammar system.

> *All students—not just African Americans—benefited from learning that African American language has a highly structured grammar system.*

Teaching about Ebonics has been a no-go zone for many teachers since the controversy over a 1996 Oakland School District resolution that recognized Black English as a language of instruction. Stanford linguistics professor John Rickford noted in his book *Spoken Soul*:

> Ebonics was vilified as "disgusting black street slang," "incorrect and substandard," "nothing more than ignorance," "lazy English," "bastardized English," "the language of illiteracy," and this "utmost ridiculous made-up language." (Rickford, 2000, p. 6)

As Rickford pointed out, the reactions of linguists were much more positive than those of most of the media and the general public. Although they disagree about its origins, "linguists from virtually all points of view agree on the systematicity of Ebonics, and on the potential value of taking it into account in teaching Ebonics speakers to read and write." (Rickford, 1997)

In an African American Literature class I recently taught at Grant High School in Portland, Ore., I introduced the Ebonics part of the language curriculum by giving the 31 students (28 of whom were black) a concept chart and asking them to fill in a definition of Ebonics, write a few examples, and note where it originated. All but one student wrote that Ebonics is slang. Most wrote that Ebonics came out of Oakland or the West Coast or the "ghetto." It was clear that their impressions were negative.

None of the black students in the group used Ebonics/AAVE exclusively. But many of them used aspects of Ebonics in both their speech and their writing. One of my goals was for students to recognize the difference between slang and Ebonics/Black English when they hear it in their school, churches, and homes—and to be able to distinguish it when they are using it. The term "Ebonics" (from ebony and phonics) was coined by Professor Robert Williams in 1973, during a conference on the language development of black children (Rickford, 2000, p. 170). In her essay, "Black English/Ebonics: What It Be Like?" renowned scholar and linguist Geneva Smitherman writes that Ebonics "is rooted in the Black American Oral Tradition and represents a synthesis of African (primarily West African) and European (primarily English) linguistic-cultural traditions" (Smitherman, 1998).

In the class, we read Rickford's essay, "Suite for Ebony and Phonics" aloud together paragraph by paragraph, stopping to discuss each part. Is Ebonics just "slang," as so many people have characterized it? No, because slang refers just to the vocabulary of a language or dialect, and even so, just to the small set of new and (usually) short-lived words like chillin ("relaxing") or homey ("close friend") which are used primarily by young people in informal contexts. Ebonics includes nonslang words like ashy (referring to the appearance of dry skin, especially in winter), which have been around for a while, and are used by people of all age groups.

Ebonics also includes distinctive patterns of pronunciation and grammar, the elements of language on which linguists tend to concentrate because they are more systematic and deep-rooted (Rickford, 1997).

We also read "From Africa to the New World and into the Space Age: An Introduction and History of Black English Structure," a chapter from Geneva Smitherman's 1977 book *Talkin and Testifyin: The Language of Black America.* Her discussion of the grammar structure of Ebonics led to a wonderful day of conjugating verbs. For example, we discussed the absence of a third person singular present tense in Ebonics (example: I draw, he draw, we draw, they draw); students then conjugate verbs using this grammar rule. The zero copula rule—the absence of is or are in a sentence—provided another model for students to practice. Smitherman gives as an example the sentence, "People crazy! People are stone crazy!" The emphasis on are in the second sentence, she points out, intensifies the feeling. I asked students to write zero copula sentences and we shared them in class.

Ebonics also includes distinctive patterns of pronunciation and grammar, the elements of language on which linguists tend to concentrate because they are more systematic and deep-rooted.

After I started teaching my students about Ebonics, many of them began to understand how assumptions about the supremacy of Standard English had created difficulties in their education.

Empowered by Linguistic Knowledge

After I started teaching my students about Ebonics, many of them began to understand how assumptions about the supremacy of Standard English had created difficulties in their education. One student, Kaanan, wrote:

> When I went to school, teachers didn't really teach me how to spell or put sentences together right. They just said sound it out, so I would spell it the way I heard it at home. Everybody around me at home spoke Ebonics, so when I sounded it out, it sounded like home and it got marked wrong. When I wrote something like, "My brother he got in trouble last night," I was marked wrong. Instead of showing me how speakers of Ebonics sometimes use both a name and a pronoun but in "Standard English" only one is used, I got marked wrong.

Another student, Sherrell, said:

> I grew up thinking Ebonics was wrong. My teachers would say, "If you ever want to get anywhere you have to learn how to talk right." ... At home, after school, break time, lunch time, we all talked our native language which was Ebonics. Our teachers were wrong for saying our language wasn't right. All I heard was Spanish and Ebonics in my neighborhood. They brainwashed me at school to be ashamed of my language and that almost took away one of the few things that African Americans had of our past life and history.

Throughout the Ebonics unit, I asked students to listen and take notes and see if they could spot the rules of Ebonics at work in the school halls, at home, or at the mall. To celebrate and acknowledge a language that so many of my students spoke without awareness, I pointed out Ebonics in class as students spoke. Often, they didn't hear it or recognize it until we held it up like a diamond for them to examine.

One day my student Ryan handed me an unexpected gift when he asked if I'd ever heard the rapper Big L's song "Ebonics." I confessed my ignorance, but I looked it up on the web and downloaded the music and lyrics. The song is clever, but because the performer misunderstands Ebonics as slang, he provided a great audience for my students to rehearse their arguments about Ebonics. In one essay, for example, Jerrell wrote:

> "Ebonics is slang shit," rapper Big L said in his song titled "Ebonics." In this song he tells a lot about the slang that young African Americans use, but this is the problem.

He is talking about slang; there is no Ebonics in his lyrics. The misconception people have is that slang and Ebonics are the same thing. The problem is that slang is just a different way of saying things. For example, in his slang you say money, you can also say bread, cheese, cheddar, cash, dough, green, duckets, Washingtons, chips, guap, and many more. However, when you use Ebonics, there is a sentence structure that you have to use. Don't get me wrong, slang and Ebonics go together like mashed potatoes and gravy, but there is a difference between the two. As my classmate said, "Slang is what I talk; Ebonics is how I speak it."

In his end-of-unit reflection, Jayme wrote that he appreciated "the knowledge that was given to us about the language that we speak and how it related to our roots in Africa." Hannah wrote, "Kids who have been taught that the way they speak is wrong their entire lives can now be confident." And I love the sassiness of Ryan's conclusion: "Ebonics is here to stay and shows no sign of fading away in either the black or white communities. In the words of Ebonics: 'It's BIN here and it's 'bout to stay.'"

Inclusive School Communities

When I took students to local universities to share their knowledge about language during our take-it-to-the-people project, Jacoa told aspiring teachers at Portland State University, "On my college application, I'm going to write that I'm fluent in three languages: English, Spanish, and Ebonics. Call me if you need more information."

As educators, when we talk about building inclusive communities in which all students can learn, we must also examine how our policies and practices continue to shame and exclude students in ways that may not be readily apparent. We signal students from the moment they step into school, whether they belong or whether we see them as trespassers. Everything in school—from the posters on the wall, to the music played at assemblies, to the books in the library—embraces students or pushes them away. Approaching students' home languages with respect is one of the most important curricular choices teachers can make.

We signal students from the moment they step into school, whether they belong or whether we see them as trespassers.

This article first appeared in the Sept. 2008 issue of *Educational Leadership*. Reprinted with permission. Learn more about ASCD at www.ascd.org.

Writer's Note: In my *Rethinking Schools* article "The Politics of Correction" (Vol. 18, No. 1), I discuss more fully how I address moving students between their home language and the language of power, Standard English.

References

LeClair, T. "'The Language Must Not Sweat': A Conversation with Toni Morrison." *New Republic* 21 Mar. 1981: 25-29.

Rickford, J. R. (2008). "Suite for Ebony and Phobics," www.stanford.edu/~rickford/papers/SuiteForEbonyAndPhonics.html

Smitherman, G. (1977). *Talkin and Testifyin: The language of black America.* Boston: Houghton Mifflin.

Smitherman, G. (1998) "Black English/Ebonics: What it be like?" The real ebonics debate. Milwaukee: Rethinking Schools.

Rickford, J. R. & Rickford R.J. (2000). *Spoken soul: The story of black english.* New York: John Wiley & Sons.

CHAPTER TEN

My Mother's Spanish

By Salvador Gabaldón

My mother, a gifted storyteller, nourished a love of language in all her children. Even before we began school, she would read to us from the Spanish translations of such classic works as Jules Verne's *Twenty Thousand Leagues Under the Sea* and Victor Hugo's *The Hunchback of Notre Dame.*

Mexican music from the radio filled our house in Los Angeles, and my mother taught us to hear the words as well as the melody. Books in Spanish and Spanish-language newspapers filled our home, and she corrected the Spanish we used in writing letters to our family in Chihuahua.

With the wisdom of a young mother, she realized that the foundation of a good education is a love of language. Knowing

IStockphoto

the importance of English in this country, she made sure we would learn it. Her contribution to that end was to give us a love for her speech, the language she knew best.

Perhaps inevitably, her two sons both became bilingual and both translated their love of language into careers as English teachers. Those of us who teach language minority students in our nation's public schools see the evidence for inter-language literacy again and again: Students who are strong readers in their native language invariably become strong readers in English.

Unfortunately, in the heat of ideological battles, voters sometimes lose their common sense. Who would have thought that Arizonans—a people who have come to respect and admire the culture of our native tribes—would vote for a law, Proposition 203, that is so harmful to our remaining native languages? Or that we would abandon the concept of local control of schools because we fear that the growing use of Spanish in our communities will somehow threaten English?

As Americans, we should know our own language better. Beautifully flexible and seductive in its power, nothing threatens English. It is the language of science, business, the internet, popular culture, and diplomacy. Anyone who feels a desperate urge to protect English is badly underestimating its strength. I have spent my career helping students to discover the splendor of the English language and the richness of its literature. I've yet to meet any group of parents who do not want English for their children.

Parents seeking bilingual education feel exactly the same way. They want English. The only difference is that, like my mother, they want Spanish for their children, too. They are wise enough to see the value of bilingualism.

Yes, Spanish has indeed become our second language, a language with its own power and beauty. It is everywhere: in bookstores, banking machines, phone messages, advertisements, and media of all types. It gives lyrical (and sometimes perplexing) names to our streets and towns, our mountains, valleys, and rivers. It flavors our foods, colors our music, deepens our ties to the land. Those who interpret Spanish as a threat rather than a marvelous resource are the poorer for it.

Sadly, their fear now impoverishes our system of education. Spanish became a convenient scapegoat, blamed for the educational struggles of the children of immigrants. It wasn't the fact that 76 percent of all such children received English-only

Those who interpret Spanish as a threat rather than a marvelous resource are the poorer for it.

instruction. It wasn't the disparity of funding between wealthy school districts and poor ones. It wasn't the lack of teacher training on language-acquisition strategies.

No, Spanish was the problem. If we could rid our schools of Spanish, then all children would acquire English "in a period not normally intended to exceed one year."

That was the promise. The reality turned out to be something very different. California launched its experiment with immersion in the late 1990s. In the first few years after their immersion programs began, school officials bragged about test-score improvements. They insisted that immersion programs were working, and that children were acquiring English with amazing speed. Then, slowly, the exuberant reports from California began to fade away. Subsequent reports barely made the news. What happened?

In February 2004, California's legislative analysts released a study based on 2.6 million test results, tracking the length of time that it took for students from various language backgrounds to become proficient in English. The students who learned English most quickly were from an Asian American group, Mandarin speakers, averaging 3.4 years. The ones who took longest were from another Asian American group, Hmong speakers, averaging 7.1 years.

The results were exactly what specialists in language acquisition had been saying all along. "English in one year" is a fantasy; literacy in two languages is a treasure.

My mom could have told them that.

This article first appeared in Latino Perspectives *(www.latinoperspectivesmagazine.com). Reprinted with permission.*

'English in one year' is a fantasy; literacy in two languages is a treasure.

CHAPTER ELEVEN

Taking a Chance with Words

Why are the Asian American kids silent in class?

By Carol A. Tateishi

I received Jeff's essay in a mailing from Joan Cone, an old friend and Bay Area Writing Project teacher-consultant who was teaching at El Cerrito High School in the San Francisco Bay Area at the time. She'd sent it to me mainly to share a powerful piece of writing but also because in my position as director of the Bay Area Writing Project, Joan had worked with me in our project's teacher research program and knew I had long been concerned by what I had noted in Bay Area high school classrooms as a lack of participation by students of Asian descent in the oral language activities of the class.

Being Japanese American, this issue was of both personal and professional interest. I was aware that high numbers of secondary

Jordin Isip

teachers whose practice I knew well, shared a belief that classroom talk in a variety of modes is a primary means by which students make sense of the world and what they are learning. But in conversations with these same teachers and in my visits to classrooms, the silent Asian American student is a familiar presence.

While teachers are concerned about this lack of participation in classroom talk, they are also often relatively accepting of these quiet students who don't pose a discipline problem, who turn in homework on time, and in general, get passing grades.

If we believe that the use of language is key to classroom learning, what might it mean if the class includes Asian American students, such as Jeff, and significant numbers of them do not participate or participate minimally day in and day out in the oral discourse of the class? How does their nonparticipation in the active talk of a class affect their learning, or does it? Why don't they participate? What do they understand about the purposes of these orally rich classroom activities? What role might their cultures and home language practices play in their nonparticipation? And, does it matter?

My interest in these questions stems from the fabric of my personal life. Growing up post-World War II in the L.A. Basin, I attended predominantly white schools (my father having bought a house by proxy after the war in an area that discriminated against people of Japanese descent, so there were few of us), but my world outside of school, mainly social life and church life, was mainly among Japanese Americans. I was raised, though, to make my way in the dominant culture, and it started at the dinner table which in my family was a place for talk, orchestrated largely by my dad, sitting at the head of the extra large table he'd built to accommodate six kids. As soon as we all sat down, his questions would start:

"How'd that test go in your math class?"

"Whatever happened to that friend of yours?"

We were a noisy bunch, all vying to keep our dad's attention for that extra minute or two. While this scene may have been common for white middle-class families in the 1950s, it wasn't for Japanese Americans, attested to by my mother, who sat quietly amidst the jabbering, having been raised as a proper Japanese child to not speak during meals. Not that my dad's upbringing was any different. What was different was his intention. The 1950s was only a decade after the internment of 110,000 people of Japanese ancestry and its shadow loomed large over our everyday lives. My dad believed one reason we were

If we believe that the use of language is key to classroom learning, what might it mean if the class includes Asian American students … and significant numbers of them do not participate or participate minimally day in and day out in the oral discourse of the class?

"sold down the river," as he would say, was that we lacked leaders who could make our case and resist government forces. His children would have the words and the confidence to speak up and use language like full-blooded Americans. And for the most part, we did develop the words and the confidence, which served us well in school. But as a teenager trying to fit in among my Japanese American friends, the same rules for speaking served me poorly. As I attempted to negotiate the linguistic borders of school and social life, my conflicting experiences gave me a heightened awareness of culturally patterned differences in the ways people speak and use language.

Now, as an educator, these experiences had taken on an expanded dimension, and I wanted to learn more. Jeff's essay made me think that he would be an interesting student to speak to, and I arranged to spend time in this particular 12th-grade class. Joan and I had talked before about the Asian American students in her classes, and she, too, wanted to learn more about the ways her students used language.

Snapshots from the Classroom

During a small group discussion on my first visit to Joan's class, I sat in Jeff's group, which happened to be made up of students who were all of Asian descent. No one spoke for the longest time while students in the other groups chattered away about the story they'd read for homework, following Joan's directions to share what they didn't understand about the story and to get help from others in their group. While I grew increasingly uncomfortable with the silence, the students seemed fine with this extended wait time. Finally, Jeff spoke, followed by Dan, and eventually the three girls in the group spoke briefly in voices barely loud enough to hear. And while it was clear they'd done the homework, their comments skirted the assigned questions, no one eager, it seemed, to divulge what they didn't understand in their readings.

I asked Jeff about this later that day. Jeff, a fourth-generation Japanese American whose father was a dentist and who, with his shock of pink hair falling over his forehead, appeared right at home among his peers, said, "I was brought up to believe it was a sign of strength to solve your problems yourself and not to impose them on others. It's really hard for me to bring questions about what I don't understand to class to have others help me find the answer." Jeff's response stopped me in my tracks as I immediately recalled learning the same thing at an early age, that silence is a sign of self-reliance and strength. I was surprised at

As I attempted to negotiate the linguistic borders of school and social life, my conflicting experiences gave me a heightened awareness of culturally patterned differences in the ways people speak and use language.

the abiding strength of this cultural value, extending to this young man whose great grandfather would have immigrated to this country at the turn of the century. In talking further with Jeff, it emerged that his reluctance to participate was compounded by the negative attitude in Japanese culture toward verbosity in men, something that he'd also learned at home. However, his answer was a point of concern, knowing Joan's belief in collaborative learning and realizing these particular students were not reaping its benefits.

In my next visit, Jeff was leading a whole-class discussion, for the first time according to Joan, of "Seventeen Syllables," a short story by Hisaye Yamamato that takes place during the 1930s in California's San Joaquin Valley. Central to the story is the relationship between an Issei (first-generation Japanese immigrant) husband and wife where the wife's writing of haiku and the social recognition of her talents make apparent the class differences between them, and challenges the husband's authority within the family. Told from the young daughter's point of view, the story reveals deep-seated emotions by the father, masked through his silence, and the truth behind her mother's move to America due to a shameful romantic liaison. The meaning of silence and the father's inability to express emotions are important themes.

Jeff pulled a desk to the front of the room and started the discussion with a few questions. Soon, other students were answering his questions and raising their own, but they appeared puzzled by the key incident in the story where the father destroys the prize given to his wife in a haiku contest:

> [H]e threw the picture on the ground and picked up the axe. Smashing the picture, glass and all (she heard the explosion faintly), he reached over for the kerosene that was used to encourage the bath fire and poured it over the wreckage.

Jeff pulled a desk to the front of the room and started the discussion with a few questions. Soon, other students were answering his questions and raising their own.

Students wondered why the father hadn't just talked to his wife. Two of the students felt that the father's silence and his abruptness with his wife leading up to this incident were inexplicable and undercut the meaning of the story. Jeff attempted to explain the father's behavior, but it seemed that Jeff was experiencing, himself, the very difficulty he was trying to explain about the father's inability to use language to reveal his thoughts and feelings. Finally, Jeff said, "That's just the way the Japanese are," and he quietly moved the desk back into the row and sat down, frustrated and deflated.

What Students Had to Say

Over time I sat in on Joan's class often and interviewed five students in depth: Jeff and Dan, both Japanese American; Christina and Sandra, who had emigrated from China when they were in elementary school; and Wanda, who had emigrated from Korea when she was in middle school. (I should add that I had started with one-to-one interviews but switched to group interviews when I found that the students seemed to feel that they were failing me by the brevity of their responses.)

For these students, speaking in class was not a simple matter. A recurrent theme throughout our interviews was "You're not supposed to say too much." Jeff was brought up believing that too much talk could "cause disrespect and harsh feelings," while Dan viewed negatively students who were "outspoken." Sandra repeatedly told me that in her family "We don't talk about feelings," and gender issues compounded the girls' reluctance to talk. Christina summarized their experiences: "In my home, women aren't supposed to speak unless they're spoken to. It's just the way I've been raised. Girls aren't supposed to talk out loud in public and it's just the way I grew up." And, in direct opposition to the way I was deliberately raised, all the girls said they weren't supposed to talk at the dinner table. In addition, the three girls, who had entered American schools as English learners, continued to worry about their language skills. Wanda commented that, "I may not be able to speak as well English as other kids, but I'm scared like, oh, probably they're going to laugh at me … so that discourages me from speaking loud in class."

For these students, speaking in class was not a simple matter.

While all the students tended to be self-conscious about expressing their thinking in class, as our interviews progressed, the students' views of speaking at home began to take on a number of shared qualities:

- Oral language tends to be used functionally.

- Speaking publicly about one's problems is discouraged.

- That restraint in talking is valued.

- You don't talk about feelings or personal experiences.

I was initially surprised that their comments about ways of speaking at home held such commonalities since there were differences among the Asian cultures represented among the students and differences in the features of each of the Asian speech communities. In addition, the students' families spanned close to

100 years of immigration to this country. It could be that the group interview setting may have contributed to this show of commonalities. Even so, the features singled out above shouldn't necessarily be generalized to all students of Asian descent.

What is relevant, though, is to examine these speech behaviors in light of Joan's beliefs about classroom talk that are very likely shared by many progressive classroom teachers, beliefs such as:

- Oral language can be used to negotiate meaning.
- Risk-taking in talk is valued.
- Speaking in class increases engagement.
- Classroom dialogue deepens learning.

When compared with the students' views, the exploratory and engaging nature of this kind of classroom talk was a far cry from the students' ways of speaking at home. In addition, the students had little opportunity to practice or learn about these other ways of speaking in public spaces except in the classroom.

What Students Say Would Help Them

When I asked about what helped or hindered them in speaking in class, the students had definite ideas. They were keenly aware of differences in the sociocultural expectations for speaking in the home and the classroom, and they were unanimous in their preference for small groups. But they felt a strong need to have group leaders, which corresponds to a point made by Professor Lily Wong Fillmore in a conversation I had with her at UC Berkeley where she spoke of a need by Asian American students to be "authored" to speak, a concept that makes sense given the hierarchical nature of many Asian American families. It's not surprising that students might look to an external authority for permission to speak or feel more comfortable with a set of rules or protocols that in themselves "author" turn-taking in speaking. (I realized, too, that this is what my dad had done for my siblings and me as we were growing up.) The students said they felt they could begin to leave behind their hesitations and self-consciousness when they were asked to speak and when the rules for speaking were clear. They felt in these instances they were complying with an external request and the content of what they said was shaped by that request. As Christina stated, "Maybe sometimes I need someone to ask me to say something instead of me moving myself into the group."

The students said they felt they could begin to leave behind their hesitations and self-consciousness when they were asked to speak and when the rules for speaking were clear.

For the students interviewed, to "just, like, join the conversation" (as Christina put it) was the hardest and most unfamiliar way to participate in small-group talk, although they noted that this approach worked for others. They said they needed help in negotiating the open, unstructured nature of the class discussion groups. For example, they were unanimous in their preference for small discussion groups, but they said a group needed to have designated leaders so that, in Sandra's view, "everyone has an equal chance to speak." At one point, Wanda described an "authoring" structure she liked that Joan had used early in the year: "In the *Shipping News*, the whole class got in a big circle. I said 'pass' because I didn't have anything to say, but everybody had a chance to say pass or speak. That was kind of nice."

The concept of "authoring" also shed light on Dan's debate team participation. I had been surprised to learn that he not only was on the team but also had actively recruited new members and was responsible, according to Joan, for the increased number of Asians Americans on the team. In my class visits, though, Dan had not spoken once in the whole-group discussions and had spoken only minimally in small-group discussions. It seemed that the formal structure of debate with its clear rules for speaking gave Dan the authority he needed to speak, liberated him to do so, and, perhaps, gave him the time to plan and craft his words.

A Lot Less Quiet

So far I have focused on the gap between oral language use in the classroom by the Asian American students I interviewed and Joan's expectations for it. I would be remiss, however, to leave a picture of black and white differences. Jeff was the one student who seemed to be straddling the two speech communities, and early on provided an interesting insight about Asian Americans and language use when viewed in a historical context:

> What I think is that Asian Americans (as a significant percentage of the population) are a relatively new minority. A lot of the time they are kept out of the mainstream or keep themselves out of the mainstream—it's kind of ingrained in you like in that "Seventeen Syllables" story where you have to kind of restrain yourself. At the same time as Asian American kids are becoming more American, I think there's less of that restraint and so gradually more Asian American kids and also adults are speaking out more. Maybe 20 years ago or something I'm sure there's quite a big difference compared to now. We're a lot less quiet now.

They said they needed help in negotiating the open, unstructured nature of the class discussion groups.

"A lot less quiet now" is a good way to describe an emerging phase that not only Jeff was experiencing but also one which seems to be just beginning to be played out in Bay Area schools and in San Francisco schools in particular. Based on anecdotal evidence from San Francisco high school teachers, their students are increasingly joining the conversation of the classroom, partly, I think, because they are "becoming more American," but also because of the district's demographics. Close to 40 percent of students are of Asian descent, districtwide, with 31.9 percent Chinese. Numbers make a difference.

While San Francisco and students like Jeff are showing promising changes, what can teachers do right now that might bring students such as those I interviewed more readily into the talk of the classroom where they can experience and practice the intellectual engagement it can provide?

Recommendations

While this beginning list of ideas only skims the surface of what is possible, they address the concerns of the students I spoke with—students who said they were raised to wait to speak out of respect for others, who needed to have a definite turn to speak or needed to be called on in order to speak, who needed better understanding of the academic and intellectual purposes of talk in school settings, and who needed scaffolded practice in venturing into talk that might reveal personal feelings and opinions or provoke argument.

Be aware and knowledgeable of the cultural barriers some students face in attempting to participate in classroom talk.

- Be aware and knowledgeable of the cultural barriers some students face in attempting to participate in classroom talk.

- Take the same kind of time and effort to teach effective classroom talk as you might for writing response groups or any kind of classroom collaborative work.

- Model strong and weak discussion groups with mock classroom enactments that highlight the why's of the talk.

- Create stable discussion groups as you would for writing groups. Take care in putting students into groups, helping them build trustful communities over time and sensitivity to cultural differences.

- Designate group leaders and develop clear guidelines and protocols with students for how the group works and how talk is conducted and why.

- Debrief the workings of small-group talk regularly to help students develop greater understanding of the dynamics of classroom talk.

Our challenge is to make the rules and purposes governing classroom talk as visible and explicit as possible so that students can acquire new literacy practices and move easily from one speech community to the next in a code-switching mode, not only for the Asian American students but for their fellow students who need to hear their thoughts and perspectives.

Final Thoughts

While my inquiry has ostensibly been about teaching and learning, the underlying question is, teaching and learning for what? More is at stake than better learning of the curriculum. There are consequences beyond academia. Already a lack of strong verbal skills is impacting Asian Americans and their communities.

Studies I've looked at point to our underrepresentation in occupations such as journalism, law, and the social sciences that require language skills and personal contact and, instead, a concentration in fields where technical knowledge rather than linguistic and social skills are at a premium. Also, the glass ceiling effect is well known among Asian Americans where candidates tend to do poorly in oral interviews where their lack of verbal fluency translates into a perceived lack of self-confidence and necessary supervisory skills.

And my "for what" question brings me back to my father and his intuitive understanding that language is connected to resistance and social justice, that language is connected to action and consequences.

It mattered in the 1940s and matters again today if Asian Americans have the words and voice to speak up for themselves and their communities. It matters if we have lawyers, writers, activists, educators, business leaders, elected officials, and ordinary citizens who understand the power of language and use it.

Right now, Asian Americans are among the fastest growing segments of the population and are expected to grow to 20 million in this country by 2020. It is increasingly important that Asian American voices, literally, become part of the ongoing dialogue that helps shape and inform who we are. A good place to start is the classroom.

Our challenge is to make the rules and purposes governing classroom talk as visible and explicit as possible.

CHAPTER TWELVE

Black English/Ebonics

What it be like?

By Geneva Smitherman

*I looked at my hands, they looked new/I looked at my feet, and they
did too/I got a new way of walkin/and a new way of talkin.*
—Traditional Black Gospel Song

The month after the Oakland School Board passed its resolution, the term "Ebonics" turned 24 years old. Yeah,
dass right, the name is over two decades old. It was
coined by a group of black scholars as a new way of talkin bout
the language of African slave descendants. Like the message of
that old Gospel tune, "Ebonics" was about transformation, about
intellectuals among the Talented Tenth striking a blow for the linguistic liberation of our people. The guru in this group of scholars

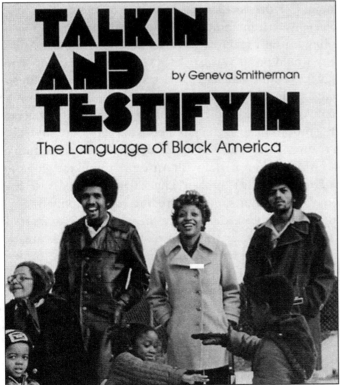

TALKIN
AND
TESTIFYIN

by Geneva Smitherman

The Language of Black America

Wayne State University Press

at that "Language and the Urban Child" conference, convened in St. Louis, Mo., in January 1973, was the brilliant clinical psychologist Dr. Robert L. Williams, now Professor Emeritus, Washington University. In the book of conference proceedings Williams published in 1975, he captures the thinking of that historical moment:

> A significant incident occurred at the conference. The black conferees were so critical of the work on the subject done by white researchers, many of whom also happened to be present, that they decided to caucus among themselves and define black language from a black perspective. It was in this caucus that the term *Ebonics* was created. [The term refers to] linguistic and paralinguistic features which on a concentric continuum represent the communicative competence of the West African, Caribbean, and United States slave descendant of African origin. It includes the various idioms, patois, argots, ideolects, and social dialects of black people, especially those who have been forced to adapt to colonial circumstances. (1975, Preface, Introduction)

The conceptual framework of 'Ebonics' represented an avenue for decolonization of the African American mind.

For this group of scholars, the conceptual framework of "Ebonics" represented an avenue for decolonization of the African American mind, a way to begin repairing the psycholinguistically maimed psyche of blacks in America. As Paulo Freire would put it 12 years later, "language variations (female language, ethnic language, dialects) are intimately interconnected with, coincide with, and express identity. They help defend one's sense of identity and they are absolutely necessary in the process of struggling for liberation" (1985, p. 186). Ebonics reaffirms the interrelatedness of language and culture and links Africans in America with Africans around the globe.

Ebonics: neither "broken" English, nor "sloppy" speech, nor merely "slang," nor some bizarre lingo spoken only by baggy-pants-wearing black kids. Rather, the variety of Ebonics spoken in the U.S. (hereafter USEB) is rooted in the Black American Oral Tradition and represents a synthesis of African (primarily West African) and European (primarily English) linguistic-cultural traditions. The linguistic shape of the words in USEB can readily be identified as standard English, i.e., the Language of Wider Communication here in the U.S. (hereafter LWC), but these words do not always have the same meaning in USEB as in LWC. Further, there are many words of direct African origin—e.g., *okay, gorilla, cola, jazz*—that are now part of LWC (often without props to us African slave descendants). However, what gives Black Language (un-huh, dat ain no typo, I meant "language") its distinctiveness is the nuanced meanings of these English words, the pronunciations, the ways in which the words are combined to form grammatical statements, and the communicative practices of the USEB-speaking community. In short, USEB may be thought of as the Africanization of American English.

In short, USEB may be thought of as the Africanization of American English.

Patterns of Ebonics

In the next section, I discuss the following patterns of USEB: 1) aspectual be; 2) stressed been; 3) multiple negation; 4) adjacency/context in possessives; 5) post-vocalic /r/ deletion; 6) copula absence; 7) camouflaged and other unique lexical forms.

Consider this statement, which comes from some black women just kickin it in the beauty shop (gloss: conversational chit-chat at a hair salon): "The Brotha be lookin good; that's what got the Sista nose open!" In this statement, *Brotha* is USEB for an African American man, *lookin good* refers to his style, his attractive appearance (not necessarily the same thing as physical beauty in USEB), *Sista* is USEB for an African American woman, and her passionate love for the Brotha is conveyed by the phrase *nose open* (in USEB, the kind of passionate love that makes you vulnerable to exploitation). *Sista nose* is standard USEB grammar for denoting possession, indicated by adjacency/context (i.e., rather than the LWC /'s, s'/). The use of be means that the quality of *lookin good* is not limited to the present moment, but reflects the Brotha's past, present, and future essence.

As in the case of Efik and other Niger-Congo languages, USEB has an aspectual verb system, conveyed by the use of the English verb be to denote iterativity (i.e., a recurring or habitual state-of-affairs; contrast *He be lookin good* with *He lookin good*, which refers to the present moment only—not the kind of *lookin good* that opens the nose!). Note further that many black writers and rap artists employ the spellings "Brotha" and "Sista." Now, they ain just tryin to be cute. These orthographic representations are used to convey a phonological pattern derived from the influence of West African languages, many of which do not have an /r/ sound. Also in these language communities, kinship terms may be used when referring to African people, whether biologically related or not.

Of course there is overlap between USEB and colloquial, everyday American English—e.g., use of "ain't," ending sentences with prepositions, double negatives. However, there are critical distinctions that separate linguistically competent USEB speakers from the wanna-bes. For example, the colloquial speaker says *gonna* or *goin to* for the LWC form going to. But the USEB speaker uses the nasalized vowel form, producing a sound close to, but not identical with, LWC *gone*, thus: "What she go (n) do now?", i.e., in LWC, "What is she going to do now?" Another example is in negation patterns. While those obsessed with the "national mania for correctness" often rail against colloquial speakers' double negatives, USEB is distinctive not only for its negative inversion, but also for its *multiple* negatives, that is, three or more negatives formed from combinations of indefinite pronouns and/or adjectives. Check out this exclamation of complex negative inversion from a devout church-goer: "Don't nobody don't know God can't tell me nothin!" i.e., in LWC, "A person who doesn't believe in God and isn't saved has no credibility with me."

As mentioned above, USEB words may look like mainstream American English, but the usage and meaning are different. This is the source of a good deal of miscommunication and misunderstanding between USEB and LWC speakers. In response to the question, "Is she married?" the USEB speaker may answer "She been married." If the speaker pronounces been without stress, it means the woman in question was once married but is now divorced. If the speaker pronounces *been* with stress, it means she married a long time ago and is still married.

Another example is the use of LWC words that are "camouflaged" (Spears, 1982). For example, in the USEB statement, "She come tellin me I'n [didn't] know what I was talkin bout," the verb *come* does not denote motion as in LWC. Rather the meaning of come in this context is one of indignation, i.e., in LWC, "She had the audacity to tell me that I didn't know what I was talking about. How dare she!" Yet another kind of cross-communication example comes from semantic inversion. Due to crossover and the popular appeal of Michael Jackson, most people are aware that *bad* in USEB translates to *good* in LWC; however, lexical items that haven't enjoyed such a high degree of crossover are problematic in these cross-cultural exchanges. For example, consider the following form of address common among many black males: "Yo, Dog!" *Dog* is a linguistic symbol of male bonding, most likely derived from the African American fraternity tradition of referring to pledges as *dogs. Yo, Dog!* was used by a Brotha on lock down (gloss:

imprisoned) to address his European American male psychiatrist as an expression of camaraderie. Turns out, though, that this white psychiatrist was not yet down (gloss: hip, understanding of the Black Cultural framework). He misinterpreted the Brotha's greeting and made an issue of the "insult."

The above are only some of the patterns in the grammatical, phonological, and semantic systems of USEB. To explore the full 360 degrees of USEB, we need to move on to styles of speaking. In fact, it is the area of communicative practices—rhetorical strategies and modes of discourse—that cuts across gender, generation, and class in the African American community. USEB speech acts may be classified as follows: 1) Call-Response; 2) Tonal Semantics; 3) Narrativizing; 4) Proverb Use/Proverbializing; 5) Signification/ Signifyin; 6) The Dozens/Snappin/Joanin. Space limitations will only permit discussion of two of these discourse modes.

Signification, or more commonly, *signifyin*, which can be rendered with or without the phonological and morpho-syntactical patterns of USEB, is a form of ritualized insult in which a speaker puts down, talks about, needles—signifies on—other speakers. In this communicative practice, the speaker deploys exaggeration, irony, and indirection as a way of saying something on two different levels at once. It is often used to send a message of social critique, a bit of social commentary on the actions or statements of someone who is in need of a wake-up call. When signifyin is done with verbal dexterity, it avoids the creation of social distance between speaker and audience because the rich humor makes you laugh to keep from crying. Like Malcolm X, who once began a speech with these words: "Mr. Moderator, Brother Lomax, Brothas and Sistas, friends and enemies." Now, you don't usually begin a speech by addressing your enemies. Thus, Malcolm's signifyin statement let his audience know that he knew inimical forces were in their midst. Or like one of the deacons at this Traditional Black Church, where the preacher would never deal with the problems and issues folk were facing on a daily basis. Rather, he was always preachin bout the pearly gates and how great thangs was gon be at dat home up in the sky. So one day this deacon said to the preacher, "Reb, you know, I got a home in Heaven, but I ain't homesick!"

Signifyin is engaged in by all age groups and by both males and females in the black community. It has the following characteristics: 1) indirection, circumlocution; 2) metaphorical-imagistic (images rooted in the everyday real world); 3) humorous, ironic; 4) rhythmic fluency; 5) teachy, but not preachy;

Signification, *or more commonly,* signifyin, *is a form of ritualized insult in which a speaker puts down, talks about, needles —signifies on— other speakers.*

6) directed at person(s) present in the speech situation (signifiers do not talk behind your back); 7) punning, play on words; 8) introduction of the semantically or logically unexpected.

Types of Signification

There are two types of Signification. One type is leveled at a person's mother (and occasionally at other relatives). Traditionally, this first type was referred to as "The Dozens"/"playin The Dozens." The second type of signifyin is aimed at a person, action, or thing, either just for fun, or for corrective criticism. Today, the two types of Signification are being conflated under a more general form of discourse, referred to as "snappin."

To fully appreciate the skill and complexity of Signification, we shall analyze in some detail a conversational excerpt involving two Sistas in a group of several at a wedding shower:

> Linda: Girl, what up with that head? [Referring to her friend's hairstyle]
>
> Betty: Ask yo momma. [Laughter from all the Sistas on this conversational set.]
>
> Linda: Oh, so you going there, huh? Well, I *DID* ask my momma. And she said, "Cain't you see that Betty look like her momma spit her out?" [Laughter from all, including Betty.]

Betty and Linda signify on each other. Instead of answering Linda's question directly, Betty decides to inform Linda that the condition of her hairstyle is none of Linda's business by responding with "Ask yo momma." The usual expectation in a conversation is that a speaker's question will be answered honestly and sincerely; thus Betty's unexpected indirection produces laughter from the listeners.

Speech act theory indicates that communication succeeds or fails as a result of the illocutionary, i.e., intended, and perlocutionary, i.e., received, effects of a message. The surface meaning of "yo momma" for those outside the USEB speech community is simply "your mother/mom." However, within the black speech community, the utterance immediately signals that an insult has been hurled. The intended and received meaning of *yo momma* is invective; the game of ritual insult begins with participants creating the most appropriate, humorous, spontaneous, creative, exaggerated/untrue retorts that they can come up with.

The source of the retort "Ask yo momma" probably stems from family patterns in which mothers are consulted ("asked") about all kinds of things, great or small. Fathers may even respond to their children's questions or requests by saying "Ask your mother." In USEB, the speaker does not intend the direct meaning, "You should go and ask your mother about this situation." Rather, given the conversational context, the speaker is indirectly saying "Let the game of The Dozens begin." Linda clearly recognizes the entry into this game as indicated by her response, "Oh, so you going there, huh?" Unskilled players, lacking a spontaneous, apposite, humorous retort, would have let the conversation end at this point. However, Linda shows adeptness in playing the game. She regroups momentarily ("Oh, so you going there, huh?") and fires back skillfully. In fact, she "caps" (gloss: wins) this exchange with a more clever retort. Although Betty's use of the intragroup expression, *ask yo momma*, is humorous and sets up a challenge, it is formulaic, simplistic, and stylized. In this instance, it cannot, and does not, beat: "Well, I DID ask my momma and she said, cain't you see that Betty look like her momma spit her out" (Troutman-Robinson and Smitherman, 1997).

Although the Rev. Jesse Jackson and Sista Maya Angelou came out in the national news and dissed the Oakland School Board's resolution, they are well-versed in USEB. Twenty years ago, in my first major work on USEB, *Talkin and Testifyin*, I quoted both at length and lauded them as linguistic role models, who are adept at capitalizing on the forms of Black Language to convey profound political messages. Like Jesse who is down wit Signification: "Pimp, punk, prostitute, preacher, Ph.D.—all the P's, you still in slavery!" Thus he conveys the message that all members of the African American community, regardless of their social status, are marginalized and disempowered, by virtue of U.S. historically institutionalized racism and skin color bias. (Jesse also uses copula absence here—"you still in slavery"—which has not been found in any of the dialects of British English that came over on the Mayflower, but which is used widely in the languages of West Africa.)

The Dozens

As mentioned above, The Dozens is one of several significant speech acts in USEB. This ritualized game of insult has analogues in West African communicative practices (see Smitherman, 1995, and the several references cited there). Also referred to as "snappin" by many members of the Hip Hop Nation, The Dozens is like "Yo momma so dumb she thought a quarterback was a refund!"

Sista Maya Angelou is so bad she don't play The Dozens, she play The Thirteens! She uses this USEB discourse mode to critique the actions of blacks and whites. Here how she do it:

> (The Thirteens Black):
> Your Momma took to shouting
> Your Poppa's gone to war,
> Your sister's in the streets
> Your brother's in the bar,
> The thirteens. Right On ...
> And you, you make me sorry
> You out here by yourself,
> I'd call you something dirty,
> But there just ain't nothing left,
> cept
> The thirteens. Right On ...
> (The Thirteens White):
> Your daughter wears a jock strap,
> Your son he wears a bra
> Your brother jonesed your cousin
> in the back seat of the car.
> The thirteens. Right On...
> Your money thinks you're something
> But if I'd learned to curse,
> I'd tell you what your name is
> But there just ain't nothing worse
> than
> The thirteens. Right On.
>
> —Angelou, 1971)

To speak Ebonics is to assume the cultural legacy of U.S. slave descendants of African origin.

African French psychiatrist Frantz Fanon taught that "every dialect, every language, is a way of thinking. To speak means to assume a culture." To speak Ebonics is to assume the cultural legacy of U.S. slave descendants of African origin. To speak Ebonics is to assert the power of this tradition in the quest to resolve the unfinished business of being African in America. While years of massive research (done in the 1960s and early '70s) on the language of this group (mostly by white scholars) did indeed debunk cognitive-linguistic deficiency theory, in its place arose social inadequacy theory.

Although the language was shown to be systematic and rule-governed, since it is not accepted by the white mainstream, difference became deficit all over again, and in the process,

Africans in America suffered further dislocation. To speak (of/on/about) Ebonics, to consciously employ this terminology and conceptual framework, as those black scholars did back in 1973, and as the Oakland School Board has done a generation later, is to be bout the business of relocating African Americans to subject position. Large and in charge, as the Hip Hoppers say, Ebonics, then and now, symbolizes a new way of talkin the walk about language and liberatory education for African Americans.

References:

Angelou, M. (1971). *Just give me a cool drink of water 'fore I die.* New York: Random House.

Fanon, F. (1967). The Negro and language. In *Black skin, white masks.* New York: Grove Press.

Freire, P. (1985). *The politics of education: Culture, power, and liberation* (D. Macedo, trans.). Massachusetts: Bergin & Garvey Publishers, Inc.

Smitherman, G. (1995). Introduction. In J. Percelay, S. Dweck, & M. Ivey, *Double snaps.* New York: William Morrow.

Smitherman, G. (1986). *Talkin and testifyin: The language of black America.* Detroit: Wayne State University Press.

Spears, A.K. (1982). The Black English semi-auxillary come. *Language, 58*(4), 850-872.

Troutman, D. & Smitherman, G. (1997). Discourse as social interaction. In T.A. van Dijk (ed.), *Discourse, ethnicity, culture, and racism* (pp.144-180). London: Sage Publications.

Williams, R.L. (ed.) (1975). *Ebonics: The true language of black folks.* St. Louis: Institute of Black Studies.

CHAPTER THIRTEEN

Ebonics and Culturally Responsive Instruction

By Lisa Delpit

The "Ebonics Debate" has created much more heat than light for most of the country. For teachers trying to determine what implications there might be for classroom practice, enlightenment has been a completely nonexistent commodity. I have been asked often enough recently, "What do you think about Ebonics? Are you for it or against it?" My answer must be neither. I can be neither for Ebonics or against Ebonics any more than I can be for or against air. It exists. It is the language spoken by many of our African American children. It is the language they heard as their mothers nursed them and changed their diapers and played peek-a-boo with them. It is the language through which they first encountered love, nurturance, and joy.

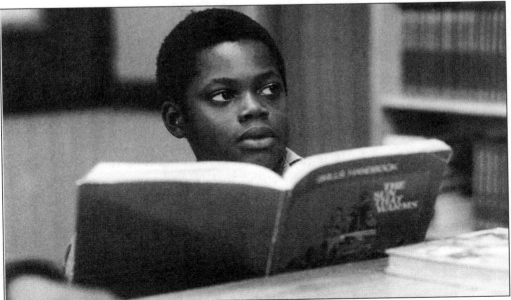

Jean-Claude Lejeune

On the other hand, most teachers of those African American children who have been least well-served by educational systems believe that their students' life chances will be further hampered if they do not learn Standard English. In the stratified society in which we live, they are absolutely correct. While having access to the politically mandated language form will not, by any means, guarantee economic success (witness the growing numbers of unemployed African Americans holding doctorates), not having access will almost certainly guarantee failure.

So what must teachers do? Should they spend their time relentlessly "correcting" their Ebonics-speaking children's language so that it might conform to what we have learned to refer to as Standard English? Despite good intentions, constant correction seldom has the desired effect. Such correction increases cognitive monitoring of speech, thereby making talking difficult. To illustrate, I have frequently taught a relatively simple new "dialect" to classes of preservice teachers. In this dialect, the phonetic element "iz" is added after the first consonant or consonant cluster in each syllable of a word. (Maybe becomes miz-ay-biz-ee and apple, iz-ap-piz-le.) After a bit of drill and practice, the students are asked to tell a partner in "iz" language why they decided to become teachers. Most only haltingly attempt a few words before lapsing into either silence or into Standard English. During a follow-up discussion, all students invariably speak of the impossibility of attempting to apply rules while trying to formulate and express a thought. Forcing speakers to monitor their language typically produces silence.

Correction may also affect students' attitudes toward their teachers. In a recent research project, middle school, inner-city students were interviewed about their attitudes toward their teachers and school. One young woman complained bitterly, "Mrs. ___ always be interrupting to make you 'talk correct' and stuff. She be butting into your conversations when you not even talking to her! She need to mind her own business." Clearly this student will be unlikely to either follow the teacher's directives or to want to imitate her speech style.

Group Identity

Issues of group identity may also affect students' oral production of a different dialect. Researcher Sharon Nelson-Barber, in a study of phonologic aspects of Pima Indian language, found that, in grades 1 through 3, the children's English most approximated the standard dialect of their teachers. But surprisingly, by

> *So what must teachers do? Should they spend their time relentlessly 'correcting' their Ebonics-speaking children's language so that it might conform to what we have learned to refer to as Standard English?*

4th grade, when one might assume growing competence in standard forms, their language moved significantly toward the local dialect. These 4th graders had the *competence* to express themselves in a more standard form, but chose, consciously or unconsciously, to use the language of those in their local environments. The researcher believes that, by ages 8 or 9, these children became aware of their group membership and its importance to their well-being, and this realization was reflected in their language.[1] They may also have become increasingly aware of the schools' negative attitude toward their community and found it necessary—through choice of linguistic form—to decide with which camp to identify.

What should teachers do about helping students acquire an additional oral form? First, they should recognize that the linguistic form a student brings to school is intimately connected with loved ones, community, and personal identity. To suggest that this form is "wrong" or, even worse, ignorant, is to suggest that something is wrong with the student and his or her family. To denigrate your language is, then, in African American terms, to "talk about your mama." Anyone who knows anything about African American culture knows the consequences of that speech act!

On the other hand, it is equally important to understand that students who do not have access to the politically popular dialect form in this country are less likely to succeed economically than their peers who do. How can both realities be embraced in classroom instruction?

It is possible and desirable to make the actual study of language diversity a part of the curriculum for all students. For younger children, discussions about the differences in the ways television characters from different cultural groups speak can provide a starting point. A collection of the many children's books written in the dialects of various cultural groups can also provide a wonderful basis for learning about linguistic diversity,[2] as can audiotaped stories narrated by individuals from different cultures, including taping books read by members of the children's home communities. Mrs. Pat, a teacher chronicled by Stanford University researcher Shirley Brice Heath, had her students become language "detectives," interviewing a variety of individuals and listening to the radio and television to discover the differences and similarities in the ways people talked.[3] Children can learn that there are many ways of saying the same thing, and that certain contexts suggest particular kinds of linguistic performances.

The linguistic form a student brings to school is intimately connected with loved ones, community, and personal identity.

Some teachers have groups of students create bilingual dictionaries of their own language form and Standard English. Both the students and the teacher become engaged in identifying terms and deciding upon the best translations. This can be done as generational dictionaries, too, given the proliferation of "youth culture" terms growing out of the Ebonics-influenced tendency for the continual regeneration of vocabulary. Contrastive grammatical structures can be studied similarly, but, of course, as the Oakland policy suggests, teachers must be aware of the grammatical structure of Ebonics before they can launch into this complex study.

Other teachers have had students become involved with standard forms through various kinds of role play. For example, memorizing parts for drama productions will allow students to practice and "get the feel" of speaking Standard English while not under the threat of correction. A master teacher of African American children in Oakland, Carrie Secret, uses this technique and extends it so that students video their practice performances and self-critique them as to the appropriate use of Standard English. (But I must add that Carrie's use of drama and oration goes much beyond acquiring Standard English. She inspires pride and community connections which are truly wondrous to behold.) The use of self-critique of recorded forms may prove even more useful than I initially realized. California State University-Hayward professor Etta Hollins has reported that just by leaving a tape recorder on during an informal class period and playing it back with no comment, students began to code-switch—moving between Standard English and Ebonics—more effectively. It appears that they may have not realized which language form they were using until they heard themselves speak on tape.

Young students can create puppet shows or role-play cartoon characters—many "superheroes" speak almost hypercorrect standard English! Playing a role eliminates the possibility of implying that the child's language is inadequate and suggests, instead, that different language forms are appropriate in different contexts. Some other teachers in New York City have had their students produce a news show every day for the rest of the school. The students take on the personae of famous newscasters, keeping in character as they develop and read their news reports. Discussions ensue about whether Tom Brokaw would have said it that way, again taking the focus off the child's speech.

Although most educators think of Black Language as primarily differing in grammar and syntax, there are other differences

Although most educators think of Black Language as primarily differing in grammar and syntax, there are other differences in oral language of which teachers should be aware in a multicultural context.

in oral language of which teachers should be aware in a multicultural context, particularly in discourse style and language use. Harvard University researcher Sarah Michaels and other researchers identified differences in children's narratives at "sharing time." [4] They found that there was a tendency among young white children to tell "topic-centered" narratives—stories focused on one event—and a tendency among black youngsters, especially girls, to tell "episodic" narratives—stories that include shifting scenes and are typically longer. While these differences are interesting in themselves, what is of greater significance is adults' responses to the differences. C.B. Cazden reports on a subsequent project in which a white adult was taped reading the oral narratives of black and white 1st graders, with all syntax dialectal markers removed.[5] Adults were asked to listen to the stories and comment about the children's likelihood of success in school. The researchers were surprised by the differential responses given by black and white adults.

Varying Reactions

In responding to the retelling of a black child's story, the white adults were uniformly negative, making such comments as "terrible story, incoherent" and "[n]ot a story at all in the sense of describing something that happened." Asked to judge this child's academic competence, all of the white adults rated her below the children who told "topic-centered" stories. Most of these adults also predicted difficulties for this child's future school career, such as, "This child might have trouble reading," that she exhibited "language problems that affect school achievement," and that "family problems" or "emotional problems" might hamper her academic progress.

This is not a story about racism, but one about cultural familiarity.

The black adults had very different reactions. They found this child's story "well formed, easy to understand, and interesting, with lots of detail and description." Even though all five of these adults mentioned the "shifts" and "associations" or "nonlinear" quality of the story, they did not find these features distracting. Three of the black adults selected the story as the best of the five they had heard, and all but one judged the child as exceptionally bright, highly verbal, and successful in school.[6]

This is not a story about racism, but one about cultural familiarity. However, when differences in narrative style produce differences in interpretation of competence, the pedagogical implications are evident. If children who produce stories based in differing discourse styles are expected to have trouble reading, and viewed as having language, family, or emotional problems, as was the case with the informants quoted by Cazden, they are unlikely to be viewed as ready for the same challenging instruction awarded students whose language patterns more closely parallel the teacher's.

Most teachers are particularly concerned about how speaking Ebonics might affect learning to read. There is little evidence that speaking another mutually intelligible language form, per se, negatively affects one's ability to learn to read.[7] For commonsensical proof, one need only reflect on nonstandard English-speaking Africans who, though enslaved, not only taught themselves to read English, but did so under threat of severe punishment or death. But children who speak Ebonics do have a more difficult time becoming proficient readers. Why? In part, appropriate instructional methodologies are frequently not adopted. There is ample evidence that children who do not come to school with knowledge about letters, sounds, and symbols need to experience some explicit instruction in these areas in order to become independent readers. Another explanation is that, where teachers' assessments of competence are influenced by the language children speak, teachers may develop low expectations for certain students and subsequently teach them less.[8] A third explanation rests in teachers' confusing the teaching of reading with the teaching of a new language form.

Reading researcher Patricia Cunningham found that teachers across the United States were more likely to correct reading miscues that were "dialect" related ("Here go a table" for "Here is a table") than those that were "nondialect" related ("Here is a dog" for "There is a dog").[9] Seventy-eight percent of the former types of miscues were corrected, compared with only 27 percent of the latter. She concludes that the teachers were acting out of ignorance, not realizing that "here go" and "here is" represent the same meaning in some black children's language.

In my observations of many classrooms, however, I have come to conclude that even when teachers recognize the similarity of meaning, they are likely to correct Ebonics-related miscues. Consider a typical example:

Text: Yesterday I washed my brother's clothes.
Student's Rendition: Yesterday I wash my bruvver close.

The subsequent exchange between student and teacher sounds something like this:

There is little evidence that speaking another mutually intelligible language form, per se, negatively affects one's ability to learn to read.

T: Wait, let's go back. What's that word again? {Points at "washed." }

S: Wash.

T: No. Look at it again. What letters do you see at the end? You see "e-d." Do you remember what we say when we see those letters on the end of the word?

S: "ed"

T: OK, but in this case we say washed. Can you say that?

S: Washed.

T: Good. Now read it again.

S: Yesterday I washed my bruvver ...

T: Wait a minute, what's that word again? {Points to "brother." }

S: Bruvver.

T: No. Look at these letters in the middle. {Points to "brother." } Remember to read what you see. Do you remember how we say that sound? Put your tongue between your teeth and say "th" ...

The lesson continues in such a fashion, the teacher proceeding to correct the student's Ebonics-influenced pronunciations and grammar while ignoring that fact that the student had to have comprehended the sentence in order to translate it into her own language. Such instruction occurs daily and blocks reading development in a number of ways. First, because children become better readers by having the opportunity to read, the overcorrection exhibited in this lesson means that this child will be less likely to become a fluent reader than other children that are not interrupted so consistently. Second, a complete focus on code and pronunciation blocks children's understanding that reading is essentially a meaning-making process. This child, who understands the text, is led to believe that she is doing something wrong. She is encouraged to think of reading not as something you do to get a message, but something you pronounce. Third, constant corrections by the teacher are likely to cause this student and others like her to resist reading and to resent the teacher.

Language researcher Robert Berdan reports that, after observing the kind of teaching routine described above in a number of settings, he incorporated the teacher behaviors into a reading instruction exercise that he used with students in a college class.[10] He put together sundry rules from a number of

This child, who understands the text, is led to believe that she is doing something wrong.

American social and regional dialects to create what he called the "language of Atlantis." Students were then called upon to read aloud in this dialect they did not know. When they made errors he interrupted them, using some of the same statements/comments he had heard elementary school teachers routinely make to their students. He concludes:

> The results were rather shocking. By the time these Ph.D. candidates in English or linguistics had read 10-20 words, I could make them sound totally illiterate. ... The first thing that goes is sentence intonation: they sound like they are reading a list from the telephone book. Comment on their pronunciation a bit more, and they begin to subvocalize, rehearsing pronunciations for themselves before they dare to say them out loud. They begin to guess at pronunciations. ... They switch letters around for no reason. They stumble; they repeat. In short, when I attack them for their failure to conform to my demands for Atlantis English pronunciations, they sound very much like the worst of the 2nd graders in any of the classrooms I have observed.
>
> They also begin to fidget. They wad up their papers, bite their fingernails, whisper, and some finally refuse to continue. They do all the things that children do while they are busily failing to learn to read.

The moral of this story is not to confuse learning a new language form with reading comprehension.

The moral of this story is not to confuse learning a new language form with reading comprehension. To do so will only confuse the child, leading her away from those intuitive understandings about language that will promote reading development, and toward a school career of resistance and a lifetime of avoiding reading.

Unlike unplanned oral language or public reading, writing lends itself to editing. While conversational talk is spontaneous and must be responsive to an immediate context, writing is a mediated process which may be written and rewritten any number of times before being introduced to public scrutiny. Consequently, writing is more amenable to rule application—one may first write freely to get one's thoughts down, and then edit to hone the message and apply specific spelling, syntactical, or punctuation rules. My college students who had such difficulty talking in the "iz" dialect, found writing it, with the rules displayed before them, a relatively easy task.

To conclude, the teacher's job is to provide access to the national "standard" as well as to understand the language the children speak sufficiently to celebrate its beauty. The verbal adroitness, the cogent and quick wit, the brilliant use of metaphor, the facility in rhythm and rhyme, evident in the language of Jesse Jackson, Whoopi Goldberg, Toni Morrison, Henry Louis Gates, Tupac Shakur, and Maya Angelou, as well as in that of many inner-city black students, may all be drawn upon to facilitate school learning. The teacher must know how to effectively teach reading and writing to students whose culture and language differ from that of the school, and must understand how and why students decide to add another language form to their repertoire. All we can do is provide students with access to additional language forms. Inevitably, each speaker will make his or her own decision about what to say in any context.

But I must end with a caveat that we keep in mind a simple truth: Despite our necessary efforts to provide access to standard English, such access will not make any of our students more intelligent. It will not teach them math or science or geography—or, for that matter, compassion, courage, or responsibility. Let us not become so overly concerned with the language *form* that we ignore academic and moral *content*. Access to the standard language may be necessary, but it is definitely not sufficient to produce intelligent, competent caretakers of the future.

©1997 Lisa Delpit *Other People's Children* (New Press: 1995).

The teacher must know how to effectively teach reading and writing to students whose culture and language differ from that of the school, and must understand how and why students decide to add another language form to their repertoire.

Endnotes

1. S. Nelson-Barber, "Phonologic Variations of Pima English," in R. St. Clair and W. Leap, (Eds.), *Language Renewal Among American Indian Tribes: Issues, Problems and Prospects* (Rosslyn, VA: National Clearinghouse for Bilingual Education, 1982).
2. Some of these books include Lucille Clifton, *All Us Come 'Cross the Water* (New York: Holt, Rinehart, and Winston, 1973); Paul Green (aided by Abbe Abbott), *I Am Eskimo—Aknik My Name* (Juneau, AK: Alaska Northwest Publishing, 1959); Howard Jacobs and Jim Rice, *Once upon a Bayou* (New Orleans, LA.: Phideaux Publications, 1983); Tim Elder, *Santa's Cajun Christmas Adventure* (Baton Rouge, LA: Little Cajun Books, 1981); and a series of biographies produced by Yukon-Koyukkuk School District of Alaska and published by Hancock House Publishers in North Vancouver, British Columbia, Canada.
3. Shirley Brice Heath, *Ways with Words* (Cambridge, Eng.: Cambridge University Press, 1983).
4. S. Michaels and C.B. Cazden, "Teacher-Child Collaboration on Oral Preparation for Literacy," in B. Schieffer (Ed.), *Acquisition of Literacy: Ethnographic Perspectives* (Norwood, NJ: Ablex, 1986).
5. C.B. Cazden, *Classroom Discourse* (Portsmouth, NH: Heinemann, 1988).
6. Ibid.

7. R. Sims, "Dialect and Reading: Toward Redefining the Issues," in J. Langer and M.T. Smith-Burke (Eds.), *Reader Meets Author/Bridging the Gap* (Newark, DE: International Reading Association, 1982).
8. Ibid.
9. Patricia M. Cunningham, "Teachers' Correction Responses to Black-Dialect Miscues Which Are Nonmeaning-Changing," *Reading Research Quarterly* 12 (1976-77).
10. Robert Berdan, "Knowledge into Practice: Delivering Research to Teachers," in M.F. Whiteman (Ed.), *Reactions to Ann Arbor: Vernacular Black English and Education* (Arlington, VA: Center for Applied Linguistics, 1980).

Defending
Bilingual Education

By Kelley Dawson Salas

"Teacher, this is crazy!"

After six days straight of standardized testing in English, her second language, Ana lost it. She laughed out loud and the rest of us laughed with her. As her 4th-grade teacher, I was expected to keep order and continue administering the test (which I did), but I could see where she was coming from. Perhaps it was the rigorous schedule: seven days of testing for three hours each morning. Perhaps it was the tedious format: listen as each test item is read aloud twice in English and twice in Spanish, then wait for all students to mark an answer, then move on to the next test item. Perhaps it was the random nature of some of the questions.

Alain Pilon

There are more English language learners than ever in U.S. schools, and yet the policies that affect their schooling make less and less sense.

Whatever it was, Ana knew it didn't make sense. That moment has become a metaphor to me. There are more English language learners than ever in U.S. schools, and yet the policies that affect their schooling make less and less sense.

About 10 percent of all U.S. students—more than five million children—are English language learners. This represents a tremendous resource and opportunity. If schools serve English language learners well, at least 10 percent of U.S. students can have highly valued skills: fluency in more than one language and an ability to work with diverse groups of people. If communities give English-speaking students the opportunity to learn side by side with students who speak other languages, an even greater number of students can learn these skills.

But there are obstacles. Although research shows that bilingual education works, top-down policies increasingly push English-only education. To make matters worse, schools serving immigrants are some of the most segregated, understaffed, underresourced schools in the country.

In our Winter 2002/03 editorial, *Rethinking Schools* wrote that "bilingual education is a human and civil right." I think all teachers should defend this right and demand equal educational opportunities for English language learners. It's not just about immigrant students: U.S. society as a whole will benefit greatly when all students have access to bilingual education, and when schools serve English language learners well.

Bilingual Education Works

Research shows that bilingual education is effective with English learners, both in helping them learn English and in supporting academic achievement in the content areas.

A synthesis of research recently published by Cambridge University Press showed that English learners do better in school when they participate in programs that are designed to help them learn English. The review also found that "almost all evaluations of K-12 students show that students who have been educated in bilingual classrooms, particularly in long-term programs that aim for a high level of bilingualism, do as well as or better on standardized tests than students in comparison groups of English-learners in English-only programs."

A synthesis of studies on language-minority students' academic achievement published in 1992 by Virginia Collier found that students do better academically in their second language when they have more instruction in their primary language, combined with balanced support in the second language.

I have seen this in action at the two-way immersion school where I teach 4th grade. Spanish-dominant students who develop good literacy skills in Spanish have a far easier time in 3rd and 4th grade when they begin to read, write, and do academic work in English. Likewise, students who struggle to read and write in Spanish do not transition easily to English reading, and they tend to lag behind in English content-area instruction. High-quality Spanish language instruction starting in kindergarten is essential. Without it, Spanish-dominant students do not get a fair chance to develop good literacy and academic skills in their first or second language.

More Need, Less Bilingual Instruction

Despite the evidence that properly implemented bilingual education works for English language learners, English learners are being pushed into English-only programs or getting less instruction in their primary languages.

Voters in three states (California, 1998; Arizona, 2000; Massachusetts, 2002) have passed referenda mandating "English-only" education and outlawing bilingual instruction. (Colorado defeated a similar referendum in 2002.) Although many parents in these states hoped to get waivers so their children could continue bilingual education, they had more luck in some places than others.

In Arizona, one third of English language learners were enrolled in bilingual education before voters passed Proposition 203 in 2000. Although Proposition 203 allowed waivers, the state's Superintendent of Public Instruction insisted on a strict interpretation of the law that denied waivers to most parents. Eventually almost all of Arizona's bilingual programs were discontinued; the National Association for Bilingual Education noted in October of 2005 that "bilingual education is simply no longer available" to English language learners in Arizona.

Prior to the passage of Question 2 in Massachusetts in 2002, 23 percent of that state's roughly 50,000 English learners were enrolled in bilingual education. By 2005, only about 5 percent were in bilingual programs. Under the law it is easier for children older than 10 to get waivers, so middle and high school students are more likely to participate in bilingual education than elementary students. Students do not need a waiver to participate in two-way bilingual programs; in 2005 there were 822 students enrolled in two-way bilingual programs.

Despite the evidence that properly implemented bilingual education works for English language learners, English learners are being pushed into English-only programs or getting less instruction in their primary languages.

Resistance Saves Some Programs

In California, the first state to pass an English-only referendum, some schools were able to continue offering bilingual education. The law required all districts to inform parents of their option to continue in bilingual education by signing a waiver; some schools and districts succeeded in getting a very high percentage of waivers and continuing their programs. But by 1999, researchers at the University of California Linguistic Minority Research Institute found that only 12 percent of English learners were in bilingual programs, compared to 29 percent before the law changed.

Researchers also found that districts that had a strong commitment to primary language programs were able to hold on to those programs after Proposition 227 passed, while districts that were "not especially supportive of primary language programs prior to 1998" were more likely to do away with primary language instruction altogether.

The "English-HURRY!" Approach

Even in places where bilingual education is still permitted, top-down pressures threaten to weaken it.

Even in places where bilingual education is still permitted (by law or by waiver), top-down pressures threaten to weaken it. Since the passage of No Child Left Behind, standardized testing in English has put pressure on schools to teach English earlier and to do it faster.

Bilingual education is still legal in Wisconsin, where I teach. Milwaukee has a districtwide developmental bilingual (also called "late-exit") program. This means that children learn to read and write first in their primary language (in our case, Spanish), and in the early grades they are taught all subjects in Spanish. Once they have gained a strong footing in Spanish, they transition to English and start to receive a larger percentage of literacy and content area instruction in English. Even after making the transition to English, students can continue to get a significant portion of their literacy and content area instruction in Spanish for as many years as they choose to stay in the bilingual program.

But since the passage of NCLB, our district's developmental bilingual program has not fared as well as one might hope. In 2002, Wisconsin did away with all of its Spanish-language standardized tests and began requiring almost all English language learners to take standardized tests in English starting in 3rd grade. (Wisconsin could have purchased and administered tests in Spanish, but chose not to do so because of the cost.)

The English tests have changed classroom instruction for bilingual students in our district. District administrators, many principals, and lots of teachers have bought into the idea that kids must learn English sooner because they must score well on English language tests. "Hurry up and teach kids to read in English! They've got to be ready to take the 3rd-grade reading test in English! They've got to be ready to take the 4th-grade WKCE (Wisconsin Knowledge Concepts Examination) in English!" Suddenly a lot of what we know about second-language acquisition has fallen by the wayside in the scramble to get kids to do well on tests so we can keep schools off the list.

At my school, the year after the law changed, I was part of a team of teachers and administrators that met for months to decide how to respond to the reality that our Spanish-dominant students would be tested in English starting in 3rd grade. We ultimately decided to transition children to English reading in the 2nd and 3rd grades. (We had previously transitioned students to reading in their second language at the end of 3rd grade and beginning of 4th grade.) Other schools in my district have also pushed the transition to English to earlier grades. Still others have reduced primary language instruction in the early grades to make room for direct instruction in English reading (for Spanish-speaking students) as early as 1st grade.

There has been little public discussion about these changes, which contradict the research because they decrease the amount of primary-language instruction and allow less time for students to establish solid literacy skills in their primary language before beginning the transition to second-language literacy. Instead of engaging in discussion about these changes, many administrators and some teachers dismiss concerns with a common refrain: "This is what we have to do to get them ready for the tests."

In a report called "The Initial Impact of Proposition 227 on the Instruction of English Learners," researchers in California described how bilingual instruction changed when English-only testing began:

> English-only testing was observed to have an extra - ordinary effect on English learner instruction, causing teachers to leapfrog much of the normal literacy instruc- tion and go directly to English word recognition or phon- ics, bereft of meaning or context. Teachers also worried greatly that if they spent time orienting the children to broader literacy activities like storytelling, story sequencing activities, reading for meaning, or writing and vocabulary

Many administrators and some teachers dismiss concerns with a common refrain: 'This is what we have to do to get them ready for the tests.'

development in the primary language, that their students would not be gaining the skills that would be tested on the standardized test in English. They feared that this could result in the school and the students suffering sanctions imposed by the law.

Thus, even in the classrooms that had been designated as bilingual, and where principals often contended that little had changed, teachers revealed that their teaching practices had indeed changed substantially and that their students were receiving much less literacy instruction in their primary language.

Ironically, NCLB does not specify what language students should be taught in, nor does it even require that students be tested in English. It specifies that students must be tested "in a valid and reliable manner," and that they should be given "reasonable accommodations," including "to the extent practicable, assessments in the language and form most likely to yield accurate data on what such students know and can do."

But states have chosen to implement the law in a variety of ways. Most states test students exclusively in English. Some states give English learners extra time to take the test. Another common accommodation is to translate or simplify the English on portions of the test. The state of California allows no accommodations for students who have been in the California schools for one year. Ten California districts have filed suit claiming this violates the NCLB's provision that students be tested in a valid and reliable manner with reasonable accommodations.

Segregation and Unequal Resources

These recent changes in language and testing policies are making a bad situation worse for English language learners, many of whom were already experiencing some of the worst educational conditions in the country.

These recent changes in language and testing policies are making a bad situation worse for English language learners, many of whom were already experiencing some of the worst educational conditions in the country.

A study published by the Urban Institute noted that the majority of English language learners are "segregated in schools serving primarily ELL and immigrant children." The study found that these "high-LEP" schools (defined as schools where Limited English Proficient students comprise 23.5 percent or more of the student body) tend to be large and urban, with a student body that is largely minority (77 percent) and largely poor (72 percent). In addition, "high-LEP schools face more difficulties filling teaching vacancies and are more likely to rely on unqualified and substitute teachers," and teachers are "more likely to have provisional, emergency, or temporary certification than are those in other schools."

Researchers at the University of California, Davis, in 2003 found similar disadvantages for the schooling of English language learners, saying they faced "intense segregation into schools and classrooms that place [English learners] at particularly high risk for educational failure."

Advocacy for Immigrants

As conditions and policies worsen for English learners, there is an urgent need for teachers, families, and language-minority communities to speak up in favor of immigrant students and bilingual education.

It is important for English learners to succeed academically and to become bilingual, especially now. Many U.S. cities have majority-minority populations, and more and more people in the United States speak languages other than English. To be able to successfully live in and lead this diverse society, people need to learn how to value and accept others. All children need to learn how to communicate with people whose language and culture are different from their own.

These abilities are highly valued, and many teenagers and adults spend years trying to develop them. Children who are raised from birth speaking a language other than English have a unique opportunity to cultivate these abilities from a young age. Our schools must help them seize that opportunity.

CHAPTER FIFTEEN

Bilingual Education Works

By Stephen Krashen

Arizona's passage of Proposition 203 aimed at dismantling bilingual education confirms, once again, that a substantial percentage of voters is unaware of the facts about bilingual education. Specifically, much of the public is unaware that bilingual education is very good for English language development.

In my book *Condemned Without a Trial: Bogus Arguments Against Bilingual Education*, I analyze five myths surrounding bilingual education. Below I address two myths that played a particularly important role in the Arizona vote, and look at some of the confusion over media reports on bilingual education, especially in California.

Jean-Claude Lejeune

Providing education in the first language can greatly help second language development.

Myth No. 1: Bilingual Education Keeps Students from Learning English

Saying that educating children in their primary language will help them learn English seems to defy common sense for many people. But providing education in the first language can greatly help second language development. It does this in two ways.

First, when teachers provide students with solid subject matter in the first language, it gives the students knowledge. This knowledge helps make the English children hear and read much more comprehensible.

A child who speaks little English (referred to as "a limited English proficient student") who is knowledgeable about history, thanks to education in the first language, will understand more in a history class taught in English than a limited English proficient child without this knowledge. The child with a background in history will learn more history, and will acquire more English, because the English heard in class will be more comprehensible.

Second, developing literacy in the first language is a shortcut to literacy in the second language. It is easier to learn to read in a language you understand; once you can read in one language, this knowledge transfers rapidly to any other language you learn to read. Once you can read, you can read.

In my interpretation of the research, programs that are set up correctly, that is, that supply background information in the primary language and that provide literacy in the primary language, and, of course, also provide instruction in the second language, typically succeed in teaching the second language.

English in these programs is introduced at the very beginning, in the form of English-as-a-Second Language (ESL) classes. As children acquire more English, and learn some academics through the first language, subject matter is introduced in English gradually, but as soon as it can be made comprehensible.

Controlled studies consistently show that children in such properly organized bilingual classes acquire at least as much English as those in all-English classes and usually acquire more (Willig, 1985; Krashen, 1996). A review of this research was done by Prof. Jay Greene of the University of Texas at Austin, using statistical tools far more precise than those used in previous reviews. Greene concluded that the use of the native language in instructing limited English proficient children has "moderate beneficial effects" and that "efforts to eliminate the use of the native language in instruction ... harm children by denying them access to beneficial approaches" (Greene, 1997).

Myth No. 2: Bilingual Education Failed in California

A great deal of confusion was caused by newspaper articles that reported that after Proposition 227 passed in California, severely restricting bilingual education, test scores went up. This was widely interpreted as a victory for all-English immersion and a defeat for bilingual education. But this conclusion is incorrect.

First, test scores always go up when a new test is introduced (Linn, Graue, and Sanders, 1990). In California, the SAT9 was introduced at the same time Proposition 227 passed. Linn et al. note that scores increase about 1.5 to 2 points per year after a new test is introduced. Thus, test score inflation accounts for about half of the increase in grades 2 and 3 in the SAT9 reading test since 1998, and all of the increase in grades 4 through 7. It also suggests that SAT9 reading scores in California have actually declined slightly in grades 8 through 11.

There is no evidence linking test score increases to dropping bilingual education.

Test scores increase for a variety of reasons, and not all of them are related to increased learning. Among the bogus means of increasing test scores are extensive training in test-taking skills and selective testing, i.e., excluding low-scoring children from taking the test. Asimov (2000) suggests that selective testing may have occurred in California. She reported that for some schools in the San Francisco area SAT9 test scores increased in those schools in which the number of students taking the test declined. According to Asimov, "questionable pairings" appeared in 22 Bay Area school districts. Such bogus means are especially likely to be used when strong carrots (financial rewards for teachers if test scores go up) and sticks (threats of school closure if scores go down) are instituted by the state, as they are in California.

Second, there is no evidence linking test score increases to dropping bilingual education. Stanford professor Kenji Hakuta and his associates found, in fact, that test scores rose in districts in California that kept bilingual education, as well as in districts that never had bilingual education (Orr, Butler, Bousquet, and Hakuta, 2000; Hakuta, 2000). Ironically, in the same state that voted to dismantle bilingual education, Arizona, limited English proficient students in bilingual education have outscored those in all-English programs on tests of English reading for the last three years (Crawford, 2000).

A major problem is that nearly all the media focus had been on one district in California—Oceanside. After Proposition 227 passed in 1998, Oceanside dropped bilingual education, enthusiastically embraced English immersion, and test scores went up.

But Hakuta and his associates have shown that gains for Oceanside's English learners were similar to gains made in many California schools that retained bilingual education.

In addition, the bilingual program that Oceanside dropped was a poor one. In an article in the Sept. 2, 2000, *Washington Post*, Oceanside superintendent Ken Noonan confirmed that Oceanside's "bilingual" program taught only in Spanish until grades 5 or 6. It was therefore not a bilingual program, but a monolingual Spanish program. As noted above, properly organized bilingual programs introduce English the first day, and teach subject matter in English as soon as it can be made comprehensible. An article, Oct. 5, 2000, in the *San Diego Union Tribune* confirmed suspicions that Oceanside's pre-Proposition 227 efforts were dismal. Before 227, "a lot of students (at Laurel Elementary School) didn't even have books," the article noted (Parnet, 2000).

Controversy in New York

Similar controversy has arisen over recent reports from New York City. The New York Board of Education issued a report on the progress of English language learners that has been interpreted by many as evidence against bilingual education. A casual look appears to show that English-only has the edge: According to the report, for those entering in kindergarten, 84 percent of those in English-only "exited" (acquired enough English to enter the mainstream) within three years, while 73 percent of those in bilingual education did so.

Students in bilingual education are more likely to be of lower socio-economic status than students in English-only programs.

One cannot conclude from these results that bilingual education did worse than English-only. As the authors of the study repeatedly note, there was no control for confounding factors. Most important is the effect of poverty. Students in bilingual education are more likely to be of lower socio-economic status than students in English-only programs (NCES, 1993). This tendency has been confirmed for New York City by Luis Reyes, a former member of the board of education in New York.

In commenting on a 1994 report from New York City, Reyes noted that "there were a number of middle-class students in the ESL program who came from countries that were more developed ... kids in the bilingual program came from where they hadn't had full schooling (Hennelly, 1995).

Children who come to the United States with more education in their home country have several important advantages. In addition to having basic food, housing, and health needs adequately met, they live in a more print rich environment, which has a tremendous impact on school success (Krashen, 1993; McQuillan, 1998). Also, many older children from privileged backgrounds have actually had "de facto" bilingual education, that is, substantial literacy development and subject matter learning in their own language before arriving in the United States. Interestingly, the Board of Education also found that those who entered with greater competence in their first language exited more quickly than those with less. This is strong evidence for the positive impact of first language development.

It is also interesting to compare the results of the 1994 study and the recent report: For those entering at kindergarten in 1994, 79 percent of all English-only students were exited after three years. In the recent report, it is 84 percent. In 1994, for bilingual education, 42 percent were exited after three years. In the recent report, it is 73 percent. This is an amazing improvement, and is counter to claims that children typically "languish" in bilingual programs for years.

Many older children from privileged backgrounds have actually had 'de facto' bilingual education.

Public Opinion

Surveys consistently reveal strong support for the use of the primary language in school (Krashen, 1996, 1999). The research by Fay Shin of California State University at Stanislaus is particularly informative. Shin did not ask people if they supported bilingual education; instead, she asked about the underlying principles. For instance, she asked whether people thought "developing literacy through the first language facilitates literacy development in English" and whether "learning subject matter through the first language helps make subject matter study in English more comprehensible." Results were encouraging; these principles apparently make good sense. Following are some of the results of Shin's surveys:

Developing literacy through the first language facilitates literacy development in English.

Percent agreement:

Hispanic parents = 53 percent (Shin and Gribbons, 1996);

Korean parents = 88 percent (Shin and Kim, 1996);

Hmong parents = 52 percent (Shin and Lee, 1996);

Administrators = 74 percent (Shin, Anton and Krashen, 1999);

Teachers = 74 percent (Shin and Krashen, 1996).

Learning subject matter through the first language makes subject matter study in English more comprehensible.

Percent agreement:

Hispanic parents = 34 percent (33 percent were "not sure") (Shin and Gribbons, 1996);

Korean parents = 47 percent (Shin and Kim, 1996);

Hmong parents = 60 percent (Shin and Lee, 1996);

Vietnamese parents = 64 percent (Young and Tran, 1999);

Administrators = 78 percent (Shin, Anton and Krashen, 1999);

Teachers = 70 percent (Shin and Krashen, 1996).

It is important to note that Shin's subjects were not recent graduates of language education programs, or bilingual teachers.

What these results show is that people agree with the principles underlying bilingual education; the problem seems to be that they are not aware that bilingual education is based on these principles.

Of course, English language development is not the only goal of bilingual education. A second worthy goal is the continuing development of the first language. Research confirms that continuing development of the first language has a positive influence on cognitive development, has practical advantages, and promotes a healthy sense of biculturalism (see, e.g., Krashen, Tse, and McQuillan, 1998). But many people still think that the bilingual education "debate" is between rational people who think that children should learn English and irrational fanatics who think children should be prevented from learning English.

If the antibilingual education movement is to be stopped, this misunderstanding needs to be corrected immediately. We need to better get out the message that bilingual educators are deeply concerned about English language development and that properly organized bilingual education programs are very helpful for English language development.

> *People agree with the principles underlying bilingual education; the problem seems to be that they are not aware that bilingual education is based on these principles.*

REFERENCES

Asimov, N. (July 22, 2000). Test scores up, test-takers down: Link between participation, improvement on school exam prompts concern. *San Francisco Chronicle.*

Crawford, J. (2000). Stanford 9 scores show a consistent edge for bilingual education. http://alec2000.org/craw1b.htm

Greene, J. (1997). A meta-analysis of the Rossell and Baker review of bilingual education research. *Bilingual Research Journal* 21(3): 103-122.

Hakuta, K. (2000). Points on SAT-9 Performance and Proposition 227. http://www.stanford.edu/~hakuta/SAT9/SAT9_2000/bullets.htm

Hennelly, R. (1995). NYC bilingual study clarified. *Multicultural Newsletter*, People's Publishing Group International.

Krashen, S. (1993). *The power of reading.* Englewood, CO: Libraries Unlimited.

Krashen, S. (1996). *Under attack: The case against bilingual education.* Culver City, CA: Language Education Associates.

Krashen, S. (1998). *Condemned without a trial: Bogus arguments against bilingual education.* Portsmouth, NH: Heinemann.

Krashen, S. & Biber, D. (1988). *On course: California's success in bilingual education.* Los Angeles: California Association for Bilingual Education.

Krashen, S., Tse, L., & McQuillan, J. (Eds.) (1998). *Heritage language development.* Culver City, CA: Language Education Associates.

Linn, R., Graue, E., & Sanders, N. (1990). Comparing state and district test results to national norms: The validity of claims that 'everyone is above average.' *Educational Measurement: Issues and Practice* 9: 5-13.

Lisi, P. & Chinn, P. Editorial. *Multicultural Perspectives*, Education Association, Maywood, NJ. 2, 2:1-2.

McQuillan, J. (1998). *The literacy crisis: False claims and real solutions.* Portsmouth, NH: Heinemann.

New York City Board of Education. (2000). ELL subcommittee research studies progress report. New York: Board of Education of the City of New York.

Orr, J. B., Y. Bousquet, M. & Hakuta, K. (2000). What can we learn about the impact of Proposition 227 from SAT9 scores? http://www.stanford.edu/~hakuta/ SAT9/SAT9_2000/index.com

Parnet, S. (October 6, 2000). Test-score gains fill schools with pride. *San Diego Union Tribune.*

Shin, F. & Kim, S. (1998). Korean parent perceptions and attitudes of bilingual education. In R. Endo, C. Park, J. Tsuchida and A. Abbayani (Eds.) *Current Issues in Asian and Pacific American Education.* Covina, CA: Pacific Asian Press.

Shin, F. & Gribbons, B. (1996). Hispanic parent perceptions and attitudes of bilingual education. *The Journal of Mexican American Educators,* pp. 16-22.

Shin, F. & Lee, B. 1996. Hmong parents: What do they think about bilingual education? *Pacific Educational Research Journal,* 8: 65-71.

Shin, F. Anton, M. & Krashen, S. (1999). K-12 administrators' views on bilingual education. *NABE News* 22(8):11-12, 29.

Young, R. & Tran, M. (1999). Vietnamese parent attitudes toward bilingual education. *Bilingual Research Journal* 23 (2, 3): 225-233.

Raising Children's Cultural Voices

By Berta Rosa Berriz

How can teachers create a learning environment that honors the diverse family cultures of students within a racist society? Further, how can teachers develop literacy in two languages within a standards-driven curriculum that dictates what each student needs to learn, regardless of cultural and linguistic differences? I work with my colleague Ramona in a large urban school system in Massachusetts. Our journey as teachers is grounded in our search for answers to these questions within our two-way bilingual program classrooms, in which native speakers of Spanish and English are taught in integrated classes in both languages.

Jean-Claude Lejeune

As 3rd-grade teachers, we are committed to quality education for inner-city youth and hold the highest expectations for our students. Our students are African Americans and Latinos whose family cultures differ significantly from mainstream U.S. culture. Thus, they move between two cultural worlds—their home culture and the mainstream culture. Becoming familiar with these two worlds is a developmental process with a double edge: Our students must strengthen their sense of pride in their family culture while at the same time building skills to succeed in mainstream culture. Part of the work of our bicultural classrooms is to live and recreate our own cultures within an integrated learning environment.

Our students must strengthen their sense of pride in their family culture while at the same time building skills to succeed in mainstream culture.

We use a team approach to create a consistent learning environment in which we model cross-cultural respect and cooperation for our students as we learn and teach together from different points of view. Our teaching combines use of the arts and a strong emphasis on writing within a web of relationships essential to our bilingual and bicultural classroom, which includes the teacher, the teacher team, the students, their families, and our community. The arts become tools that celebrate the cultural identity of our students, develop their cultural voices, and strengthen their connection with their family and community. Writing links children's personal experiences to academic learning. This weave of symbols from family cultures and the community becomes the foundation for the development of dual literacy within a standards-driven curriculum.

Two-Way Structure

In our program, the language of instruction is separated by classroom. There are two classrooms with one teacher for each language. I always use English in my classroom and Ramona always uses Spanish in hers. Two groups of students spend an equal amount of time in each language, rotating between Spanish and English classrooms biweekly. Each class group has a mix of students who speak Spanish or English as their native language. Students are becoming bilingual to varying degrees, depending on how long they have been in the two-way program. Teachers speak only one language, while students may use either language as they are acquiring the new language.

The language immersion in our classrooms is supported by team teaching. The team spends time coordinating the development of the curriculum so that it develops sequentially. We do not repeat teaching content. Students follow the development of ideas in one language at a time. For example, a child may start the math investigations unit on patterns in Spanish and finish it in English. In other cases, an entire unit will be presented in one language, and then we move to studying the next unit in the other language. In each classroom, students who are at ease in both languages are resources to their peers in the learning process. Both languages are used as a tool for students to explore and interact with their world.

The integration of students from diverse cultural and linguistic backgrounds is achieved through cooperative learning groups. We do not believe in tracking or ability grouping. Children learn and play together with their peers, many of whom are neighbors in their community. Learning together, they are protected from the harm that segregated student groupings may cause to their spirit and ability to learn. In our child-centered classrooms, the children are language resources for one another. We take care to group students with mixed abilities in each cooperative group. For example, social studies curriculum includes building skills for cooperative learning, cross-cultural understanding, and conflict resolution. Each group will have members who are strong in English, Spanish, reading, writing, drawing, and so on. In our collaborative learning environment, differences are good and necessary for the success of the challenging work of learning two languages.

In our child-centered classrooms, the children are language resources for one another.

There are many principles contributing to the effectiveness of our program, in particular, our use of the arts to develop students' cultural voices, our integrated approach to learning, and our belief that learning happens in a web of relationships, not only among peers but within the wider scope of the community. [For a more complete explanation, see my chapter in the book *Lifting Every Voice: Pedagogy and Politics of Bilingualism*, edited by Zeynep F. Bekont (Cambridge: Harvard Education Publishing Group, 2000), 71-94.]

In this article, I would like to concentrate on how we use writing as the gateway to literacy.

Writing Is a Gateway

Writing, the creation of symbol on a page, is an important step toward literacy. In our classrooms, writing accompanies the arts in the development of biliteracy. Artistic expression and writing are connected in that they are both symbol systems. In the process of making art, a child spends time with images before they take on shape, color, and texture in an art piece. In the same way, writing requires that a child spend time with ideas and bring them out in conversation before they take shape in a manuscript. Both forms of self-expression, arts and writing, have common requisites: a safe place to explore, a personal place to move from, and a community place to share both the process and the message. Many of the writing activities in our 3rd-grade classrooms are based on art projects.

Autobiographical writing, journals, and publishing are three major components of our writing program. Autobiographical writing builds on a personal story and develops academic knowledge of Standard English. Journals provide a safe place to express personal concerns, try out new ideas, and have exchanges in writing with the teacher. Publishing promotes effective communication through writing for general audiences.

Autobiographical writing is key to the positive cultural identity formation of children who have been inhibited by negative immigration experiences or by racism.

Autobiographical writing is key to the positive cultural identity formation of children who have been inhibited by negative immigration experiences or by racism. Student autobiographies are deepened over the course of the year and represent self-discovery, family history, and future dreams. Autobiographies encourage children to reconnect with family stories and name the values in those stories that sustain them. It is significant that the experts on this writing assignment are also the protagonists. Yismilka's words from the introduction to her autobiography exemplify both depth in self-expression and quality writing in her second language:

> I see the world as a dark place. If people depended on helping and saving, we could make a vast difference. The world is a good place to grow in. If we stick together the large difference can take us to an incredible blossom.

We use "sheltering" strategies to enhance the quality of autobiographical writing. One sheltering language development strategy highlights students' prior knowledge in conversations held before writing. For example, sheltering for autobiographical writing may include building descriptive language through talk about family pictures or drawings. In the process of writing their autobiographies, students talk to their classmates about the family pictures. Using oral language, children elaborate with detail as they develop descriptive language for their written life stories. These ideas can be graphically organized for further development around a central theme. Word banks organized on large chart paper categories—such as nouns (names), verbs (actions), adjectives (descriptions), or by topic—such as colors, feelings, textures, or geographical locations—are always on display and are added to by students as their vocabulary expands. Sheltering strategies also include the use of repetitive phrases such as "I know that it is a piñata because ... ." Students are asked to repeat the phrase and fill in as many descriptions of a piñata as they can. Invented spelling, oral dictation, and illustrated response to questions are also part of sheltering strategies for students who are beginning to develop literacy.

Another strong support for good autobiographical writing is simply discussing with students the criteria for evaluating a writing piece. For example, students were preparing artist statements for a schoolwide exhibit that would form part of their autobiographies. In writing, they had to describe the scene that was represented on their family quilt square. The best artist statements would meet the task (stay focused), use a variety of sentence structures, use details, use descriptive language (including smells, colors, adjectives, adverbs), and use good basic mechanics (spacing, margins, indentations, capital letters, spelling, and punctuation). We used a sample quilt square and generated lists of words that would visually describe the art piece by categories such as colors, textures, background, and foreground. The second part of the assignment required students to describe the art-making process. In preparation, they dictated a list of actions involved in making their quilt square. The list generated a repetitive pattern of sentences: "I chose the color ... because it ... ." Clarifying the assignment, using visual cues, generating lists of words, and using repetitive language patterns are sheltering strategies that enable second-language learners to write effectively. These student-generated lists are resources for the whole class as they compose. The words and ideas have been experienced orally, visually, dramatically, and in writing. This allows for reciprocity between students and teachers. Both players are participants in the learning process and vocabulary development.

A variety of genuine writing experiences is woven throughout our day by the frequent use of journals, which accompany many of our classroom activities: morning journals, math journals, science journals, end-of-the-day journals—though different in content, all of these journals provide a safe place for students to try out ideas. I respond to the journals regularly. The personal nature of these exchanges allows me to build friendships with my students and a sense of trust. The interactive morning journal opens the day with a personal dialogue and is written freestyle. Poems or illustrations may be the communicative

A variety of genuine writing experiences is woven throughout our day by the frequent use of journals, which accompany many of our classroom activities.

symbol system on any given morning. There is something peaceful and gentle about morning journal time. While music plays softly, children sit quietly at their desks and make their transition from home to the work of school as they read and respond to my comments. Both reading and writing form part of our written conversations. The following is a poem from a student's morning journal:

> Shhhhh.
> Listen! to the sound
> Higher than the ground
> We are black,
> We are white
> they are not so tight.
> We are Puerto Rican,
> We are Dominican,
> We are Chinese,
> We are Cuban,
> We will hold hands and stand.
> We are Japanese,
> We are Indian,
> We are together forever.
> Together forever.
> —from "I Am Black," by Myeshia

End-of-the-day journals are strictly academic in nature. A special book with a beautiful cover and quality paper is purchased for this purpose. At the end of the day, one student leads the class in a discussion that generates three main ideas that were learned during the day. Three other students write these in complete sentences on the board. The day closes as students enter their summary of the learning for the day in their end-of-the-day journals. Content-area journals, such as literature-response and math journals, also provide a review and confirmation of the main ideas covered in a lesson or unit.

Real-world Audiences

Our many forms of journaling are important tools for written communication, review, and documentation of academic gains. In telling, writing, and presenting themselves to the world, students realize reciprocity in learning—that is, that students are also teachers.

Bringing student writing to real-world audiences through publishing or the internet also promotes effective communication

In telling, writing, and presenting themselves to the world, students realize reciprocity in learning—that is, that students are also teachers.

skills. One such publication project over the internet resulted when 3rd- and 5th-graders in our school worked together on math stories in their math journals, writing stories about their everyday lives with numbers. News about a bilingual internet exchange project called *De Orilla a Orilla* inspired our students. A group of teachers in New York, California, and Puerto Rico were facilitating exchanges between Spanish and English bilingual students through the internet. Students wanted to participate even though we did not have internet access in the classroom.

Our students' math journals contain stories and describe ways of thinking about math. They write, for example, about how they solved a problem, and include real-life math stories. They enjoyed their math journals and wanted to share them with other students. We decided to participate in *De Orilla a Orilla* by using the internet connection on my computer at home. Students prepared the following announcement for the project on the internet:

Our students' math journals contain stories and describe ways of thinking about math.

Math Journals Take Us Across Grades and Across Cyberspace Warm Greetings from Chilly Boston:

> We are students in 3rd- and 5th-grade classes in a two-way bilingual program in Greater Boston. You might be wondering what it means to be a two-way bilingual program (two x bi = multi?). We are African American and Latino kids who are learning about one another's cultures and languages. We study math, science, and social studies in Spanish and English. In math class we have been keeping a math journal and writing math stories with the ideas we are discovering in math class.
> Here are some ideas we have been writing about:

The Community We Have Multiplied

> In math class we were multiplying, multiplying, multiplying. We read *Anno's Mysterious Multiplying Jar.* We wrote our own versions of the Multiplying Jar set in our own communities. Would you like to write with us? Please send us your stories and let us know if you would like to read ours.

I sent the message from my computer at home. A few weeks later, I printed the responses and brought them into class. Although the exchange was difficult to maintain without classroom access to the internet, this collaboration across grade levels strengthened the writing for both groups as they presented their work to an international audience. The literacy circle is complete when children take what they have learned in the classroom and use it in their experiences with the outside world.

Another example of student publishing was preparing student stories in book form for the classroom library. Including quality student writing in the multicultural library inspired children to write their own versions of stories that were popular with the class. One reading group was reading science fiction with animal characters. Their favorite was *Catwings*, by Ursula LeGuin. This story takes place in an urban setting; the wings saved the cats from a terrible fate. Stories sprouted from our students about urban animal families with liberating anatomy. Final edited versions were included in the library for classmates to read.

To summarize, as classroom teachers we emphasize varied ways of developing literacy through writing. Autobiographies, journals, and publishing projects encourage children to express themselves through writing. Second-language learners benefit from sheltering strategies to support the development of their academic language. Children write to be read when their work is validated through publishing.

Excerpted from "Raising Children's Cultural Voices," Lifting Every Voice: Pedagogy and Politics of Bilingualism, *pp. 71-94. Copyright © 2000 by the President and Fellows of Harvard College. All rights reserved.*

CHAPTER SEVENTEEN

And Then
I Went to School

By Joe Suina

I lived with my grandmother when I was 5 through 9 years of age. It was the early 1950s when electricity had not yet entered our Pueblo homes. The village day school and health clinic were first to have it, and to the unsuspecting Cochiti, this was the approach of a new era in their uncomplicated lives.

Transportation was simple. Two good horses and a sturdy wagon met the daily needs of a villager. Only five, maybe six individuals possessed an automobile in the Pueblo of 400. A flatbed truck fixed with side rails and a canvas top made the usual Saturday morning trip to Santa Fe. It was always loaded

IStockphoto

beyond capacity with people and their wares headed for town for a few staples. The straining old truck with its escort of a dozen barking dogs made a noisy exit, northbound from the village.

A Sense of Closeness

During those years, grandmother and I lived beside the plaza in a one-room house. Inside, we had a traditional fireplace, a makeshift cabinet for our few tin cups and bowls, and a wooden crate carried our two buckets of all-purpose water. At the innermost part of the room were two rolls of bedding—thick quilts, sheepskin, and assorted—which we used as comfortable sitting couches by day and unrolled for sleeping by night. A wooden pole the length of one side of the room was suspended about ten inches from the vigas and draped with a modest collection of colorful shawls, blankets, and sashes, making this part of the room most interesting. In one corner sat a bulky metal trunk for our ceremonial wear and a few valuables. A dresser which was traded for her well-known pottery held the few articles of clothing we owned and the "goody bag"—an old flour sack Grandma always kept filled with brown candy, store-bought cookies, and Fig Newtons. These were saturated with a sharp odor of moth balls. Nevertheless, they made a fine snack with coffee before we turned in for the night. Tucked securely beneath my blankets, I listened to one of her stories about how it was when she was a little girl. These accounts appeared so old fashioned compared to the way we lived. Sometimes she softly sang a song from a ceremony. In this way, I went off to sleep each night.

Earlier in the evening we would make our way to a relative's house if someone had not already come to visit us. There, I'd play with the children while the adults caught up on all the latest news. Ten-cent comic books were finding their way into the Pueblo homes. Exchanging "old" comics for "new" ones was a serious matter that involved adults as well. Adults favored mystery and romance stories. For us children these were the first links to the world beyond the Pueblo. We enjoyed looking at them and role-playing our favorite hero rounding up the villains. Grandmother once made me a cape to leap tall buildings with. It seems everyone preferred being a cowboy rather than an Indian since cowboys were always victorious. Sometimes stories were related to both children and adults at these get-togethers. They were highlighted by refreshments of coffee and sweet bread or fruit pies baked in the outdoor oven. Winter months would most likely include roasted piñon nuts and dried deer meat for all to

For us children these were the first links to the world beyond the Pueblo.

share. These evening gatherings and the sense of closeness diminished as radios and televisions increased over the following years. It was never to be the same again.

The winter months are among my fondest memories. A warm fire crackled and danced brightly in the fireplace, and the aroma of delicious stew filled our one-room house. The thick adobe walls wrapped around the two of us protectingly during the long freezing nights. To me, the house was just right. Grandmother's affection completed the warmth and security I will always remember.

Being the only child at grandmother's, I had lots of attention and plenty of reasons to feel good about myself. As a preschooler, I already had chores of chopping firewood and hauling in fresh water each day. After "heavy work" I would run to her and flex what I was convinced were my gigantic biceps. Grandmother would state that at the rate I was going I would soon attain the status of a man like the adult males in the village. Her shower of praise made me feel like the Mr. Indian Universe of all time. At age 5, I suppose I was as close to that concept of myself as anyone.

In spite of her many years, grandmother was highly active in the village ceremonial setting. She was a member of an important women's society and attended every traditional function, taking me along to many of them. I'd wear one of my colorful shirts she made by hand for just such occasions. Grandmother taught me appropriate behavior at these events. Through modeling she showed me how to pray properly. Barefooted, I greeted the sun each morning with a handful of cornmeal. At night I'd look to the stars in wonderment and let a prayer slip through my lips. On meeting someone, grandmother would say, "Smile and greet. Grunt if you must, but don't pretend they're not there." On food and material things, she would say, "There is enough for everyone to share and it all comes from above, my child." I learned to appreciate cooperation in nature and with my fellow men early in life. I felt very much a part of the world and our way of life. I knew I had a place in it, and I felt good about it.

I felt very much a part of the world and our way of life. I knew I had a place in it, and I felt good about it.

And Then I Went to School

At age 6, like the rest of the Cochiti 6-year-olds that year, I had to begin my schooling. It was a new and bewildering experience— one I will not forget. The strange surrounding, new ideas about time and expectations, and the foreign tongue were at times overwhelming to us beginners. It took some effort to return the second day and many times thereafter.

To begin with, unlike my grandmother, the teacher did not have pretty brown skin and a colorful dress. She wasn't plump and friendly. Her clothes were of one color and drab. Her pale and skinny form made me worry that she was very ill. In the village, being more pale than usual was a sure sign of an oncoming fever or some such disorder. I thought that explained why she didn't have time just for me and the disappointed looks and orders she seemed always to direct my way. I didn't think she was so smart since she couldn't understand my language. "Surely that was why we had to leave our 'Indian' at home." But then I didn't feel so bright either. All I could say in her language was "Yes, teacher," "My name is Joseph Henry," and "When is lunch?" The teacher's odor took some getting used to also. In fact, many times it made me sick right before lunch. Later I learned from the girls this smell was something she wore called perfume.

An Artificial Classroom

The classroom, too, had its odd characteristics. It was terribly huge and smelled of medicine like the village clinic I feared so much. The walls and ceiling were artificial and uncaring. They were too far from me and I felt naked. Those fluorescent light tubes made an eerie drone and blinked suspiciously over me, quite a contrast to the fire and sunlight my eyes were accustomed to. I thought maybe the lighting did not seem right because it was man-made, and it wasn't natural. Our confinement to rows of desks was another unnatural demand made on our active little bodies. We had to sit at these hard things for what seemed like forever before relief (recess) came midway through the morning and afternoon. Running carefree in the village and fields was but a sweet memory of days gone by. We all went home for lunch since we lived a short walk from school. It took coaxing, and sometimes bribing, to get me to return and complete the remainder of the school day.

School was a painful experience during those early years.

School was a painful experience during those early years. The English language and the new set of values caused me much anxiety and embarrassment. I couldn't comprehend everything that was happening, but I could understand very well when I messed up or wasn't doing so well. Negative messages were communicated too effectively and I became more and more unsure of myself. How I wished I could understand other things in school just as well.

The conflict was not only in school performance but in many other areas of my life as well. For example, many of us students had a problem with head lice due to the "unsanitary conditions in our homes." Consequently, we received a harsh shampooing which was rough on both the scalp and the ego. Cleanliness was crucial, and a washing of this sort indicated to the class that one came from a home setting which was not healthy. I recall one such treatment and afterwards being humiliated before my peers with a statement that I had "She'na" (lice) so tough that I must have been born with them. Needless to say, my Super Indian self-image was no longer intact.

"Leave Your Indian at Home"

My language, too, was questioned right from the beginning of my school career. "Leave your Indian at home!" was like a school trademark. Speaking it accidentally or otherwise was punishable by a dirty look or a whack with a ruler. This reprimand was for speaking the language of my people which meant so much to me. It was the language of my grandmother, and I spoke it well. With it, I sang beautiful songs and prayed from my heart. At that young and tender age, it was most difficult for me to comprehend why I had to part with my language. And yet at home I was encouraged to attend school so that I might have a better life in the future. I knew I had a good village life already, but this awareness dwindled each day I was in school.

As the weeks turned to months, I learned English more and more. It may appear that comprehension would be easier. It got easier to understand, all right. I understood that everything I had, and was a part of, was not nearly as good as the white man's. School was determined to undo me in everything from my sheepskin bedding to the dances and ceremonies which I had learned to have faith in and cherish. One day I dozed off in class after a sacred all-night ceremony. I was startled awake by a sharp jerk on my ear, and informed coldly, "That ought to teach you to attend 'those things' again." Later, all alone, I cried. I couldn't understand why or what I was caught up in. I was receiving two very different messages; both were intended for my welfare.

Values in lifestyle were dictated in various ways. The Dick and Jane reading series in the primary grades presented me pictures of a home with a pitched roof, straight walls, and sidewalks. I could not identify with these from my Pueblo world. However, it was clear I didn't have these things, and what I did have did not measure up. At night, long after grandmother went to sleep, I would lie awake staring at our crooked adobe walls casting uneven shadows from the light of the fireplace. The walls were no longer just right

> *School was determined to undo me in everything from my sheepskin bedding to the dances and ceremonies which I had learned to have faith in and cherish.*

My life was no longer just right. I was ashamed of being who I was, and I wanted to change right then and there.

for me. My life was no longer just right. I was ashamed of being who I was, and I wanted to change right then and there. Somehow it became very important to have straight walls, clean hair and teeth, and a spotted dog to chase after. I even became critical of, and hateful toward, my bony, fleabag of a dog. I loved the familiar and cozy environment at grandmother's house, but now I imagined it could be a heck of a lot better if only I had a white-man's house with a bed, a nice couch, and a clock. In school books, all the child characters ever did was run at leisure after the dog or kite. They were always happy. As for me, all I seemed to do at home was go for buckets of water and cut up sticks for a lousy fire. Didn't the teacher say drinking coffee would stunt my growth? Why couldn't I have nice tall glasses of milk so I could have strong bones and white teeth like those kids in the books? Did my grandmother really care about my well-being?

Torn Away

I had to leave my beloved village of Cochiti for my education beyond 6. I left to attend a Bureau of Indian Affairs (BIA) boarding school 30 miles from home. Shined shoes and pressed shirt and pants were the order of the day. I managed to adjust to this just as I had to most of the things the school shoved at me or took away from me. Adjusting to leaving home and the village was tough enough. It seemed the older I got, the further I got from the ways I was so much a part of. Since my parents did not own an automobile, I saw them only once a month when they came in the community truck. They never failed to come supplied with "eats" for me. I enjoyed the outdoor oven bread, dried meat, and tamales they usually brought. It took a while to get accustomed to the diet of the school. Being in town with strange tribes under one roof was frightening and often very lonely. I longed for my grandmother and my younger brothers and sisters. I longed for my house. I longed to take part in a Buffalo Dance. I longed to be free.

I came home for the four-day Thanksgiving break. At first, home did not feel right anymore. It was much too small and stuffy. The lack of running water and bathroom facilities was too inconvenient. Everything got dusty so quickly, and hardly anyone spoke English. It occurred to me then that I was beginning to take on the whiteman's ways that belittled my own. However, it didn't take long to "get back with it." Once I reestablished my relationships with family, relatives, and friends, I knew I was where I came from. I knew where I belonged.

Leaving for the boarding school the following Sunday evening was one of the saddest events in my entire life. Although I had enjoyed myself immensely the last few days, I realized then that life would never be the same again. I could not turn back the time just as I could not do away with school and the ways of the whiteman. They were here to stay and would creep more and more into my life. The effort to make sense of both worlds together was painful, and I had no choice but to do so. The schools, television, automobiles, and many other outside ways and values had chipped away at the simple cooperative life I began to grow in. The people of Cochiti were changing. The winter evening gatherings, the exchanging of stories, and even the performing of certain ceremonies were already only a memory that someone commented about now and then. Still, the two worlds were very different and the demands of both were ever present. The whiteman's was flashy, less personal, but very comfortable. The Cochiti were both attracted and pushed toward these new ways which they had little to say about. There was no choice left but to compete with the whiteman on his terms for survival. To do that I knew I had to give up part of my life.

SECTION III

Transnational Identities, Multicultural Classrooms

What Happened to the Golden Door?

How my students taught me about immigration

By Linda Christensen

At Eureka High School, immigration equaled Ellis Island. We watched old black-and-white film strips of Northern Europeans filing through dimly lit buildings. My textbooks were laced with pictures of the Statue of Liberty opening her arms to poor immigrants who had been granted an opportunity to "pull themselves up by their bootstraps" when they passed through America's door:

> Give me your tired, your poor,
> Your huddled masses yearning to breathe free,
> The wretched refuse of your teeming shores.
> Send these, the homeless, tempest-tost, to me,
> I lift my lamp beside the golden door.

Jean-Claude Lejeune

Years later when I visited Angel Island in San Francisco Bay, I learned about another immigration that hadn't been mentioned in my high school or college texts.

I felt pride at being part of a country that helped the unfortunate, including my own family.

Years later when I visited Angel Island in San Francisco Bay, I learned about another immigration that hadn't been mentioned in my high school or college texts. I walked through the deserted barracks where painted walls covered the poems of immigrant Chinese who viewed the "Golden Mountain" through a barbed wire fence. I felt angry that yet another portion of U.S. history had been hidden from me. Between 1910 and 1940, the "tired, poor, wretched refuse" from Asian shores were imprisoned on Angel Island before being accepted as "resident aliens" or rejected at the "golden door." As historian Ronald Takaki notes, "Their quarters were crowded and unsanitary, resembling a slum. 'When we arrived,' said one of them, 'they locked us up like criminals in compartments like the cages in the zoo.'"[1] Turning their anger and frustration into words, the Chinese carved poems on the building's wooden walls. Their poems stood in stark contradiction to the Statue of Liberty's promise:

America has power, but not justice.
In prison, we were victimized as if we
were guilty.
Given no opportunity to explain, it was
really brutal.
I bow my head in reflection but there is
nothing I can do.[2]

All Europeans were eligible for citizenship once they passed through Ellis Island, a right denied to Asians until the mid-1940s.

In 1995 when California voters passed Proposition 187, I decided to teach about immigration, not just the traditional version, but the more dangerous and unspoken immigration that denies access to large numbers of potential immigrants based on color or politics.

Beyond these political reasons, I had personal and educational reasons to teach this unit. It was the last quarter of the year in Literature in U.S. History, a combined junior level untracked history and English class that met 90 minutes a day for the entire year. The days had warmed up and the students smelled summer. If I said the word "essay," "interior monologue," or "role play," I could hear a collective moan rise from the circle and settle like stinky fog around my head.

For three quarters, my planning book had been filled with lessons attempting to teach students how to become critical readers of history and literature. They'd written essays, critiques, short stories, personal narratives, poems, and interior monologues analyzing their own lives as well as the history and contemporary issues that continue to deprive Native Americans of land and economic opportunities. They'd also reflected critically on the enslavement of Africans, starting with life in Africa before slavery as well as forced immigration and resistance. We examined the literature and history of the Harlem Renaissance, the Civil Rights Movement, and contemporary issues. They read and critiqued presidential speeches, historical and contemporary novels and poems written by people from a variety of backgrounds. They were ready to do their own investigation and teaching—putting into practice their analytical skills.

Fourth quarter I wanted them to conduct "real" research— not the scurry-to-the-library-and-find-the-closest-encyclopedia-and-copy-it-word-for-word kind of research, but research that made them ask questions about immigration policies, quotas, and personal stories that couldn't be lifted from a single text. I wanted them to learn to use the library, search for books, look up alternative sources, find the Ethnic NewsWatch, search the Oregon Historical Society's clipping files, photo files, and rare documents room. I wanted them to interview people, read novels and poetry that told the immigrant's story in a more personal way. Through this kind of thorough research, I hoped they would develop an ear for what is unsaid in political speeches and newspaper articles, that they would learn to ask questions when their neighbors or people on the bus began an anti-immigrant rap.

I wanted them to interview people, read novels and poetry that told the immigrant's story in a more personal way.

Setting the Stage

I started fourth quarter by outlining my goals and expectations. I do this each term, so students know what kinds of pieces must be in their portfolio, for example, a literary essay comparing two novels, an essay exploring a historical issue, a poem that includes details from history, etc. As part of the opening of the quarter ceremonies, I passed out an outline of their upcoming project. I wanted a lengthy deadline so students would have the opportunity to work the entire quarter on the project.

Before students started their research, I modeled how I wanted the lessons taught by presenting Chinese and Japanese immigration. While students who come through the Jefferson network of elementary, middle, and high schools get at least surface background knowledge of Native Americans and African Americans, they appear to know less about Asian or Latino literature or history. In fact, students are often surprised that the Japanese and Chinese faced any prejudice.[3]

During the lessons on Japanese Americans, students examined Executive Order 9066 signed by President Roosevelt, which gave the military the right to force Japanese Americans from their homes and businesses into camps surrounded by barbed wire and guard towers. Because these "resident aliens" and U.S. citizens were allowed to take only what they could carry to the "camps," they were forced to sell most of their possessions in a short period of time. Students read "Echoes of Pearl Harbor," a chapter from *Nisei Daughter* by Monica Sone, where she describes her family burning their Japanese poetry, kimonos, breaking their Japanese records, destroying anything that could make them look like they cherished their Japanese heritage. Students wrote moving poetry and interior monologues imagining they were forced to leave their homes, businesses, and treasured possessions. "Becoming American," was written by Khalilah Joseph:[4]

> I looked into the eyes of my Japanese doll
> and knew I could not surrender her
> to the fury of the fire.
> My mother threw out the poetry
> she loved;
> my brother gave the fire his sword.
> We worked hours
> to vanish any traces of the Asian world
> from our home.
> Who could ask us
> to destroy
> gifts from a world that molded
> and shaped us?
> If I ate hamburgers
> and apple pies,
> if I wore jeans,
> then would I be American?"

I came across *Beyond Words: Images from America's Concentration Camps*, a fascinating book of personal testimony and artwork produced in the camps: black-and-white drawings, watercolors, oil paintings, and pieces of interviews that gave me a window into the lives of the imprisoned Japanese. While I showed slides of the artwork, students I prompted ahead of time read "Legends from Camp" by Lawson Inada, "The Question of Loyalty," by Mitsuye Yamada, and segments of the internees'

Students wrote moving poetry and interior monologues imagining they were forced to leave their homes, businesses, and treasured possessions.

interviews that matched pictures on screen. With images and words of the prisoners in their minds, students wrote their own poems. Thu Throung's poem is called "Japanese Prisoners":

> Guards watch us.
> They wrap us around
> in barbed wire fences
> like an orange's meat
> that never grows outside its skin.
> If the orange's skin breaks,
> the juice drains out.
> Just like the Japanese behind the
>   wire fence.

We watched and critiqued the somewhat flawed film *Come See the Paradise*,[5] and talked about the laws that forbade Japanese nationals from becoming citizens or owning land. Students read loyalty oaths imprisoned Japanese American citizens were forced to sign. After learning about the "No No Boys," men who refused to sign the oath, and their subsequent imprisonment in federal penitentiaries, students argued about whether or not they would have signed the loyalty oath if they'd been interned.[6]

Students also looked at the number of immigrant Chinese allowed in the country compared to European immigrants. For example, in 1943 when Congress repealed the Chinese Exclusion Act because of China's alliance with the United States against the Japanese, 105 Chinese were allowed to enter Angel Island while 66,000 English immigrants passed through Ellis Island.[7]

The Research Begins

Students started on their own projects during the same time period I presented the Chinese and Japanese immigration. They had two 30-minute sessions the first week to discuss what they knew, itemize what they needed to find, and list the resources they had (people to interview, books at home, potential videos to use, outside resources like Vietnamese, Russian, or Latino teachers or districtwide coordinators.) During the following weeks, while I continued my presentations, they were given varied amounts of time to conduct research: 45 minutes to prepare for the library, a full day at the library, additional 90-minute periods as we got closer to deadline, etc.

At the end of each period of "research/preparation" time, students turned their information in to me so I could see if they made headway, ran into a block, needed a push or help. During this research period, I moved between groups, listening in, asking questions, making lists of questions they raised, but didn't answer, questioning literary choices when a piece was by a writer from the immigration group but didn't deal with any of the issues we were studying.

During this time, it was not unusual to see some of my students gathered around a television in the hallway outside my door or in the library as they watched and critiqued videos, looking for potential sections to show to the class. Travis, Roman, and Sophia, who were individual researchers, could be seen translating notes or cassette tapes for their stories. Sometimes they met to talk over stories or ideas for their presentation.

The Mexican group had the most members—too many, really. They watched videos together and then split the rest of the work: Danica and Komar collected and read books to find a story; Shannon researched Cesar Chavez and wrote a profile to hand out to the class; Heather gathered information for a debate on Proposition 187; Stephanie and Stacey coordinated the group, collecting information from each subgroup, fitting research into a coherent lesson plan, and creating a writing lesson that would pull information together for the class; Rosa, the only group member fluent in Spanish, talked with recent immigrants in ESL classes and the Latino coordinator to find speakers, videos, and stories to feed to her group.

Before I end up sounding like a movie script starring Michelle Pfeiffer, let me quickly insert into this idyllic classroom a word or two of other things you might see: kids whining and competing for my attention, RIGHT NOW; students gossiping about a fight, a guess-who's-going-out-with ..., an upcoming game, or a movie they saw last night; a sly student attempting to take advantage of the chaos to catch up on math or Spanish; the slippery students who said they were going to the library or to see an ESL coordinator, but who actually sneaked into the teachers' cafeteria for coffee or outside for a smoke. There were also two students who attended regularly and might have learned something through other people's work, but who produced no work themselves, and a few others who rode the backs of their group's work, contributing a little in spurts, but not making the sustained efforts of most students. The ESL coordinators and librarians and I developed an easy communication system regarding passes. I called students and parents at home to talk about their lack of work. While the calls pushed the back-riding students who made some effort, I failed to bring the "slackers" into the research fold.

Besides the usual chaos a teacher might expect when turning over the curriculum to students, I simultaneously hit another problem. I'd set up immigrant groups that I knew would have some interesting and contradictory stories because I was familiar with their history and literature. While students did accept some of the groups I'd proposed: Mexican, Haitian, Cambodian, Irish, and Vietnamese, others argued vehemently that they be allowed to choose the immigrant group they would study. Our previous lessons on resistance and solidarity had certainly taken root within each of the class members, and I was the object of their solidarity. A few wanted to research their own family's immigration stories: Greek, Jewish, Macedonian, and Russian. Several African American students wanted to study immigrants from Africa or from the African Diaspora. Most were happy to study Haiti, one of my original groups; one student chose to study Eritrea, since Portland has a larger population of Eritreans than Haitians. I agreed; in fact, he made an excellent choice. We ended our first rounds with the following research groups: Cambodians, Eritreans,[8] Greeks, Haitians, Irish, Jewish, Macedonians, Mexicans, Russians, and Vietnamese. This first dialogue marked the end of my control over the history and literature presented in class. And I was nervous because I knew almost nothing about Greek and Macedonian immigration and not much more about the Russians.

This first dialogue marked the end of my control over the history and literature presented in class.

Ultimately, the contrast between groups made for great discussion. In my class of 31 students, three had immigrated from Vietnam, one from Russia, one from Cambodia; several students were second generation Americans from Greece, Ireland, Nicaragua, and Mexico; half of the class' ancestors had been enslaved Africans, and one girl's grandmother was the only surviving member of her family after the Holocaust. But I can imagine a more homogenous classroom where this might not be the case. In my high school English class over 20 years ago, 29 students were white and one was black. Around Portland today, I can cite similar profiles. These ratios would have made me demand more diversity in the research if all students wanted to study their own heritage. I do think it is important to negotiate the curriculum with students, and I'm sure some students would be more interested in researching their own past than researching the past of others, but sometimes, in order to surface issues of race and class inequality, it is necessary to move beyond our personal histories.

Research Problems

Prior to the beginning of the unit, I spent time in the public library and the Oregon Historical Society (OHS) library, finding sources, articles, books, practicing computer research programs, before bringing my students across town. OHS officials were friendly and helpful, but told me that I couldn't bring the entire class to their library: I'd have to bring one or two at a time after school or on Saturdays. And they closed at 5 p.m.

In addition to limited library time, I discovered that the easily accessible research materials did not have a critical page in their spines; they just restated the textbook version. I wanted students to learn the "whole truth," not just a watered-down version that left out facts that might complicate the issues. I figured that part of research is getting lots of material and then deciding what is important to present so that others hear a fuller truth. But when I discovered that much of what students were reading only told one side of the immigration story—the same side I learned in high school—I made an effort to put other facts in students' hands as well. We searched computer files of Ethnic NewsWatch and alternative news and magazine sources. Although many students dutifully read the computer-generated articles, most of these pieces were too academic or required extensive background knowledge to understand. If we had relied solely on these sources of information—either textbook or alternative—many students would have come away with material that they might have been able to cite and copy into a readable paper, but they wouldn't have understood much about the underlying political situations their immigrant group faced.

After the library research, I linked students with people or information that might provide facts and stories not available in the library. The Haitian group, for example, read articles but hadn't comprehended what was going on: Who was Papa Doc? How was the United States involved? What was happening with Aristide? I distributed copies of the Network of Educators on the Americas' (NECA) booklet *Teaching About Haiti*, which gave them historical and political analysis they needed in order to make sense of the newspaper and magazine articles. The novel *Krik? Krak!* by Edwidge Danticat developed their personal connection; she gave faces and voices to the people on the boats, to those who lived in fear. The names in the newspaper became real: Aristide, Tontons Macoutes, boat people, refugees. (The group's enthusiasm for the novel caught on. I'd purchased five copies,

> I wanted students to learn the 'whole truth,' not just a watered-down version that left out facts that might complicate the issues.

and there were arguments over who got to read *Krik? Krak!* after group members finished.)

Students became wonderfully devious researchers, using their own connections to gain information. They learned to find back doors when the front doors closed and windows when all of the doors were locked. But sometimes these backdoor, through-the-window type researches posed another problem: What if personal history omitted vital historical facts and perspectives? While I could help students who studied immigrant groups that I knew something about, I had little time to read and research the Macedonians, Greeks, and Russians. Travis was thoroughly confused when his research revealed a snarled web of history involving Greece, Bulgaria, and a historic trade route through the mountains. His research took him back to 146 B.C., when Rome conquered the Kingdom of Macedonia, and forward to today. He wanted to know why his grandfather immigrated. Instead of untangling the web of Macedonian history, he spent time with his grandfather, talking, asking questions, going through photo albums, relying on his personal relationships to decode the past. He arranged for a day at the Macedonian lodge, where he interviewed men his grandfather's age about their immigration experiences. Because of my own limited knowledge of events in Macedonia, I let him. This was history via personal story—how much or how little of the history was included, I wasn't sure.

Likewise, when Meghan and I met one Saturday at the Oregon Historical Society, we discovered the letters James Mullany, an Irish immigrant, wrote to his sister in Ireland in the mid-1800s. In one letter, he pleaded with his sister not to mention that he was Catholic: "their [sic] is a strong prejudice against them here on account of the people here thinking it was the Priests that caused the Indian war three or four years ago."[9] Interesting. But in another letter he wrote of the Snake Indians who attacked a train of 45 whites, "only 15 survived but some of them died of starvation … [A] company of soldiers … found them living of [sic] the bodyes [sic] of them that were killed by the [I]ndians."[10] Could we count these letters as historic evidence? Whose voices weren't included? What stories might the Snake Indians have told?

Students using voices of immigrants or novels to tell the history created a dilemma for me: What happens when personal narratives exclude the stories of large groups of other people or neglect important historical facts? When and how do I intervene? If students tell only their own stories or draw on personal testimonies, is that "inaccurate" history? As an English teacher who

> *Students became wonderfully devious researchers, using their own connections to gain information.*

weaves literature and history together, who values personal stories as eyewitness accounts of events and who encourages students to "tell their stories," I began to question my own assumptions.

The Vietnamese group, occupying Tri's corner between the windows and closet, underscored my "history versus personal story" dilemma. Their student-told account emphasized a pro-American stance around the Vietnam War but said nothing, for example, of U.S. support for French colonialism, its creation of "South Vietnam," or its devastating bombardment of the Vietnamese countryside. How could I challenge the story these students grew up hearing from parents and elders in their community?

With Meghan's research, we'd studied historical accounts of Native Americans in the Northwest, so we knew that Mullany's letters lacked facts about land takeovers and Indian massacres. But I didn't have time to teach the unit on Vietnam that Bill Bigelow and I developed when we taught the class together, so I also worried that the rest of the class would come away without an understanding of the key role the United States played in the Vietnam War; and without that understanding, how would they be able to critique other U.S. interventions?

I talked with Cang, Tri and Thu and gave them resources: a timeline that reviewed deepening U.S. involvement in Vietnam and numerous readings from a critical standpoint. I also introduced them to the film *Hearts and Minds*, which features testimony from numerous critics of the war, as well as prominent U.S. antiwar activists like Daniel Ellsberg. Without a sustained dialogue, this insertion seemed weak and invasive, more so than my talks with Travis and Meghan, because their research was at a greater distance from their lives. But I learned a lesson: Personal story does not always equal history. This lingers as a vexing teaching dilemma.

I learned a lesson: Personal story does not always equal history. This lingers as a vexing teaching dilemma.

The Presentation

Once presentation deadlines hit, students argued over dates and order—who got to go first, last, etc. Our biggest struggle came around the issue of time. Students lobbied for longer time slots. The Mexican group was especially ardent. They'd found great movies as well as short stories, informational videos, and a guest speaker from PCUN, the local farm workers union, about working conditions and the boycott of Garden Burgers, a veggie burger sold in stores and restaurants across the country. They figured they needed at least a week, possibly two. We had five weeks left: four for presentations and a last sacred week to finish portfolios and evaluations. Rosa said, "Look how many days you used when you taught us about the Japanese and Chinese. Two weeks on each! Aren't the Latinos as important as the Asians?" They bargained with single person groups, like the Russians and Greeks, for part of their time.

A week or so prior to presentations, groups submitted detailed lesson plans. I met formally with each group to make sure all requirements were covered, but also questioned choices. During previous weeks, I'd read every proposed story and novel selection, watched each video, went over writing assignments: I didn't want any surprises on their teaching day.

The power of my students' teaching was not in just the individual presentations, where students provided historical information in a variety of mostly interesting and unique lesson plans, but also in the juxtaposition of these histories and stories. Students created a jazz improvisation, overlaying voices of pain and struggle and triumph with heroic attempts to escape war, poverty, or traditions that pinched women too narrowly into scripted roles. Their historical research and variety of voices taught about a more varied history of immigration than I'd ever attempted to do in the past.

The power of my students' teaching was not in just the individual presentations, but also in the juxtaposition of these histories and stories.

But the presentations were also like improvisation in that they were not as tightly connected and controlled as a rehearsed piece I would have conducted. There were off notes and unfinished strands that seemed promising but didn't deliver an analysis that could have strengthened student understanding of immigration. Few students found research on quotas, few had time left in their presentation to engage in a discussion that linked or compared their group to another. The Haitian group, for example, tied our past studies of Columbus and the Taínos to present Haiti, but didn't develop the history of Duvalier or Aristide or the involvement of the United States.

Although presentations varied in length and depth, most gave us at least a look at a culture many students weren't familiar with, and at best, a strong sense that not only did racial and political background determine who gets into this country, but also how they live once they arrive.

The Cambodian group arranged for Sokpha's mother to come to class, as well as a viewing of the film *The Killing Fields*. Sokpha's mother told of her life in Cambodia, of hiding in the deep tunnels her father built to keep them safe from U.S. bombs, of her fear of snakes at the bottom of the tunnel that scared her almost as much as the bombs. She talked about the Khmer Rouge, the Vietnamese, and the United States. On her father's deathbed, he said, "Go to America. Leave Cambodia." She did. Shoeless, nine months pregnant with Sokpha, and carrying a three-year-old on her back, she walked for three days and three nights from Cambodia into Thailand, dodging land mines that killed some of her fellow travelers. She also spoke of difficulties here—how her lack of language skills have kept her from finding a good job, her reliance on Sokpha, the breakdown of their culture, the Americanization of her children.

The Haitians presented background history tying the modern struggle in Haiti with previous history lessons; their strengths were chilling descriptions of the refugees, their choice of story, their research into Haitian culture, and their writing assignment. Read aloud by a male and a female student, the two-voice story, "Children of the Sea," portrayed a political young man who dared to speak out against the Haitian government, writing to his lover as he rides a sinking boat in search of refuge in the United States. His lover writes of the increased military violence of the Tontons Macoutes, who make parents have sex with their children, rape and torture suspected supporters of Aristide.

Cang, from the Vietnamese group, recounted Vietnam's history through a timeline. Thu's stories of escape and life in the refugee camps created nightmare scenes for her fellow students of drownings, rapes, and the difficulties of families who got separated. Tri pointed out the geographical settlements of immigrant Vietnamese and their induction into the United States. He talked about the struggle of the Vietnamese shrimp fishermen in the Gulf, the attempts of the KKK to drive the fishermen out of the region,[11] and the creation of Little Saigon in California, a space where the Vietnamese have forged a community inside the United States, not unlike many immigrants who came before them.

The student writing assignments generated excellent poems and personal narratives.

The student writing assignments generated excellent poems and personal narratives. After Sophia spoke about her mother's experiences, she said her inheritance from her mother was the strength to pursue her goals even when she faces opposition. Her assignment for the class: "Write about something you treasure from your family. It might be an heirloom, like a ring, but it can also be a story, a memory, a tradition, a personal trait. Write it as a poem, a personal narrative, or a story." Komar Harvey wrote an essay about his family's love of music:

> You can hear music on the porch before you enter our house. Tunes climb through those old vinyl windows and mailbox and drift into everybody's ears in the neighborhood. If you came during the holiday season you could hear

the Christmas bells chiming through the static of that old crackling phonograph needle. You hear the rumbling voice of Charles Brown as if he were digging a hole up in the living room, 'Bells will be ringing' ... Nobody graces our door during those Christmas months without a little Charles ringing his bells in their ears.

After talking about the efforts of his grandfather's struggles to get to the United States, Travis asked students to write a personal narrative about an obstacle they overcame in their life. Cang wrote about his difficulty learning English in the face of classmates' ridicule. His narrative had a profound effect on students. I have not changed or corrected his language because it is part of the story:

> [After he left Vietnam, he was in the Philippines.] In 1989 we came to America. That's when I started to go to school. I went to all of the classes I had, but I felt the blonde and white-skinned people not respected me. They make joke over the way I talk ... I'll never give up, I say to myself ... One day I'm going to be just like them on talking and writing, but I never get to that part of my life until now. Even if I can understand the word, but still I can't pronounce it, if I do pronounce it, it won't end up right. Truly, I speak Vietnamese at home all the time, that's why I get used to the Vietnamese words more than English, but I'll never give up what I have learned. I will succeed with my second language.

The Mexican group took several days for their presentation. They taught about the theft of Mexican land by the United States, immigration border patrols, the effect of toxic sprays on migrant workers, the migrants' living conditions in Oregon. During this time, we also debated Proposition 187: Should the United States deny services to undocumented immigrants? Then the presenters asked the class to write a persuasive essay taking a point of view on the question.

One day we watched the movie *Mi Familia*, about a "Mexican" family whose original homeland was in California. As we watched, we ate tamales and sweet tacos that Rosa and her mother-in-law lugged up three flights of stairs. Then we wrote food poems that tied us to our culture. Sarah LePage's "Matzah Balls" is a tribute to her grandmother:

> Grandma's hands,
> wise, soft, and old,
> mold the Matzah meal
> between the curves of each palm.
> She transforms our heritage

into perfect little spheres.
Like a magician
she shapes our culture
as our people do.
This is her triumph.
She lays the bowl aside
revealing her tired hands,
each wrinkle a time
she sacrificed something for our family.

Evaluation

On our last day, students over-whelmingly voted that immigration was the unit they both learned the most from and cared the most about.

On our last day, students overwhelmingly voted that immigration was the unit they both learned the most from and cared the most about. Komar, the first to speak, said, "I never realized that Cambodians were different from Vietnamese. Sokpha's family went through a lot to get here, so did Tri's, Thu's and Cang's." Stacey, a member of the Haitian group added, "I learned that the United States isn't just black and white. I learned that my people are not the only ones who have suffered in this country." Khalilah noted that she hadn't realized what research really meant until she struggled to find information about the Haitians. While others added similar points about various groups or presentations they learned from, Travis summed up the conversation by saying, "I didn't know anything about Proposition 187 or the discrimination immigrants have faced because that wasn't part of my family's history. I didn't know that there was discrimination about who got in and who was kept out of the United States, and now I do."

I felt that students learned from each other about immigrants' uneven and unfair treatment. The Statue of Liberty's flame and rhetoric had met with a history, told by students, that dimmed her light. But they had also learned lessons that would alter their interactions with the "Chinese"—actually Korean—store keeper at the intersection of Martin Luther King Jr. and Fremont. At Jefferson, one of the most offensive scenes I have witnessed in the hallways or classrooms is the silencing of immigrant Asian, Russian, and Mexican students as they speak their own languages or struggle to speak English. Throughout the year, Cang, Thu, and Tri's personal testimony during discussions or read-arounds about the pain of that silencing as well as their stories about fighting with their parents or setting off fire crackers in their school in Vietnam created much more awareness in our classroom than any lecture could have. I credit our study of history, for example, the Mexican-American War, as part of that change, but through this student-led unit on immigration, I watched students crack through stereotypes they had nurtured about others. Students who sat by their lockers on C-floor were no longer lumped together under the title "Chinese"; they became Vietnamese, Cambodian, Laotian. Students no longer mimicked the sound of their speech as a put-down. Latino students who spoke Spanish near the door on the west side of the building were no longer seen as outsiders who moved into the neighborhood with loud cars and lots of children, but as political exiles in a land that had once belonged to their ancestors. The Russian students who moved together like a small boat through the halls of Jefferson were no longer odd, but seekers of religious freedom.

Throughout fourth quarter, I tossed and turned at night questioning my judgment about asking students to teach such an important part of history—and the consequence that much history would not be taught. But after hearing their enthusiasm and their changed perceptions about their classmates, the world, and research, I put my critique temporarily on hold. Turning over the classroom circle to my students allowed them to become the "experts" and me to become their student. While I lost control and power over the curriculum and was forced to question some key assumptions of my teaching, I gained an incredible amount of knowledge—and so did they.

Bibliography

Asian Women United of California (1989). *Making waves: An anthology of writings by and about Asian American women.* Boston, MA: Beacon Press.

Chin, F., Chan, J. P., Inada, L.F., & Wong, S. (1991). *Aiiieeeee! An anthology of Chinese American and Japanese American literature.* New York, NY: Penguin Books.

Danticat, E. (1991). *Krik? krak!* New York, NY: Vintage Books.

Gesensway, D. & Roseman, M. (1987). *Beyond words: Images from America's concentration camps.* Ithaca, NY: Cornell University Press.

Harvey, K., Joseph, K., LePage, S. (1996). We treasure music. *Rites of passage.* Portland, OR: Jefferson High School.

Houston, J.W. & Houston, J.D. (1973). *Farewell to Manzanar.* Boston: San Francisco Book Company/Houghton Mifflin.

Inada, L.F. (1993). *Legends from camp.* Minneapolis, MN: Coffee House Press.

Kim, E.H. (1982). *Asian American literature.* Philadelphia, PA: Temple University Press.

Lai, H.M., Lim, G., & Yung, J. (1986). *Island: Poetry and history of Chinese immigrants on Angel Island 1910 – 1940.* San Francisco, CA: San Francisco Study Center.

Lowe, F. (1988). *Carved in silence.* San Francisco, CA: National Asian American Telecommunications Association.

Okada, J. (1957). *No-no boy.* Boston: Charles E. Tuttle Co.

Sone, M. (1953). *Nisei daughter.* Seattle, WA: University of Washington Press.

Sunshine, C.A. & Menkhart, D. (1994). *Teaching about Haiti* (3rd ed.). Washington, DC: Network of Educators on the Americas.

Takaki, R. (1989). *Strangers from a different shore: A history of Asian Americans.* New York: Viking Penguin.

Yamada, M. (1976). *Camp notes.* San Lorenzo, CA: Shameless Hussy Press.

Endnotes

1. Takaki, R. (1989). *Strangers from a different shore: A history of Asian Americans.* New York: Viking Penguin. (p. 237)
2. Lai, H.M., Lim, G., & Yung, J. (1986). *Island: Poetry and history of Chinese immigrants on Angel Island 1910 – 1940.* San Francisco, CA: San Francisco Study Center. (p. 58)
3. I have to thank my former student Mira Shimabukuro, who pointed out my own lack of attention to these groups, and Lawson Inada, professor at Southern Oregon State College, who served as my mentor in these studies.
4. Many of the student poems used in this article are printed in our literary magazine, *Rites of Passage.*
5. For example, like many films about an oppressed people, *Come See the Paradise,* features a white man in the lead role.
6. Wakatsuki Houston, J. & Houston, J.D. (1973) *Farewell to Manzanar.* Boston: San Francisco Book Company/Houghton Mifflin. (p. 58)
7. Lowe, F. (1988). *Carved in silence.* San Francisco: National Asian American Telecommunications Association.
8. The student studying Eritreans left school, so I will not report on his project.
9. Letters from James Mullany to his sister Mary Mullany, August 5, 1860. Oregon Historical Society Mss 2417, p. 10.
10. Mullany, November 5, 1860, p.14.
11. See the film *Alamo Bay,* which despite its "white hero main character" flaw, does tell some of the story of Vietnamese immigrant fishermen.

CHAPTER NINETEEN

Bringing Globalization Home

By Jody Sokolower

"Globalization is complicated," I admitted to my 12th-grade economics class, all immigrants, all English language learners. "But migration is a key aspect of globalization, and every single one of you is an expert on migration. So we're going to start our study of globalization with migration."

I believed that starting with my students' own immigration experiences would push them to a deeper emotional level. In my experience, deep emotions lead to deep learning. But I was worried, too. The class included students from Mexico and El Salvador who came to this country out of economic desperation. Other students, including individuals from Yemen, Japan, and

Gale Geltner, Times of War and Peace

Pakistan, came from more privileged backgrounds. I hoped I could lead in a way that the diversity would enrich our learning, not feed tensions based on class or culture.

It's difficult to find good social science text sources for English language learners (ELLs). Writers and publishers tend to "accommodate" ELL students by eliminating the complexity and contradictions in the content. But limited English doesn't mean limited capacity for critical thinking. I usually look for strong materials and then expand, rewrite, or excerpt as needed. I knew I wanted to use *Rethinking Globalization: Teaching for Justice in an Unjust World* as the basis for my curriculum, but it needed adaptation for English language learners.

The first challenge was providing a definition of globalization that would tie the course together. My experience in a mainstream class the year before was that many students "got" pieces of globalization—like sweatshops and the World Trade Organization (WTO)—but never saw the system as a whole. They got the trees, but not the forest. I hoped that explaining the definition up front, posting it on the wall, and referring back to it periodically would help students keep both trees and forest in view. Unfortunately, there's no simple, quick definition of globalization. After comparing definitions in a range of books and websites, I ended up writing my own:

Unfortunately, there's no simple, quick definition of globalization.

Globalization—More than ever before in history, there is one world economy. This pressure toward one world economy is called globalization. Globalization is the struggle for control of the earth's resources—natural resources, human resources, and capital resources. There are eight elements of globalization:

1. Migration.

2. Big companies are international companies.

3. Resources are international.

4. Free trade agreements.

5. World Bank and International Monetary Fund (IMF).

6. Sweatshops.

7. Environmental problems.

8. Increased communication among peoples—the basis for resistance.

Before I introduced the definition, we did a gallery walk: I created collages with three to five images representing each of the elements of globalization and posted them around the room. I asked students to circulate and look at each collage. Then I asked the following questions: What are five important details you see in this collage? What do you think this collage is about? What questions do you have about this collage? What questions does this collage raise about the world? We had a lively discussion of each collage and it helped me begin to explain the elements of globalization.

Then, as I promised that first day, we began with migration. We watched *Uprooted: Refugees of the Global Economy*, which introduces globalization in the context of three migration stories: Maricel from the Philippines, Luckner from Haiti, and Jessy and Jaime from Bolivia. As we watched the video, I asked students to take notes: Why did these people have to leave their countries? What were their thoughts and feelings about migrating? What problems did they have as immigrants? Is anything about their experiences similar to yours? Each time I stopped the video for discussion, common threads emerged: "Even though Maricel studied hard in school, there were no jobs for her—that's just like in Pakistan." "Jessy and Jaime missed their children so much—my father didn't see us for 12 years." "My uncle's factory in El Salvador moved to Nicaragua—like Luckner's moved to China." "Everyone in the movie has problems with immigration papers—in my family some of us have papers to be here and some of us don't—I feel scared all the time." I used this opportunity to open a discussion about the many reasons why some immigrants don't have legal documents. "In this class," I concluded, "everyone is welcome, and we don't want to put anyone in danger. Please be careful what you ask and what you share. And can we agree that what we discuss in class stays in class?" Everyone agreed.

Then we started to collect our own information. I sent students home with global migration oral interview worksheets. Their assignment was to interview a parent or older relative who had migrated to the United States. The interview questions were keyed to the elements of globalization. For example: What are the most important economic and natural resources in your country? Which resources are publicly owned? Privately owned? How has the economy changed in the past 20 years? Why did you migrate to the United States? I encouraged students to interview family members in their first language and then translate the answers into English.

My expectations for this activity were modest. I figured we'd gather some information about natural resources and industry that we could use later in the semester, and collect data on why people migrate. I included questions about which resources are

Why did these people have to leave their countries? What were their thoughts and feelings about migrating? What problems did they have as immigrants? Is anything about their experiences similar to yours?

publicly and privately owned to lay groundwork for our study of the World Bank and International Monetary Fund (IMF) later in the semester, but I expected many question marks on the surveys.

Two days later, when students returned with the completed surveys, we posted the information on butcher paper and compiled it by region. As they waited for their chance to write their responses on one of the charts, the students spontaneously clustered in groups, watching the findings go up and tracking patterns. One pattern that emerged was how often families were separated by migration. Another was the career sacrifices parents make: Beza's father had been a principal in Ethiopia but works as a teacher's aide here; Maria's father was an engineer in Pakistan, but here he does clerical work.

I was amazed at the depth of information we received and the time that parents and other relatives spent in sharing a wealth of experience and knowledge. We got great information on resources, public and private ownership, changes in the economy—everything. As an engineer in Pakistan, Maria's father had a professional's understanding of energy resources. José's cousin knew firsthand about the North American Free Trade Agreement (NAFTA) and how he and his family were forced off their land in Mexico when the price of corn fell year after year. Every family had personal stories and specific pieces of information that contributed to the global picture we were creating.

High school educators don't talk much about the importance of the connection between home learning and school learning. The enthusiasm my students and their families demonstrated for this project made me realize what a mistake it is to ignore families as resources. This is particularly true for immigrant students, who sometimes feel they must leave their family and culture behind to "make it" in the United States.

One part of the survey that elicited rich results was the question "How has immigration to the United States affected your family?" Hamza's father said, "[The positive effects are that] my family is getting a good education, jobs, and dreams come true. [The negative effects are that] my family has to work full-time during their studies. We have less time to spend in the house. We have less time to sit together and talk." During our class discussion Delia said, "I never knew what it was like for my father when he first came from Mexico until I just asked him now. I had no idea how hard it was."

I asked the students to use the information from their survey as background for writing the story of their own migration or the story of one of the people they interviewed. And I requested that

The enthusiasm my students and their families demonstrated for this project made me realize what a mistake it is to ignore families as resources.

all the stories be written in first person. I read them a couple sample immigration stories and gave them a word count (400 words). When the stories were complete, we read them aloud in small groups.

Building Community

Asking students to share the complexity and pain of their families' migrations was a risk, but it did push class discussions to a deeper level as students shared their feelings and the feelings of their families. This deeper level of connection with the material built class community. As one student said in her end-of-year evaluation, "When I am sharing my ideas with the group, I feel very friendly because people are talking very nicely to each other—with respect, no racism." It also enabled the students to engage with academic material that was very difficult for their level of English language development. The most marked result from my perspective was their willingness, spring of senior year, to think critically about the world economy.

One of the many strengths of *Rethinking Globalization* is the emphasis on rooting globalization in the history of colonialism. During our very first discussions of globalization, José asked, "Why are some countries so much richer than others?" Astri asked, "Why do some countries have so many resources and others so few?" I wanted to make sure that every student understood that power and wealth in the current situation is based on what happened during centuries of colonialism and imperialism.

The center of our study of colonialism was the "Six Building Blocks of Colonialism": stealing resources, cash crops, factories instead of crafts, drawing borders, holding up the hierarchy and west is best (adapted from *Rethinking Globalization*, p. 35). After we discussed the building blocks, students created booklets with drawings that illustrated each building block. From looking at the drawings, I could tell at a glance whether they understood the concepts.

Then we headed for the library. The assignment was to pick a country that was colonized and create a poster explaining how each of the six building blocks applied to that country's history. The students worked in teams of two or three. Many of them chose their own countries and they brought their prior knowledge of colonialism to the patterns we discussed in class. The class discussion was broadened by history learned in schools in Pakistan, Mexico, Indonesia, Taiwan, China, Brazil, Yemen, and Japan. Faryal wrote the following:

> *Asking students to share the complexity and pain of their families' migrations was a risk, but it did push class discussions to a deeper level as students shared their feelings and the feelings of their families.*

It connects with my life because Pakistan and India were one country when the British came to take over. The British people made it very hard for my people and made conflict between them. Pakistan and India got separated. Some Indian people stayed in Pakistan with the Muslim people, and most of the Pakistani people are in India and can't come to live with their own people. I learned a lot from this topic because now I actually know how and why everything happened.

Tackling "Free Trade"

One of the most complicated aspects of globalization is the role of the World Bank and the IMF.

One of the most complicated aspects of globalization is the role of the World Bank and the IMF. I was searching for a concrete and personal way to introduce structural adjustment policies and the IMF when my cousin reminded me that credit card debt balloons in very similar ways to IMF debt. What's more important for young adults to understand than the pitfalls of those seductive pieces of plastic?

I downloaded a couple of credit card offers aimed at college students. We went through them line by line, defining terms and reading the small print together. Raymond, calculator in hand, showed us on the board what happens if you charge $1,000, miss a payment, and then pay the minimum amount each month for a year.

This worked well as an introduction to *Life and Debt in Jamaica*, an excellent video on the role of the IMF, World Bank, and WTO policies on post-colonial Jamaica. The impact of IMF policies on the dairy industry, farming, banana plantations, and manufacturing are all illustrated in depth. Michael Manley, former president of Jamaica, explains why he felt he had to accept the IMF loan and conditions; IMF and World Bank leaders explain why they believe their policies are good for Jamaica; and Jamaican farmers, workers, and economists describe the impact on their lives and on the country. The voiceovers and accents are difficult for English language learners, so we went slowly and stopped frequently for interpretation and discussion. As we watched the video, students created dialogue journals. On the left side of the page, they recorded quotations and described significant images from the video. On the right side, they wrote personal reflections and reactions. Alvin applied his new understanding of free trade policies to migration from his homeland, Hong Kong:

In some countries, there are a lot of people with no jobs because their businesses were destroyed by free trade.

Because of the problem of getting jobs, people immigrate to other countries and settle down there. In Hong Kong in 1997, the year it was returned to China, people were scared there would be a financial storm because free trade is changing China. That's why people started immigrating to Canada or somewhere else.

One student's reflections took the form of a poem:

> Debt is like a deep and dark circle,
> It has a way in, not a way out.
> Debt is like a deep and dark circle,
> It puts conditions on you.
> Debt is like a deep and dark circle,
> It makes you non-independent.
> Debt is like a deep and dark circle,
> It always goes up, but lets you go down.
> Debt is like a deep and dark circle,
> But you can come out by being together.

At the end of the semester, I gave the class a choice of culminating activities. Somewhat to my surprise, the students decided to create a text for English language learners on globalization. We brainstormed a list of the most important things we learned over the semester, and the students narrowed the list down to eight chapters:

1. What Is Economics?

2. Migration: We Are Part of Globalization

3. Colonialism: The Roots of Globalization

4. What Is Globalization?

5. The IMF and Poor Countries in Debt

6. Sweatshops, Free Trade, and Fair Trade

7. Globalization Means the Whole World Can Fight for Justice

8. Economics Is the Fight for Resources: The War in Iraq

I developed a framework for the chapters and an assignment sheet, and the students divided themselves into eight groups. Each group was responsible for developing a list of the information that should be included in their chapter and for assigning sections. In addition to the core information, each chapter included personal reflections, an illustration, focus questions, vocabulary, and activities. By now we were well into May of their senior year, but every-

Somewhat to my surprise, the students decided to create a text for English language learners on globalization.

one wrote at least two drafts of their section and a reflection as well as collaborating with their teammates on the other pieces. The students submitted their final drafts on diskette or via email; I compiled and edited the final text. When we were finished, we had a 53-page spiral-bound book, *Globalization: Economics in the 21st Century, Immigrant Students Teach Students.*

My favorite part of the book is the reflections at the end of each chapter because there I can see the critical thinking process. For example, here Shoaib reflects on Chapter 4, "What Is Globalization?"

> The big countries are getting stronger and more powerful, and small countries are getting weaker. The big countries are taking air, land, and a lot of resources from other countries. After learning all about globalization and the dilemmas of global trade, my point of view is that the world is getting worse and worse. With no tariffs on products, it seems like big countries have most of the power in the world. It is destroying the world economy. If I were the president of the United States, I would change all the world and make everyone equal. I would make the whole world one country and live in peace.

Next Steps

Of course the next step is to use the student-generated textbook with the next generation of students. Ideally there would be a progression, with each new class using the previous year's text as a springboard for their own. Stay tuned. ...

On the end-of-year evaluation, I asked students what skills they thought they had improved. More than half of the responses were specifically related to critical thinking about the world. For example, "I've become more aware and sensitive about the changes of people's lives because of economic problems." "We understand what is the real meaning of migration. It was important to me because I also migrated to another country." But the most exciting response was the suggestion from several students that we should have returned to look at the economies of their home countries in the light of their new understanding of globalization. Their eagerness to apply what we learned to re-analyzing the situation of their home countries is the best evidence of what we accomplished.

One aspect of the curriculum that didn't work as well as I had hoped was the unit on resistance. After so much appalling information on the injustices of globalization, I hoped my stu-

Their eagerness to apply what we learned to re-analyzing the situation of their home countries is the best evidence of what we accomplished.

dents would feel excited by the opportunities that increased global connection provides for international solidarity. We read articles, researched organizations on the internet, and watched several videos, but this section lacked the fire and intensity of other parts of the semester. Next time I will integrate resistance into each unit; when it's tacked on at the end, it just doesn't work. I will also prioritize bringing in speakers (or maybe we'll take a field trip to Bolivia!). One of my colleagues had an additional suggestion: Students need explicit support in going from classes with progressive, critical perspectives to "the rest of the world." In other words, I need to help them navigate the distance between the view of globalization we studied and the one they may encounter in their next economics class.

Students need explicit support in going from classes with progressive, critical perspectives to 'the rest of the world.'

When I decided to use the students' own migration as the starting point for studying globalization, I was operating partly on instinct. I hoped it would engage students at the beginning, but I saw migration as an isolated "element," one detached piece of the globalization story. I didn't really grasp myself how central it was to the global web. It took the students and their parents to show me the way. Here is how Rizwana, Mariam, and Yaneli described the connection in their introduction to their chapter, "Migration Is Part of Globalization":

> Migration is part of the world economy today. It is a big piece of globalization. The changes in the world economy are good for some countries and bad for other countries. If there are no jobs in your own country or if there is a war, many people have to migrate to other places in the world. That is part of globalization. Because we are a class of students who were all immigrants to the United States, our family stories are a good way to begin to understand globalization.

We closed the year by writing poems to express our hopes for the future. Here is Delia's:

The world shall be one nation
    Where there is no discrimination for skin color
    Where the word humanity has presence
    As the water sparkling through the mountains
    The world shall be unity
    As the ants lining together form a group
    Working for each other and helping each other
    The world shall be never defeated
    It shall be so strong that even

Wars or natural disasters won't
Make it fall down
There shall be a world where
The words war, hatred and ambition
Don't exist
Because the world shall be love, peace
Freedom and friendship.

Resources

BOOKS:

Bigelow, B., & Peterson, B. (Eds.) (2002). *Rethinking globalization: Teaching for justice in an unjust world.* Milwaukee: Rethinking Schools.

Cho, E., Paszy Puente, F., Louie, M., & Khokha, S. (2004). *Bridge: Building a race and immigration dialogue in the global economy.* Berkeley, CA: Inkworks Press.

VIDEOS:

Uprooted: Refugees of the Global Economy. National Network for Immigrant Rights and the Interfaith Coalition for Immigrant Rights, 2002. Bilingual with English/Spanish subtitles.

Life and Debt. Stephanie Black, director. New Yorker Films, 2001.

Zoned for Slavery: The Child Behind the Label. National Labor Committee, 1995.

CHAPTER TWENTY

Arranged Marriages, Rearranged Ideas

By Stan Karp

Jihana was one of my favorite students. By the time she was a senior, we had been together for three years, first in a sophomore English class and then through two years of journalism electives where students produced school publications and learned desktop publishing. Jihana's bright-eyed intelligence and can-do enthusiasm made her a teacher's dream. Her daily greeting in our busy journalism office was, "Hi, Mr. Karp, what needs to be done?" I used to joke that she'd get straight A's until the end of her senior year when I'd have to fail her so she couldn't graduate and leave. It was corny, but she always laughed. Jihana was one of a growing number of Bengali students in my Paterson, N.J. high school. Along with increasing numbers of Latin American, Caribbean, Middle Eastern, Central European,

Donna DeCesare

and other immigrants, these new communities had transformed the school in the 20 years I'd been there as a teacher. What had once been a predominantly white, then later a primarily black and Latino student population was now thoroughly international. The teaching staff, however, remained mostly white, with a limited number of teachers of color.

Increasingly, some of my best students each year were young Bengali women. Some, like Jihana, covered their heads with scarves in keeping with Muslim tradition. A few wore the full veil. Others wore no special dress. Many seemed reserved and studious. Others gradually adopted the more assertive, outgoing styles of the citywise teens around them.

An Arranged Marriage

By the time Jihana was a senior it was natural for me to ask, during one of the many extra periods she spent in the journalism office, what her postgraduation plans were. She said she wanted to go to college, perhaps to study medicine, and was considering several schools. But, she added, a lot depended on whether she had to get married.

I knew enough about Jihana, and about the Bengali community, to know that she wasn't referring to a premature wedding prompted by an unplanned pregnancy, but to the possibility of an arranged marriage. Jihana made it pretty clear that she wasn't ready to get married. She was anxious to go to college and to move out of a household where she felt she had too many cleaning chores and childcare duties and not enough personal freedom. She said the outcome partly depended on what happened with her sister, who was several years older and also a candidate for marriage, and on whether her family decided to send them both back to Bangladesh in the summer for possible matches. I listened sympathetically and made schoolteacher noises about how smart I thought she was and how I hoped she'd get the opportunity to attend college. Unsure of just what my role, as a white, male, high school teacher, could possibly be in this situation, I halfheartedly offered to speak to her family about her college potential if she thought it would help. Jihana smiled politely and said she'd keep me posted. I went home thinking about Jihana's situation. I was upset, even angered, by the thought that this young woman's promising prospects and educational future could be sidetracked by a cultural practice that seemed to me hopelessly unreasonable and unfair. No matter how I tried to come to terms with it, the custom of arranged marriages was

Unsure of just what my role, as a white, male, high school teacher, could possibly be in this situation, I halfheartedly offered to speak to her family about her college potential.

completely alien to my own sensibilities and to my expectations for my students. I kept thinking of how my own high-school-aged daughter, raised at home—and at least nominally at school—to think in terms of gender equality and independence, would laugh in my face if I ever sat her down and tried to tell her my plans for her marital future.

I also thought, and not for the first time, about what my responsibilities were as a public school teacher, and how I should manage this mix of my own strongly held personal opinions, concern for my students' well-being, and respect for the cultural differences that were increasingly evident in my school community.

As both a political activist and a classroom teacher, I'd wrestled with these issues often. On the one hand, I'd come to believe that effective classroom teaching, especially in schools with a history of failure and pervasive student alienation, was inherently "political," in the sense that it had to take the social context of schooling and of students' lives as a primary point of departure. I tried to encourage students to "talk back" to the world we studied, and, wherever possible, to take action in response to ideas and issues. These premises informed any number of choices I made daily about curriculum, classroom organization, and how to channel in particular directions the "oppositional energy" I found in most teenagers. It also meant I frequently tried to take real situations in my students' lives, both in and out of school, as starting points for research, writing, and class discussion. At the same time, I know it is neither appropriate nor fair for teachers to restrict the curriculum to only those views and ideas that they personally agree with. Since teachers have power over students, it's especially necessary to be sensitive to issues of intimidation, the rights of dissent, personal privacy, and freedom of choice. In some ways, the closer issues hit to home, as in Jihana's situation, the more careful teachers must be, particularly where racial, cultural, and class differences are involved. At first glance, Jihana's problem seemed personal and private, not readily the stuff of classroom discussion. It had social roots and cultural dimensions like other student concerns that had become the subject of class assignments or research. But it seemed to call for an individual, personal response on my part, rather than a pedagogical one, and I had real trouble imagining what that response should be.

I also thought about how I should manage this mix of my own strongly held personal opinions, concern for my students' well-being, and respect for the cultural differences that were increasingly evident in my school community.

Reluctant to Intervene

As a rule, I have generally been reluctant to intervene at home when it comes to handling personal and family issues with my teenage students. Though I've always supported parents' participation in their children's education, for me this usually has meant support for parent participation in governance and policymaking processes, or finding ways to include parent and family experience in my curriculum.

But when personal (as opposed to strictly academic) problems arise with secondary-age students, I've always hesitated to "call home" too quickly. Most of the 15- to 18-year-olds I deal with are emerging adults who've been semi-independent to varying degrees for years: holding down jobs, assuming family responsibilities, traveling the world, dealing with the courts and immigration authorities, and even coping with parenthood themselves. Others come from difficult family situations that are not always supportive or, not infrequently, may even be the source of the problems they choose to share with me. In the normal course of a year, it's not unusual for me to deal with teenagers who are wrestling with everything from homelessness, pregnancy, and sexual identity to depression, domestic violence, and drug abuse.

When my students bring such issues to me, I've always felt that my first allegiance was to them, to listen sympathetically and to offer whatever advice or access to services I could manage, and not, primarily, to act as a surrogate for, or even mediator with, parental authority. Yes, there have been occasions when my judgment, or the legal responsibilities that are periodically spelled out in nervous memos from central office, compel me to pick up the phone or make a home visit. But in general I take my signal about whether home intervention on my part makes sense from my students, and most of the time it doesn't. There have also been times when I've passed on information about where to get birth control or other kinds of counseling services (for example, for gay teens) that I knew might not be fully endorsed at home.

The problem was figuring out the dividing line between responding to the needs of my students and interfering inappropriately with 'other people's children.'

In Jihana's case I tried to imagine what I could possibly say to her family about the situation: "Hi, I'm Jihana's teacher, and as a politically progressive, pro-feminist, privileged white male, I think your plans for Jihana are a medieval abomination."

I don't think so.

But the more I thought about it, the more I realized that the problem wasn't finding more diplomatic ways to voice my opinions; the problem was figuring out the dividing line between responding to the needs of my students and interfering inappropriately with "other people's children." I also thought about another student I had some 10 years earlier, Rafia, who faced this same situation. Rafia was the youngest of four daughters in a Bengali family. Smart, sophisticated beyond her years, and ambitious, Rafia was anxious to go to college despite her family's objections. As I encouraged her and helped her fill out applications during her junior and senior years, it was Rafia who first made me aware that many Bengali families did not think girls should go to college, and that she and her sisters were facing, with varying degrees of dread, the prospect of arranged marriages. I was horrified at the idea, and said so. In fact, as I recall, my main reaction consisted of expressing my outrage that women were oppressed this way in her culture. I told her I didn't think anyone had the right to tell her who to marry, and that it was much more important for her future to go to college than to please her parents. I even suggested that it was more important to choose college than to avoid a break with her family, and that, even if they got upset, they would probably get over it. I somewhat flippantly told her she could stay at my house for a while if she decided to run away.

Learning a Lesson

When Jihana's story jogged my memory, it was with more than a little embarrassment that I recalled how my reaction to Rafia had been foolish, and not a little arrogant. At the time I had acted as if the most important response to Rafia's dilemma was to show her that not everyone was as "backward" as her parents, and that there were swell, "enlightened" folks like myself who believed in her right to shape her own future and education. In effect I was showing off the "superior" values and "advanced" thinking of "progressive Western culture," especially of radicals like myself, and contrasting it to the "underdeveloped practices" of her own community, which I encouraged her to reject. I had also reacted as if what I thought and how I felt about the issues raised by her predicament were of paramount importance, and should be the point of departure for my response. Looking back, it seemed that the problem wasn't that I was wrong to oppose the custom of arranged marriages or to make my opinions known, but that I did it in a way that was essentially self-serving, and as a practical matter, not very helpful. I had basically denounced what I, as an outsider, saw as "deficient" in her culture and encouraged her to turn her back on it.

Looking back, it seemed that the problem wasn't that I was wrong to oppose the custom of arranged marriages or to make my opinions known, but that I did it in a way that was essentially self-serving.

While my sympathies may have been well-meant, my advice was culturally insensitive and wildly impractical. And it probably just reinforced Rafia's sense of alienation and being trapped.

Fortunately, Rafia was sharp enough to appreciate my personal support and ignore my advice. Instead of running away or openly breaking with her family, she steadfastly argued for her chance to attend college while continuing to excel in school. Eventually, she got her father's permission to go to college (though she was forced to study engineering instead of the humanities she preferred). The experience had stayed with me over the years, and now that a similar situation had arisen, I was anxious to do better by Jihana. A couple of weeks passed after our first conversation, and it became clear that nothing decisive would happen with Jihana's situation until the summer came. Still looking for a way to lend support, one day I suggested to Jihana that she consider writing a story about arranged marriages for our student magazine. I mentioned briefly my experience with Rafia and asked how the growing community of female Bengali students in the high school felt about this and related issues. Instead of dwelling on my own opinions, I tried to emphasize that she wasn't the only one facing these issues, and that she could perform a service for both Bengali students and the rest of the school by focusing on a set of concerns that had gotten little attention. Jihana seemed interested but hesitant. She was a good writer but generally took less ambitious assignments, like covering school news or activities. She expressed some concern that her family would be offended if they found out, and that, in the tightly-knit Bengali community, it might be hard to keep it a secret even if she published a piece anonymously. I asked her to think it over and told her she could get credit for writing the article even if she decided in the end not to publish it. I also told her, as I told all my students, that we could consider the implications or consequences of going public later, but she should write what she really thought and not censor herself in advance.

I was hoping to use the tremendous potential that writing has, not only to help students express their ideas and feelings but also to help them develop the skills, and sometimes the distance, needed to analyze complicated topics and clarify issues.

I was hoping to use the tremendous potential that writing has, not only to help students express their ideas and feelings but also to help them develop the skills, and sometimes the distance, needed to analyze complicated topics and clarify issues. While I hoped Jihana would eventually publish, it seemed valuable to have her organize and express her thoughts for her own purposes as well. After a few days, and after double-checking that she wouldn't have to publish the piece if she wasn't comfortable, she agreed. She asked for help making an outline, so we arranged a story conference.

A Broader Context

When we started discussing how to organize the article, Jihana said she wanted to deal first with stereotypes and misconceptions that

Westerners had about Muslims. She said she wanted to put the issue of arranged marriages in a broader context of Muslim culture, which had a variety of customs and practices that she felt were misunderstood. Muslim women were not "slaves," she said, and not everyone did things the same way. When it came to marriage, there was a range of practices, and in many cases, Muslim women did have choices and varying degrees of input into the decision.

This led to a discussion of women and marriage customs in general, and how women have faced oppression and male supremacy in all cultures. We also talked about the generational conflict between young Bengalis (and other younger immigrants) raised in the United States, and their parents, rooted in more traditional "old country" customs, and how this exacerbated the struggle over marriage practices. Jihana told me stories about families that had been torn apart by these differences, as well as others where parents and children had found common ground and happy endings. As we talked, several things started to become clear. By locating the issue of arranged marriages inside the broader issue of women's rights, which cuts across all cultures and countries, it became easier for Jihana to address the topic without "stigmatizing" her own community. If Bengali women had to wrestle with arranged marriages and male dominance, the supposedly more "liberated" sexual culture of the United States presented women with its own set of problems: higher levels of sexual assault, single teenage parenthood, divorce, and domestic violence. Generational conflict between old ways and new also cut across cultures and made the issue seem more universal, again allowing it to be addressed in a context that didn't demonize one particular group.

Finally, it was clear that speaking on behalf of Bengali women, instead of just against the practice of arranged marriages, tended to make Jihana feel more empowered than isolated. She was still determined to question the imposition of marital arrangements against the woman's will, but would do so in the context of defending Muslim culture against stereotypes and as part of a critique of women's oppression as a whole. Added to the protection she felt from not having to publish her work if she chose not to, assuming this positive stance on behalf of herself and her peers seemed to give her the safe space she needed from which to address these difficult issues. By the end of our conversation, she seemed ready to go. Within a week or two, Jihana was back with her article. "Do Muslim women have any rights?" she began.

By locating the issue of arranged marriages inside the broader issue of women's rights, which cuts across all cultures and countries, it became easier for Jihana to address the topic without 'stigmatizing' her own community.

> Do they make their own decisions? Are they allowed to think? Are they prisoners in their own homes? There are many stereotypes held by Westerners about the position and role of Muslim women. ... These notions are based upon the lack of knowledge Westerners have of Islam.
>
> Women, regardless of their culture or society, have suffered tremendously over inequality and have had to fight for a firm place in their society. During the Roman civilization, a woman was considered to be a slave. The Greeks bought and sold their women as merchandise rather than accept them as human beings. Early Christianity regarded their women as "temptresses," responsible for the fall of Adam.
>
> In pre-Islamic times, as well as in certain places today, a female child is thought of as a cause for unhappiness and grief. Baby girls were sometimes buried alive after birth. But gaps in wealth, education, and justice between men and women can be found everywhere and just can't be explained by religion.

Jihana went on to discuss "some issues about the rights of a Muslim woman [that] stem from the issue of marriage." She wrote about the varying degrees of choice women may have in different families, the generational conflict, the problems associated with patterns of marriage in the United States. ("Some Muslim families say that while the Westerners seem to be 'more free,' their society is not working too well.") She cited examples to show that, "as in all marriages, whether arranged or not, some work and some do not."

Though many of the Bengali students Jihana spoke to declined to be quoted by name, she did find one senior who "extremely disagrees with arranged marriages" and who thought "all Muslim women should be given an opportunity and the privilege to choose the person that they want to spend the rest of their lives with."

After exploring the issues from several sides, Jihana came to a balancing act that suggested her own personal struggle:

> Arranged marriages and other Muslim customs of life, like the covering of the body and not dating, may seem to be burdensome to women of most Western cultures, but for Muslim women it's their way of life. We were brought up to follow and believe that these practices were the right ways of life. It is up to us as individuals to see that we follow what is expected of us. ...The Muslim religion, in my opinion, can include double standards. ... In many cases males are allowed to do certain things that females can't. ...

For example, when a male does get married without his parents' permission, it is OK, but if a female does the same thing it is not OK. This is so because in the Holy Koran it states that a woman has to follow certain things. For example, it is a woman's duty and obligation to bring up her children according to the ways of Islam. She has to look after the family and has absolute control over domestic affairs. She must wear a covering cloak when meeting adult men outside her family. She is her husband's helpmate. Islam recognizes the leadership of a man over a woman, but that does not mean domination.

In conclusion, women should have the freedom and right to do something they're interested in doing or accomplishing. They should go forward with their education if they want to continue it, with the help and support to do so. Women can cook and clean, but they could also do more.

At bottom, Jihana's "balancing act" was an affirmative statement about her place and her rights in her community. And though writing the article didn't resolve her dilemma, it did, I think, support her in her efforts to speak up for herself, and offered a way for her to develop some useful perspectives on her situation. It also helped focus attention on issues that she and her Bengali peers were wrestling with inside the school community.

At bottom, Jihana's 'balancing act' was an affirmative statement about her place and her rights in her community.

New Pride

Though Jihana had originally balked at the idea of publication, by the time she was done she used the computer skills she'd learned in class to create a two-page layout for our magazine with her article, her byline, and her picture under the title, "Muslim Women: Where Do We Belong?" She seemed proud of it, and so was I, especially as I reflected on what I'd learned myself.

Switching the focus from my own reactions to my student's point of view, and developing a deeper appreciation of the need to deal with issues of cultural difference with more humility and care, had led me to a more effective and more appropriate response. I was still just as opposed as ever to arranged marriages, and still saw contradictions in Jihana's balancing act about the codes of Islam. But because I hadn't begun with an attack on the cultural norms of her community, I had managed to find a way that, to some degree at least, both supported and empowered her. As it turned out, Jihana's willingness to raise such issues was not limited to our magazine. One morning in the spring, I found her working feverishly in the journalism office on a list of "Bengali Concerns" for the next Student Government Association meeting. The list had a tone familiar from earlier days of student activism, but it had specifics I'd never seen before. It read:

1. How come there aren't more Bengali SGA members?

2. There is a lack of Bengali students involved in school activities. We need more participation and more representation of the Bengali people.

3. We need Bengali-speaking guidance counselors and teachers.

4. We need Bengali mentors.

5. How come the history teachers never teach about Bangladesh and its culture when they teach world history?

6. Why isn't there Bengali student representation when the school presents a panel of students to represent the school?

7. How come all the newsletters that go home from the school are either in Spanish or in English? How come you can't send letters home that are in Bengali? That way the parents will know what is going on in their children's school. The lack of communication with the Bengali parents is a reason why many don't attend the Home-School Council meetings.

New Steps for Jihana

Around the same time that these concerns were being presented to the student government, preparations were underway for an assembly presentation of Bengali dance and traditional dress. Like many other schools, my high school was still in the relatively superficial stages of addressing multicultural issues, and tended toward food festivals and holiday celebrations. But the assembly program tapped the energy of many Bengali students, and Jihana had gotten involved. One afternoon, soon after our magazine had appeared, she came to the journalism office and asked if I could fax a copy of her article to a reporter from a local newspaper. She said she'd been interviewed in connection with the upcoming assembly program, but had left some things out. "I was trying to explain myself to the reporter and couldn't get the words out right," she said. "I told him I had written an article explaining what I thought, and it was all in there. I promised to send it to him." The article she had been hesitant to write and reluctant to publish had become a personal position statement.

Like many other schools, my high school was still in the relatively superficial stages of addressing multicultural issues, and tended toward food festivals and holiday celebrations.

As we headed into the last weeks of the school year, I occasionally asked Jihana if there were any new developments. There weren't any on the marriage front, but she did get accepted to several colleges and began to make plans to attend a state university. When we parted at year's end, I made her promise to let me know how things turned out. About a month later, I returned from a trip to find a slightly ambiguous message. Jihana had called to say hello and to invite me to a wedding. Taken aback, and fearing that this might be her way of letting me know that marriage had won out over college, I called her at home. She was in good spirits and busy getting ready to move into the dorms on her new campus. The invitation was to her sister's wedding, Jihana explained, and if I could come I'd get a chance to see some more of how Bengali marriage customs worked. Unfortunately, I wasn't able to attend, but Jihana promised to show me the proceedings on videotape.

In September Jihana started college classes. A few weeks later, I got a note describing her new life. "College is OK," she wrote, "not that great as everyone said it would be. Maybe it is just me. I never realized how difficult my classes would be and so large in lectures!! I am taking an Arabic class so that I can be trilingual!

"I have to go home every weekend, but I don't mind," she wrote. "I have a new status in my family; everyone respects me more, and I also don't have to do any more housework. Isn't that great??!!" I had to agree that it was.

The names of students in this article have been changed

CHAPTER TWENTY-ONE

Welcoming Kalenna

An early childhood teacher strives to make all her students feel at home

By Laura Linda Negri-Pool

When I was a child, our home was filled with the sounds of Spanish, mariachi music, and boisterous conversations. At home, my Nana cooked enchiladas, menudo, and tamales. During family celebrations we broke piñatas, danced, and hung papel picados. I was surrounded by six siblings, multiple cousins, tíos, and tías. My home was filled with light, color, art, texture, and love.

My school, in contrast, was drab, white, and unappealing.

I recall only one time when my Mexican American identity was validated during elementary school. When I was in 3rd grade, my mother organized a Cinco de Mayo event at our

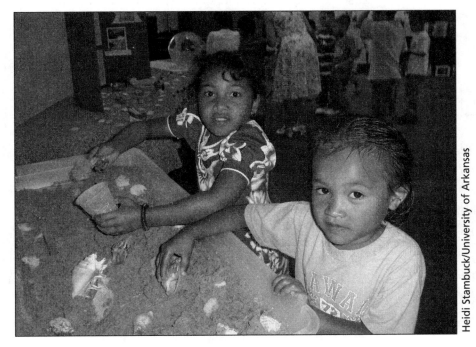

Heidi Stambuck/University of Arkansas

school. My father, siblings, and I cut out the papel picados, made the piñatas, formed the papier mâché sculptures, and created paper flowers. Seeing my culture represented at school made me feel at home there for the first time.

I want my students to have more than one memory like that. I've taught preschool for 27 years, and I feel passionate about embracing families from nondominant cultures into the early childhood communities I work in.

As the result of a personal process of identity and cultural reclamation, I came to understand how my personal experiences influence this passion.

My experiences inspired me to find ways to make other marginalized children and families see themselves and their lives reflected in our classroom community.

Welcoming Kalenna

One fall day a few years ago, I held an open house to welcome the new children and families enrolled in our preschool program. When Kalenna entered our classroom, I immediately felt an affinity with her. Kalenna's dark, thick hair and chocolate brown skin set her apart from most of the other 14 children in the class. Our community college lab school served predominantly European American children whose parents were taking classes. Her mother, Diane, spoke with an accent that made me wonder if English was not her first language.

"Do you speak a language in addition to English?" I asked Diane.

She smiled and answered, "Marshallese." Our journey had begun.

I sensed Diane's feeling of relief and surprise when I asked about her language history. I knew from my own experiences what it was like to not be seen, to be treated with a question mark. I wondered how many times others had asked her, as they had me, "what she was" rather than respectfully and authentically inquiring about her. My question was an open and honest acknowledgment of her differences.

Over the next few months, I tried to infuse our classroom environment with the sounds, textures, and objects that surrounded Kalenna in her home.

First I had to learn about the Marshall Islands. I had no idea where or what the Marshall Islands were, let alone anything about the Marshallese language and culture. I started with a map, where I learned that the Marshall Islands are a col-

Over the next few months, I tried to infuse our classroom environment with the sounds, textures, and objects that surrounded Kalenna in her home.

lection of 1,225 islands and islets in Micronesia. From the internet, I learned about the ongoing struggle of the Marshallese people to maintain their language and culture given their history of domination by Germany, Japan, and the United States. Following World War II, the United States conducted nuclear tests on the islands—including Bikini Atoll. These tests exposed many inhabitants to high radiation levels.

After gaining some knowledge of her origins, I was able to begin to speak more confidently with Kalenna's family. I began regular conversations with Diane, each of us sharing information about our family and culture.

I discovered a website with Marshallese music and language. I printed a list of simple words and phrases and brought it to the classroom. I showed Diane what I had found and asked her to translate a song into Marshallese. Each morning the children, student teachers, and I sang a greeting song utilizing the home languages of the children and adults present in our classroom, including Spanish, Chinese, and Afrikaans. Diane taught us how to sing our good morning song in Marshallese.

I asked Diane if she could help me locate items from the Marshall Islands that the students might use in the classroom. She brought in a hat, a basket, clothing, a hairpiece, and a necklace. We incorporated them into our dramatic play area. The children frequently wore the hairpiece and hat. The large basket with shells held an assortment of classroom materials throughout the year. The children loved wearing the seashell necklaces. They knew that the items belonged to Kalenna and treated them with care and respect.

I invited Diane to record the book *No, David*, by David Solomon, on audiotape in Marshallese. The book was a favorite in our classroom due in part to the artwork, the simple text, and message of unconditional love. In the story, a little boy repeatedly gets in trouble for typical misbehaviors, including making a mess, overfilling the bathtub, and playing with a baseball in the house. The story concludes with the mother expressing her enduring love for him despite his antics. The children already could "read" each page in English. I partnered Diane with a mom who spoke Spanish. Together they recorded the book in their home languages. The mothers joined us at circle time to read the book aloud and to allow us to hear their voices on tape. From then on, Kalenna listened frequently to her mother's voice reading *Jaab, David*.

After gaining some knowledge of her origins, I was able to begin to speak more confidently with Kalenna's family.

Bridging Cultures

One of my best memories of Kalenna is of the day she brought some of "her music" to class. I had invited her mother to share music that they listened to at home, in part because I was having difficulty locating Marshallese music.

Kalenna and I went to the CD player and began to listen. At first we listened to it as background music while the students played. Later Kalenna went to the large rug area. I began to move to the music and told her how much I liked it. Then she began to dance. As she danced, a magnificent smile appeared on her face. She clearly had a specific routine that she'd learned for that particular song. I began to mimic her movements. When the song ended, I rewound the tape and started it again. She began to teach me the moves. We laughed and moved, reveling in our intimate shared enjoyment. The other children watched, pausing in their own play to see our scene unfold. Later, some came and joined us. Kalenna's delight was evident as our dance continued. I had finally touched her where she lived.

A few years ago a former teacher of mine told me that he always pictured my face while reading of a young Mexican woman in the novel *The Pearl*. I was shocked. I never knew that he saw me as Mexican, that he associated me with the language, the culture, and the stories. I was touched, yet felt a loss. The loss was about not having my identity validated some 25 years earlier.

How I yearned to have a teacher who could see me, hear me, and dance with me.

You're Asian. How Could You Fail Math?

Unmasking the myth of the model minority

By Benji Chang and Wayne Au

Have you ever sat next to an Asian student in class and wondered how she managed to consistently get straight A's while you struggled to maintain a B-minus average?

—from *Top of the Class: How Asian Parents Raise High Achievers—and How You Can Too*

In January 1966, William Petersen penned an article for *The New York Times Magazine* entitled, "Success Story: Japanese American Style." In it, he praised the Japanese American community for its apparent ability to successfully assimilate into mainstream American culture, and literally dubbed Japanese Americans a "model minority"—the first popular usage of the term.

Jordin Isip

207

By the 1980s, *Newsweek, The New Republic, Fortune, Parade, U.S. News and World Report*, and *Time* all had run articles on the subject of Asian American success in schools and society, and the Myth of the Model Minority was born. The Myth of the Model Minority asserts that, due to their adherence to traditional, Asian cultural values, Asian American students are supposed to be devoted, obedient to authority, respectful of teachers, smart, good at math and science, diligent, hard workers, cooperative, well-behaved, docile, college-bound, quiet, and opportunistic.

Top of the Class (quoted above) is a perfect modern example. Published in 2005, the authors claim to offer readers 17 "secrets" that Asian parents supposedly use to develop high school graduates who earn A-pluses and head to Ivy League colleges. It's a marketing concept built purely on the popular belief in the Myth of the Model Minority.

However, in both of our experiences as public school teachers and education activists, we've seen our share of Asian American students do poorly in school, get actively involved in gangs, drop out, or exhibit any number of other indicators of school failure not usually associated with "model minorities."

A critical unmasking of this racist myth is needed because it both negatively affects the classroom lives of Asian American students and contributes to the justification of race and class inequality in schools and society.

On the most basic level, the Myth of the Model Minority masks the diversity that exists within the Asian American community.

Masking Diversity

On the most basic level, the Myth of the Model Minority masks the diversity that exists within the Asian American community. The racial category of "Asian" is itself emblematic of the problem. Asia contains nearly four billion people and over 50 countries, including those as diverse as Turkey, Japan, India, the Philippines, and Indonesia.

The racial category of "Asian" is also historically problematic. Similar to those categories used to name peoples from Africa and the Americas, the definition of Asia as a continent (and race) and division of Asians into various nations was developed to serve the needs of European and U.S. colonialism and imperialism.

The category of Asian gets even fuzzier in the context of the United States, since there are over 50 ways to officially qualify as an Asian American according to government standards. Pacific Islanders and "mixed race" Asians are also regularly squished together under the banner of Asian or Asian Pacific Islander (which, out of respect for the sovereignty of Pacific peoples, we refuse to do here).

Masking the Class Divide

The Myth of the Model Minority, however, masks another form of diversity—that of economic class division. As Jamie Lew explains in her 2007 book, *Asian Americans in Class*, there are increasing numbers of working-class Korean American students in New York City performing more poorly in schools than their middle-class counterparts.

Similarly, Vivian Louie found class-based differences in her study of Chinese American students. Her research indicated that middle-class Chinese American mothers tended to have more time, resources, and educational experience to help their children through school and into college than mothers from working-class Chinese American families, who had longer work hours, lower-paying jobs, and lower levels of education.

These class differences are sometimes rooted in specific immigrant histories and are connected to the 1965 Immigration Act. The Act not only opened up the United States to large numbers of Asian immigrants, but, among a handful of other criteria, it granted preference to educated professionals and those committing to invest at least $40,000 in a business once they arrived.

As a consequence, some Asian immigrants, even those within the same ethnic community, enter the United States with high levels of education and/or with economic capital attained in their countries of origin. Others enter the United States with little or no education or money at all. These educational and financial heritages make an important difference in how well children gain access to educational resources in the United States.

In other words, whether we are talking about African American, white, Latina/o, indigenous, or "model minority" Asian American students, the first rule of educational inequality still applies: Class matters.

> *The Myth of the Model Minority, however, masks another form of diversity—that of economic class division.*

Masking Ethnic Inequity

To add to the complexity of Asian American diversity, many of the class differences amongst Asian Americans also correlate with ethnic differences. According to the 2000 census, 53.3 percent of Cambodians, 59.6 percent of Hmong, 49.6 percent of Laotians, and 38.1 percent of Vietnamese over 25 years of age have less than a high school education. In contrast, 13.3 percent of Asian Indians, 12.7 percent of Filipinos, 8.9 percent of Japanese, and 13.7 percent of Koreans over 25 years of age have less than a high school education.

These educational disparities are particularly striking considering that, for instance, 37.8 percent of Hmong, almost 30 percent of Cambodians, and 18.5 percent of Laotians have incomes below the poverty line (compared to 12.4 percent of the total U.S. population). Indeed, the 2000 census reveals relatively consistent high education rates and income amongst South Asian, Korean, and Chinese Americans, and relatively low education rates and low income amongst Cambodian, Lao, and Hmong Americans. Hence, the Myth of the Model Minority serves to obscure the struggles of poor or "undereducated" families working to gain a decent education for their children.

Masking Economic Circumstance

One of the most cited statistics proving the Myth of the Model minority is that Asian Americans even out-earn whites in income. What is obscured in this "fact" is that it is only true when we compare Asian American *household* income to white *household* income, and the reality is that Asian Americans make less per person compared to whites. Statistically, the average household size for Asian Americans is 3.3 people, while for whites it is 2.5 people.

Consequently, Asian American households are more likely than white households to have more than one income earner, and almost twice as likely to have three income earners. When we take these issues into account, Asian American individuals earn $2,000 on average less than white individuals.

The statistics on Asian American income are further skewed upward when we look at the economies of the states where the majority live. The three states with the highest proportion of Asian Americans, Hawai'i, California, and New York, all have median income levels in the top third of states. This means that, regardless of statistically higher household incomes, the high cost of living in states with large Asian American populations guarantees that Asian Americans, on average, are more likely to have less disposable income and lower living standards than whites.

Masking Racism

While the above statistics may be remarkable in the face of the Myth of the Model Minority, they also point to another serious problem: The myth is regularly used as a social and political wedge against blacks, Latina/os, and other racial groups in the United States.

The racist logic of the model minority wedge is simple. If, according to the myth, Asian Americans are academically and

The myth is regularly used as a social and political wedge against blacks, Latina/os, and other racial groups in the United States.

socially successful due to particular cultural or racial strengths, then lower test scores, lower GPAs, and lower graduation rates of other groups like African Americans and Latina/os can be attributed to their cultural or racial weaknesses.

Or, as one high school guidance counselor in Stacey J. Lee's book, *Unraveling the Model Minority Stereotype*, puts it, "Asians like … M.I.T., Princeton. They tend to go to good schools … I wish our blacks would take advantage of things instead of sticking to sports and entertainment."

The Myth of the Model Minority also causes Asian American students to struggle with the racist expectations the myth imposes upon them. An Asian American high school student in Lee's book explains, "When you get bad grades, people look at you really strangely because you are sort of distorting the way they see an Asian."

The Myth of the Model Minority also causes Asian American students to struggle with the racist expectations the myth imposes upon them.

Unfortunately, some East and South Asian Americans uphold the myth because it allows them to justify their own relative educational and social success in terms of individual or cultural drive, while simultaneously allowing them to distance themselves from what they see as African American, Latina/o, indigenous, and Southeast Asian American educational failure.

As Jamie Lew observes, the Myth of the Model Minority "attributes academic success and failure to individual merit and cultural orientation, while underestimating important structural and institutional resources that all children need in order to achieve academically." In doing so, the Myth of the Model Minority upholds notions of racial and cultural inferiority of other lower achieving groups, as it masks the existence of racism and class exploitation in this country.

The Challenge of Educating Asian America

One of the difficulties of unmasking the Myth of the Model Minority is that the diversity of the Asian American experience poses substantial challenges, particularly in relation to how race, culture, and ethnicity are typically considered by educators.

For instance, Asian American students challenge the categories commonly associated with the black-brown-white spectrum of race. Many Asian American students follow educational pathways usually attributed to white, middle-class, suburban students, while many others follow pathways usually attributed to black and Latina/o, working-class, urban students.

Other Asian American groups challenge typical racial categories in their own identities. Pilipinos,[1] for instance, don't quite fit into the typical categories of South, East, or Southeast Asian, nor do they quite fit the category of Pacific Islander. Further, some argue that Pilipinos have a lineage that is more closely related to Latina/os because they were in fact colonized by Spain. Consequently, because of their particular circumstances, many Pilipinos more strongly identify with being brown than anything else. As another example, many high-achieving, middle-class South Asians consider themselves "brown," especially after the discrimination endured after 9/11.

Asian American students also challenge typical notions of immigration and language by blurring the typical dichotomies of native language vs. English and immigrant vs. American-born. Some Southeast Asian refugees, like those from Laos, may develop fluency in multiple languages and attend universities, even as their parents are low-income and do not speak English. On the other hand, there are groups of Pilipinos who grow up highly American-ized, who have been taught English their whole lives, but who have some of the highest dropout and suicide rates.

Asian American students also challenge popularly accepted multicultural teaching strategies because they are often a numer-ical minority in classrooms, and multicultural teaching strategies designed to meet the needs of classroom majorities can leave out the culturally specific needs of Asian American students. These can include the language acquisition needs of students who come from character-based languages (e.g., Chinese, Japanese), social and ideological differences of students from majority Muslim nations (e.g., Pakistan, Indonesia), and psychological issues that emerge from student families traumatized by U.S. interven-tion/war policies (e.g., Korea, Vietnam, Thailand).

From the Fukienese Chinese student in an urban Philadel-phia classroom with mostly black or Latino/a students, to the Hmong student who sits with two or three peers in a mostly white school in rural Wisconsin, to the Pilipino student in a San Diego suburb with predominantly Pilipino classmates and some white peers, Asian American youth do not fit neatly into the typ-ical boxes of our educational system.

Unmasking the Myth in Our Classrooms

Despite the diversity and complexity inherent in working with Asian American populations, there are many things that educa-tors can do to challenge the Myth of the Model Minority. Simi-lar to other communities of color, effective steps include recruiting more educators from Asian American backgrounds,

Asian American students also challenge typical notions of immigration and language by blurring the typical dichotomies of native language vs. English and immigrant vs. American-born.

promoting multilingual communication in instruction and parent involvement, and developing relationships between parents, community groups, and schools.

Within the classroom, teachers can make use of several strategies to counter the Myth of the Model Minority in their own classrooms. The following list offers a starting point to address the realities of Asian American students' lives.

Don't automatically assume that your Asian American students are "good" students (or "bad," for that matter), and get to know them.

Personally get to know students and their family's practices, which widely vary from home to home, despite their "membership" in specific ethnic or linguistic groups. Start by researching the specific histories and cultures of the students in your classroom to better understand the historical and political contexts of their communities. Also, bring the lives of all of your students, Asian Americans included, into your classroom. Have them consider, reflect, and write about how their home lives and experiences intersect with their school lives and experiences.

Bring the lives of all of your students, Asian Americans included, into your classroom.

Develop strategies to personally engage with students and their communities, whether through lunchtime interactions or visits to their homes, community centers, and cultural or political events. While we recognize the limited resources of all teachers, learning about your Asian American students and their communities takes the same energy and commitment as learning to work with any specific group of students.

Rethink how you interpret and act upon the silence of Asian American students in your classroom.

Asian American student silence can mean many things, from resistance to teachers, to disengagement from work, to a lack of understanding of concepts, to thoughtful engagement and consideration, to insecurity speaking English, to insecurity in their grasp of classroom content. Rather than assume that Asian American student silence means any one thing, assess the meaning of silence by personally checking in with the student individually.

Teach about unsung Asian American heroes.

Teachers might include the stories of real-life woman warriors Yuri Kochiyama and Grace Lee Boggs, for instance. Kochiyama has been involved in a range of efforts, from working closely with Malcolm X in Harlem, to Puerto Rican sovereignty, to freeing political prisoners like Mumia Abu Jamal. Boggs' efforts have included work with famed Marxist Humanist Raya Dunayevskaya, organized labor, and the Detroit Freedom Summer schools.

Or perhaps teach about Ehren Watada, the first commissioned officer to publicly refuse to go to war in Iraq because he believes the war is illegal and would make him a party to war crimes. Learning about heroes like these can help students broaden the range of what it means to be Asian American.

Highlight ways in which Asian Americans challenge racism and stereotypes.

Schools should challenge racist caricatures of Asians and Asian Americans, including viewing them as penny-pinching convenience store owners, religious terrorists, kung fu fighting mobsters, academic super-nerds, and exotic, submissive women.

Schools should challenge racist caricatures of Asians and Asian Americans.

One way to do this is to introduce students to stereotype-defying examples, such as Kochiyama, Boggs, and Watada. There are also many youth and multi-generational organizations of Asian Americans fighting for social justice in the U.S. These include Khmer Girls in Action (KGA, Long Beach), and the Committee Against Anti-Asian Violence/Organizing Asian Communities (CAAAV, New York).

These organizations are extremely important examples of how youth can be proactive in challenging some of the issues that affect our communities, and their work challenges the stereotypes of Asian Americans as silent and obedient.

Illustrate historical, political, and cultural intersections between Asian Americans and other groups.

There are historical and current examples of shared experiences between Asian Americans and other communities. For instance, teachers could highlight the key role of Asian Americans in collective struggles for social justice in the United States. Possible examples include: Philip Veracruz and other Pilipino farm workers who were the backbone and catalyst for the labor campaigns of Cesar Chavez and the United Farm Workers in the late 1960s and early 1970s; Chinese students and families who challenged the racism of public schools in the *Lau v. Nichols* case of the 1970s that provided the legal basis for guaranteeing the rights of English language learners and bilingual education; Asian American college students who in 1967-69 organized with blacks, Latina/os, and Native Americans at San Francisco State University in a multiethnic struggle to establish the first ethnic studies program in the nation, united under the banner of "Third World Liberation."

Weave the historical struggles, culture, and art of Asian American communities into your classroom.

As part of a curriculum that is grounded in the lives of all of our students, teachers can highlight Asian American history, culture, and art in their classroom practices to help Asian American students develop not only positive self-identity, but also empathy between Asian Americans and other racial, cultural, or ethnic groups. Teachers might use novels by Carlos Bulosan, John Okada, Nora Okja Keller, Lê Thi Diem Thúy, Jessica Hagedorn, Jhumpa Lahiri, or Shawn Wong; poetry by Lawson Inada, Li-Young Li, Marilyn Chin, Nick Carbón, or Sesshu Foster; spoken word by Reggie Cabico, Ishle Park, Beau Sia, or I Was Born With Two Tongues; hip-hop music by Blue Scholars, Skim, Native Guns, Himalayan Project, or Kuttin Kandi; and history texts by Ron Takaki, Sucheng Chan, Peter Kwong, or Gary Okihiro.

By believing in a 'positive' stereotype we ultimately give credence to an entire way of thinking about race and culture, one that upholds the stereotypic racial and cultural inferiority of African Americans and Latina/os and maintains white supremacy.

When it comes to dealing with Asian Americans in education, it is all too common for people to ask, "What's wrong with the Myth of the Model Minority? Isn't it a positive stereotype?" What many miss is that there are no "positive" stereotypes, because by believing in a "positive" stereotype, as, admittedly, even many Asian Americans do, we ultimately give credence to an entire way of thinking about race and culture, one that upholds the stereotypic racial and cultural inferiority of African Americans and Latina/os and maintains white supremacy.

The Myth of the Model Minority not only does a disservice to Asian American diversity and identity, it serves to justify an entire system of race and class inequality. It is perhaps for this reason, above all else, that the Myth of the Model Minority needs to be unmasked in our classrooms and used to challenge the legacies of racism and other forms of inequality that exist in our schools and society today.

Endnote:

1. Pilipino is a term used by some activists in the Pilipino American community as means of challenging the way that Spanish and U.S. colonization of the islands also colonized the language by renaming them the Philippines after King Phillip, and introducing the anglicized "f" sound which did not exist in the indigenous languages there.

Edwina Left Behind

By Sören Wuerth

The woman from the state education department had come to show us "the data." She stood in an auditorium, in front of Ketchikan school district's some 300 teachers and staff and began a choppy Powerpoint presentation describing the standards on how students should soon be judged.

The official, dressed in a black blouse and black sport jacket, called herself a "recovering" math and middle school teacher.

During her presentation, which I'd seen before, we were quizzed on the meaning of acronyms and asked multiple-choice questions about No Child Left Behind. Judging from comments and muffled heckling behind me, I was not the only teacher who considered the education department's presentation demeaning.

Sören Wuerth

As I listened, I reflected on Edwina, a student in the 12th-grade language arts class I taught last year in the remote Cu'pik Eskimo village of Chevak. Chevak School is the dominant feature in the rural, western Alaska village. Just over 300 students shuffle from small, modular homes to the K-12 school, leaning into the wind most of the year to get there, crossing swells of snow drifts in the winter.

Edwina was tough. She had a round face, always wore the same sweatshirt and oval glasses, and maneuvered through two communities rife with drugs and alcohol like a running back moving past hapless opponents.

Edwina's family lived in the coastal village of Hooper Bay, but she attended Chevak's school 20 miles inland, hoping her education would be superior to that of the neighboring village. On weekends, she'd leave her grandmother's place and drive a snowmobile 40 miles across frozen tundra, in weather that dipped to 60 below, to visit her home village. Edwina beat up boys who picked on her brothers, swore, and chewed tobacco. She turned to her schoolwork with the same rugged self-assurance.

A senior, Edwina needed to pass the state's High School Graduation Qualifying Exam to receive a diploma. Early in the year, I downloaded practice tests the state education department offered on its site. The sample test was three years old and students were so familiar with it they had many of the answers memorized.

Edwina didn't complain. She took the test seriously, as she did most of her school assignments. She remained after class to finish projects, always smiling, easily falling into laughter. She was a good writer. One of her stories, detailing the time she got lost riding through a blizzard behind her father on his snowmobile, eventually appeared in a journal of high school writing. A disciplined student, Edwina maintained a straight-A average throughout her school career. When a storm gripped the village and other students decided not to go to school, Edwina would invariably trudge through wind-packed snow to ensure an immaculate attendance record.

As the woman from the state droned on about formulaic assessment, I thought of how, as far as the state was concerned, Edwina's entire education—all that she'd learned and all that she had endured to obtain it—would come down to one test.

Kids in the village struggle to memorize vocabulary and concepts with which they have no connection. A counselor in my village told me the story of an elementary student who began crying during a test. When the counselor asked her what was wrong, the

---

Edwina was tough. She had a round face, always wore the same sweatshirt and oval glasses, and maneuvered through two communities rife with drugs and alcohol like a running back moving past hapless opponents.

girl pointed to the word "curb" and said she didn't know what it meant. In her community, on a dusty knoll above thousands of acres of barren tundra, residents travel on dirt paths with four-wheelers and snowmobiles.

It seems every teacher who has worked in Alaska's rural school system has a story of the cultural ignorance of standardized tests. A question that stumped a student in my wife's 2nd-grade class asked for the best choice on how to get to a hospital: boat, ambulance, or airplane. Since the nearest hospital is 300 miles away, the student circled the logical, yet "incorrect," answer: airplane.

In Alaska, only about 40 percent of Native students graduate from high school, compared to almost 70 percent for all other ethnicities combined. There were 13 dropouts in Chevak the year I taught there. Generally, white students pass high-stakes tests at double the rate of their Native counterparts. In the region encompassing Chevak, an area the size of Iowa and dotted with more than 50 villages, only about a quarter of the students pass reading tests.

Edwina had lived her entire life in the remote villages of Hooper Bay and Chevak. It's a desolate region where the wind blows almost constantly across a vast delta of winding rivers, sloughs, and subarctic tundra. Edwina had to work hard to support her family. Her anna (grandma) and atta (grandpa) as well as other family members relied on her to help prepare food, cook, wash laundry, run to the village store, and perform hundreds of other tasks.

She tried to stay awake in class and, when I joked with her once about her sleepiness, she erupted in uncharacteristic anger: "I've been up all night working, babysitting, helping my anna and atta!"

Yet, the state graduation-qualifying exam would not ask about her snowmobiling experience, subsistence hunting on the frozen ocean, collecting driftwood, or preparing a traditional sauna called a "steam."

Worried about previous years' lackluster test results, Edwina took a supplementary class, from another teacher, designed specifically to "teach to the test." In my classroom, I deviated from language arts units geared toward critical thinking, inquiry-based learning, and cultural literacy, and devoted several weeks of classroom instruction to review test strategies, test content, and preparation. We analyzed sample tests, practiced using the process of elimination to discard distracting choices, and even discussed cultural biases in test questions.

But in a village where kids are raised with a linguistically distinct form of English—called village English—and where young

It seems every teacher who has worked in Alaska's rural school system has a story of the cultural ignorance of standardized tests.

people struggle daily with the effects of economic hardship, domestic violence, and cultural disintegration, tests that ask students to compare personal digital assistants are irrelevant. Alaska Natives in rural villages have far greater concerns. With Alaska's Native communities suffering from the highest rates of Fetal Alcohol Syndrome, teen suicide, and child abuse in the nation, staying healthy—and even alive—is the paramount motive.

I tried to take these real concerns into consideration in my classroom by making learning relevant to conditions my students faced in their communities while maintaining high expectations in an academically rigorous curriculum. We read books by Native American authors such as Sherman Alexie, reconstructed traditional narratives into plays, and analyzed comparisons between "home" language and Standard English.

I conducted a grant-writing unit so students could realize an authentic outcome for composition. Edwina wrote an introduction to a grant that was ultimately awarded to her senior class.

Little did I know, however, how severely high-stakes tests would undercut my efforts to motivate my Alaska Native students for reading and writing.

Little did I know, however, how severely high-stakes tests would undercut my efforts to motivate my Alaska Native students for reading and writing.

Near the end of the year, the counselor came into my classroom. She stood solemnly by the door, as someone would who is about to deliver the news of a death in the family. She held the test results and waited until students were sitting down.

When the seniors looked at their test scores, some seemed unfazed by the results. Edwina, however, said she felt sick.

Because she didn't pass the test, Edwina didn't get a diploma when she graduated later that spring. None of her female classmates did.

Edwina wrote a letter about her shattered hopes and her view of schools—how she'd "been working hard in school all this time" since kindergarten, how she wanted to earn the diploma her older sister never received, how she's afraid she'll end up living with her mother the rest of her life. When she read her letter aloud, other students in class fell silent.

I suggested she send her letter to the editor of the Bethel paper, but drawing attention to oneself and one's problems is not customary among the Cu'pik Eskimo.

In Ketchikan, the department of education representative closed her presentation, saying, "Everyone's goal is to increase student achievement."

Edwina accomplished that goal. The state and the school district failed her.

CHAPTER TWENTY-FOUR

Language Lessons
Using student assistants to bridge culture and language

By Denise Hanson-Rautiainen

"I know another language and can teach it to others who are learning the language that I know. Being a Teaching Assistant has been a beautiful experience. I have met people in this class who are very nice also … I met new friends. I see that they are happy with the things that I taught them."

—Glenda, a 15-year-old student from Peru

For the past three years, I have used native Spanish-speaking students as teaching assistants in my Spanish classes. I've found it challenges the white norm prevalent at my high school, and could also be one piece of a strategy to help close our district's achievement gap. By working as teaching assistants, native Spanish speakers gain skills, status, and all students are deeply exposed to cultures and languages.

West High School in Madison, Wis., a school of more than 2,100 students, is about 65 percent white. Latinos, many of them

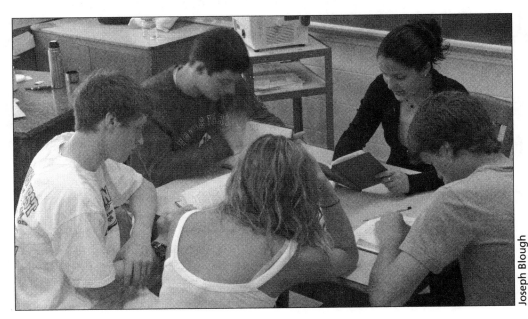

Joseph Blough

immigrants, are the fastest growing group in the school, as they are throughout the district; they now make up 10 percent of West's students. Latino student achievement has been low relative to their white peers.

Just two years ago, only 60 percent of West's Latino students graduated, as compared to 96 percent for white students.

Uncomfortable Fit

West High School has more than 200 students from about 40 countries enrolled in its English as a second language program. Although these students speak a total of 20 languages, more than half speak Spanish as their first language. And while many of these students speak Spanish fluently, few have the same confidence or skill when it comes to reading and writing.

As a longtime Spanish teacher, it has always concerned me that most ESL students seem marginalized in the school. Over time, I realized that ESL students connect fairly easily with each other, especially with other speakers of their native language. They often form close relationships with ESL teachers and staff. Yet, they tend to remain sheltered in a small community within the school, and English speakers rarely form friendships with them.

As a longtime Spanish teacher, it has always concerned me that most ESL students seem marginalized in the school.

Over the years, I have worked to bridge this gap by opening up my Spanish classrooms to native Spanish speakers. I've encouraged and even recruited them to take my classes. I felt their presence would enhance our classroom both culturally and linguistically. I also hoped that this would facilitate students making friends outside of their own ethnic groups. Unfortunately, my push to move native Spanish speakers into my classroom often backfired when other students made comments to native Spanish speakers along these lines: "What are you doing in this class? You already know Spanish" or worse: "You should know Spanish." At an age when peer approval is particularly important, comments like these can be hurtful.

Many Spanish-speaking students have told me they not only failed in the traditional Spanish classes, they felt stupid for doing so. I began to understand how these experiences with Spanish classes designed for nonnative speakers could actually harm the native speakers' desire to improve their own Spanish language skills. Partly due to my experience working with native speakers ill-served by the standard Spanish curriculum, West now offers a Spanish for Spanish Speakers class, which I currently teach.

Having native Spanish speakers in my classroom underscored for the native English speakers that English speakers have multiple opportunities to improve their native language throughout their school experience—an advantage most of their Latino peers do not have. This often comes up when a native English speaker asks me why a Spanish speaker would be taking Spanish—and that question comes up frequently, usually in a one-on-one situation. I tell them that, as native English speakers, they have taken English classes since they were in elementary school. It is clear to me, and borne out by research, that native Spanish speakers need to know their language not just socially, but academically. While the opportunity to be a TA gives Spanish speakers a new social standing in the school, it is also important for them to have the chance to study their language with their peers—again, one of the motivating factors for me to advocate the Spanish for Spanish Speakers course.

All of my TA students come from areas of the Americas that have been economically and politically ravaged, both by U.S. policy as well as by internal political upheavals. Many of them come from poor families, and even those of middle-class backgrounds have seen education in their countries take a backseat to the more immediate needs of food, shelter, and safety. Many of these students quickly learn basic English, but they never acquire the fundamentals they will need to pursue education beyond high school. At the same time, they lack a strong background in Spanish language literacy. Because they've yet to master either language, everyday academic performance is an ongoing struggle.

Students as Teachers

At West High, teaching assistantships were traditionally offered to high-achieving students, particularly in the sciences and math. Being able to list a TAship on a transcript was a sign of academic status. I sought to confer that same status on native Spanish speakers, too long regarded only in the context of what they do not know. I believed native English speakers would benefit from authentic oral practice and the native Spanish speakers would become more literate in Spanish. This turned out to be the case as the native Spanish speakers had to know enough about Spanish to be able to explain different grammatical and linguistic points to the students in the class. An added benefit was that native English speakers would become more familiar with the geography, history, and culture of the teaching assistant's country of origin. Teaching assistants at Madison West receive credit (without a grade) for the class, increasing the likelihood they will graduate.

I believed native English speakers would benefit from authentic oral practice and the native Spanish speakers would become more literate in Spanish.

Teaching assistants participate in Spanish classes in multiple ways. On the first day, I tell my students that they can ask the assistants anything they want as long as they ask in Spanish. My classes range from Spanish 1 to 3, so the students are all over the map in terms of ability. Students have the opportunity to hear the distinct accents of the assistants, as well as learn some background information about each TA.

One problem for teaching assistants is they are initially uncertain about their role. They have to adjust to the enhanced status as knowledge providers, as well as to define their new relationship with the students. It's a struggle for some, but I've found my native Spanish students rise to the challenge and show empathy for their English-speaking peers. Omar, a TA from Mexico, remembers how hard it was at first:

> At the beginning, I was kind of unsure of what level they were at, and I didn't want to start just talking in Spanish to them because I think, like, I can speak really fast and that was kind of a problem. ... I would use these words that they don't really know yet. And that was a big thing, having to use the words that they learned in class and not only the words that I know ... once I'd been in the class for a while, it just got easier.

As the students begin to think of themselves as teachers, they begin to understand themselves as leaders.

As the students begin to think of themselves as teachers, they begin to understand themselves as leaders. Raúl, another TA, saw it this way:

> I learned to take more responsibilities because you are a TA, you're a teacher assistant, it's like a job. If there is one student who is not really getting the class or something like that, then Ms. Hanson is like, "OK, you're going to give him special attention so he can understand." You feel like, OK, if he fails, I fail.

Sharing Home Cultures

Each TA does a formal presentation about his or her home country that also includes a lot of personal information about the TA. I ask them to talk about their own experiences growing up, and also about what it was like to come to the United States. For example, Claudio, a freshman TA from Nicaragua, told his peers about the long Contra war in his country. It is something all Nicaraguans learn about, even though the war was coming to an end just as Claudio was born. After Claudio's presentation, I invited his father, Roberto, who fought with the Sandinistas, to speak with the class. I asked students ahead of time to take notes and ask questions of the guest speaker—a fairly significant task for my students to carry out in Spanish. Roberto now comes to my Spanish classes once a year to talk about Nicaragua, usually after I have prepared my class with readings and/or a movie.

Each year, my Mexican TAs teach about a core celebration of their culture, the annual Day of the Dead. They bring in pictures of ofrendas, an offering that incorporates food, drink, flowers, candles, and pictures to celebrate the souls of deceased relatives. Several students talked about the difference between the traditional approach to death in the United States and the way that it is understood in Mexico. Zaira, a Mexican TA who has been here for less than two years, took a major role in this class period. "It was fun for me to share with the other students," she said. "They all were surprised that we actually put out food for our ancestors—they're still a big part of our lives, and that's not so true here. I like the way that we remember, and celebrate, our ancestors, and I'm proud of it, and I think the other students really got that."

The teaching assistants are able to teach in a nonthreatening way that does not involve formal assessment or grades. In addition, there is a lot of informal exchange of experiences. Claudio helped organize a student walkout in support of the April 10, 2006, demonstration for immigrant rights. We talked about the walkout in each of my Spanish classes, and the organizers—Claudio and Rafael, also a former TA—came to speak to the classes about the walkout. They explained to the Spanish classes that they themselves didn't have to worry about legal documents, but many Latino kids at school do not have documents and so constantly live with uncertainty. They also talked about how the conditions in many countries, including Mexico and Central America, are so difficult that many people feel that going to the United States is their only option.

Having Rafael and Claudio talk about the immigration issue made it possible for my other students to relate to the Latino students in a way that wouldn't have happened if I had been the only one broaching the subject. In subsequent classes, we talked about the importance of supporting the march, and why it was crucial that all students—not just Latino students—be present in the march. Having the teaching assistants in the class made the march much more personal and important to many of my students. I believe their presence in class resulted in the majority of my native English students joining the walkout.

The teaching assistants are able to teach in a nonthreatening way that does not involve formal assessment or grades.

Bicultural Friendships

Almost all the assistants report that the U.S.-born students now greet them regularly in the hallway, and they no longer feel so isolated. One assistant, a 17-year-old male from Peru, told me how near the beginning of the year he felt that two African-American girls in the class didn't like him, wouldn't greet him, and even said "bad things" to him in the halls. As the year went on, he said they started to ask him questions in class. By spring, he told me: "They say, 'Hey.' They're affectionate; they give you their hand or a hug or they joke with you. They pass you in the hall and are with their friends and they say, 'Look, it's my friend Joaquín, my Spanish teacher.' I like it."

Another TA, Pablo, said he may now have more "North American friends than Latino friends."

Throughout this experiment, my teaching assistants have taken on additional leadership roles.

Throughout this experiment, my teaching assistants have taken on additional leadership roles. They seek out future assistants and give me suggestions for expanding the program. They often talk about how this program should continue and extend to all Spanish classes. I am convinced that placing Latino students in leadership roles has had a powerful impact on both the lives of my students and TAs, as well as on the greater school community.

CHAPTER TWENTY-FIVE

Putting a Human Face on the Immigration Debate

By Steven Picht-Trujillo and Paola Suchsland

While politicians debate immigration policy, many of our high schools in Southern California and across the country are places where immigration issues are not just academic, abstract discussions but rather the real-life drama that many of our students face on a daily basis. For those of us working with immigrant populations, we have in our students living examples that we can use to bring the immigration issue to the forefront and teach all of our students, both immigrants and descendants of immigrants, so that they can have a better understanding of the issue as it relates to their fellow students and their community. This past school year at our high

Michael Duffy

school we joined forces to teach a unit on immigration to our students, using our students' own immigration experiences to form a curriculum that we will be able to use in future classes.

We teach at Valencia High School, in Placentia, Calif., on the northern edge of Orange County. Traditionally considered a conservative "white" enclave of Southern California, Placentia is undergoing major demographic changes. Valencia High School, the oldest of Placentia's three high schools, was established 70 years ago and now serves a student population of over 2,500. English language learners constitute 22 percent of the student body, and just over half the school's students are Latino. However, Valencia is diverse, with 31 percent of the students officially categorized as "white" (non-Hispanic, including a variety of immigrant Europeans such as Germans, Romanians, and Albanians, as well as Lebanese, Indians, Pakistanis, and others); 12 percent Asian (Korean, Vietnamese, Chinese, and Filipino students predominate); and 3 percent black (African American as well as African and Caribbean immigrants). Our school's population reflects the huge demographic shift that has occurred throughout Orange County over the past 20 years; the result is that our county is now decidedly less "white" than the stereotypical image depicted in television programs such as "The OC" and "Laguna Beach."

To be admitted to a university in the California State University system, a student must have two years of study in a language other than English; and to enter the University of California system, a student must have at least three years of study. Therefore, we have a large percentage of students studying Spanish, followed by French and Japanese.

Steve teaches first- and third-year Spanish to students from various ethnic backgrounds, while Paola, a native of Mexico, teaches second- and third-year classes in Spanish for native speakers. The vast majority of her students are first- or second-generation immigrants from Mexico, some of whom arrived only recently. As teachers in the same department, we always look for ways to have our students interact, as this cross-class engagement has language and cultural benefits for both groups.

The 2006 U.S. House of Representatives bill that declared all undocumented immigrants to be felons and imposing draconian penalties on those knowingly assisting such immigrants triggered an intense debate in the school. Since a number of our school's students participated in the 2006 May Day marches in Orange County and Los Angeles in support of immigrants' rights, we decided that this year we wanted to engage students in several joint

> *As teachers in the same department, we always look for ways to have our students interact, as this cross-class engagement has language and cultural benefits for both groups.*

lessons to increase their understanding of these issues. We especially wanted to make them more aware of the circumstances facing many of our students whose families have recently immigrated from Latin America.

To align our lessons with the California Standards for Foreign Language Instruction, Steve chose to begin our "Immigration Unit," as we called it, during the chapter in his class's Spanish 3 textbooks entitled "La riqueza cultural" ("Cultural Richness"), which teaches vocabulary and grammar within the context of the immigrant experience and our students' cultural heritage. Students learn how to express topics dealing with the challenges associated with arrival in a new country, talking about future plans and goals, discussing their accomplishments and successes, and expressing intention and purpose. This chapter comes late in our second semester and coincided perfectly with the one-year anniversary of the May 1st marches. Likewise, "La Experiencia Migrante" ("The Migrant Experience"), a unit in Paola's textbook, includes poems and short stories depicting the lives and struggles of immigrants' families coming to the United States. Some of Paola's students live with the constant worry of either being deported or having their parents deported.

Against this backdrop, we began to put together lessons and activities to have our students become more aware of the realities of immigrants and their contributions to American society, and to promote greater appreciation of the commonalities we share in our pursuit of the American dream. All activities, projects, readings, and films that we used during this unit aligned with both the language and culture standards. Since this was our first year to teach this unit, we often created as we went along, but the end result laid the groundwork for what we feel will be an outstanding unit next year.

To begin this unit, we brought our classes together to have our students read excerpts from Francisco Jiménez's book *Cajas de cartón*, an account of the author's experiences as an immigrant child in California during the 1940s. We chose this text in order to draw parallels between undocumented immigrants of that period with those of today. The first time our classes met together we read sections aloud in Spanish in small groups, with Paola's students helping Steve's with their pronunciation and comprehension. It was also a chance for our students to get to know each other and to feel comfortable with one another.

Another activity that our two classes shared was the bilingual skits prepared by the students. We combined our classes to form

We began to put together lessons and activities to have our students become more aware of the realities of immigrants and their contributions to American society.

groups of four to five students, with at least two native speakers in each group. Students wrote and prepared short skits that they later presented to the combined classes. Each group randomly drew from a list of situations and prepared their skits in Spanish (or English if it fit the situation). We came up with the topics based on real-life events that were being reported in the news.

The topics included: 1) a family in Mexico discusses the pros and cons of immigrating to the United States; 2) politicians on both sides of the spectrum debate immigrant issues; 3) an encounter between Minutemen and immigrants at the U.S.-Mexico border; 4) a family in California receives a deportation order and decides whether the U.S.-born children will stay or leave; 5) a raid at a California business that employs undocumented workers.

All of these situations were either derived from news articles that we had read or were gleaned from our own experiences living in Orange County, home to an estimated 185,000 undocumented immigrants.

Each group of students randomly chose one of the five topics that were written on slips of paper. Immediately some groups responded positively to their selected topics while others expressed disappointment and wanted to change to a different topic. We had each group keep their selected topic and challenged everyone to make the effort of putting themselves in the shoes of others and to act accordingly, even if it meant taking a role completely opposite from their own closely held beliefs. As they started to work in their groups, many of the students from both classes seemed uneasy and tried to make light of their topics, jokingly taking extreme positions with each other in order to gauge the attitudes of the other students in their groups. However, as their work progressed it became obvious to us that they were putting their efforts into developing their roles and working to create cogent arguments either for or against immigrants' rights. An additional challenge for many of Steve's students was to prepare a role in Spanish that would convey the emotional intensity that came so easily for Paola's students. After working together for nearly a full class period, the students seemed ready to begin presenting, so we planned to start the skits in the next day's class, reserving the entire hour for the presentations and discussion.

As we anticipated, many of these topics struck a nerve with Paola's immigrant students, and some of the presentations became very emotional. We noticed how some of Paola's students were especially animated as they took on the role of the perpetrator instead of the victim in their situations (e.g., the immigration

We challenged everyone to make the effort of putting themselves in the shoes of others and to act accordingly, even if it meant taking a role completely opposite from their own closely held beliefs.

officer or the manager who refuses to pay fair salaries to undocumented workers). Still, we also saw mixed feelings of frustration and kindness from my students, who had difficulty arguing anti-immigrant positions in front of their peers. One of Steve's students had taken an adversarial role in her skit as a politician arguing against immigrants and stopped several times in order to address the class directly, saying, "I don't really feel this way, I'm just playing a role." During the presentation of the skits there seemed to be a feeling of mutual respect and understanding, and we had no discipline or behavior problems.

During this unit Steve wanted to engage his students in a project that would not only put their language skills to use but that would give them cause to reflect on their own immigrant heritage, regardless of whether they or their own parents were immigrants or their family had been in the United States for centuries. To reach this aim he decided on posters in which they would include graphic representations of their heritage (photos, maps, flags, drawings, cultural artifacts, etc.) along with an original written piece. The written portion could be in the form of a personal letter, a diary entry, a newspaper article, or a short essay written in the first person as if the student were their immigrant ancestor, a parent, or themselves. The only stipulation was that they incorporate vocabulary from our textbook and show command of the grammatical structures that they employed in their writing.

In Steve's case, his maternal ancestors were not actually immigrants to the United States; rather, the United States came to them after the Mexican-American War and subjugated them under the oft-violated terms of the Treaty of Guadalupe Hidalgo. Therefore, while we used the term *inmigrante* during this unit, he explained to his students that we were using the word as an all-encompassing term to include anyone who wasn't indigenous to the United States, regardless of the circumstances under which their ancestors arrived here. Steve had no Native American or African American students in his class during this unit, but that would bring a whole other voice to the discussion that he hopes we can develop in next year's class.

For Steve's students whose ancestors may have come to the United States 100 or more years ago, the project required that they use their creative powers to make educated assumptions about the circumstances surrounding their chosen ancestor's reasons for coming to the United States, based on what they might have learned in their U.S. or world history classes, or perhaps from parents or family members. Often, these students had to make up the

We also saw mixed feelings of frustration and kindness from my students, who had difficulty arguing anti-immigrant positions in front of their peers.

ancestor, but doing so helped them understand why that ancestor would have made the sacrifices of leaving his or her native land to come to a new country. Most of Paola's students are from recently immigrated families so their documents often related to a parent or grandparent.

After creating their posters, students presented them to the class, after which they were put up on the walls in both of our classrooms. One of our aims was for Paola's students to see Steve's in a different light and to understand that most of them too were descended from people who came to this country in search of the same opportunities. While we didn't formally assess their responses this time around, we were happy to see her students actively engaged in poring over the posters, and we will definitely include more discussion to gauge their responses in our next unit. Some of the written documents on the posters were written as letters from the immigrant ancestor (or parent, as many of them were) to a loved one left behind. Many of these were touching accounts of the challenges the person faced in a new land, and sometimes expressed regret for having left parents or loved ones behind. Other documents were written as diary entries, expressing the pain of discrimination and marginalization in what was supposed to be a land of liberty for all. The posters' vibrancy and creativity made Steve's classroom into a virtual art gallery for the last month of school and students were eager to see each other's posters and read their accounts.

All of Paola's students wrote a personal narrative in Spanish about their family's circumstances of coming to the United States, including reasons for leaving their homeland, challenges they faced after arrival, and hopes for the future. When she assigned the personal narratives she had her students use fictional names so that only she would know who wrote which narrative. She also had them change the names of the characters involved in their stories to avoid any accidental divulging of the authorship of any given piece. These narratives were especially poignant, as they talked about the hardships involved in crossing through the desert or being smuggled by ruthless coyotes or living with the fear of being deported or having their families torn apart.

About a third of her class, mostly recent immigrant students, had a difficult time writing about events that were still fresh wounds in their hearts.

When Paola assigned the personal narratives to her students, some were hesitant but excited to be able to tell others their story. On the other hand, about a third of her class, mostly recent immigrant students, had a difficult time writing about events that were still fresh wounds in their hearts. We realized then that many of the personal stories had no happy endings. Paola had to encourage her students, especially the ones having trouble writing or who did not want to tell their story, to use writing as a tool that would allow them to heal their inner scars. The students were given the option to undertake an alternative assignment more generically related to immigration if they did not want to pen their personal experiences, and indeed there was one student who in the beginning refused to put his experience on paper. But after seeing his fellow classmates focused on writing their accounts he told Paola, "Ms. Ledezma, my family has suffered a lot and I have to tell their story so others will know how they suffered."

As Paola had hoped, students were able to complete and share their personal narratives in class because of the encouragement to write. To groups of five or six students, she randomly handed out essays to read aloud and then discuss, but the authors' identities were not divulged.

These narratives are valuable documents and will be useful for our unit next year when we have our students read them in the target language and realize that these amazing stories are from their classmates' lives. These, more than anything, put a human face on the immigration issue and in the future we hope will help students understand that regardless of whether a person immigrates to this country with documents or without, the motivation is the same: to secure the best opportunities for us and our families.

During our frequent lunch conversations, we often discussed the immigration situation, especially as it relates to undocumented immigrants. Steve sometimes had to deal with his own students' negative and derisive comments about Mexican immigrants, while Paola was comfortable discussing immigration issues openly with her students, with whom she could easily relate. It was during those conversations that we realized that we needed to create a unit to empower both of our classes to become agents of change. For Paola's students, by putting themselves in the shoes of others, they gained a better understanding of those who fight against undocumented immigrants and they learned to discuss and defend their own positions in the immigration debate in both English and Spanish. For Steve's students, they came away with a deeper understanding of the issues and how they relate to their fellow classmates. As one student commented, "I never really thought about these things before, but now I realize that when they talk about immigrants in the news, they're talking about my friends and classmates."

The Brazilian education theorist and activist Paulo Freire once said that, "Washing one's hands of the conflict between the power-

We realized that we needed to create a unit to empower both of our classes to become agents of change.

With this unit we tried to get our students to understand the position of the powerless in the immigration debate.

ful and the powerless means to side with the powerful, not to be neutral." With this unit we tried to get our students to understand the position of the powerless in the immigration debate. On the one hand, Steve's students are siding with the powerful since they remained relatively uninformed on the immigration debate even though many of them are from families who have immigrated to the United States legally and enjoy a certain level of economic success. Since many of them live without the constant fear of losing everything and being deported, many had never given this issue a second thought until we discussed it in class.

By not using their voice and being heard, Paola's students were likewise siding with the powerful. This unit was an opportunity for them to raise their voices and to begin their first steps toward empowerment. Most of them immigrated to this country without documents or were born in the United States to undocumented parents. Prior to this unit, the national debate surrounding immigration was becoming more intense, so Paola brought in articles from the Spanish-language press about various proposals for immigration reform, and her students were eager to talk about the issue. Her classroom became what she liked to call a "sanctuary city" as she sought to create a loving and welcoming environment where her students would feel safe talking about their experiences. For her as a Mexican immigrant and having been undocumented herself for over five years, she could relate to their fears and frustrations.

One of our fears in doing this unit was the anticipation of combining our classes. We had previously brought students together in an earlier unit to create plays depicting Aztec legends, so they were already somewhat familiar with each other, but not in the context of dealing with a controversial topic such as this. For this unit, Paola confided to Steve that she worried about how our students would respond, especially because more than half her students are English language learners and had said how hard it was for them to speak English with Steve's students. His students too had reservations. They felt like the native Spanish speakers made fun of them for their poor Spanish skills. Also, we were apprehensive about our students' parents: How would they react? Would they complain about the unit and our politicizing of the subject matter, insisting that we just stick to the curriculum? We prepared for the worst by always having the unit's objectives and the standards ready to justify our work.

Moreover, we had to challenge ourselves to present multiple sides of the arguments and not appear to force our personal agenda on students. Paola, once undocumented herself, was concerned that her personal situation might prevent students from expressing opposing points of view. She had shared her personal story with her students and had told them about her support for the legalization of millions of immigrants in the United States. Through our personal and professional experiences working with immigrant students, as well as the personal relationships we have with undocumented friends and relatives outside of the classroom, we are both passionate about the immigration issue and we feared that a class discussion about such a heated topic could result in chaos and/or disciplinary problems. Thankfully, our fears never materialized and the experience turned out to be overwhelmingly positive. Contrary to our fears, discussions never got out of hand, nor did we have to deal with irate parents. The curriculum provided students ample opportunity to put themselves in someone else's shoes.

Putting a human face on immigration issues has been one of our most challenging tasks, and at the same time has been one of the most rewarding experiences that we have had in our relatively short teaching careers. As teachers who strive to be agents of change, there came a moment when we realized that we could not just dispassionately talk about the issue, but rather we needed to act upon it by bringing it into our classrooms. By doing so we hope we have planted the seeds so that our students can begin to effect change in their communities and work to change attitudes of those around them. As language teachers we don't always have opportunities to raise students' social awareness or to address global social justice issues, so for us this unit was the opportunity we were waiting for. We hope that it is just the beginning.

Putting a human face on immigration issues has been one of our most challenging tasks, and at the same time has been one of the most rewarding experiences that we have had in our relatively short teaching careers.

RESOURCES

Readings
During this unit we had our students read a book excerpt dealing with immigration issues from the 1940s along with a contemporary article about the experience of a Mexican family in San Diego. These readings were the initial activity for this unit and were used in order to give students a feel for how these issues have not changed substantially in the United States since the early 20th century.

Cajas de cartón: relatos de la vida peregrina de un niño campesino, by
  Francisco Jiménez, Chapter 1: "Bajo la alambrada." This book is the author's account of his family's illegal entry into the United States from Mexico during the 1940s. (Available in English: *The Circuit*, by Francisco Jiménez, Chapter 1: "Under the Wire.")

"Column One: A family's painful split decision." *Los Angeles Times* article from April 27, 2007, by Anna Gorman, tells the story of parents who were deported to Tijuana, leaving their three U.S.-born children in San Diego so that the children might have greater opportunities in life.

Films

During this unit we watched three films relating to immigrants from Latin America, in which our students were able to meet a handful of immigrants and learn their stories.

El Norte, by Gregory Nava. (In Spanish, English, and Mayan languages with English subtitles) This film tells the story of a Guatemalan brother and sister who flee their country's civil war during the 1980s and shows the harrowing events crossing the U.S.-Mexican border as they immigrate to Los Angeles. Edited version for classroom use available from Teacher's Discovery, www.teachersdiscovery.com.

Immigration. This is an episode of Morgan Spurlock's FX Network series "30 Days" that deals with an undocumented immigrant family in Los Angeles and the anti-immigrant Minuteman who lives with them for 30 days. The program sparked a number of lively in-class debates and discussions. (In both English and Spanish with English subtitles) Available from iTunes.

Farmingville. This is a PBS P.O.V. documentary by Carlos Sandoval and Catherine Tambini dealing with the impact of undocumented immigrants on a suburban New York community and the community's sometimes-violent reaction to their presence. Available from www.amazon.com. This documentary is primarily in English with some Spanish (English subtitles).

The Puerto Rican Vejigante

Teaching art in its social and cultural context

By Patty Bode

I n my public school art room I constantly feel pressured to make the biggest splash in the shortest period of time. School schedules often pinch at art classroom time, leaving little space for in-depth studies in the curriculum of the cultural contexts that produce art-making.

Yet, years ago I embarked on a journey to contextualize each art lesson within the sociopolitical influences in which the art is created. I picture my curriculum as concentric circles, like a splash in a pond, with the study of a specific art form in the center, and the students' knowledge, my curiosity, and the expertise of the community bubbling outward. This process began while I was an elementary school art teacher and continues today in my middle school art room and my summer arts camp for teenagers.

The Vejigante Mask

"Can we make those?" my students called out, as we studied the colorful Vejigante masks of Puerto Rico in a video.

"Yes we can make these masks," I assured them. "Let's figure out what the Vejigante mask is all about. That will help us build our own mask interpretations."

For each slide that flashed on the screen, I asked my students, "What do you notice? What do you wonder?"

Jasmina jumped in, "I notice lots of spots. They painted them with spots, on every mask. I wonder why?"

"I see lots of horns, I notice they are scary," said Orlando.

"I notice that each mask is different; some look kinda the same, but they are all different," Richie added.

"I see fangs, teeth, horns, big mouths, and flared nostrils," Sarah said. "I wonder how they made so many teeth on that one?"

The Vejigante character from Puerto Rico is a crowd-pleaser, both on the island during Carnival, and here in Amherst, Mass., in my middle school art room. But most of my students have limited knowledge of Puerto Rico. Of the 700 students in this school only about 9 percent of my students identify as Latino or Hispanic, and most of those students who identify as such are Puerto Rican. The Puerto Rican community is one of the fastest growing of all the communities of color in this school district. Yet many students, from all cultural backgrounds in this school population, have not learned much about Puerto Rican art in the school setting.

Exploring the history, traditions and cross-cultural influences of the Vejigante mask provides a context for understanding the intersection of the African, European, and indigenous Taíno cultures in the Caribbean.

Many students in the Puerto Rican community have grown up here in New England where the dominant culture in the schools has made Puerto Rico's rich history and culture invisible. Exploring the history, traditions, and cross-cultural influences of the Vejigante mask provides a context for understanding the intersection of the African, European, and indigenous Taíno cultures in the Caribbean. Art-making in this context enhances a more comprehensive understanding of Puerto Rican arts, culture, and history.

The following is a glimpse into the organic evolution of my art curriculum that started years ago with a well-intentioned—yet superficial—multicultural focus, and which continues to evolve and develop into a deliberate intent to teach about the Puerto Rican experience in a broader context.

I began to develop a curriculum about the Vejigante years ago, but the more I worked on it, the more I began to question the image of Puerto Rico that my students were internalizing. In follow-up lessons, students from 1st grade to 7th grade would identify Puerto Rico as "the island where they make Vejigante masks!" Yes, that is true, but did they think that everyone on the island spent their time designing and wearing Vejigante masks? Did they understand the specificity of this folk character to certain traditions, regions, and events? I do not want my students to assume that "folk art" existed on the island in a void without any previous historical context. I do not want to denigrate this beautiful tradition to the status of a mere "tourist curriculum" by exploiting the attractive color and character of the custom. And I wanted the students to understand the significance of the intersection of Spanish and African cultures in the endearing character of the Vejigante—so it was more than an appealing "exotic" character to replicate in art class.

Art in Context

The challenge was to teach about the masks in a historical and cultural context of folk arts, while keeping my art class active and hands-on. After we spent the first part of the class period studying the Vejigante masks through slides and video, I demonstrated how to begin making the mask. As the students watched me shape the oak tag and listened to me explain skills in paper cutting, folding, and scoring, I also talked with them about what they remember from the video. "Does anybody remember when and where the Vejigante masks are worn in Puerto Rico?" Some students responded with guesses, some responded with clear memory of the video.

After a recent class session, I was confident that my students were very much aware that the Vejigante is an artifact of social context, when Alejandro and Sarah grabbed their masks and started chasing their classmates with loud scary roars. They were imitating the gestures we had read about and viewed on the video. "Alejandro," I shouted over the roars, "you are dressed as a Vejigante, what time of year is it in Puerto Rico?"

"February, it is festival in this town!" He yelled.

"Sarah, where are you in Puerto Rico?"

"We're in Ponce, Ms. Bode, because my mask is made of papier mâché and it has fangs—it's not the coconut-shell kind from Loíza!"

The challenge was to teach about the masks in a historical and cultural context of folk arts, while keeping my art class active and hands-on.

This classroom dialogue drew upon the work of Edwin Fontánez whose *Legend of the Vejigante* video and *The Vejigante and the Folk Festivals of Puerto Rico* book (Exit Studios, 1996) provide a sociohistorical context of the vejigante tradition. By using his work in conjunction with the book *Vejigante/Masquerader* by Lulu Delacre, (Scholastic, 1993) students learned about the towns of Ponce and Loíza Aldea, where the vejigante tradition thrives. The mask makers in the town of Loíza Aldea, whose population is predominantly Afro-Puerto Rican, carve the masks from coconut shells, a style derived directly from African traditions. We compared these coconut shell masks to the papier mâché masks in Ponce which are linked to the European tradition, and usually painted with chromatic acrylic paints. The comparisons of the towns, the demographics of their populations, and their styles of mask reveal some of the social context of art-making, and illustrate Puerto Rico's history of race and class stratification. We extended our research about the town of Loíza to learn that this community has maintained African traditions over the years in many aspects of life such as cooking, language, and religion. This leads us into a discussion of race, and heightens awareness of the multiracial heritage of Puerto Rico.

"A nice place to take a vacation"

As I moved around the art room assisting with goopy glue strips of papier mâché and trouble shooting with attaching horns and fangs, I overheard some non-Puerto Rican students saying things like, "Puerto Rico is a nice place to take a vacation." I think to myself, while this may be true, if that is all they know about Puerto Rico, they're missing a lot.

I firmly believe that folk arts play a critical role in the maintenance and nurturing of culture.

This limited understanding of some of my students led me to underscore the value of folk arts, by placing them within the context of other art traditions. I firmly believe that folk arts play a critical role in the maintenance and nurturing of culture. I began to compare and to teach folk arts in the context of contemporary arts, to offer students a fuller picture of the arts of Puerto Rico. I wonder: Do my students have a grasp on folk art as a tradition passed down through generations of families and communities? Do they realize that there were multiple other realms of art created by artists at the universities, galleries, and community art centers both on the island and the mainland? Do they see this connection between Puerto Rican artists in New York and throughout the United States to artists on the island? Are they viewing folk arts and the Vejigante as the only example of Puerto Rican artistic expression?

Throughout our days in the art room, as we worked on our masks, I tried to address these concerns. I showed slides of contemporary artwork such as Juan Sánchez's innovative imagery he labels "Ricanstructions" juxtaposed with slides of several Vejigante masks. Students asked questions about the Sánchez work: "Why does he write about racism and injustice all over his artwork?" "Why does he paint the United States flag in opposite colors?" "Does he make Vejigante masks, too?" I responded with some answers and with some questions: "No, he does not make Vejigante masks; he works more with painting and collage. Why do you think he writes about racism and injustice? Why do you think he paints the United States flag in opposite colors?"

His work inspired discussion about the relevance of history for all contemporary artists. Aviva said, "Maybe he thinks the United States is doing the opposite of what it promised. ... Maybe he feels that racism is the opposite of United States' symbols." These insightful comments led me to utilize examples from several other contemporary Puerto Rican artists, such as Carlos Irizarry's "Transculturalization of the Puerto Rican," which comments on Puerto Rican identity and Soraida Martinez's creation of "verdadism." These artists and images—along with my students' observations—set the stage for discussions on the role of race and class in the Puerto Rican community and the wider United States society, and how it is expressed through art. I emphasized to my students that they, too, are contemporary artists, and I encouraged them to address their concerns about justice and injustice through their art.

I emphasized to my students that they, too, are contemporary artists, and I encouraged them to address their concerns about justice and injustice through their art.

When I discussed race and diversity, I emphasized the vibrant and resilient heritage of the Puerto Rican community, while simultaneously looking at the hard reality of marginalization of the culture in the United States. U.S. business interests have wreaked havoc on the environment, language, and livelihood of many Puerto Ricans throughout the 20th century and to the present.

While my students are busily fashioning masks in my art room in Amherst, Mass., I read aloud current front-page news articles about the bombing practice near the island of Vieques in Puerto Rico and the debate surrounding the U.S. military presence there. A deeper understanding of the Vejigante creates an avenue for understanding the political debates and the different perspectives of the Puerto Rican people surrounding these debates. I was reading this news article, while we were painting our masks, and I invited the students to voice their opinions on the military action around Vieques. We had such a lively discussion, we had to make a rule about "using words" and "no paint splashing" to emphasize one's opinion.

We decided that when we were finished with our Vejigante masks we would each make a painting/collage inspired by the style of Juan Sánchez, in which we would articulate a social political passion of each student's choice. Since this art activity was open-ended, some students chose to stay with Puerto Rican themes and emphasized the Vieques-military debate. Others directed their creativity into a spectrum of social and political statements, such as child labor in the globalized economy, U.S. consumption of fossil fuel and its global and environmental effects, and capitalist control of artistic expression in the music and radio industry, among many others.

The evolution of my curriculum led me to realize that one art form is never enough to teach the entire history of a people.

The evolution of my curriculum led me to realize that one art form is never enough to teach the entire history of a people. I am wary of the danger of using only one example such as the Vejigante to represent all of Puerto Rico's folk arts.

I am also cautious about trying to take on these tasks as a lone art teacher within the confines of the art room. As an art teacher, I do not want to participate in the "colonization" of any artworks or cultures. If Puerto Rico needs to be more visible and more contextualized in art class, then it needs to be so in the entire school curriculum. I certainly cannot accomplish this goal with one art unit, and I absolutely cannot do it alone. This is a complex endeavor.

Getting Help

I needed help. As I developed this unit over the years, I sought out discussions and collaborations with colleagues who teach social studies, language arts, and world languages to integrate curriculum. I also met with parents, grandparents, and community members in an effort to represent their voices in the curriculum. Some of these discussions were informal chats in the school hallway; others were organized community meetings. And we integrated what we learned into our art class. Each day, while students were developing their masks, I asked them what they knew about Puerto Rico. One day after watching a video in social studies, Alicia explained the debate over Puerto Rico's status as a commonwealth, a state, or an independent country. Another day Isaiah retold a folktale they read in English class. I asked how this information has affected the art traditions, leading us back to our Vejigante study. I made a large chart paper list of what we know, and another classroom list of our questions. This list helped me develop the curriculum, and reminded us how much more there is to learn in art class and in other classes. In these discussions, many students turned and stared at the Puerto Rican students in the class. I wonder if they expected them to be experts on all aspects of Puerto Rican history. I realized this is another misconception I needed to address.

Not every Puerto Rican identifies with the tradition of the Vejigante or even knows about it. Puerto Rican students who have lived most of their lives here in the United States have very different experiences from those who have arrived recently from the island. Each community has unique experiences, and each family develops its own perspective on those experiences. My classroom experience reflects this diversity: Some Puerto Rican students had their first introduction to the Vejigante in my classroom, while others are the grandchildren of famous mask-makers on the island.

In the midst of this unit, some of my students reminded me: "That's not the Puerto Rico that I know." I responded, "Yes there are so many different communities and experiences in Puerto Rico! Tell me about the Puerto Rico that you know. Let's learn more about that." That is why I find it so valuable to draw on student knowledge and experience. When using one specific Puerto Rican art form, I find it essential to place that artwork in its location and history, to emphasize the diversity of the island and the arts it produces. I strive to keep in the foreground that no culture is a monolith, and that no single art form can adequately represent an entire culture. Especially because I am not Puerto Rican, I tell my students, "I am in the process of learning, researching, and exploring, and I need your help." This helps to level the playing field for all students—Puerto Rican or not—to view each other as resources, and to draw on the expertise of students and families as well as academic resources.

When my students heard about a devastating hurricane in Puerto Rico several years ago, they were motivated to hold bake sales to assist in the relief effort. When they heard about the struggle with the military in Vieques, they were curious to hear more and to voice their opinions.

I use the study of the Vejigante mask in my art class to stimulate students' interest in Puerto Rican culture and to heighten their awareness of the politics surrounding Puerto Rico's history. In my struggle to contextualize this art activity, I have found students from all backgrounds in all grade levels hungry to learn more. Parents, grandparents, caregivers, and community members are eager to share artifacts, stories, and knowledge. This unit will continue to expand as long as my teaching career progresses.

When using one specific Puerto Rican art form, I find it essential to place that artwork in its location and history, to emphasize the diversity of the island and the arts it produces.

SECTION IV

Confronting Race in the Classroom

CHAPTER TWENTY-SEVEN

Decolonizing the Classroom

Lessons in multicultural education

By Wayne Au

When I was in 9th grade, I had Mr. Anderson for honors World History. Mr. Anderson was one of those teachers that all the honors and AP-track parents wanted their kids to have. He had a reputation for academic rigor, of preparing teenagers for their stratospheric climb towards being a National Merit Scholar slated to attend an Ivy League college.

Like many history teachers, Mr. Anderson talked about his trips to places we studied. During our unit on China, I remember him telling us stories about his trip there, including the exciting fruit he ate, something he called "lee-chee."

Jordin Isip

I knew what he was talking about. I loved lychee. Available only about six weeks a year and costing up to $8 a pound, lychees were a rare treat in my family. After my parents divorced, my father would take me to San Francisco's Chinatown during summer visits, where we bought bunches of the syrupy sweet fruit with translucent flesh. Sitting in the park, cracking the lychee's rough, deep red skin and feeling its juices drip down our chins and fingers, my father told me stories of his childhood in Hawaii, about how he would sneak into the lychee groves to get the precious fruit at the risk of getting shot by farmers guarding their crops.

Sitting in the park, cracking the lychee's rough, deep red skin and feeling its juices drip down our chins and fingers, my father told me stories of his childhood in Hawaii.

But in my family, we said it differently. We called it "LIE-chee." Knowing that the translation between Chinese and English is difficult and imprecise, I raised my hand and tried to tell Mr. Anderson how my family pronounced it. He wasn't having it. This white teacher had been to China and knew better. So he told me (and the class) that I was simply wrong, that I didn't know what I was talking about. Never mind my memories of lychee, never mind my father's stories, and never mind that my Chinese grandmother, aunts, uncles, and cousins all pronounced it LIE-chee.

Now that I have been both a high school teacher and a teacher of teachers, when I reflect back on his class, I see that Mr. Anderson taught us some basic lessons about multicultural education, albeit by negative example. For instance, in Mr. Anderson's class, student knowledge about communities, cultures, and diversity didn't matter, especially if it contradicted his own. Further, Mr. Anderson's contempt for student knowledge revealed no sense of curiosity about the experiences and stories that might lead to a different perspective than his. The lesson to learn here is that multicultural education should be grounded in the lives of students, not only because such a perspective provides a diversity of viewpoints, but also because it honors students' identities and experiences.

Another related lesson to take away from Mr. Anderson's negative example is that multicultural education should seek to draw on the knowledge, perspectives, and voices of the actual communities being studied. In Mr. Anderson's class, my own authentic cultural knowledge and perspective as a Chinese American had no value, and he actively disregarded my own lived experiences. Again, Mr. Anderson was contemptuous of student knowledge and he disregarded the importance of building from kids' lives and prior experiences.

Mr. Anderson's example also teaches us that, because it is connected to students' lives, multicultural education has to be based on dialogue—both amongst students and between students and teachers. As students in Mr. Anderson's class we were always on the outside looking in, and he and the textbooks were the sole authorities. There was no dialogue, only monologue.

The final lesson to draw from Mr. Anderson is that, when classes are not grounded in the lives of students, do not include the voices and knowledge of communities being studied, and are not based in dialogue, they create environments where not only are white students miseducated, but students of color feel as if their very identities are under attack.

Multicultural Education on the Down Low

I had to get my real multicultural education on the down low, outside of classes like Mr. Anderson's. I went to Garfield High School, located in Seattle's historically African American neighborhood, the Central District. Garfield has been known for many years as Seattle's "black high school," and back in the 1970s there was a strong Black Panther Party presence both in the neighborhood and in the school itself. Garfield, always a basketball powerhouse, also boasts a rich connection to African American culture and music, with names like Quincy Jones and Jimi Hendrix still haunting the hallways.

By the time I got there in the late 1980s, Garfield had become a flagship for the Seattle Public Schools. It housed the district's AP program, maintained a world-renowned jazz band, was the district's science magnet high school, and provided a model of Seattle's desegregation busing system (of which I was a part). Totaling around 1,600 students, Garfield's student body hovered at about 50 percent African American and 50 percent white, with a few Latinos and Asian Americans like myself sprinkled in.

Given Garfield's history, position in the community, and commitment to racially integrated education, you might think that real multicultural education took place in most classes. Sadly, it didn't. There was one teacher, Mr. Davis, who taught two "secret" classes at my school: one section of Harlem Renaissance and one section of African Studies.

To get into Mr. Davis' classes, you first had to learn (by word of mouth) the true content of his classes, which were listed plainly in the schedule as Language Arts 10b and Social Studies elective. Second you had to convince your counselor that yes, you really did want to be in Mr. Davis' class, that yes, you really knew what you were getting into.

For the first time in my schooling experience, I was one of only two non-African American students in a class. In Mr. Davis'

For the first time in my schooling experience, I was one of only two non-African American students in a class.

classes we looked at the politics of Blackness through the poetry and literature of the Harlem Renaissance and hashed through segregation, desegregation, and African American identity in U.S. history. We read about how Greek civilization was built upon a legacy of knowledge that had already existed in Egypt. And then we learned that Egypt wasn't really "Egypt." From an African-centric standpoint it was actually called Kemet, with its own rich cultural worldview, symbolism, and creation stories.

I sat in this decidedly African-centric, predominantly African American cultural space, trying to sort through my own cultural identity as a mixed white and Chinese American young man, my own connection with African American culture, and my own sense of education and the politics of race. And I'm sure my presence also left many of my African American classmates questioning. I mean, what was this half-Asian kid doing in the black studies classes anyway? Why does he care? Isn't race and racism mainly about black and white? Do Chinese Americans, let alone half-bloods, even count as people of color? Struggling with these questions (and many more), all of us were asked to stretch.

To be sure, an African-centric course cannot be "multicultural" in and of itself. African-centered is just that, African-centered. But in the real-life context of a school like Garfield, Mr. Davis' classes embodied multicultural education: it was grounded in the lives, identities, and histories of students; it provided critical and alternative perspectives on history that we were not getting in our other classes; and it openly addressed the issue of racism.

> Multicultural education is fundamentally based in a critique of school knowledge that has historically been Eurocentric.

Again, now having worked with very diverse populations of students, I see that Mr. Davis' classes also taught me about multicultural education. For instance, his class illustrated how multicultural education is fundamentally based in a critique of school knowledge that has historically been Eurocentric. For example, it was in his class that we learned that "civilization" did not start in Europe, that other nations and cultures had great civilizations that pre-dated their Western counterpart. Challenging such Eurocentrism also spoke to the cultural and political imperative to resist Eurocentric curriculum, as Mr. Davis saw his course as a positive and supportive intervention in the identity development and self-esteem for the students in his classes. Finally, inherent in Mr. Davis' instruction is the lesson that it is important to critically question what textbooks and teachers say about the world.

Mr. Davis' classes also offer a lesson on how multicultural education invites students to engage with real social issues. In his courses my classmates and I connected our burgeoning historical understandings of race and racism to contemporary issues. We argued about interracial dating, black nationalism, racism, and education. In this way, multicultural education inherently connects learning to the world outside of our classrooms.

Another lesson to be gained from Mr. Davis' example is that multicultural education creates a space for students to meaningfully engage with each other. It was through such struggle over social and political issues that I developed substantive relationships with my African American classmates—relationships that I do not think could have developed in my other, more Eurocentric classes that were either populated predominantly by white kids or simply did not create the space to really engage students of color.

Finally, it is crucial to acknowledge that Mr. Davis' classes helped me learn that multicultural education is rigorous. In African Studies and Harlem Renaissance we read serious texts like George G.M. James' *Stolen Legacy* to learn about ancient Egypt's effect on ancient Greek civilization, or Joel Augustus Rogers' *From Superman to Man* to gain historical perspectives of U.S. race relations.

Multicultural Education and Rigor

The connection between multicultural education and rigor is important because one of the consistent critiques against multicultural education is that it isn't "real" education, that it isn't rigorous. However, the idea that multicultural education represents a lowering of standards or represents a neglect of academic rigor is false.

Let's compare Mr. Davis' and Mr. Anderson's classes. As with most "rigorous," upper-track classes, the central pieces of rigor I remember from Mr. Anderson's "honors" World History class consisted of an immense amount of textbook reading, chapter questions, and a research paper. And such courses are rigorous in particular ways. Certainly they have formal and strict requirements, and Mr. Anderson's class, like most others of its kind, was demanding in terms of workload. We were always kept busy.

Now as a professor of education, when I critically reflect on these types of "honors" or "advanced" classes, I think that, although they require significant amounts of work, they are not necessarily *intellectually* rigorous. Instead it often asks for memorization and textbook reading comprehension, not critical analysis. Knowledge is multifaceted and simply reading tough books does not mean that students are engaged in understanding the complexities of any particular historical episode or time period.

The idea that multicultural education represents a lowering of standards or represents a neglect of academic rigor is false.

Take teaching about the U.S. war with Mexico, for instance. A typical class would focus solely on the actions of governments—U.S. and Mexican alike. A multicultural perspective asks about the Irish American soldiers, Mexican women in conquered territories, black and white abolitionists who opposed the war, soldiers who embraced and also rejected the war, Mexican cadets who jumped to their death rather than surrender to invading U.S. troops, etc. A multicultural perspective is not only inherently more interesting, it is also more complex—and more fully truthful, if we dare use that word. Further, academic rigor is impossible without the multiple perspectives that multicultural education provides because without it, we miss huge pieces of history, culture, and society—leaving huge gaps in our knowledge about the world.

A multicultural perspective is not only inherently more interesting, it is also more complex—and more fully truthful, if we dare use that word.

Mr. Anderson's class miseducated us about the world too. For instance, in addition to the textbook readings for our unit on Africa, Mr. Anderson had us watch the movie *The Gods Must Be Crazy*. In this movie an African San is befuddled by Western technology and makes a buffoon of himself. Through my 9th-grade eyes, I saw the colonizers' view of the African-native-as-primitive, of darker peoples as idiotic and childlike.

Mr. Anderson didn't really teach about this film. He just showed it as an "entertaining" way for 14-year-olds to learn about Africa. So we never learned about how such a film could justify the system of apartheid in South Africa by portraying the San people as incompetent and unable to be incorporated into a democratic society. We never learned how such a film might rationalize the idea that the San needed "benevolent" white rulers to take care of them.

My African Studies course with Mr. Davis, however, was different, and despite its tag as being "regular," its perspective made it more intellectually rigorous than my "honors" history classes because, as all good multicultural education should do, we were asked to consider the variety of our own experiences and relate them to the complexities of history and society.

I remember struggling to write a paper for Mr. Davis that explained the relationship between race, poverty, and education in the United States. While in many ways this topic was probably beyond my mid-teen reach, in many ways it wasn't: The relationship between race, poverty, and education was something I was trying to understand (and still am), and writing a paper about it pushed me in my writing and my thinking. Assignments like this made me think hard in my "regular" African Studies class, whereas my "honors" World History class asked for very little thinking at all—just lots of work. More importantly, this assignment illustrates how a multicultural curriculum honors the experiences and curiosity of students so that their own questions about these issues are encouraged and honored as a way of fueling their academic inquiry.

This rigorous need for multicultural perspectives raises another critical lesson: Multicultural education cannot be relegated to individual classes. Mr. Davis' classes were important because they existed within a context where most other classes were Eurocentric, so they became spaces of multicultural resistance. But ideally all classes at Garfield—social studies, language arts, math, science, art, etc.—should have taken multicultural education seriously if they really wanted to be rigorous and if they really wanted to engage all students in learning. For that matter, all classes for all students, from prekindergarten on, should take multicultural education seriously. Then, students would generally be in a position to more actively and collectively resist classroom colonization and smarter in that they could take up a more critical analysis of all course content.

Multicultural education cannot be relegated to individual classes.

The Struggle for Multicultural Education

Sadly, college-bound students at Garfield certainly didn't fight to get Mr. Davis' classes on their transcripts. Instead they would forego Harlem Renaissance and African Studies in order to stay in AP and on the honors track. Things haven't changed all that much since I was in high school, because in today's context of high-stakes education, multicultural education is still viewed as not academically rigorous, not "real" education, and not worthy of being included in the curriculum in its own right.

The lowly status of multicultural curriculum has also meant a constant fight to justify its existence. Take again for instance the African Studies class at Garfield. Ten years after I had walked the halls as a student, I returned to Garfield as a teacher. To my great pleasure, African Studies was given to me as part of my teaching load.

Not surprisingly, I found that many teachers in the social studies department openly sneered at the African Studies course, and the department chair—seeing that Mr. Davis had left to become a principal—thought it would be a good chance to get rid of the class. In his mind, it had no value. What the department chair couldn't see, and what I knew as a legacy student of that very same class, was that African Studies created an irreplaceable space

Multicultural education is rooted in an anti-racist struggle over whose knowledge and experiences should be included in the curriculum.

to engage in the politics of Blackness that existed nowhere else at Garfield. Further, African Studies was an irreplaceable space where students' cultures were respected, where students learned to think in terms of multiple social experiences, where traditional narratives and explanations were complicated by race and culture. After a protracted and sometimes nasty fight, the African Studies course survived (and I enjoyed teaching it), but there shouldn't have been a fight to begin with. My experience fighting for African Studies taught me another lesson: Multicultural education is rooted in an anti-racist struggle over whose knowledge and experiences should be included in the curriculum.

The Need for Multicultural Education

I think the biggest lesson in multicultural education I've learned from my experiences as a student, teacher, and teacher educator, is that it is a valuable and necessary orientation towards teaching and learning that needs to be embraced by all educators. Every institution I've ever worked in has been resistant to multicultural education in some way, shape, or form, and I'm tired of having to justify it, tired of having to prove its worth. As a person of color I take offense at the idea that my history, my perspective on the world as an individual and a representative member of a community does not matter.

As a teacher educator I encounter on a daily basis the consequences of schooling that is not multicultural. Many of my students know little of the histories and cultures of the students that they will end up teaching. What's more, they don't know that they don't know, and I fear that many of them will enter communities of color as an army of Mr. Andersons, damaging the young people they're trusted to educate. Hopefully, the lessons in multicultural education they learn in my classes will help them become more like Mr. Davis, teachers who can lead a struggle against racism in their classrooms.

CHAPTER TWENTY-EIGHT

Brown Kids Can't
Be in Our Club

By Rita Tenorio

A few years before I became the princpal at La Escuela Fratney in Milwaukee, I sat down one day with seven of the children in my 1st-grade class. It was early in the year and we were getting to know each other. We talked about how we were alike, how we were different. "Our skin is different," one of the children said. I asked everyone to put their hands together on the table, so we could see all the different colors.

One of my African American students, LaRhonda*, simply would not. Scowling, she slid her hands beneath the table top, unwilling to have her color compared to the others.

It was a reaction I had seen before. I teach at La Escuela Fratney, an ethnically diverse school in a racially mixed working-class

IStockphoto

Milwaukee neighborhood. My students typically include black kids, white kids, and Latinos. They have many things in common. Recess is their favorite time of day. Friendships are a priority. They want to "belong" to a group and they are very conscious of where they fit in a social sense.

And they all "know" that it is better to be light-skinned than dark-skinned.

Even though my students have only six or seven years of life experience by the time they reach my classroom, the centuries-old legacies of bias and racism in our country have already made an impact on their lives. I have seen fair-skinned children deliberately change places in a circle if African American children sit down next to them. An English speaker won't play with a Latino child because, he says, "He talks funny." On the playground, a group of white girls won't let their darker-skinned peers join in their games, explaining matter-of-factly: "Brown kids can't be in our club."

As teachers, we have to acknowledge that we live in a racist society and that children typically mirror the attitudes of that society. Between the ages of 2 and 5, children not only become aware of racial differences, but begin to make judgments based on that awareness. They do this even though they may not be able to understand, in an intellectual way, the complexities of race and bias as issues.

Teachers have a responsibility to recognize the influence of racism on themselves and their students. And we can help children learn the skills and strategies they will need to counteract it in their lives. At Fratney, our 1st-grade teaching teams have put those ideas at the center of our practice.

Are They Too Young for This?

Many people would say that children at this age are too young to deal with these serious issues. I too had real questions at first about what was actually possible with young children. Can you have "real" conversations with 6-year-olds about power, privilege, and racism in our society? Can you make them aware of the effects that racism and injustice have in our lives? Can they really understand their role in the classroom community?

The answer to all of these questions is "yes." Even very young children can explore and understand the attitudes they and their classmates bring to school each day. They have real issues and opinions to share, and many, many questions of their own to ask. In this way they can begin to challenge some of the assumptions

> *Even though my students have only six or seven years of life experience by the time they reach my classroom, the centuries-old legacies of bias and racism in our country have already made an impact on their lives.*

that influence their behavior toward classmates who don't look or talk the same way they do.

Children at this age can explore rules and learn about collecting data, making inferences, and forming conclusions. They can compare and contrast the experiences of people and think about what it means. They can, that is, if they are given the opportunity.

At Fratney, which serves 400 students from kindergarten through 5th grade, we discuss issues of social justice with all of our students. During the past several years, those of us teaching 1st grade have developed a series of activities and projects that help us to discuss issues of race and social justice in a meaningful, age-appropriate way.

We strive to build classroom community by learning about each other's lives and families. We ask our students to collect and share information about their families and ancestry. For example, we might talk about how they got their names, how their families came to live in Milwaukee, which holidays they celebrate and how. And at every step we help the children to explore the nature of racial and cultural differences and to overcome simplistic notions of "who's better" or who is "like us" and who isn't.

These activities include:

Me Pockets

This is always a class favorite. Each child takes home a letter-sized clear plastic sleeve, the kind used to display baseball cards. We ask students to fill the pockets with photos, pictures, drawings, or anything else that will help us know more about them and the things that are important in their lives. They return the pockets within a week and put them into a three-ring binder that becomes the favorite classroom book to read and re-read.

The individual pockets reflect the cultural and socioeconomic diversity of the families. Some students put lots of photos or computer images in their pockets. Others cut pictures out of magazines or make drawings. Our experience is that every family is anxious to share in some way, and family members take time to help their children develop the project.

If someone doesn't bring their Me Pocket sheet back, the teachers step in to help them find pictures or make the drawings they need to add their page to the binder.

I'm always amazed at how quickly the children learn the details about each other's lives from this project: who has a pet,

> *Children at this age can explore rules and learn about collecting data, making inferences, and forming conclusions.*

who takes dance classes, who likes to eat macaroni and cheese. The children know there are differences among them, but they also love to share the things that are alike.

"Look, Rachel has two brothers, just like me."

"I didn't know that Jamal's family likes to camp. We do too!"

Each of the teachers also completes a Me Pocket sheet. The students love looking at the picture of me as a first grader, seeing my husband and children, and learning that chocolate cake is my favorite food.

Partner Questions

Each day we take time to teach the social skills of communicating ideas with others and listening to another person's perspective.

Each day we take time to teach the social skills of communicating ideas with others and listening to another person's perspective. We use this time to "practice" those skills with role-playing activities and problem-solving situations they or we bring to the group. For example, we might ask such questions as: What is the meanest thing anyone has ever said to you? Why do you think some people like to use put-downs? The children take a few minutes to talk about this with a partner. Afterwards some are willing to share with the whole group. We might then role-play the situation as a group and look for ways to respond, such as speaking back to insults.

"Someone Special"

By the end of October, during the time of Halloween, Día de los Muertos, and All Souls' Day, we learn about how people remember their ancestors and others who have died or who are far away. We set up a table and students are encouraged to bring in pictures or artifacts to display. They bring a remarkable variety of things: jewelry, a trophy won by a departed relative, a postcard that person sent them, or perhaps the program from a funeral. And they bring many, many stories. Again, the teachers also participate and share stories of those who have gone before us. We get great responses from our students and from their families.

Let's Talk About Skin

Another important conversation I have with my students focuses on the varieties of skin color we have in our group. Usually when we begin this discussion, some children are uncomfortable about saying "what they are" or describing the color of their skin. In particular, children with very dark skin—like LaRhonda, who would not even put her hands on the table—are often reluctant to join in. Meanwhile, the white kids often boast about being "pink." Though we've never talked about this in class before, there is definitely a strong implication that it is better to be lighter.

Many children are amazed that this topic is put out on the table for discussion. The looks in their eyes, their frequent reluctance to begin the discussion, tell me that this is a very personal topic.

As part of the lesson, we ask the students if they have ever heard anyone say something bad or mean about another person's skin color. The hands shoot up.

"My mom says that you can't trust black people."

"My sister won't talk to the Puerto Rican kids on the bus."

"Mara said that I couldn't play, that I was too black to be her friend."

They continue to raise their hands and this conversation goes on for a while. We talk about ways we've heard others use people's skin color to make fun of them or put them down. We talk about what to do in those situations.

As we continue to discuss issues of race, we teachers often introduce our personal experiences. I tell them about the first time I realized that black and white people were treated differently. I share my experience being one of the few Latinas in my school. And we try to ask questions that really intrigue the students, that invite them to try and look at things with a different perspective, to learn something new about the human experience and be open-minded to that idea: Do people choose their colors? Where do you get your skin color? Is it better to be one color than another? Lots of our conversations revolve around a story or a piece of literature.

With a little work, we can expand this discussion of skin color in ways that incorporate math lessons, map lessons, and other curricular areas. We've done surveys to see how many of our ancestors came from warm places or cold places. We ask children to interview their relatives to find out where the family came from. We create a bulletin board display that we use to compare and learn about the huge variety of places our students' relatives are from. We graph the data of whose family came from warm places, who from cold, who from both, or don't know.

Skin Color and Science

Our class discussions of skin color set the stage for lots of "scientific" observations.

As part of the lesson, we ask the students if they have ever heard anyone say something bad or mean about another person's skin color.

For example, I bring in a large variety of paint chips from a local hardware store. The students love examining and sorting the many shades of beige and brown. It takes a while for them to find the one that is most like their own skin color.

In the story *The Colors of Us*, by Karen Katz, Lena learns from her mother that "brown" is a whole range of colors. Like the characters in the story, we take red, yellow, black, and white paint and mix them in various combinations until we've each found the color of our own skin. Then we display our "research" as part of our science fair project.

In another exercise, inspired by Sheila Hamanaka's *All the Colors of the Earth*, students are asked to find words to describe the color of their skin, and to find something at home that matches their skin color. Then we display the pieces of wood and fabric, the little bags of cinnamon and coffee, the dolls and ceramic pieces that "match" us.

As we continue these explorations, dealing concretely with a topic that so many have never heard discussed in such a manner, students begin to see past society's labels. It is always amazing to children that friends who call themselves "black," for example, can actually have very light skin. Or that children who perceive themselves as "Puerto Rican" can be darker than some of the African American children.

Writing About Our Colors

As children begin to understand the idea of internalizing another's point of view, they can apply that understanding by examining different ideas and alternatives to their own experiences. As they learn to express themselves through reading and writing, they can learn to challenge stereotypes and speak back to unfair behavior and comments.

Once students have had a chance to reflect on skin color, they write about it. Annie wrote: "I like my skin color. It is like peachy cream." James wrote: "My color is the same as my dad's. I think the new baby will have this color too." And Keila wrote: "When I was born, my color was brown skin and white skin mixed together."

When LaRhonda wrote about mixing the colors to match her skin, she said: "We put black, white, red, and yellow [together]. I like the color of my skin." How far she had come since the day she would not show us her hands.

As they learn to express themselves through reading and writing, they can l earn to challenge stereotypes and speak back to unfair behavior and comments.

Tackling Issues

These activities have an impact. Parents have spoken to us about the positive impression that these activities have made on the children. Many children have taken their first steps toward awareness of race. They are not afraid to discuss it. They now have more ways in which to think about and describe themselves.

Yet these activities are no guarantee that children have internalized anti-racist ideas. So much depends on the other forces in their lives. We are still working on making these activities better: doing them sooner in the year, integrating them into other subjects, deepening the conversations, finding other stories or activities to support them. Each year's group is different, and we need to incorporate their experiences and understandings. I learn something new every time. They challenge my consciousness too.

We rely on our schools to be the place for a multicultural, multiracial experience for our children. We want to believe that learning together will help our students to become more understanding and respectful of differences. Yet so often we do not address these issues head-on. It is unlikely that sensitivity and tolerance will develop, that children will bridge the gaps they bring to school from their earliest days, without specific instruction.

Personally, I want to see more than tolerance developed. I want children to see themselves as the future citizens of this city. I want them to gain the knowledge to be successful in this society. Beyond that, though, I want them to understand that they have the power to transform society.

When students see connections between home and school, when lessons challenge them to look at the issue of race from multiple perspectives, we take the first steps in this process.

It is unlikely that sensitivity and tolerance will develop, that children will bridge the gaps they bring to school from their earliest days, without specific instruction.

What Color
Is Beautiful?

By Alejandro Segura-Mora

Most of my kindergarten students have already been picked up by their parents. Two children still sit on the mat in the cafeteria lobby, waiting. Occasionally, one of them stands to look through the door's opaque windows to see if they can make out a parent coming. Ernesto*, the darkest child in my class, unexpectedly shares in Spanish, "Maestro, my mom is giving me pills to turn me white."

"Is that right?" I respond, also in Spanish. "And why do you want to be white?"

"Because I don't like my color," he says.

"I think your color is very beautiful and you are beautiful as well," I say. I try to conceal how his comment saddens and alarms me, because I want to encourage his sharing.

"I don't like to be dark," he explains.

His mother, who is slightly darker than he, walks in the door. Ernesto rushes to take her hand and leaves for home.

Childhood Memories

Ernesto's comment takes me back to an incident in my childhood. My mom is holding me by the hand, my baby brother in her other arm, my other three brothers and my sister following along. We are going to church and I am happy. I skip all the way, certain that I have found a solution to end my brothers' insults.

"You're a monkey," they tell me whenever they are mad at me. I am the only one in my family with curly hair. In addition to "monkey," my brothers baptize me with other derogatory names—such as Simio (Ape), Chineca (a twisted and distorted personification of being curly, and even more negative by the feminization with an "a" at the end), and Urco, the captain of all apes in the television program *The Planet of the Apes*.

As we enter the church, my mom walks us to the front of the altar to pray before the white saints, the crucified white Jesus, and his mother. Before that day, I hadn't bought into the God story. After all, why would God give a child curly hair? But that day there is hope. I close my eyes and pray with a conviction that would have brought rain to a desert.

"God, if you really exist, please make my hair straight," I pray. "I hate it curly and you know it's hard. So at the count of three, please take these curls and make them straight. One, two, three."

With great suspense I open my eyes. I reach for my hair. Anticipating the feel of straight hair, I stroke my head, only to feel my curls. Tears sting my eyes. As I head for one of the benches, I whisper, "I knew God didn't exist."

For Ernesto, the pill was his God; for me, God was my pill. I wonder how Ernesto will deal with the failure of his pill.

A Teachable Moment

I can't help but wonder how other teachers might have dealt with Ernesto's comments. Would they have ignored him? Would they have dismissed him with a, "Stop talking like that!" Would they have felt sorry for him because they agree with him?

As teachers, we are cultural workers, whether we are aware of it or not. If teachers don't question the culture and values being

As teachers, we are cultural workers, whether we are aware of it or not.

promoted in the classroom, they socialize their students to accept the uneven power relations of our society along lines of race, class, gender, and ability. Yet teachers can—and should—challenge the values of white privilege and instead promote values of self-love.

Young students, because of their honesty and willingness to talk about issues, provide many opportunities for teachers to take seemingly minor incidents and turn them into powerful teaching moments. I am grateful for Ernesto's sincerity and trust in sharing with me. Without knowing it, Ernesto opened the door to a lively dialogue in our classroom about white privilege.

To resurface the dialogue on beauty and skin color, I chose a children's book which deals with resistance to white privilege (a genre defined, in part, by its scarcity). The book is *Niña Bonita*, written by Ana María Machado and illustrated by Rosana Fara (1996, available in English from Kane/Miller Book Publishers). The book tells the story of an albino bunny who loves the beauty of a girl's dark skin and wants to find out how he can get black fur. I knew the title of the book would give away the author's bias, so I covered the title. I wanted to find out, before reading the book, how children perceived the cover illustration of the dark-skinned girl.

"If you think this little girl is pretty, raise your hand," I said. Fourteen hands went up.

"If you think she is ugly, raise your hand," I then asked. Fifteen voted for ugly, among them Ernesto.

I was not surprised that half my students thought the little girl was ugly. Actually, I was expecting a higher number, given the tidal wave of white dolls which make their way into our classroom on Fridays, our Sharing Day, and previous comments by children in which they indicated that dark is ugly.

After asking my students why they thought the girl on the book cover was ugly, one student responded, "Because she has black color and her hair is really curly." Ernesto added, "Because she is black-skinned."

"But you are dark like her," Stephanie quickly rebutted to Ernesto, while several students nodded in agreement. "How come you don't like her?"

"Because I don't like black girls," Ernesto quickly responded. Several students affirmed Ernesto's statement with "yes" and "that's right."

"All children are pretty," Stephanie replied in defense.

Carlos then added, "If you behave good, then your skin color can change."

Young students, because of their honesty and willingness to talk about issues, provide many opportunities for teachers to take seemingly minor incidents and turn them into powerful teaching moments.

"Are you saying that if you are good, you can turn darker?" I asked, trying to make sure the other students had understood what he meant.

"White!" responded Carlos.

"No, you can't change your color," several students responded. "That can't be done!"

"How do you know that your color can change?" I asked, hoping Carlos would expand on his answer.

"My mom told me," he said.

"And would you like to change your skin color?" I asked.

"No," he said. He smiled shyly as he replied and I wondered if he may have wished he was not dark-skinned but didn't want to say so.

Carlos's mother's statements about changing skin color reminded me of instances in my family and community when a new baby is born. "Oh, look at him, how pretty and blond-looking he is," they say if the baby has European features and coloring. And if the babies came out dark, like Ernesto? Then the comments are, "¡Ay! Pobrecito, salió tan prietito"—which translated means, "Poor baby, he came out so dark."

I hear similar comments from co-workers in our school's staff lounge. A typical statement: "Did you see Raul in my class? He has the most beautiful green eyes."

It is no surprise that so many students must fight an uphill battle against the values of white privilege; still other students choose not to battle at all.

It is no surprise that so many students must fight an uphill battle against white supremacist values; still other students choose not to battle at all.

Challenging the Students

In an attempt to have students explain why they think the black girl in *Niña Bonita* is ugly, I ask them, "If you think she is ugly for having dark skin, why do you think her dark skin makes her ugly?"

"I don't like the color black," volunteers Yvette, "because it looks dark and you can't see in the dark."

"Because when I turn off the light," explains Marco, "everything is dark and I am afraid."

Although most of my kindergarten students could not articulate the social worthlessness of being dark-skinned in this society, I was amazed by their willingness to struggle with an issue that so many adults, teachers included, ignore, avoid, and pretend does not exist. At the same time, it was clear that many of my students had already internalized the values of white privilege.

At the end of our discussion, I took another vote to see how students were reacting to *Niña Bonita*; I also wanted to ask individual students why they had voted the way they had. This second time, 18 students said the black girl was pretty and only 11 said she was ugly. Ernesto still voted for "ugly."

"Why do you think she is ugly?" I asked, but this time the students didn't volunteer responses. Perhaps they were sensing that I did not value negative answers as much as I did comments by students who fell in love with *Niña Bonita*. In their defense of dark skin, some students offered explanations such as, "Her color is dark and pretty," "All girls are pretty," and "I like the color black."

Our discussion of *Niña Bonita* may have led four students to modify their values of beauty and ugliness in relation to skin color. Maybe these four students just wanted to please their teacher. What is certain, however, is that the book and our discussion caused some students to look at the issue in a new way.

Equally important, *Niña Bonita* became a powerful tool to initiate discussion on an issue which will affect my students, and myself, for a lifetime. Throughout the school year, the class continued our dialogue on the notions of beauty and ugliness. (One other book that I have found useful to spark discussion is The Ugly Duckling. This fairy tale, which is one of the most popular among early elementary teachers and children, is often used uncritically. It tells the story of a little duckling who is "ugly" because his plumage is dark. Happiness comes only when the duckling turns into a beautiful, spotless white swan. I chose to use this book in particular because the plot is a representation of the author's value of beauty as being essentially white. I want my students to understand that they can disagree with and challenge authors of books, and not receive their messages as god-given.)

When I have such discussions with my students, I often feel like instantly including my opinion. But I try to allow my students to debate the issue first. After they have spoken, I ask them about their views and push them to clarify their statements. One reason I like working with children is that teaching is always a type of experiment, because the students constantly surprise me with their candid responses. These responses then modify how I will continue the discussion.

I struggle, however, with knowing that as a teacher I am in a position of power in relation to my young students. It is easy to make students stop using the dominant ideology and adopt the ideology of another teacher, in this case my ideology. In this society, in which we have been accustomed to deal with issues in either-or terms, children (like many adults) tend to adopt one ideology in place of another, but not necessarily in a way in which

I struggle, however, with knowing that as a teacher I am in a position of power in relation to my young students.

they actually think through the issues involved. I struggle with how to get my students to begin to look critically at the many unequal power relations in our society, relations which, even at the age of 5, have already shaped even whether they love or hate their skin color and consequently themselves.

At the end of our reading and discussion of the book, I shared my feelings with my students.

"I agree with the author calling this girl 'Niña Bonita' because she is absolutely beautiful," I say. "Her skin color is beautiful."

While I caressed my face and kissed my cinnamon-colored hands several times happily and passionately, so that they could see my love for my skin color, I told them, "My skin color is beautiful, too."

I pointed to one of my light-complexioned students and said, "Gerardo also has beautiful skin color and so does Ernesto. But Gerardo cannot be out in the sun for a long time because his skin will begin to burn. I can stay out in the sun longer because my darker skin color gives me more protection against sunburn. But Ernesto can stay out in the sun longer than both of us because his beautiful dark skin gives him even more protection."

Despite our several class discussions on beauty, ugliness, and skin color Ernesto did not appear to change his mind. But, hopefully, his mind will not forget our discussions.

Ernesto probably still takes his magic pills, which, his mother later explained, are Flintstones Vitamin C. But I hope that every time he pops one into his mouth, he remembers how his classmates challenged the view that to be beautiful one has to be white. I want Ernesto to always remember, as will I, Lorena's comment: "Dark-skinned children are beautiful and I have dark skin, too."

* Names have been changed.

REFLECTION ACTIVITY

If this is an individual reflection, reflect on, and respond to, the following question.

If you are having a group discussion, write and share your individual response to the following question:

If your skin could speak, what would it say?

> *Despite our several class discussions on beauty, ugliness, and skin color Ernesto did not appear to change his mind. But, hopefully, his mind will not forget our discussions.*

Race: Some Teachable
–and Uncomfortable–
Moments

By Heidi Tolentino

"You can never know what it's like to be black," Carlen said sharply. The class went silent.

It was the fourth week of school and my juniors had just begun Sue Monk Kidd's *The Secret Life of Bees*. The novel is set in South Carolina in the mid-1960s. Something intrigued me about the perspective and the interracial relationships during such social upheaval. I chose this book because I love the characters, but also because it opens the door to discussions of racial justice—both historically and today.

Zach Bartel

> *One of my aims is to help students— especially my predominantly white students—recognize that life in our society confronts us with choices about whether and how we will act to counter racism.*

Growing up the only Asian American student in my community, I promised myself that I would never walk away from issues of race in a classroom setting. Thus, for my 11th-grade American Literature class, I choose multicultural literature that explores how race plays out in characters' lives, which I hope will in turn trigger discussions about how race plays out in *our* lives. One of my aims is to help students—especially my predominantly white students—recognize that life in our society confronts us with choices about whether and how we will act to counter racism. Too often, "racism" is reduced to how people treat one another on an interpersonal level. But I wanted them to think in broader terms about this country's history of legislated racism and the lingering patterns of inequality produced by that history. Some of this curriculum I can map out in advance in lesson plans, but part of this work is improvisational, and I know I need to be alert to the unpredictable, and sometimes uncomfortable, ways that students respond to this teaching.

As part of Portland's annual "curriculum camp," I worked with a group of high school teachers to create a unit around *The Secret Life of Bees* as a stepping stone for teaching about the human effects of institutionalized racism. I began the unit in my 11th-grade language arts classes at Portland's Cleveland High School, an urban school, but one that is over 75 percent European American. My students and I were early in the unit and just beginning our exploration of the impact of segregation in the lives of characters in the novel.

I opened our reading of *The Secret Life of Bees* by examining the dichotomy between the lives of whites and blacks in the South during the 1960s. I used Spike Lee's documentary *Four Little Girls* to help students gain insight into the chasm between the two communities. The film focuses on the bombing of the 16th St. Church in Birmingham, Ala., by white supremacists. This African American church was the center of civil rights activity there at the time of the bombing; the congregation was focused on helping black citizens gain the right to vote. Four young girls were murdered and Spike Lee focuses both on the repercussions of their deaths and how members of the community honored their lives through continuing civil rights activism. I chose this film to begin our unit because it is a powerful look at the blatant and violent racism that existed in 1965 and the struggle of African Americans and their white allies to fight for equal rights through their push to register African American voters. This was our starting point.

Shortly after watching the film, I initiated a discussion on a scene from *The Secret Life of Bees* in which Rosaline, one of the book's African American characters, is arrested while on her way to register to vote. We reflected on what we'd learned about work for voting rights, and I brought out copies of the Louisiana voting rights test given to African Americans who tried to register. [A PDF of this test is available at www.rethinkingschools.org/img/archive/17_02/Vote_test.pdf.]

We examined the tricks used in the test to keep African Americans from voting. I set the scene for them: "Imagine the fear that must have come with walking through that door, seeing the men with rifles standing a few feet behind you, and being handed a test, given 10 minutes to finish, and realizing that there was no way for you to pass." The students were appalled and kept pointing out new questions for us to examine and to try and decode them, and finally concluded that there was no way to decode trick questions. They couldn't take their eyes off the document.

As students put the tests away, I noticed Evan watching the clock from his desk, and I walked over and joked, "Stop counting down the minutes until you can run from the classroom." He shushed me and told me he was timing Jessie to see if she could finish the test in 10 minutes. She wrote frantically as she sat hunched over the paper. Without glancing up she said, "I want to know what it was like."

Suddenly, from across the room I heard, "You can never know what it's like. You will never understand." I turned quickly to see the fury on the face of one of my African American students as she glared at Jessie. Jessie looked up from the test, her pencil poised over the paper, and stared across the room.

I knew I had to make a choice quickly and either cut off discussion or open the door all the way. I decided to let it swing wide open. I said: "Talking about issues of race is so difficult. It's painful. Most adults don't want to touch it and will silence others when they do. But I've found that at our school students will discuss it, and I want to give you room to do so. You need to know that when you say something in this class, you have to be ready to explain yourself and have an open discussion about it as a class."

I motioned to the student who had confronted Jessie and said, "Carlen, tell us what you meant." I sat down at a student desk and the room went completely silent. The students sat rigidly at their desks, and the tension in the room was palpable.

Carlen took a deep breath, leaned forward, and said pointedly to Jessie who was seated directly across from her, "You can

> *Suddenly, from across the room I heard, 'You can never know what it's like. You will never understand.'*

never know what it's like to be black." Her face became more serious with each word, her tone angry. "I also don't understand why white people always say, 'I want to know what you're feeling and know what it feels like.' You don't want to know what it feels like to walk down the street and have white women clutch their purses. You don't want to know what it's like to be different every single day. You can't want to know because it's horrible."

Jessie pushed her blond hair back from her face and came right back at her and said, "But should I just remain ignorant then? Don't you think it's important for me to try and understand so that things can change? Race is a huge issue in 2006 and things haven't changed and I think we have to learn to change things." Her voice shook just the slightest bit, but she looked determined. No one made a sound.

"But there is nothing you can do to understand it. You are white and you will always be white and you won't ever know what it's like to be me." Carlen never shouted, but the intensity of her words filled the room.

"But don't I have to try? Shouldn't I try?" Jessie's voice sounded desperate.

"But, why? What will it change?" Carlen sat back in her seat and I felt 34 pairs of eyes turn my way.

The girls looked at each other for a moment, and I stepped toward them. I told them how much I appreciated their honesty and that I wanted them to feel that they could always stop our discussions to be honest about what they were feeling and thinking. I explained that we were not going to end this conversation for good—we would come back to it over and over so they should reflect on today and think about what they'd heard, felt, and thought. In retrospect, I wish I had stopped the class and had them journal about what occurred so that they could gain some perspective in the moment. But, if I had, the following discussion may never have happened.

Just as a student continued our read-aloud, I noticed a hand out of the corner of my eye. In my gut, I knew that something was coming.

The 'N' Word

I breathed a sigh of relief as we returned to the book and Rosaline, who was on her way to register to vote. Before we began to read, I explained that in the next section and in sections to come, the N-word would be used, and I wanted them to understand my policy around that word. I explained that because of its painful history, I ask students not to say the word when we read aloud. Instead, I have them say N. I also explained that we would naturally never use that word in the classroom at any time or toward anyone. Just as a student continued our read-aloud, I noticed a hand out of the corner of my eye. In my gut, I knew that something was coming. I'd known the student for two years and I knew his penchant for creating chaos, but I asked anyway. "Joe, do you have a question about the book?"

"No, but I have a question about the N-word. Why can black people use it and white people can't?"

Voices exploded from every corner of the room. "Are you a complete idiot for bringing that up now?" "Why are you trying to start something?" "What is wrong with you?"

I silenced the class and, with an inner grimace, thanked Joe for asking such a difficult question. What I really wanted to say was, "We don't have time for that question now. Just don't use the N-word." But I knew that this was a pivotal point in my year and if I wanted to push kids, I had to push myself. I asked the students to close their books.

Internally I was shaking. *What was I going to say? How did I let it get this far? Why wasn't I prepared for this?* I had five seconds to come up with something.

I explained to students that words that are historically used against a community in hate are often taken back by that community and turned around and used as words of power. I told them about my 6th-grade experience when I told my parents that we played "smear the queer" at school that day and how my parents almost jumped out of their chairs trying to cover my mouth. They explained why that word was never to be used again in our house because it was derogatory and disrespectful. I never forgot that, so when a friend of mine used "queer" years later when talking about her own community, I was taken aback. I asked her about its use and she explained how the gay and lesbian community had taken it back and used it as a word of power. I told kids that the N-word had an even more horrific past and so much pain connected to it and we had to be careful when dealing with it.

Joe was not appeased. He peered out at me from behind his glasses, "But why can't white people use it?"

I explained that even within the African American community, there was a split about whether or not to use the N-word and that the debate was heated and might always be that way. I noticed some students raising their hands, waving them around, and I had to make another split-second decision. I knew that they wanted to put their two cents in about the topic, and I was usually open to hearing what everyone had to say, but this was different. We had already had an intense blowup and two of my

Internally I was shaking. What was I going to say? How did I let it get this far? Why wasn't I prepared for this? I had five seconds to come up with something.

African American students looked uncomfortable and were not making eye contact with anyone.

I knew what it felt like to be one of the only students of color in a classroom and to have to wait for other students to make comments that were stereotypical and painful. I knew the feeling in the pit of my stomach as I waited for the comment and knew everyone was looking at me and waiting for my reaction. So I continued: "But if you are not a member of that community and have never had that word used against you in hate, you don't get to be part of the debate." The hands slowly lowered. "The African American community can discuss its use and debate its power, but we won't use that word here and I hope you won't use it anywhere."

The class was silent for a few moments. No one spoke or moved and they seemed to ponder what I was saying. In solidarity with my African American students, I had shut down a discussion that most of the class wanted to have, and I wasn't sure that I had made the right choice; I followed my instincts and they were the only thing that I had in that moment. There were only a few minutes left in class, and I reminded them that this would not be our last discussion and that they should continue to bring up these important questions. I reiterated their reading homework and the bell rang.

In solidarity with my African American students, I had shut down a discussion that most of the class wanted to have, and I wasn't sure that I had made the right choice.

Second Thoughts

Before Carlen left the room, Jessie walked over to her and said, "I'm sorry, Carlen. I hope you know that I wasn't trying to make you angry. I just really wanted to know what it felt like." Carlen simply nodded.

I asked Carlen to stay after class so that I could talk to her because she looked upset. After the students filed out, Carlen and I sat down and she began to cry. "I hate this. I hate having to deal with this. Why does it happen over and over?" I hugged her and we sat there for a moment. "Why do I always have to defend people of color? Why do I always have to explain?" I wanted to comfort Carlen, but my internal struggles were so heavy from such an intense class and the fear that I had done and said everything wrong, that I was at a loss for the right words.

I told Carlen, "I'm so proud of you for how openly you spoke and how willing you were to go to that place."

"But it didn't help. It never helps."

"I think it helped more than you will ever know. You got people thinking. But you didn't get to say everything, and I think you need to write about it. I want you to go home and write down everything that comes to mind about today. Reflect on it and get as angry as you need to. We'll meet tomorrow and talk about it again."

Carlen nodded and seemed to relax a bit. I sent her to the library to write and I went to my desk and put my head down. I was overwhelmed both emotionally and physically. I took a moment to email Carlen's mom because I wanted her to know what to expect when Carlen came home. I needed someone to talk to, and I needed some help in processing the day.

I found our school campus monitor, Joann. She had been my ally for the past three years. Like me, she had grown up mixed-race (African American and European American) and was also the only person of color in her community. We had spent hours talking about issues of race and how to work with students around those issues. Outside of school, she worked with African American writers in the community and African American at-risk youth and had amazing insight into how to confront difficult topics.

So I asked her, "When I encourage students to think about race in an almost all-white classroom, do I do it on the backs of my students of color? Do I force them to carry a load that is too heavy just to help white students begin to deal with their own issues of race? It was too heavy for me, so am I just doing the same thing to them?"

When I encourage students to think about race in an almost all-white classroom, do I do it on the backs of my students of color? Do I force them to carry a load that is too heavy just to help white students begin to deal with their own issues of race?

She reminded me that many, perhaps most, teachers feel so much discomfort confronting issues of race that they try to avoid it in their classes. I was talking about race in a way that not everyone was willing to take on and it was always going to be uncomfortable—for students *and* for me. But hadn't we said that we worked with kids because of what we both experienced in our youth? Students of color were forced to carry the load of racism every day because racism is entangled in every aspect of their lives. As educators we have to find ways to be their allies and be sensitive to how our work in the classroom affects them.

Carlen's Story

The next day, Carlen returned with a letter that she wrote to the class. I asked her if I could read it aloud and she agreed. The following is an edited version of what she wrote:

> Yesterday in class was very intense for everyone because of the subject matter and no matter how many times you can say you were comfortable sitting there, it is a fact that no one was. I don't regret anything I said yesterday because I meant every word. When Jessie said that she wanted to take the test to get a feel for what it was like, my

first reaction was to give her the benefit of the doubt and to think of it as just a statement. That was only half of my brain saying to keep my mouth shut … the impulse part of me always speaks up and I commented back as everyone knows. But I shouldn't have forgotten that Ms. T. makes everything a discussion. Although I am not the only person of color in the classroom, I always have something to say … and yesterday I did. Honestly, I was about to cry because I am tired of having to talk about racism and tired of having to feel this way once again because I always get offended. It hurts to have to think about the people out there that don't think you deserve to be in a classroom with them or to even be alive. It makes me feel like as a black person I am stripped of my rights, confidence, value, and self-image every time I have to open a book or see a movie about slavery or racism. After class and the discussion was over, Ms. T and I talked. I was really upset and I hate to admit it, but I cried. It didn't upset me that Jessie made that statement or that it became a big deal. I was upset because I will never be able to explain to anyone who isn't a person of color what it is really like. I can't just walk in a store and not be watched or followed. I can't make people feel safe around me when they assume that I want to steal something of theirs. I don't get automatic respect from white people; I have to try even harder because someone always has a stereotype. I make jokes all the time, but it's only because I wish it made me feel better about who I am and the race I am. I'm not saying I am ashamed and I have never wanted to be white. I just wish I didn't have to be so different or so judged. But everything having to do with the subject just makes me want to leave the room, but I can't let my people down by not getting through it. … Hopefully yesterday taught everyone something. But I also realize it only makes me stronger every day. I hope you all don't hate me and I hope you understand where I am coming from and who I am as a person. But, to end it with four encouraging words …

Peace and love, everyone,
Carlen

I talked to them about the idea of sympathy versus empathy—that it is not possible for us to feel what people in other times or circumstances felt, but that it's crucial that we attempt to understand how the conditions in people's lives affect them.

Students were silent after I finished reading. They applauded Carlen and thanked her for her writing. I talked to them about the idea of sympathy versus empathy—that it is not possible for us to *feel* what people in other times or circumstances felt, but that it's crucial that we attempt to *understand* how the conditions in people's lives affect them. And from this empathy we can consider ways that we can work to make the world a more just place for everyone.

Looking back, I wish that I had stopped myself before handing students my conclusions, and instead asked them to write a reflection about what had happened the day before. It could have been something that they wrote to me or something that they wrote to Carlen or to Jessie, which I would read and give to them later. I missed an opportunity to use their writing as a means for them to reflect on crucial issues. I want students to gain insight because *they* come to realizations, not because I tell them. This writing might not have elicited realizations, but it would have given them an opportunity to express what they felt and wondered, which could have led to a valuable discussion.

Jessie

After class I stopped Jessie as she was leaving and commended her for what she had said the day before. I told her that I knew how strong Carlen's anger must have felt, yet she did not back down. I was so impressed by her courage. She told me that she wished she hadn't started the conflict and that she hadn't meant anything by it, but she really wanted to explain what had motivated her. She gave me a thoughtful look before she left but didn't say any more.

My own role in prompting the blowup in class continued to gnaw at me. Hadn't I put Jessie in that situation? Hadn't I asked her, and the entire class, to "imagine the fear" of people who took the voting test? Hadn't Jessie simply done what I'd asked of all my students? Wasn't this attempt at historical imagination a crucial component of social justice teaching?

Perhaps. And yet Jessie's attempt to imagine the impact of racism in people's lives felt presumptuous to Carlen—like Jessie was proposing to understand something that her white privilege would never permit her truly to grasp.

But what about Jessie? How did the exchange affect her? Jessie and I didn't talk at length about the incident until the last day of school when I shared a draft of this article with her. Jessie explained that she felt "cornered" that day and had felt unable to express what she truly meant or felt. I think that she was politely telling me that I hadn't helped open a space for her to speak. I'd allowed the conversation to happen, but hadn't made it safe enough for her to express her intent or her confusion. She told me that she wished that she had been brave enough to speak her peace and help the class understand that she wasn't trying to "be black," but rather hoped to understand the severity of the situation so that she could better understand the extent to which institutionalized racism affects an individual's daily life.

> *My own role in prompting the blowup in class continued to gnaw at me.*

Jessie and Carlen's responses were both legitimate; how does my teaching honor each of these? This is an issue I'm still pondering.

Lessons Learned

I learned many things from this experience both about my teaching and about myself. I realized that I hadn't appreciated how uncomfortable it can be to teach about race, even though I considered myself an anti-racist teacher. It's one thing to map out lesson plans on a novel about the Civil Rights Movement, but students' reactions cannot be "scripted" in the same way that a lesson plan can be. Anti-racist teaching requires a willingness to go where students' responses take us. I have to be willing to go deeper than just interactions between characters in a book.

I realized that I have to keep myself from being bound by my own calendar and recognize when students are engaged. I have to remember that learning comes in the cracks when we are open and willing to deal with the uncomfortable conversations, the unpredictable questions, and the spontaneous outbursts. I can choose books, films, and other resources that create opportunities to discuss racism, but that is not enough without being open to allowing the tough conversations to happen. I have to be willing to make mistakes and not have all of the answers and let my students learn without me always leading them there. I have to be willing to deal with the unexpected if I want to truly be an anti-racist teacher.

Exploring
Race Relations

By Lisa Espinosa

"I don't want my daughter going to the high school with all the blacks."

That's what one of my students' mothers said when I first began teaching. While her comment took me aback, it wasn't the first time I had heard such racist comments from people in the Latino community.

Although I had not heard my own students, most of whom are Mexican Americans, make blatant racist comments, I had heard adults mention "loud black people" or express fear of black people moving into the community. My own parents were caring people, but they had biases and prejudices against blacks—

Edel Rodriguez

279

mostly stemming from lack of education and experience. I wondered how this racial divide affected my students.

I had chosen to teach in a predominantly Mexican community in Chicago because, as a Mexican American woman, I felt a connection to the students there. I hoped to use our shared culture as a means of validating my 7th graders' experiences. And I wanted to help my students become more politically aware by exposing them to issues and ideas I didn't encounter until college.

Comments such as the one my student's mother made reminded me that part of teaching my students about who they are in the world and how to overcome oppression means helping them see the commonalities between their struggles and those of other people of color.

But starting a dialogue about it with them wasn't easy. I did not want to disrespect my students' families, and I did not want my students to perceive me as doing so. I had struggled with this issue before and believed that by bringing in my personal experiences I could help my students feel more comfortable. But I must admit that sharing my own family's biases was not something I enjoyed. I couldn't help feeling as if talking about this made me somehow disloyal to my family—and maybe even my culture.

I am very proud of my Mexican American heritage, and I want to help foster that pride in my students. At the same time, I feel people of color need to unite to fight against the oppression and systemic racism in our society. In the current political climate—with attacks on public schools, immigrants, the poor, and new tax breaks for the wealthy—it is easy for people of color to narrow their vision and "fight for scraps" instead of joining together to fight against common oppression. In fact, those in power in our society count on the divisions among the powerless to maintain their positions.

In order to introduce my students to these concepts, I began integrating content into my curriculum that I believed would help them see connections between the struggles of blacks and Latinos in this country. I hoped that this would help them develop a sense of alliance between themselves and African Americans.

This is the story of some of the efforts I have made—sometimes only partially successful ones—to teach about issues of racism and to begin a conversation with my students about their own racial biases. These are not snapshots of amazing transformations among my students, but glimpses of efforts I've made to challenge my students—and myself—to examine a topic that often goes unacknowledged.

> *Part of teaching my students about who they are in the world and how to overcome oppression means helping them see the commonalities between their struggles and those of other people of color.*

A Process of Discovery

Examining racial biases has been a learning experience for my students, but it has been just as much a process of discovery for me. Growing up in a working-class Mexican immigrant household, I didn't listen to National Public Radio and read the *New York Times*. I didn't know about progressive causes because there was nobody to inform me about them. Unlike my parents, I was able to go to college. But, during college, I was also busy raising my children, so my main concern was making sure I stayed in school and graduated. Because of my background, I continually feel as if I'm trying to play catch up—even when it comes to knowing about my own cultural history. So, when I teach my students about the Chicano Movement, in many ways, I'm learning right along with them.

But whoever is doing the teaching, one thing is certain: Racism still affects the lives of African Americans and Latinos (as well as other people of color).

But whoever is doing the teaching, one thing is certain: Racism still affects the lives of African Americans and Latinos (as well as other people of color). According to *Minding the Gap*, a 2003 report funded by the Human Relations Foundation of Chicago, the Jane Addams Policy Initiative, and the Center for Urban Research and Learning at Loyola University, Latinos and African Americans in the Chicago area continue to face disparities in areas such as housing, economic opportunity, access to public transportation, and health care. In 2001, for example, African Americans in Chicago were five times more likely to be denied conventional mortgages than whites, while Latinos were two-and-a-half times more likely than whites to be denied. While income levels grew for all racial groups in Illinois between 1990 and 2000, Latino and African American men still earn less than half of their Asian and white counterparts. And Latinos (29 percent) and African Americans (24 percent) in Illinois have the highest rates of nonelderly persons without health insurance.

These numbers demonstrate that systemic injustices continue to affect both blacks and Latinos. But for a person growing up in a racially isolated neighborhood, it's sometimes hard to get that perspective. I grew up in a very segregated community in Chicago in the 1980s, and I don't remember ever having black classmates in the public elementary school I attended. Today many students in Chicago public schools face similar circumstances: In 2003, 50 years after the *Brown v. Board of Education* decision, 343 of Chicago's 602 schools are racially isolated, with 90 percent or more of their students sharing the same racial background, according to statistics from the Chicago Board of

When I asked my students how many of them had black friends, few raised their hands.

Education. When I asked my students how many of them had black friends, few raised their hands. Some had had African American teachers at school, but most have had little, if any, personal interaction with black people.

I tried to do three things in my class throughout the year: provide background knowledge about the history of racism and discrimination in this country and how that has led to the inequalities that exist today; look at current issues that affect people of color; and examine how the media creates and perpetuates negative images of people of color. Here I will focus on curriculum that I developed around certain resources that I gathered, most of which focus on the African American experience. Because I was doing this as part of my language arts class, where I need to cover many other topics, I can't always explore these topics as deeply as I would like.

One of the resources I used to discuss current issues affecting poor urban youth in our city is the book *Our America: Life and Death on the South Side of Chicago*, by LeAlan Jones and Lloyd Newman. This book, which grew out of two radio documentaries, examines life in a public housing development from the perspectives of two African American teenagers, 13-year-old LeAlan Jones and 14-year-old Lloyd Newman. (Along with the book we listened to the original radio documentary.) To provide some historical background about the Civil Rights Movement, I used the book *Freedom's Children: Young Civil Rights Activists Tell Their Own Stories*, by Ellen Levine. Finally, to examine how the media creates and perpetuates stereotypes of African Americans, we watched the documentary *Ethnic Notions* and read relevant articles in magazines and newspapers.

Our America

The book *Our America* was at the center of our unit. This book helped me raise some current issues that affect poor urban youth, such as inadequate housing, lack of community resources, and the prevalence of violence in their community. I required all my students to keep a dialogue journal. Through reading the journal entries I was able to get a sense of how they were connecting with LeAlan and Lloyd, the protagonists of the book. LeAlan and Lloyd write a lot about the lack of resources in their community and the biases that people who were not from their community have against them. These were things I knew my students could relate to. Many of them compared LeAlan's and Lloyd's environment with their own.

Several students wrote about the death of a 5-year-old boy in the book. Although I never forced my students to share their writing, as the unit progressed they became more comfortable sharing. Lilia,* who had recently been in a car accident that seriously injured her mother and killed her 3-year-old nephew, wrote, "It was sad because I've seen a person dead already and it reminded me of the accident that I was in." She read this aloud in class, and although it made me sad that she had experienced such a tragedy, I felt it could be healing for her to begin sharing some of her feelings about it.

Many students wanted to discuss how economic and social circumstances can lead children to resort to disruptive and even violent behavior. Angelica wrote, "This made me think that some kids were treated wrong and maybe in school they act all tough but what they really want is love and friendship." Although these reflections did not deal directly with race, the fact that my students were empathizing with LeAlan and Lloyd was an important beginning.

Ethnic Notions

To begin a conversation about the origins of stereotyping and misrepresentation of African Americans, we watched the documentary *Ethnic Notions*. Although the language of the video is difficult, with sufficient teacher guidance it can be a valuable teaching tool. It depicts different images that have been used throughout this country's history to represent African Americans. For example, blacks were either depicted as docile—"the happy slave"—as a defense of slavery, or as savages after the Civil War to justify the need to go back to the "good old times in the southern plantation."

Because the video *Ethnic Notions* is so complex, it is helpful to show it over the course of several days. I used words from the film as our weekly vocabulary, and wrote comprehension questions to help guide my students along the way. I also reviewed with them the different historical periods that the video references: antebellum (pre-Civil War), Civil War, Reconstruction, and Redemption.

To understand some of the concepts in *Ethnic Notions*, students need to have some familiarity with the idea of media representation. Since we had started the year looking at media depictions of men and women, my students were already familiar with these concepts. Before watching the video, I explained to my students that the video was going to explore different portrayals

Many students wanted to discuss how economic and social circumstances can lead children to resort to disruptive and even violent behavior.

of African Americans throughout different historical periods in this country. Although using this video was a time-consuming process, I believe that it is worth the time and energy, and it's a film we often refer back to throughout the year.

To connect the negative media images of African Americans in *Ethnic Notions* to current portrayals of Latinos in the media, I brought in copies of the "Ask Dame Edna" column in the February 2003 issue of *Vanity Fair* that had caused a stir among Latinos across the country. In the column, which is a spoof of advice columns, Dame Edna "jokingly" responds to a dilemma from a fictionalized reader who says she wants to learn French, but everyone keeps telling her to learn Spanish instead. Dame Edna responds, in part: "Who speaks [Spanish] that you are really desperate to talk to? The help? Your leaf blower?"

Like many other readers, my students did not think her comments were funny or appropriate. Some of them wrote letters to the editors of the magazine. Alberto wrote, "I think *Vanity Fair* was wrong in putting Selma Hayek on the cover of the magazine and at the same time printing Dame Edna's comment. They tried to get Hispanics to buy their magazine but at the same time, they insult Hispanics with such a racist comment. I believe *Vanity Fair* owes Hispanics an apology." Javier wrote, "When I read it, it made me feel bad … and if you just say it was a joke, well it was a joke that hurt feelings." And Mara wrote, "I love my culture and when I grow up I will find a way to make Hispanics look great in front of everybody's face."

> Mara wrote, 'I love my culture and when I grow up I will find a way to make Hispanics look great in front of everybody's face.'

Historical Context

After we explored past and current media representations, I thought it would help to provide some background on the Civil Rights Movement. The book *Freedom's Children: Young Civil Rights Activists Tell Their Own Stories* helped me to provide historical background that my students could relate to. It includes first-person accounts from activists who were teenagers during the Civil Rights Movement and photographs of the teenagers and major events.

Because we were pressed for time, I decided to read the first chapter together in class and then divide the six remaining chapters among the six reading groups in my class. I had each group summarize the major facts of one event and choose one teenager from the corresponding chapter to read and write about.

Looking back, I realize that my students needed more guidance with each chapter. Next time I teach this, I'll provide a set of questions for each chapter. When the groups finished that assignment, I asked them to design posters that included facts about the events and words from the young activists. Then I had them teach their classmates about what they'd learned. Although my students wanted to create skits for each of their chapters, finishing this project took much longer than I anticipated, so we postponed that idea. These activities helped my students get a better sense of the impact of the Civil Rights Movement and the role teenagers can play in creating social change. It also set the stage for our later discussion of the Chicano Movement and allowed us to later compare and contrast the two movements.

In a class discussion, I asked my students whether they thought building alliances with other people of color, specifically African Americans, was important. Miriam said, "I think it would be good to start alliances because they probably don't know many Mexicans and we could teach them not to believe all the stereotypes about us and we could learn too." Judging by the students' journals, I think my efforts were paying off. Eddie wrote, "We would have more power working together." Jacinto wrote, "I think it is important because the more united you are the more you get done." And Iris added, "I think they should form an alliance because the bigger we are, the better things we will probably get from the government."

As a result of this last conversation, we are planning to start a correspondence with a 7th-grade class of predominantly African American students. My students are very excited about this.

I don't want to give the impression that some of my students haven't been resistant to the idea that building solidarity with African Americans is important. For example, there have been times when students have expressed a belief that Latinos need to help themselves and that African Americans "already get too much help." But these are exactly the kinds of ideas I'm trying to address in my classroom. In a sense, these kinds of comments give me a chance to further educate my students.

In her book *De Colores Means All of Us*, Elizabeth Martinez writes, "Building alliances calls for us to break down the walls of mutual prejudice that exist. To do so we need to hammer out strong tools. One is simply education: learning about each other's history, current experience and culture, beginning very young." By exploring media depictions of African Americans and Latinos and the history of the Civil Rights Movement, I feel we're headed in the right direction.

In a class discussion, I asked my students whether they thought building alliances with other people of color, specifically African Americans, was important.

CHAPTER THIRTY-TWO

Reconstructing Race

By Nathaniel W. Smith

"I really just think it's so terrible that people judge other people for their race. I don't see how they can be so stupid! I don't care if you're black, yellow, or green. I only see people as people."

When one of my students made this comment, his classmates applauded. Yet he was the same student who, not a day later, noticed that one of our classroom windows had a broken handle. He laughed, saying the school was "so damn ghetto." And he openly talked about rap music as "complete crap. It's not even music—even I can get on a microphone and just talk!"

I wondered how I would even begin to get at the contradictions in this student's mind.

Courtesy of Greg French Collection with assistance from Greg Fried

Yes, we should "all get along," as another student once earnestly implored. But before we can, we must first understand the degree to which we don't get along. This seemed especially difficult considering the population I was working with. I taught in Central Bucks School District in Bucks County, Penn., which is approximately 98 percent white, and 95 percent middle-class or higher. There was not much in the way of racial and socioeconomic diversity among my 10th- and 12th-grade students, who were tracked into honors, standard, and basic classes.

Comments like the ones above were not those of a few idiosyncratic individuals, they were refrains, repeated again and again, often in the exact same wording. I wanted to develop a curriculum that made race enormous, difficult, and personal, when many students defined it as stupid, simple, and external.

As a white teacher in a predominantly white school I wanted to help students see their own whiteness and the ways it has shaped their lives. I wanted to confront my students' perceptions that "I don't think it has anything to do with me—I don't even have a race. I'm just normal." I thought I would begin by helping them understand race as a specifically social construct.

As a white teacher in a predominantly white school I wanted to help students see their own whiteness and the ways it has shaped their lives.

The Breakthrough

"Mr. Smith, why are you teaching us history in our English class?" Students wondered why, in a course on American Literature, I would devote multiple days to discussions of race. I explained to the students the interrelation of literature and the societies in which the authors lived, often pointing out that one couldn't understand modern music without understanding modern times.

As my course contained a unit on slave narratives and another on the Harlem Renaissance, I justified race discussion as requisite to understanding the context of the literature. So by the time our semester together had come and gone, I had taught several lessons that addressed the concepts of race, the historical development of race, and the challenges to race presented by the constant creation of multiracial people.

I had found readings and role plays, personal accounts, and documentary films. We acted out and discussed Twain's controversial *Pudd'nhead Wilson*, created graphic novels representing the autobiographies of Frederick Douglass and Harriet Jacobs, and even watched samples of the PBS film *Race: The Power of an Illusion*. Like many teachers with a passion, I bent the rules of the district curriculum requirements in favor of lessons I thought more pressing. But with all these lessons I ran into the same problem.

Constructing race, the daily practice of ascribing roles and identities to physical features, is a matter of active perception. If race affects the way you are treated by others in the world, it necessarily depends upon what race they suppose you to be. My curricular premise is that individuals can discover and address their own racism more effectively when they understand that all race categories are political lines drawn in the sands of cultural and genetic diffusion and evolution.

I can say it clearly enough, but lectures never bring the result I'm really after. If race is perceptual, it must be challenged on the level of perception. My lessons based on reading and discussion failed to produce activities that revealed to students how they construct race through their own vision and sense of identity.

Then in February 2002, I was doing some background research on Frederick Douglass, and I stumbled across Gregory Fried's article "True Pictures." (It's available on the web at www.common-place.org/vol-02/no-02/fried/) The pictures he had found were the perfect starting point.

Before we began, I told the students we were going to start working with slave narratives soon, and I thought this would be a good exercise for laying the groundwork. As I handed each student one of two photographs, I explained that these were taken around the time of emancipation (1863, to be precise), and that Frederick Douglass had hoped to use them to educate people against slavery.

Then I gave them three minutes to write a description of the photo. "Describe it, explain what's happening and who the characters are. Then explain how you think it might have been used in an antislavery campaign. If this were an antislavery campaign ad, what might be the slogan?" I avoided mentioning the race of the people in the photographs. The students spent the next few minutes reacting to these pictures. Though I cut off the original captions, I included the names for ease of discussion after.

Afterward, I asked them to share what they wrote. Students guessed that the picture of Isaac and Rosa arm in arm is symbolic of an interracial harmony campaign, a Benetton-style depiction of black and white together in youthful innocence. "The white girl and the black boy together arm in arm is a sort of vision for the future—there's hope for us to all live together," wrote one student.

Someone else suggested that Isaac and Rosa show that "the little white girl is safe playing with the little black boy."

For the second picture, students had a range of explanations, though often again the idea of safety emerges: "It shows that a black man can know more than a white person—he can

> *Constructing race, the daily practice of ascribing roles and identities to physical features, is a matter of active perception.*

teach them to read. And it sort of says, these white kids are safe with this black man."

Alternatively, some students argued, "the white kids are teaching the black man to read, kind of saying that he can learn just as well as white people and should be given a chance."

In addition to using this activity with my own classes of predominantly white students, I've also used it with classes of adults. Every time groups of people have debated these photos, they have described the pictures as photos of black and white people together.

Once students aired their reactions, I revealed to them that every person pictured was an emancipated slave. They had all been socially known as black, made to live as slaves. They were unable to own property, unable to vote, unable to pursue their rights through legal institutions. So, I asked my students: Were they in fact black, or were they white?

Though the debate was a stuttering one at this point, students began to engage in some disagreement. Before moving on, I tried to point out one constant in this exercise: When we're not thinking about race, we guess race and attach significance to it. Though I never asked anyone the race of the people pictured, all respondents (without exception) included it in their descriptions. Their interpretations of the meaning of the photos were all completely dependent on the assumed racial identities of the subjects. This point makes it much harder for students later to claim they don't see race at all.

> *Though I never asked anyone the race of the people pictured, all respondents (without exception) included it in their descriptions.*

"Is Mr. Smith a White Guy?"

I then changed the topic, volunteering to be a contemporary example. "OK, so the next question is: Is Mr. Smith a white man? Yes or no?" I asked. "Raise your hand if you think Mr. Smith is a white guy."

Across all the groups I've worked with, only one person has ever suggested that they thought I might have been mixed—because I have curly hair. "So, without asking, and without knowing my parents or how I might identify, everyone here has quietly agreed that I'm white. So how do you know?"

On the board I made a list of the things that made me white to them. Kids had a lot of fun with this (though it was tough to avoid reacting to the descriptions, as some were quite unflattering); it's a rare opportunity to pick apart their teacher's appearance. "You have a thin nose! White skin! Thin lips! Blonde hair! Blue eyes! You talk white! You walk like a white man! You wear khakis and a button-up shirt! European ancestors!" The list of evidence was long, and the students threw out comments faster than I could write them on the board.

Once the list was up, I turned it around. "So, of all these things, which ones are indispensable? Which ones make me absolutely white?" I challenged each one. "If I had fuller lips, would I still be white? Are there white people with brown or black hair? Are there white people with brown eyes? White people who speak 'ebonics'—are they still white? If a black man wears a button-up shirt, is it harder to tell that he's black?" We went down the list until the students were unable to defend my whiteness. Still, they vehemently argued: "You just know."

Again I asked, "But what about Isaac and Rosa? Why didn't we 'just know' with them?"

Following this exercise, the ensuing debate has always been deep and often heated, tightly focused on what qualifies people for their race. No one tried to claim they didn't "see" the race of the teacher or the people pictured—they had already revealed assumptions about race in their answers. All the students assumed and interpreted race, regardless of whether they considered themselves prejudiced, regardless of whether they were looking at an emancipated slave in an old photograph or a white teacher standing in front of the classroom.

With the rug pulled out from under the categories, we then moved on to discussing how, with all this uncertainty, we ever decide that a person is of a specific race. Using the traits students listed for categorizing my race, I suggested that all the qualities fit under one of three headings: color, culture, or ancestry. I then asked them, which of these provides the key? Is one category more important than the others? Students break down along unpredictable lines and bring forth some very interesting answers. One of the most strongly defended criteria is color.

A few questions quickly defeated the color argument. Students said I was white because of my white skin, so I held up a piece of blank paper. "So if I'm not exactly white in color, how white do I have to be to fit?" If students reversed it and claimed that "black people are people with black skin," I asked them to define the exact range of tones. What about darkly tanned white people? Thanks to tanning salons, there's often someone who identifies as being white in the room with skin darker than that of Malcolm X, who they all agreed was black. And what of the emancipated slaves in the pictures? Most came to accept that people with darker skin may be white, and people with very light

All the students assumed and interpreted race, regardless of whether they considered themselves prejudiced, regardless of whether they were looking at an emancipated slave in an old photograph or a white teacher standing in front of the classroom.

skin may be black. Inevitably, the kids argued about Michael Jackson, and the conversation took on a life of its own.

I offered similar challenges to those who would ground race in culture. My students often mocked white students who "wish they were black." I had students explain to me how a person "acts black." What are the behaviors? "They try to talk ebonics. They're always blasting DMX in the parking lot! They wear low baggy pants with their boxers hanging out. I know someone like that who's always trying to convince people she is black!"

If a person has adopted black culture, would we say that person is acting black? Wouldn't he or she just become black? What if this black-acting person had a black great-grandparent they didn't even know about? Who would argue that a "black-acting" person with African ancestry is not in fact black?

In the face of these ambiguities, students often drew the line at the most "scientific" seeming category—genetics. "You can look like whatever, but you either have African ancestors or you don't," is a typical student remark.

I asked about adoptees. Imagine I was adopted and didn't know my ancestry. Imagine that tomorrow I meet my real parents and one of them is black. Is it possible for a person to be black and not even know it? If this happened, would I be right to come to school tomorrow and say I am black? If not, does that mean black is something other than having African ancestry? If yes, then how could everyone have assumed I was white? I find students often split right down the middle as to whether I would be legitimately black or white in that scenario.

Another response to the ancestry argument revolved around historic black figures. I asked students if Malcolm X and Frederick Douglass were black men, and they said yes. Then I revealed to them that both men had European ancestry. If ancestry is the key to race, why doesn't that ancestry make them white? Why is it that in the game of race, even the slightest African ancestry trumps European ancestry? And in my case, students say they know I'm white because I have European ancestry—but how does one "see" ancestry?

In fact, one sees only physical traits—not the familial lines or genes from which they might be derived.

In fact, one sees only physical traits—not the familial lines or genes from which they might be derived. Here students came full circle to the point of admitting that ancestry does not clearly correlate with race—skin tone and culture matter a lot too. So the argument is circular: A person is black because we decide they are black enough, and there is no single defining quality one must possess.

My purpose wasn't to clarify race, but to blow it apart. To do that I had to bring out the complex challenges that exist on all sides of the race definition. The point was to raise questions and make a mess rather than let students off with neat and easy answers. No more raising your hand just to say, "Racism is bad."

But at this point I needed to be aware of a real danger. Students, particularly those white students who feel excluded in race discussions, may try to run with the principle that "race isn't real."

As one student said, "This just proves that all this race stuff is a bunch of people worked up about nothing." Obviously, this was not my intended result. So we got into a conversation about the word "real."

I said to the students, "Many people will say that God is not real. As with race, there is no 'scientific' evidence. Let's imagine for a moment those people are right, that there isn't a god. Even if that's true, think of the role the idea of God has played in world history. Think of all the huge religious organizations in almost every country, and the influence those religions have had in the world. Think of how many people refer to God every morning in the Pledge of Allegiance, how God is written on every coin and bill in the United States. Even if God is just something people made up—does that mean it hasn't affected us?" Even the most irreligious of students agreed that the idea of God affected them; in fact I've found the atheist-identified students to be quite upset about how often they are reminded of their status as outsiders. There is a parallel to those who would rather not see race, those who wish it would go away—wishing doesn't make it so. No matter whether race is grounded in science or ideology, it has a long and powerful history, one that has determined the shape of our society in ways no individual can escape.

My purpose wasn't to clarify race, but to blow it apart.

Bringing It Home, Literally

Once students had some time to soak in these ideas, I ended with an exercise that literally brought the lesson home. Before doing so, I gave some words of introduction, as this piece could serve to alienate some students if not handled delicately. I explained to students that often we think only of certain populations as not knowing their heritage. It is a widely acknowledged tragedy of slavery that so many family lines were severed and cannot be retraced. This is likewise the case with many populations who may have fled oppressive circumstances in their countries of origin. When one thinks of people not knowing their heritage, one might think of adoptees first. But the truth of the matter is, few if any of us truly know our heritage in the way we imagine it. Think of all the people who describe themselves as "Irish and German" or some other two- or three-part combination. Can this really capture the genetic history of any individual?

For this exercise, I produced a simple blank diagram of the family tree, reaching back five generations. I then ask students to fill in the names of every relative they can. If one looks at the spreading numbers of ancestors—32 great-great-great-grandparents, 16 great-great-grandparents, eight great-grandparents, four grandparents, and two parents—there are 62 progenitors to name. I have yet to meet a student who could name them all. If one could, it still wouldn't identify the race of those individuals, even if there were pictures of them all.

The point was simply to visualize the vast numbers of people that came before us, and the inadequacy of the simplified descriptions most of us inherit.

I tried to minimize the discomfort for students who may have hesitations about revealing this kind of information by emphasizing that we are all on the same ground when it comes to our ancestry. None of us knows "where we come from," even if we know our parents and grandparents. I didn't ask students to share their trees, or even to feel compelled to fill them in there and then. The point was simply to visualize the vast numbers of people that came before us, and the inadequacy of the simplified descriptions most of us inherit.

I grew up being told I was Scots-Irish and a little bit of Native American, but when I started to examine this tree and ask my family members, I discovered many countries of origin that had not been told to me (Hessian, German, and British), several branches of the tree for which there was no information, and absolutely no confirmation of the "bit of Native American" that I had always been told of.

As a group we then discussed the significance of the holes in all our knowledge. If being African American means having African ancestry, how many of us know whether we are African American? How do any of us know we are any specific race at all? Some students will begin insisting on their whiteness, but most quickly realize they have no evidence to stand on. As one student said, "I don't know—maybe I am black—or African American, or whatever, for all I know."

Another of my students, the same one who said he didn't see race, came back to me a week after the lesson. "Mr. Smith, I went home and asked my grandmother how we know we're white. I asked her if she knew if we had any black ancestors. She got really angry and started yelling that 'of course we don't have any n– –s in the family!' I didn't expect her to care so much about it. I quit asking about it after a while, but she never did say she had any evidence. When I showed her that [ancestry chart], she couldn't fill it out either. She tore it up." I worried I might have caused a family rift, or that I might be explaining myself to the principal soon, but at the same time I couldn't help but be happy that my student had taken it upon himself to seek answers—and he was sharp enough to recognize that no answer satisfies.

Of course, there are dangers. In my experience, no single lesson is received and applied the same way across all students, or even any two students. Some students will shut down in the face of this mess-making—others will select from the many potential implications the one they most want to hear, "race isn't real." It's a danger, though I would argue all educational practice is fraught with danger.

I believe it is promising to bring high school students to this level of thinking about race. If it is not an immutable, biological fact, then race must be a changing social fact. And if it has changed in the past, it can be changed now. Whatever dissatisfies us about the issue does not have to be accepted, looked at with resignation, and considered an inevitable part of our lives. Though it hardly guarantees that all students adopt a conscious, activist, anti-racist stance, it arms them against simple and reductive thinking about race, which is always dangerous regardless of the intent.

If it is not an immutable, biological fact, then race must be a changing social fact.

Presidents and Slaves

Helping students
find the truth

By Bob Peterson

During a lesson about George Washington and the American Revolution, I explained to my 5th graders that Washington owned 317 slaves. One student added that Thomas Jefferson also was a slave owner. And then, in part to be funny and in part expressing anger—over vote fraud involving African Americans in the then-recent 2000 election and the U.S. Supreme Court's subsequent delivery of the presidency to George W. Bush—one of my students shouted, "Bush is a slave owner, too!" "No, Bush doesn't own slaves," I calmly explained. "Slavery was finally ended in this country in 1865."

Short exchanges such as this often pass quickly and we move onto another topic. But this time one student asked: "Well, which presidents were slave owners?"

She had me stumped. "That's a good question," I said. "I don't know." Thus began a combined social studies, math, and language arts project in which I learned along with my students, and which culminated in a fascinating exchange between my students and the publishers of their U.S. history textbook.

After I admitted that I had no clue exactly which presidents owned slaves, I threw the challenge back to the students. "How can we find out?" I asked.

"Look in a history book," said one. "Check the internet," added another. I realized that I had entered one of those "teachable moments" when students show genuine interest in exploring a particular topic. Yet I had few materials about presidents and slaves, and no immediate idea of how to engage 25 students on the subject.

I also recognized that this was a great opportunity to create my own curriculum, which might help students look critically at texts while encouraging their active participation in doing meaningful research. Such an approach stands in sharp contrast to the "memorize the presidents" instruction that I suffered through growing up, and which too many students probably still endure. I seized the opportunity.

First, I had a student write down the question—"Which presidents were slave owners?"—in our class notebook, "Questions We Have." I then suggested that a few students form an "action research group," which in my classroom means an ad hoc group of interested students researching a topic and then doing something with what they learn. I asked for volunteers willing to work during recess. Several boys raised their hands, surprising me because I would have guessed that some of them would have much preferred going outside to staying indoors researching.

Action Research by Students

At recess time, Raul and Edwin were immediately in my face. "When are we going to start the action research on the slave presidents?" they demanded. I told them to look in the back of our school dictionaries for a list of U.S. presidents while I got out some large construction paper. The dictionaries, like our social studies text, had little pictures of each president with some basic information. "Why doesn't it show Clinton?" Edwin commented. "He's been president forever." I think, yeah, Clinton's been president four fifths of this 10-year-old's life. But I kept that thought to myself and instead replied "The book is old." "Why don't they just tell whether they have slaves here in this list of presidents?"

After I admitted that I had no clue exactly which presidents owned slaves, I threw the challenge back to the students.

asked Edwin. "They tell other things about presidents." "Good question," I said. "Why do you think they don't tell?"

"I don't know, probably because they don't know themselves." "Maybe so," I responded. "Here's what I'd like you to do. Since slavery was abolished when Lincoln was president, and since he was the 16th president, draw 16 lines equal distance from each other and list all the presidents from Washington to Lincoln, and then a yes-and-no column so we can check off whether they owned slaves."

I was soon to find out that filling in those columns was easier said than done.

When my students and I began investigating which presidents owned slaves, our attempts focused on traditional history textbooks and student-friendly websites from the White House and the Smithsonian Institution. These efforts turned up virtually nothing. We then pursued two different sources of information: history books written for adults and more in-depth websites.

I brought in two books that were somewhat helpful: James Loewen's *Lies My Teacher Told Me* (Simon and Schuster, 1995) and Kenneth O'Reilly's *Nixon's Piano: Presidents and Racial Politics from Washington to Clinton* (Free Press, 1995). By using the indexes and reading the text out loud, we uncovered facts about some of the presidents. We also used the web search engines Google and AltaVista and searched on the words "presidents" and "slavery." We soon learned we had to be more specific and include the president's name and "slavery"—for example, "President George Washington" and "slavery." Some results were student-friendly, such as the mention of Washington's slaves (and some of their escapes) at www.mountvernon.org/education/slavery. There was also a bill of sale for a slave signed by Dolly Madison, the wife of president James Madison (for a link to the document see www.rethinkingschools.org/rsr). Many websites had a large amount of text and were beyond the reading level of many of my students. So I cut and pasted long articles into word processing documents so we could search for the word "slave" to see if there was any specific mention of slave ownership.

In their research, students often asked, "How do we know this is true? Our history books aren't telling the truth, why should we think this does?" I explained the difference between primary and secondary sources and how a primary source—like a bill of sale or original list of slaves—was pretty solid evidence. To help ensure accuracy, the students decided that if we used secondary sources, we needed to find at least two different citations.

When my students and I began investigating which presidents owned slaves, our attempts focused on traditional history textbooks and student-friendly websites. These efforts turned up virtually nothing.

Bits and Pieces of Information

In the next several days the students, with my help, looked at various sources. We checked our school's children's books about presidents, our social studies textbook, a 1975 *World Book Encyclopedia,* and a CD-ROM encyclopedia. We found nothing about presidents as slave owners. I had a hunch about which presidents owned slaves, based on what I knew in general about the presidents, but I wanted "proof" before we put a check in the "yes" box. And though my students wanted to add a third column—explaining how many slaves each slave-owning president had—that proved impossible. Even when we did find information about which presidents owned slaves, the numbers changed depending on how many slaves had been bought, sold, born, or died.

In our research, most of the information dealt with presidential attitudes and policies toward slavery. It was difficult to find specific information on which presidents owned slaves.

In our research, most of the information dealt with presidential attitudes and policies toward slavery. It was difficult to find specific information on which presidents owned slaves. To help the investigation, I checked out a few books for them from our local university library. Overall, our best resource was the internet. The best sites required adult help to find and evaluate, and I became so engrossed in the project that I spent a considerable amount of time at home surfing the web. The "student-friendly" websites with information about presidents—such as the White House's gallery of presidents (www.whitehouse.gov/history/presidents)—don't mention that Washington and Jefferson enslaved African Americans. Other popular sites with the same glaring lack of information are the Smithsonian Institution (http://educate.si.edu/president) and the National Museum of American History (http://www.americanhistory.si.edu/presidency). As we did the research, I regularly asked, "Why do you think this doesn't mention that the president owned slaves?" Students' responses varied, including "They're stupid;" "They don't want us kids to know the truth;" "They think we're too young to know;" and "They don't know themselves." (Given more time, we might have explored this matter further, looking at who produces textbooks and why they might not include information about presidents' attitudes about racism and slavery.) During our research, my students and I found bits and pieces of information about presidents and slavery. But we never found that one magic resource, be it book or website, that had the information readily available. Ultimately, though, we came up with credible data. I'm a history buff, and had thought I was on top of the question of presidents and slavery. I was quite amazed, and didn't hide my amazement from our action research team, when they discovered that two presidents who served after Lincoln—Andrew Johnson and Ulysses S. Grant—had been slave owners. While the students taped an extension on their chart, I explained that I was not totally surprised about Johnson because he had been a Southerner. But it was a shock that Grant had owned slaves. "He was the commander of the Union army in the Civil War," I explained. "When I first learned about the Civil War in elementary school, Grant and Lincoln were portrayed as saviors of the Union and freers of slaves." When I told the entire class how Grant's slave-owning past had surprised me, Tanya, an African American student, raised her hand and said, "That's nothing. Lincoln was a slave owner, too." I asked for her source of information and she said she had heard that Lincoln didn't like blacks. I thanked her for raising the point, and told the class that while it was commonly accepted by historians that Lincoln was not a slave owner, his attitudes toward blacks and slavery were a source of much debate. I noted that just because a president didn't own slaves didn't mean that he supported freedom for slaves or equal treatment of people of different races.

I went into a bit of detail on Lincoln, in part to counter the all-too-common simplification that Lincoln unequivocally opposed slavery and supported freedom for blacks. I explained that while it's commonly believed that Lincoln freed enslaved Americans when he signed the Emancipation Proclamation, the document actually frees slaves only in states and regions under rebellion—it did not free slaves in any of the slaveholding states and regions that remained in the Union. In other words, Lincoln "freed" slaves everywhere he had no authority and withheld freedom everywhere he did. Earlier, in Lincoln's first inaugural address in March of 1861, he promised slaveholders that he would support a constitutional amendment forever protecting slavery in the states where it then existed—if only those states would remain in the Union.

Slave-Owning Presidents

By the time we finished our research, the students had found that 10 of the first 18 presidents were slave owners: George Washington, Thomas Jefferson, James Madison, James Monroe, Andrew Jackson, John Tyler, James K. Polk, Zachary Taylor, Andrew Johnson, and Ulysses S. Grant. Those who didn't: John Adams, John Quincy Adams, Martin Van Buren, William Henry Harrison, Millard Fillmore, Franklin Pierce, James Buchanan, and, despite Tanya's assertion, Abraham Lincoln. The student researchers

By the time we finished our research, the students had found that 10 of the first 18 presidents were slave owners.

were excited to present their findings to their classmates, and decided to do so as part of a math class. I made blank charts for each student in the class, and they filled in information provided by the action research team: the names of presidents, the dates of their years in office, the total number of years in office, and whether they had owned slaves. Our chart started with George Washington, who assumed office in 1789, and ended in 1877 when the last president who had owned slaves, Ulysses Grant, left office.

We then used the data to discuss this topic of presidents and slave-owning within the structure of ongoing math topics in my class: "What do the data tell us?" and "How can we construct new knowledge with the data?" Students, for example, added up the total number of years in which the United States had a slave-owning president in office, and compared that total to the number of years in which there were non-slave-owning presidents in office. We figured out that in 69 percent of the years between 1789 and 1877, the United States had a president who had been a slave owner. One student observed that only slave-owning presidents served more than one term. "Why didn't they let presidents who didn't own slaves serve two terms?" another student pondered.

Using the data, the students made bar graphs and circle graphs to display the information. When they wrote written reflections on the math lesson, they connected math to content. One boy wrote: "I learned to convert fractions to percent so I know that 10/18 is the same as 55.5 percent. That's how many of the first 18 presidents owned slaves." Another girl observed, "I learned how to make pie charts and that so many more presidents owned slaves than the presidents who didn't own slaves." During a subsequent social studies lesson, the three students who had done most of the research explained their frustrations in getting information. "They hardly ever want to mention it [slaves owned by presidents]," explained one student. "We had to search and search." Specific objectives for this mini-unit, such as reviewing the use of percent, emerged as the lessons themselves unfolded. But its main purpose was to help students to critically examine the actions of early leaders of the United States and to become skeptical of textbooks and government websites as sources that present the entire picture. I figure that if kids start questioning the "official story" early on, they will be more open to alternative viewpoints later. While discovering which presidents were slave owners is not an in-depth analysis, it pokes an important hole in the god-like mystique that surrounds the "founding fathers." If students learn how to be critical of the icons of American past, hopefully it will give them

While discovering which presidents were slave owners is not an in-depth analysis, it pokes an important hole in the god-like mystique that surrounds the 'founding fathers.'

permission and tools to be critical of the elites of America today. Besides uncovering some hard-to-find and uncomfortable historical truths, I also wanted to encourage my students to think about why these facts were so hard to find, and to develop a healthy skepticism of official sources of information. I showed them two quotations about Thomas Jefferson. One was from a recently published 5th-grade history textbook, *United States: Adventures in Time and Place* (Macmillan/McGraw Hill, 1998) which read: "Jefferson owned several slaves in his lifetime and lived in a slave-owning colony. Yet he often spoke out against slavery. 'Nothing is more certainly written in the book of fate than that these people are to be free'" (p. 314). The other quotation was from James Loewen's *Lies My Teacher Told Me.*

Loewen writes:

> Textbooks stress that Jefferson was a humane master, privately tormented by slavery and opposed to its expansion, not the type to destroy families by selling slaves. In truth, by 1820 Jefferson had become an ardent advocate of the expansion of slavery to the western territories. And he never let his ambivalence about slavery affect his private life. Jefferson was an average master who had his slaves whipped and sold into the Deep South as examples to induce other slaves to obey. By 1822, Jefferson owned 267 slaves. During his long life, of hundreds of different slaves he owned, he freed only three and five more at his death—all blood relatives of his. (p. 140)

We talked about the different perspective each quote had toward Jefferson and toward what students should learn. My students' attention immediately turned to the set of spanking new history textbooks that had been delivered to our classroom that year as part of the districtwide social studies adoption. Some students assumed that our new textbook United States (Harcourt Brace, 2000) was equally as bad as the one I quoted from. One student suggested we just throw the books away. But I quickly pointed out they were expensive, and that we could learn from them even if they had problems and omissions.

I then explained what an omission was, and suggested that we become "textbook detectives" and investigate what our new social studies text said about Jefferson and slavery. I reviewed how to use an index and divided all page references for Jefferson among small groups of students. The groups read the pages, noted any references to Jefferson owning slaves, and then reported back to the class. Not one group found a single reference. Not surprisingly, the

I then explained what an omission was, and suggested that we become 'textbook detectives' and investigate what our new social studies text said about Jefferson and slavery.

students were angry when they realized how the text omitted such important information. "They should tell the truth!" one student fumed.

No Mention of Racism

I wanted students to see that the textbook's omissions were not an anomaly, but part of a pattern of ignoring racism in America—in the past and in the present. In the next lesson, I started by writing the word "racism" on the board. I asked the kids to look up "racism" in the index of their social studies book. Nothing. "Racial discrimination." Nothing.

"Our school should get a different book," one student suggested. "Good idea," I said, "but it's not so easy." I told my students that I had served on a committee that had looked at the major textbooks published for 5th graders and that none of them had dealt with racism or slavery and presidents.

Students had a variety of responses:

"Let's throw them out."

"Let's use the internet."

"Write a letter to the people who did the books." I focused in on the letter-writing suggestion and reminded them that before we did so, we had to be certain that our criticisms were correct. The students then agreed that in small groups they would use the textbook's index and read what was said about all the first 18 presidents, just as we had done previously with Jefferson. None of the groups found any mention of a president owning a slave.

Letters as Critique and Action

In subsequent days, some students wrote letters to the textbook publisher. Michelle, a white girl, was particularly detailed. She wrote: "I am 11 years old and I like to read and write. When I am reading I notice every little word and in your social studies book I realize that the word "racism" is not in your book. You're acting like it is a bad word for those kids who read it." She went on to criticize the book for not mentioning that any presidents had slaves: "I see that you do not mention that some of the presidents had slaves. But some of them did. Like George Washington had 317 slaves. So did Thomas Jefferson. He had 267 slaves." She continued: "If you want to teach children the truth, then you should write the truth." (Michelle's letter and some of the student-made charts were also printed in our school newspaper.)

We mailed off the letters, and moved on to new lessons. Weeks passed with no response and eventually the students

I wanted students to see that the textbook's omissions were not an anomaly, but part of a pattern of ignoring racism in America—in the past and in the present.

stopped asking if the publishers had written back. Then one day a fancy-looking envelope appeared in my mailbox addressed to Michelle Williams. She excitedly opened the letter and read it to the class.

Harcourt School Publishers Vice President Donald Lankiewicz had responded to Michelle at length. He wrote that "while the word 'racism' does not appear, the subject of unfair treatment of people because of their race is addressed on page 467." He also argued: "There are many facts about the presidents that are not included in the text simply because we do not have room for them all."

Michelle wrote back to Lankiewicz, thanking him but expressing disappointment.

"In a history book you shouldn't have to wait till page 467 to learn about unfair treatment," she wrote. As to his claim that there wasn't room for all the facts about the presidents, Michelle responded: "Adding more pages is good for the kids because they should know the right things from the wrong. It is not like you are limited to certain amount of pages. ... All I ask you is that you write the word 'racism' in the book and add some more pages in the book so you can put most of the truth about the presidents."

Michelle never received a reply.

Improving the Lesson

Michelle and the other students left 5th grade soon after the letter exchange. In the flurry of end-of-year activities, I didn't take as much time to process the project as I might have. Nor did I adequately explore with students the fact that most non-slave-owning presidents exhibited proslavery attitudes and promoted pro-slavery policies.

But the larger issue, which critical teachers struggle to address, is why textbook publishers and schools in general do such a poor job of helping students make sense of the difficult issues of race. We do students a disservice when we sanitize history and sweep uncomfortable truths under the rug. We leave them less prepared to deal with the difficult issues they will face in their personal, political, and social lives. Granted, these are extremely complicated issues that don't have a single correct response. But it's important to begin with a respect for the truth and for the capacity of people of all ages to expand their understanding of the past and the present, and to open their hearts and minds to an ever-broadening concept of social justice.

We do students a disservice when we sanitize history and sweep uncomfortable truths under the rug.

I believe my students learned a lot from their research on presidents and slaves—and clearly know more than most Americans about which of the first 18 presidents owned slaves. I'm also hopeful they learned the importance of looking critically at all sources of information. I know one student, Tanya, did. On the last day of school she came up to me and amid the congratulatory goodbyes and said, "I still think Lincoln owned slaves."

"You are a smart girl but you are wrong about that one," I responded. "We'll see," she said, "You didn't know Grant had slaves when the school year started! Why should I always believe what my teacher says?"

Some of the students' names in this article have been changed.

Author's Note: About two years after I completed the research on slave-owning presidents with my students, a wonderful website called UnderstandingPrejudice.org was put up by folks at Wesleyan University. This site includes extensive information on presidents who owned slaves (see www.understandingprejudice.org/slavery). I learned from this website that three presidents not on my list also owned slaves: Martin Van Buren, William Henry Harrison, and James Buchanan. I was grateful for the additional information on this website, which opens up all sorts of new teaching possibilities.

CHAPTER THIRTY-FOUR

From Snarling Dogs
to Bloody Sunday

By Kate Lyman

"I'm not teaching about civil rights this year," my colleague asserted.

"Not teaching about civil rights?" I responded. My
teaching buddy and partner had teamed with me in tackling
"controversial issues" at the 2nd/3rd-grade level—AIDS, the "discovery" of America, and homophobia, to name a few. I couldn't
believe that she was not going to join me in planning the civil
rights unit.

My partner explained that a parent of a child who was continuing in her 2nd/3rd-grade combination class had objected to
the unit on civil rights the previous year. "There was too much
violence," she had said. Her daughter had been frightened.

Bettmann/CORBIS

Knowing that I would miss our joint planning sessions and sharing of materials and ideas, I nevertheless decided to go ahead with the unit.

My own experience growing up in an exclusively white and economically privileged suburb of Milwaukee had isolated me from the issues of the Civil Rights Movement. When, as a high school student in the 1960s, I finally became informed in a U.S. history class about the events in the South and the segregation and discrimination in my own city, I was appalled. I started on the long road to try to better understand issues of racism and to do what I could to act on the inequities in our society.

Unlike the suburb I grew up in, my school attendance area is culturally, politically, and socially diverse. Over 50 percent of the students come from families of color, most of them low-income. There are also low-income and working-class white families, and a smattering of middle-class families from a new development.

I had previously received a generally positive response to the civil rights unit. Parents had shared resources, such as a battered but prized painting of Rosa Parks. One grandmother came in to teach us freedom songs and talk about her efforts in the 1960s to organize an NAACP chapter in Oklahoma. My former principal and a few teachers had disapproved of teaching such deep and heavy issues to young children. However, I could recall only one negative comment from a parent: "Why are you still teaching black history when it's past February?" In fact, even though I generally started the unit on or around the observance of Martin Luther King's birthday, related activities integrated into all subject areas extended past January and February and, depending on student interest and the depth of the projects, into the first few weeks of March.

I planned the civil rights unit within the context of a discussion of Human Rights and Children's Rights, in honor of the upcoming 50th anniversary of the United Nations Universal Declaration of Human Rights, signed on Dec. 11, 1949. It was during that discussion that my students had agreed that among basic rights for children is the right "to not be judged by the color of our skin." This idea was a logical lead-in to the Civil Rights Movement.

We began by reading biographies about Martin Luther King Jr. and gave him his due as a strong and gifted leader. But I also wanted to go beyond the platitudes often taught in elementary classes. I discarded worksheets in my files that summed up the Civil Rights Movement in simplistic language

> I had previously received a generally positive response to the civil rights unit. Parents had shared resources, such as a battered but prized painting of Rosa Parks.

such as "Dr. King decided to help the black people and white people get along better."

One especially useful book was *I Have a Dream*, by Margaret Davidson, and for 14 days we read a chapter a day from the book. While written in clear and fairly simple language, the book goes way beyond others in its genre in the complexity of its coverage of the Civil Rights Movement.

We used a variety of books, videos, poetry, and music to follow the history of racial discrimination and segregation. We studied not only King but many other people who worked together to overturn unfair laws and practices, especially the children: Ruby Bridges, the Little Rock Nine, the children in the Birmingham children's march, the students in the sit-ins, and Sheyann Webb, the 8-year-old voting rights activist in Selma.

Sections from the PBS documentary series *Eyes on the Prize* were invaluable in helping my students witness history. They were entranced by the 1957 footage of the nine Little Rock high school students who faced angry mobs as they desegregated Central High. They cheered when one of the students, Minniejean Brown, got so infuriated with the daily intimidation that she finally poured a bowl of chili on her harasser's head. They watched with awe as the children in Birmingham, Ala., in 1963 joined the protests against segregated facilities and then stood their ground even as they were being slammed against the wall by the power of the hoses held by Bull Connor's firefighters.

My students were especially captivated by the story of the Birmingham children's crusade. The class participated in a role play about how these high school students helped desegregate public facilities in the city.

Jerome, an African American student with a gift for the dramatic, made a remarkable Martin Luther King. Imitating King's style for oratory, Jerome addressed his classmates who were playing the children gathered in the church after their first encounter with police brutality. Repeating the lines I gave him from the book *I Have a Dream*, he challenged the crowd, "Don't get bitter. Don't get tired. Are we tired?" The students role playing the Birmingham children responded before I had a chance to give them their lines. "NO!" they shouted, standing up and shaking their fists.

A Parent's Concern

I was halfway through the unit, feeling good about how the kids were conceptualizing the conviction of the civil rights activists —as well as how their enthusiasm was extending into reading,

We studied not only King but many other people who worked together to overturn unfair laws and practices, especially the children: Ruby Bridges, the Little Rock Nine, the children in the Birmingham children's march, the students in the sit-ins, and Sheyann Webb, the 8- year-old voting rights activist in Selma.

writing, and math activities—when Joanne, one of the eight African Americans in the class, handed me a letter from her mom. The letter expressed opposition to the civil rights unit, pointing out that Joanne had never witnessed hatred and brutality toward blacks. Joanne, she said, had "no experience with police and guns, snarling dogs, hatred, people who spit and/or throw soup at others." Joanne felt afraid at bedtime because of the "true stories" she remembered from the books and movies.

I had anticipated that such issues might come up, and had tried to take steps to deal with the children's reaction to the violence of racism. For example, before we began the Emmett Till section in *Eyes on the Prize*, we had discussed how scary some of these historical events were. Third-grade students, who had been exposed to some of the content the year before, shared some feelings of fear, but also affirmed that they wanted to learn more about what they had been introduced to in 2nd grade. I assured the class that acts that the Ku Klux Klan and others had committed with impunity could not go unpunished today.

I also knew I couldn't pretend that racial hatred is a thing of the past, however. I knew that many of my students were aware of the racist acts of violence reported in the national news. I also knew that many encounter racist name-calling or other biased acts in school and in their neighborhoods.

I hadn't seen signs that Joanne had been upset; in fact, her contributions to class discussions revealed a fascination with the topic. However, I was glad that Joanne's mom had communicated to me a problem that I might have missed.

As Joanne's mom had suggested, and in fact, as I would have done anyway, I took Joanne aside to talk with her. She said that the story of Emmett Till had bothered her, but that the rest had been OK. Cheerful and positive, as usual, Joanne dismissed my concern, and said she wanted to learn more.

I asked her to let me know if something was troubling her. I decided to watch her closely for signs of distress or withdrawal and to ask her frequently if she was doing all right. I also said she had the option to leave if the content disturbed her. But then I received another communication from her parents that she was to be excused from all books, movies, and poems that showed hatred toward blacks. I thought back to my teaching partner's reason for not teaching about the Civil Rights Movement.

I thought of a few other parents and one other teacher (all middle-class African Americans, like Joanne's mom) who had

Third-grade students, who had been exposed to some of the content the year before, shared some feelings of fear, but also affirmed that they wanted to learn more.

told me that they didn't want slavery or racism taught about in schools because that was all behind them and they didn't want it dredged up. It was too painful. It was over. It made them out to be victims. Joanne's mom said that she wanted her daughter to know only the positive parts of the movement—the love and the happiness—not the snarling dogs and hatred toward blacks.

I was in a quandary. Was it possible to teach in any depth about the Civil Rights Movement without including the violence and the racism? On the other hand, as a white teacher, was it presumptuous of me to decide to teach something that offended an African American parent? I knew that I couldn't put myself in her or Joanne's shoes. I can't know what it is like to be a racial minority is this country. And as a parent of three children, I know that parents have insight into their children that a teacher might lack.

I was in a quandary. Was it possible to teach in any depth about the Civil Rights Movement without including the violence and the racism?

I respect the right of parents to communicate their concerns and, if possible, I try to address them by altering what I do in the classroom. However, I knew that my obligation went beyond Joanne and her parents. I needed to think about what was best for all my students.

Assessing the Reactions of the Students

I watched my students carefully. It soon became apparent that my African American and biracial students (9 out of 25) were gaining strength and self-confidence during the unit. They were participating more frequently in class, sharing information that they had learned from the many books available in the class and relating what they were learning about the Civil Rights Movement to their own lives.

I knew I had to think of Joanne. But I also had to think of Keisha, Jasmine, Monique, and Jerome.

Take Keisha, who had often drifted off to sleep through our other units and when called on would ramble. During the unit, she suddenly found her voice. In preparation for our enactment of the Birmingham children's march, for example, I talked to the class about what it meant to be "in character" in a drama. I told them to think about how they would feel if they were the people marching for their rights.

"I know," broke in Keisha, "You would be serious. You wouldn't be acting silly or nothing, because this is about getting your freedom. And you are marching for your mother or your father or your sister or your brother or for your children or your grandchildren, not just for yourself."

The next morning, Keisha brought in a friend from another class. "I have something to share," Keisha said. "Yesterday, at the Community Center, LaToya and me made up a speech, like Martin Luther King."

Her friend pulled out a rumpled sheet of paper and they proceeded to present their speech to the class:

> Martin Luther King Jr. and Me. Martin had a dream that black people would be treated equally. But I have a dream that we would hold hands and study together, read together, and play together. I have a dream that we would go to the mall together, come to school together, and learn together as one. One day Rosa Parks refused to give up her seat on the bus to a white person. Things have gotten better now. Thank you.

Keisha later chose to do her human rights biography project on Harriet Tubman. She read all the books she could find on the topic and wrote her longest, most coherent piece in her journal on Tubman. And once, when the class was having a particularly difficult time settling down, Keisha yelled out, "Hey, would you all be acting like this if Martin Luther King was here?"

Jasmine, a biracial girl with a long history of discipline problems at the school, took to heart the story of 6-year-old Ruby Bridges. Jasmine surprised me one morning with a life-sized portrait of Ruby Bridges that she had made in the after-school program by taping together smaller pieces of paper. She wrote about Ruby Bridges in her journal and in a letter to Wisconsin Gov. Tommy Thompson on another topic, she asked, "Have you heard of Ruby Bridges?"

One day, Jasmine approached me in confidence, "Kate, you might not know this, because it's a secret, but I'll tell you something I've been doing."

"I'd like to know, Jasmine," I responded, expecting a confession of some wrongdoing.

"Well, Kate, sometimes, when I'm sitting at my table, I just pretend I'm Ruby Bridges. I pretend that the other kids sitting at my table are those people yelling at me because I'm black and they don't want me in their school. And, just like Ruby, I ignore them and just go on doing my work. I do it real good, just like Ruby. I was doing it just before at math time."

And then there were Monique and Jerome. Previously two of my biggest troublemakers, during this unit they became the two I could count on to be on task for reading, writing, and other activities. Monique, who had previously disrupted numerous

Jasmine surprised me one morning with a life-sized portrait of Ruby Bridges that she had made in the after-school program by taping together smaller pieces of paper.

group discussions or cooperative projects, suddenly became the model student: "Shhhhh, everybody!" she'd admonish. "I want to hear this!"

Jerome found a connection from home. "My mom told me that we all need to learn about this because it could happen again," he said. He told the class about when the people next door to his apartment house had put up a sign to prevent kids from cutting through their yard on their way to school. The sign had said, "Private. Stay out of our yard. No niggers."

Many of the other students talked about how they, too, would have been discriminated against if they had lived in the South during Jim Crow. (I also had four Hmong students, one Cambodian American, two Filipino Americans, two born in Mexico, and one with a Mexican-Indian grandparent.) "I would have had to use the 'colored only' drinking fountain because I'm part Filipino," Anita would remind the class. At the drawing table I heard one girl say, "You know, we would all have been discriminated against, because I'm part Mexican, you are Hmong, and you are both black."

I also watched the reactions of the European American students. There were fewer white kids than children of color in the class and, although we had learned about many brave white activists, the whites were definitely not shown in a positive light in most of the material. I watched to see if the European Americans were engaged in our discussions and if they showed any signs of discomfort. Chris was tentative at first, hanging back, sometimes fooling around with another white boy. But then he started to participate more and more in the discussions and role plays. As we were watching a video, *My Past Is My Own*, in which a white teenage gang assaults the black students at a lunch counter sit-in, Chris moved close to where I was sitting.

"I don't like this part," he confided in me. "If those kids were friends of mine, I'd tell them, 'Hey, leave them alone. What you're doing isn't right.'"

The next day, Chris decided to write a letter to Rosa Parks relating his admiration for her courage.

> *Chris and many of the other white kids in our school come with attitudes that are the products of the racism that divides our neighborhood.*

Chris and many of the other white kids in our school come with attitudes that are the products of the racism that divides our neighborhood. I came to the conclusion that they, as much as, or even more than, the children of color, needed to hear the story of the racial hatred and the saving power of a nonviolent movement. There may come a time when they find the courage to say, "What you're doing isn't right."

Despite the positive changes I witnessed in many of my students, the opposition of Joanne's parents kept nagging at me. We kept in touch through notes and conversations. I heard, on the one hand, that they supported what I was doing; yet Joanne was still to be kept out of all activities related to the unit. I talked over the situation with colleagues and friends, including the principal, who encouraged me to go on with the unit. (In the 1st grade, a parent had complained to the principal that the teacher had not gone into enough depth in presenting the history of civil rights.)

I also spoke with an African American man, the grandfather of a student, who had presented to my class several years ago. He had proudly brought in a huge photograph of the Edmund Pettus Bridge and had told how he joined the voting rights march on "Bloody Sunday," March 7, 1965, and crossed that bridge only to be attacked by local and Alabama state police officers armed with weapons and tear gas. I invited him back to speak to the class and also asked his opinion on my dilemma, sketching out the objections to the civil rights unit. His voice, heretofore somewhat soft and distant, became strident.

"Hey, that's what we were all marching for!" he said. "We were marching for the right for our kids and all kids to learn about the history of black folks. And it's not like it's over and done with. They might try to keep their kid from knowing about it now, but sooner or later they'll will find out and then it will be a shock. Better to learn now what we were all fighting for!"

I decided to also ask the opinion of my students. I was finding it hard to put off questions of why Joanne was dismissed to work in the library each time we worked on the unit. Even though I assigned different work for Joanne, some members of the class were protesting that she was playing on the computers while they were working on their writing and reading. One day, when Joanne was out of the room, I told the class that Joanne's parents objected to her learning about the Civil Rights Movement.

I also asked the class if they thought it was an important topic. The consensus was that it was "very, very important." The reasons came out faster than I could record them: "So if that stuff happened again, we could calm down and be strong." ... "It might happen again and then we'd have to go and march." ... "The KKK is still alive and they don't like blacks and Filipinos." ... "It makes us smarter to learn about this, and then if we have kids and they wanted to learn about it, we could teach them." ... "When we go to another grade, we will know not to call people names like Darkie." ... "If you learn about it, you get to go to higher grades

One day, when Joanne was out of the room, I told the class that Joanne's parents objected to her learning about the Civil Rights Movement.

and get to go to college." ... "Dr. King, he was trying to tell us that we could have a better life." ... "We want no more segregation, no more fights, no more KKK burning down houses." ... "So it don't happen no more."

We went on with our work. At this point in the unit, the focus was on presenting a student-written screenplay of *Selma, Lord, Selma* (which in turn was based on the Disney television special). Not wanting Joanne to miss what was becoming an even more central part of our curriculum, I suggested to Joanne's parents that they watch the tape of the television special. Since it was shown on "Wonderful World of Disney," I figured I couldn't go wrong there. I also gave them copies to read of the screenplay that the class had written. I again was told that Joanne could not participate.

The rest of the students, however, immersed themselves in the drama. Jasmine transformed herself into the role of Sheyann Webb, the brave 8-year-old participant in the Selma voting rights movement. She held her head high and sang "Ain't Gonna Let Nobody Turn Me 'Round" with a voice pure in tone, perfect in pitch, and strong in conviction. Monique turned all her energies into not only acting the part of Rachel West, Sheyann's friend, but also keeping the rest of the class on task and in role. Jerome continued as Martin Luther King, changing the words of his speech every practice but never failing to perform the part of the orator and leader of the people. It was clear that the play was cementing the history of the Civil Rights Movement in the minds and hearts of every student.

Several days before the final performance, Joanne's parents approached me in the hall. They wanted her to participate, although they were concerned it might be too late. They never explained what had led them to change their minds. I knew that Joanne was feeling left out, especially since the class had also been working on their play in their music and movement classes.

Several days before the final performance, Joanne's parents approached me in the hall. They wanted her to participate, although they were concerned it might be too late.

Despite my earnest efforts to excuse Joanne to the library whenever we read or discussed material related to civil rights, Joanne, a very bright and curious girl, had not only managed to pick up a lot of information, but had also learned the songs in the play. Joanne took on her role as a voting rights activist in *Selma, Lord, Selma* as smoothly as if she had been practicing it for three weeks with the rest of the class. She not only marched to the courthouse, singing "Kumbaya" and demanding the right to vote, but she also participated in a slow-motion pantomime of the "Bloody Sunday" confrontation, as marchers attempting to cross the Edmund Pettus Bridge were met with the troopers' sticks, cattle prods, and tear gas.

After Joanne and the others recover from the violent attack and rise to the occasion of singing "Ain't Gonna Let Nobody Turn Me 'Round," this time with added significance to the words, Jasmine (Sheyann) narrates: "We were singing and telling the world that we hadn't been whipped, that we had won. We had really won. After all, we had won."

The Lessons of Selma

The Selma story instructs us that out of unspeakable violence and defeat can come resolution and victory. Out of Bloody Sunday came renewed participation and power in the Civil Rights Movement, resulting in the Voting Rights Act of 1965 and the success of the second Selma to Montgomery march.

Can the Civil Rights Movement be taught without teaching about segregation, racial hatred, and violence? I don't think so.

Can the Civil Rights Movement be taught without teaching about segregation, racial hatred, and violence? I don't think so. It is against the backdrop of the firehoses and the snarling dogs that the Birmingham children found their strength to sing, even as they were hauled off to jail. When Martin Luther King was denied the right to sit in the front of a shoe store or to play with his white friends, the seeds of his leadership were planted. It does not make sense to teach the Civil Rights Movement without teaching about the separate bathrooms and KKK. Furthermore, to do so wouldn't be history. It would be a lie.

Despite the controversy my unit engendered, I did not regret my decision to proceed. Even though the behavior and academic focus of students like Keisha, Jasmine, Jerome, and Monique did not remain at that peak, they still remembered those weeks as the best part of the school year. And as we moved into learning about the struggles of other groups of people for equal rights, or as we talked about issues of justice and tolerance in the classroom, we always had the Civil Rights Movement to look back to for inspiration.

As Keisha said in her end-of-the-year evaluation: "I liked giving my speech in class about Martin Luther King and Rosa Parks, too. They fought for freedom and the right to vote. They are so cool to do that and march and give us freedom. [If they hadn't done that,] me and you would not be together today and be learning."

The names of the children were changed to protect their identities.

CHAPTER THIRTY-FIVE

On the Road to Cultural Bias

A critique of "The Oregon Trail" CD-ROM

By Bill Bigelow

The critics all agree: *The Oregon Trail* is one of the greatest educational computer games ever produced. In 1992, *Prides' Guide to Educational Software* awarded it five stars for being "a wholesome, absorbing historical simulation," and "multiethnic," to boot.

Oregon Trail II is the "best history simulation we've seen to date," according to a review by Warren Buckleitner, editor of *Children's Software Review Newsletter*. Susan Schilling, a key developer of *Oregon Trail* who was later hired by *Star Wars* filmmaker George Lucas to head Lucas Learning Ltd., promised new interactive CD-ROMs targeted at children and concentrated in math and language arts.

Getty Images/The Bridgeman Art Library

Because interactive CD-ROMs like *The Oregon Trail* are encyclopedic in the amount of information they offer, and because they allow students a seemingly endless number of choices, they may appear educationally progressive. CD-ROMs seem tailor-made for the classrooms of tomorrow. They are hands-on and "student-centered." They are generally interdisciplinary—for example, *Oregon Trail II* blends reading, writing, history, geography, math, science, and health. And they are useful in multiage classrooms because they allow students of various knowledge levels to "play" and learn.

But like the walls of a maze, the choices built into interactive CD-ROMs also channel participants in very definite directions. The CD-ROMs are programmed by people—people with particular cultural biases—and children who play the computer games encounter the biases of the programmers (Bowers, 1988). Just as we would not invite a stranger into our classrooms and then leave the room, teachers need to become aware of the political perspectives of CD-ROMs, and need to equip our students to "read" them critically.

At one level, this article is a critical review of the *Oregon Trail* CD-ROMs. I ask what knowledge is highlighted and what is hidden as students play the game. But I also reflect on the nature of the curricula, and suggest some questions teachers can ask before choosing to use them with our students. And I offer some classroom activities that might begin to develop students' critical computer literacy.

Playing the Game

In both *Oregon Trail* and *Oregon Trail II*, students become members of families and wagon trains crossing the Plains in the 1840s or 1850s on the way to the Oregon Territory. A player's objective, according to the game guidebook, is to safely reach the Oregon Territory with one's family, thereby "increasing one's options for economic success."

The enormous number of choices offered in any one session—what to buy for the journey; the kind of wagon to take; whether to use horses, oxen, or mules; the size of the wagon train with which to travel; whom to "talk" to along the way; when and where to hunt; when to rest; how fast to travel—is a kind of gentle seduction to students. It invites them to "try on this world view; see how it fits." In an interactive CD-ROM, you don't merely identify with a particular character, you actually adopt his or her frame of reference and act as if you were that character

Just as we would not invite a stranger into our classrooms and then leave the room, teachers need to become aware of the political perspectives of CD-ROMs, and need to equip our students to "read" them critically.

(Provenzo, 1991). In *Oregon Trail*, a player quickly bonds to the "pioneer" maneuvering through the "wilderness."

In preparation for this article, I've played *Oregon Trail II* until my eyes became blurry. I can see its attraction to teachers. One can't play the game without learning a lot about the geography from Missouri to Oregon. (However, I hope I never have to ford another virtual river ever again.) Reading the trail guide as one plays teaches much about the ailments confronted on the Oregon Trail, and some of the treatments. Students can learn a tremendous amount about the details of life for the trekkers to Oregon: the kinds of wagons required, supplies needed, vegetation encountered along the route, and so forth. And the game has a certain multicultural and gender-fair veneer that, however limited, contrasts favorably with the white male-dominated texts of yesteryear.

But as much as the game teaches, it mis-teaches more. In fundamental respects, *Oregon Trail* is sexist, racist, culturally insensitive, and contemptuous of the earth. It imparts bad values and wrong history.

In fundamental respects, Oregon Trail *is sexist, racist, culturally insensitive, and contemptuous of the earth.*

They Look Like Women, But ...

To its credit, *Oregon Trail* includes large numbers of women. Although I didn't count, women appear to make up roughly half the people students encounter as they play. But this surface equity is misleading. Women may be present, but gender is not acknowledged as an issue in *Oregon Trail*. In the opening sequences, the game requires students to select a profession, special skills they possess, the kind of wagon to take, the city they'll depart from, etc. Class is recognized as an issue—bankers begin with more money than saddlemakers, for example—but not gender or race—a player cannot choose these.

Without acknowledging it, *Oregon Trail* maneuvers students into thinking and acting as if they were all males—and, as we'll see, white males. The game highlights a male lifestyle and poses problems that historically fell within the male domain: whether and where to hunt, which route to take, whether and what to trade, to caulk a wagon or ford a river. However, as I began to read more feminist scholarship on the Oregon Trail, I realized that women and men experienced the Trail very differently. It's clear from reading women's diaries of the period that women played little or no role in deciding whether to embark on the trip, where to camp, which routes to take and the like. In real life, women's decisions revolved around how to maintain a semblance of community under great stress, how "to preserve the home in transit" (Faragher and Stansell, 1992; Schlissel, 1992; Kesselman, 1976). Women decided where to look for firewood or buffalo chips, how and what to cook using hot rocks, how to care for the children, and how to resolve conflicts between travelers, especially the men.

These were real-life decisions, but, with the exception of treating illness, they're missing from *The Oregon Trail*. Students are rarely required to think about the intricacies of preserving "the home in transit" for 2,000 miles. An *Oregon Trail* information box on the screen informs a player when "morale" is high or low, but other than making better male-oriented decisions, what's a player to do? *Oregon Trail* offers no opportunities to encounter the choices of the Trail as women of the time would have encountered them, and to make decisions that might enhance community, and thus "morale." As Lillian Schlissel concludes in her study, *Women's Diaries of the Westward Journey* (1992): "If ever there was a time when men and women turned their psychic energies toward opposite visions, the overland journey was that time. Sitting side by side on a wagon seat, a man and a woman felt different needs as they stared at the endless road that led into the New Country." (p. 15)

Similarly, Oregon Trail fails to represent the texture of community life on the Trail.

Similarly, *Oregon Trail* fails to represent the texture of community life on the Trail. Students confront a seemingly endless stream of problems posed by *Oregon Trail* programmers, but rarely encounter the details of life, especially that of women's lives. By contrast, in an article in the book *America's Working Women* (1976), Amy Kesselman includes a passage from the diary of one female trekker, Catherine Haun, in 1849:

> We women folk visited from wagon to wagon or congenial friends spent an hour walking ever westward, and talking over our home life "back in the states" telling of the loved ones left behind; voicing our hopes for the future in the far west and even whispering, a little friendly gossip of pioneer life. High teas were not popular but tatting, knitting, crocheting, exchanging recipes for cooking beans or dried apples or swopping food for the sake of variety kept us in practice of feminine occupations and diversions. (Kesselman, 1976, p. 71)

The male orientation of *Oregon Trail* is brought into sharp relief in the game's handling of Independence Day commemoration. Students as pioneers are asked if they wish to "Celebrate the Fourth!" Click on this option, and one hears loud "Yahoos" and guns firing. Compare this to the communal preparations described in Enoch Conyers' 1852 diary (but not in *The Oregon Trail*):

A little further on is a group of young ladies seated on the grass talking over the problem of manufacturing "Old Glory" to wave over our festivities. The question arose as to where we are to obtain the material for the flag. One lady brought forth a sheet. This gave the ladies an idea. Quick as thought another brought a skirt for the red stripes … Another lady ran to her tent and brought forth a blue jacket, saying: "Here, take this; it will do for the field." Needles and thread were soon secured and the ladies went at their task with a will, one lady remarking that "necessity is the mother of invention," and the answer came back, "yes, and the ladies of our company are equal to the task." (Hill, 1989, p. 58)

The contrast between the "yahoos" gunfire of *Oregon Trail* and the collective female exhilaration described in the diary excerpt is striking. This comparison alerted me to something so obvious that it took me awhile to recognize. In *Oregon Trail*, people don't talk to each other, they all talk to you, the player. Everyone in the *Oregon Trail*-constructed world aims her or his conversation at you—underscoring the simulation's individualistic ideology that all the world exists for you, controller of the mouse. An *Oregon Trail* more alert to feminist insights and women's experiences would highlight relations between people, would focus on how the experience affects our feelings about each other, would feature how women worked with one another to survive and weave community, as women's diary entries clearly reveal.

As I indicated, large numbers of women appear throughout the *Oregon Trail* simulation, and they often give good advice, perhaps better advice than the men we encounter. But *Oregon Trail's* abundance of women, and its apparent effort to be gender-fair, masks an essential problem: The choice-structure of the simulation privileges men's experience and virtually erases women's experience.

The choice-structure of the simulation privileges men's experience and virtually erases women's experience.

African Americans as Tokens

From the game's beginning, when a player starts off in Independence or St. Joseph, Mo., African Americans dot the *Oregon Trail* landscape. However, by and large they are no more than black-colored white people. Even though Missouri was a slave state throughout the entire *Oregon Trail* period, I never encountered the term "slavery" while playing the game. I found race explicitly acknowledged in only one exchange, when I "talked" to an African American woman along the trail: "I'm Isabella. I'm traveling with the Raleighs and their people. My job is to keep after the cows and watch the children. My husband Fred is the ox-driver—best there is." Are they free? Are they enslaved? Are we to assume the Raleighs are white? I asked to know more: "I was born in Delaware. My father used to tell me stories of Africa and promised one day we'd find ourselves going home. But I don't know if I'm getting closer or farther away with all this walking." The end. Like Missouri, Delaware was a slave state in antebellum days, but this is not shared with students. Isabella offers provocative details, but they hide more than they reveal about her identity and culture.

Oregon Trail's treatment of African Americans reflects a very superficial multiculturalism. Black people are present, but their lives aren't. Attending to matters of race requires more than including lots of black faces, or having little girls "talk black"—"I think it's time we be moving on now." (This little girl reappears from time to time to repeat these same words. A man who looks Mexican likewise shows up frequently to say, with heavy accent: "Time is a-wasting. Let's head out!")

Even though one's life prospects and worldview in the 1840s and 1850s—as today—were dramatically shaped by one's race, this factor is invisible in *Oregon Trail*. Players know their occupations but not their racial identities, even though this knowledge is vital to decisions participants would make before leaving on the journey as well as along the way.

For example, many of the constitutions of societies that sponsored wagon trains specifically excluded blacks from making the trip west. Nonetheless, as Elizabeth McLagan points out in her history of blacks in Oregon, *A Peculiar Paradise* (1980), blacks did travel the Oregon Trail, some as slaves, some as servants, and at least some, like George Bush, as well-to-do pioneers. Race may not have seemed important to the *Oregon Trail* programmers, but race mattered a great deal to Bush: Along the Trail, he confided to another emigrant that if he experienced too much prejudice in Oregon, he would travel south to California or New Mexico and seek protection from the Mexican government. (p. 19)

And Bush had reason to be apprehensive: African Americans arriving in Oregon Territory during the 1840s and 1850s were greeted by laws barring blacks from residency. Black exclusion laws were passed twice in Oregon Territory in the 1840s, and a clause in the Oregon state constitution barring black residency was ratified in 1857—a clause, incidentally, not removed until 1926.

Upon completion of one of my simulated *Oregon Trail* journeys, I clicked to see how I turned out: "In 1855, Bill built a home

Oregon Trail's treatment of African Americans reflects a very superficial multiculturalism.

on 463 acres of land in the Rogue River Valley of Oregon," experienced only "moderate success" and later moved to Medford, "establishing a small business that proved more stable and satisfying." Although the *Oregon Trail* simulation never acknowledges it, "Bill" must have been white, because in 1850 the U.S. Congress passed the Oregon Donation Land Act granting 640 acres to free white males and their wives—only. It is unlikely that a black man, much less a black woman, would have been granted land in 1855 or been allowed to start a business in Medford some years later.

Why were whites so insistent that blacks not live in Oregon? The preamble of one black exclusion bill explained that "situated as the people of Oregon are, in the midst of an Indian population, it would be highly dangerous to allow free negroes and mulattoes to reside in the territory or to intermix with the Indians, instilling in their minds feelings of hostility against the white race. ..." (McLagan, 1980, p. 26). And Samuel Thurston, a delegate to Congress from Oregon Territory explained in 1850 why blacks should not be entitled to homestead in Oregon:

> The negroes associate with the Indians and intermarry, and, if their free ingress is encouraged or allowed, there would a relationship spring up between them and the different tribes, and a mixed race would ensue inimical to the whites; and the Indians being led on by the negro who is better acquainted with the customs, language, and manners of the whites, than the Indian, these savages would become much more formidable than they otherwise would, and long and bloody wars would be the fruits of the comingling of the races. It is the principle of self preservation that justifies the action of the Oregon legislature. (pp. 30-31)

Thurston's argument carried the day. But *Oregon Trail* programmers have framed the issues so that race seems irrelevant. Thus, once students-as-pioneers arrive in Oregon, most of them will live happily after ever—never considering the impact that race would have on life conditions.

Just Passing Through?

Oregon Trail programmers are careful not to portray Indians as the "enemy" of westward trekkers. However, the simulation's superficial sympathy for Native groups masks a profound insensitivity to Indian cultures and to the earth that sustained these cultures. The simulation guidebook lists numerous Indian nations by name—and respectfully calls them "nations." The *Oregon Trail* guidebook explains that emigrants' fear of Indians is "greatly exaggerated":

Once students-as-pioneers arrive in Oregon, most of them will live happily after ever—never considering the impact that race would have on life conditions.

Some travelers have been known to cross the entire breadth of the continent from the Missouri River to the Sierra Nevadas without ever laying eye on an Indian, except perhaps for occasional brief sightings from a distance.

This is all well and good, for it is probably best for all parties concerned for emigrants and Indians to avoid contact with each other. Such meetings are often the source of misunderstandings, sometimes with regrettable consequences.

Emigrants often spread disease, according to the guidebook, which made the Indians "distrust and dislike" the emigrants. The guidebook further warns *Oregon Trail* players not to overhunt game in any one place as "few things will incur the wrath of the Indian peoples more than an overstayed welcome accompanied by the egregious waste of the natural resources upon which they depend."

What orientation is highlighted and what is hidden in the simulation programmed for students to follow? The ideology embedded in *Oregon Trail I* and *II* is selfish and goal-driven: Care about indigenous people insofar as you need to avoid "misunderstanding" and incurring the wrath of potentially hostile natives. *Oregon Trail* promotes an anthropocentric, earth-as-natural-resource outlook. Nature is a thing to be consumed or overcome as people traverse the country in search of success in a faraway land. The simulation's structure coerces children into identifying with white settlers and dismissing nonwhite others. It contributes to the broader curricular racialization of identity students absorb—learning who constitutes the normalized "we" and who is excluded.

Oregon Trail players need not take into account the lives of others unless it's necessary to do so in order to accomplish their personal objectives. Thus the cultures of Plains Indians are backgrounded. The game marginalizes their view of the earth. Contrast, for example, the Indians' term "mother earth" with the *Oregon Trail* term "natural resource."

The metaphor of earth as mother suggests humans in a reciprocal relationship with a natural world that is alive, nourishing us, sustaining us. A resource is a thing to be used. It exists for us, outside of us, and we have no obligations in return.

The consequences of the Oregon Trail for the Plains Indians, the Indians of the Northwest and for the earth were devastating. In fairness, as they play *Oregon Trail*, students may hear some of the details of this upheaval.

For example, on one trip I encountered a "Pawnee Village." Had I paid attention to the warning in the guidebook to "avoid

The ideology embedded in Oregon Trail I *and* II *is selfish and goal-driven: Care about indigenous people insofar as you need to avoid 'misunderstanding' and incurring the wrath of potentially hostile natives.*

contact" I would have ignored it and continued on my trip. But I entered and "talked" to the people I encountered there. A Pawnee woman: "Why do you bother me? I don't want to trade. The things that we get from the white travelers don't make up for all that we lose." I click to hear more. "We didn't know the whooping cough, measles, or the smallpox until your people brought them to us. Our medicine cannot cure these strange diseases, and our children are dying." I click on "Do you have any advice?" Angrily, she says, "No. I just want you to leave us alone." The implication is that if I just "leave them alone" and continue on the trail I can pursue my dream without hurting the Indians.

However, this interpretation misses the fact that the Oregon Trail itself, not just contact with the so-called pioneers, devastated Indian cultures and the ecology of which those cultures were an integral part. For example, pioneers—let's begin to call them their Lakota name, Wasi'chu, "greedy persons"—cut down all the cottonwood trees found along the rich bottomlands of plains rivers—trees which "offered crucial protection during winter blizzards as well as concealing a village's smoke from its enemies. In lean seasons, horses fed on its bark, which was surprisingly nourishing" (Davidson and Lytle, 1992, p. 114).

The Oregon Trail created serious wood shortages, which even the Wasi'chu acknowledged. "By the Mormon guide we here expected to find the last timber," wrote overlander A.W. Harlan, describing the Platte River, "but all had been used up by others ahead of us so we must go about 200 miles without any provisions cooked up." A few weeks later, in sight of the Black Hills, Harlan wrote: "[W]e have passed many cottonwood stumps but no timber. ..." (p. 115)

Wasi'chu rifles also killed tremendous numbers of buffalo that Plains Indians depended upon for survival. One traveler in the 1850s wrote that "the valley of the Platte for 200 miles presents the aspect of the vicinity of a slaughter yard, dotted all over with skeletons of buffaloes" (ibid, p. 117). Very soon after the beginning of the Oregon Trail the buffalo learned to avoid the Trail, their herds migrating both south and north. Edward Lazarus points out in *Black Hills/White Justice: The Sioux Nation Versus the United States—1775 to the Present*: "But the Oregon Trail did more than move the buffalo; it destroyed the hunting pattern of the Sioux, forcing them to follow the herds to the fringes of their domain and to expose themselves to the raids of their enemies" (1991, p. 14).

The Oregon Trail itself, not just contact with the so-called pioneers, devastated Indian cultures and the ecology of which those cultures were an integral part.

However, wrapped in their cocoons of self-interest, *Oregon Trail* players push on, oblivious to the mayhem and misery they cause in their westward drive. This is surely an unintended, and yet intrinsic, part of the game's message: Pursue your goal as an autonomous individual, ignore the social and ecological consequences. Look out for number one.

No Violence Here

Oregon Trail never suggests to its simulated pioneers that they should seek permission of Indian nations to travel through their territory. And from this key omission flow other omissions. The simulation doesn't inform players that because of the disruptions wrought by the daily intrusions of the westward migration, Plains Indians regularly demanded tribute from the trekkers. As John Unruh Jr. writes in *The Plains Across*:

> The natives explicitly emphasized that the throngs of overlanders were killing and scaring away buffalo and other wild game, overgrazing prairie grasses, exhausting the small quantity of available timber, and depleting water resources. The tribute payments ... were demanded mainly by the Sac and Fox, Kickapoo, Pawnee, and Sioux Indians—the tribes closest to the Missouri River frontier and therefore those feeling most keenly the pressures of white men increasingly impinging upon their domains. (1993, p. 169)

Wasi'chu travelers resented this Indian-imposed taxation and their resentment frequently turned to hostility and violence, especially in the later years of the Trail. The Pawnees were "hateful wretches," wrote Dr. Thomas Wolfe in 1852, for demanding a 25-cent toll at a bridge across Shell Creek near the North Platte River (ibid, p. 171). Shell Creek and other crossings became flashpoints that escalated into violent skirmishes resulting in the deaths of settlers and Indians.

Despite the increasing violence along the Oregon Trail, one choice *Oregon Trail* programmers don't offer students-as-trekkers is the choice to harm Indians. Doubtless MECC, producer of *Oregon Trail*, is not anxious to promote racism toward Native peoples. However, because simulation players can't hurt or even speak ill of Indians, the game fails to alert students that white hostility was one feature of the westward migration. The omission is significant because the sanitized, nonviolent *Oregon Trail* fails to equip students to reflect on the origins of conflicts between whites and Indians. Nor does it offer students any insights into the racial antagonism that fueled this violence. In all my play of *Oregon Trail*

Oregon Trail never suggests to its simulated pioneers that they should seek permission of Indian nations to travel through their territory.

I can't recall any blatant racism directed at Indians. But as John Unruh Jr. points out: "The callous attitude of cultural and racial superiority so many overlanders exemplified was of considerable significance in producing the volatile milieu in which more and more tragedies occurred." (p. 186)

The End of the Trail

> Soon there will come from the rising sun a different kind of man from any you have yet seen, who will bring with them a book and will teach you everything, after that the world will fall to pieces.
>
> — Spokan Prophet, 1790
> (*Limerick*, 1987, p. 39)

Someone can spend two or three hours—or more—playing one game of *Oregon Trail* before finally reaching Oregon Territory. Once we arrive, the game awards us points and tells us how our life in Oregon turned out. And yet it fails to raise vital questions about our right to be there in the first place, and what happened to the people who were there first.

In its section on the "Destination," the guidebook offers students its wisdom on how they should view life in a new land. It's a passage that underscores the messages students absorb while engaged in the simulation. These comforting words of advice and social vision are worth quoting at length:

> Once you reach the end of your journey, you should go to the nearest large town to establish your land claim. If there are no large towns in the area, simply find an unclaimed tract of land and settle down. ... As they say, possession is nine tenths of the law, and if you have settled and worked land that hasn't yet been claimed by anyone else, you should have little or no trouble legally establishing your claim at a later time.
>
> As more and more Americans move into the region, more cities and towns will spring up, further increasing one's options for economic success. Rest assured in the facts that men and women who are willing to work hard will find their labors richly rewarded, and that you, by going west, are helping to spread American civilization from ocean to ocean across this great continent, building a glorious future for generations to come!

The Lakota scholar/activist Vine Deloria Jr. in his book, *Indians of the Pacific Northwest* (1977), offers a less sanguine perspective than that included in the CD-ROM guidebook. People coming in on the Oregon Trail "simply arrived on the scene and

Oregon Trail fails to raise vital questions about our right to be there in the first place, and what happened to the people who were there first.

started building. If there were Indians or previous settlers on the spot they were promptly run off under one pretext or another. Lawlessness and thievery dominated the area". (p. 53) From 1850 on, using provisions of the Oregon Donation Act, thousands of "pioneers" invaded "with impunity."

As Deloria points out, there were some in Congress who were aware that they were encouraging settlers to steal Indian land, and so shortly after, Congress passed the Indian Treaty Act requiring the United States to get formal agreements from Indian tribes. Anson Dart, appointed to secure land concessions, pursued this objective in a despicable fashion. For example, he refused to have the treaties translated into the Indians' languages, instead favoring "Chinook jargon," a nonlanguage of fewer than 300 words good for trading, giving orders, and little else. Dart's mandate was to move all the Indians east of the Cascades, but he decided some tribes, like the Tillamooks and Chinooks, should keep small amounts of land as cheap labor reserves:

> Almost without exception, I have found [the Indians] anxious to work at employment at common labor and willing too, to work at prices much below that demanded by the whites. The Indians make all the rails used in fencing, and at this time do the boating upon the rivers: In consideration, therefore, of the usefulness as labourers in the settlements, it was believed to be far better for the Country that they should not be removed from the settled portion of Oregon if it were possible to do so. (Deloria, 1977, p. 51)

In southwestern Oregon white vigilantes didn't wait for treaty niceties to be consummated. Between 1852 and 1856 self-proclaimed Volunteers attacked Indians for alleged misdeeds, or simply because they were Indians.

Meanwhile, in southwestern Oregon white vigilantes didn't wait for treaty niceties to be consummated. Between 1852 and 1856 self-proclaimed Volunteers attacked Indians for alleged misdeeds, or simply because they were Indians. In August of 1853, one Martin Angel rode into the Rogue River valley gold mining town of Jacksonville shouting, "Nits breed lice. We have been killing Indians in the valley all day," and "Exterminate the whole race." Minutes later a mob of about 800 white men hanged a 7-year-old Indian boy.

In October 1855, a group of whites massacred 23 Indian men, women, and children. This incident began the Rogue Indian war, which lasted until June 1856 (Beckham, 1991, p. 103). Recall that this is the same region and the same year in one *Oregon Trail* session where "Bill" built a home and experienced "moderate success"—but thanks to the *Oregon Trail* programmers, learned nothing of the social conflicts swirling around him.

Nor did Bill learn that, even as a white person, he could protest the outrages committed against the Rogue River Valley Indians as did one anonymous "Volunteer" in a passionate 1853 letter to the *Oregon Statesman* newspaper:

> A few years since the whole valley was theirs [the Indians'] alone. No white man's foot had ever trod it. They believed it theirs forever. But the gold digger come, with his pan and his pick and shovel, and hundreds followed. And they saw in astonishment their streams muddied, towns built, their valley fenced and taken. And where their squaws dug camus, their winter food, and their children were wont to gambol, they saw dug and plowed, and their own food sown by the hand of nature, rooted out forever, and the ground it occupied appropriated to the rearing of vegetables for the white man. Perhaps no malice yet entered the Indian breast. But when he was weary of hunting in the mountains without success, and was hungry, and approached the white man's tent for bread; where instead of bread he received curses and kicks, ye treaty kicking men—ye Indian exterminators think of these things. (Applegate and O'Donnell, 1994, p. 34)

Oregon Trail hides the nature of the Euro-American invasion in at least two ways. In the first place, the *Oregon Trail* CD-ROM simply fails to inform simulation participants what happened between settlers and Indians. To the *Oregon Trail* player, it doesn't feel like an invasion; it doesn't feel wrong. After one of my arrivals, in 1848, "Life in the new land turned out to be happy and successful for Bill, who always cherished bittersweet but proud memories of the months spent on the *Oregon Trail*." (This struck me as a rather odd account, given that I had lost all three of my children on the trip.)

Oregon Trail hides the nature of the Euro-American invasion.

The only person that matters is the simulation player, in this case, Bill. I was never told whether life turned out equally "happy and successful" for the Klamaths, Yakamas, Cayuses, Nez Percés, Wallawallas, and all the others who occupied this land generations before the Wasi'chu arrived.

The second way the nature of the white invasion is hidden has to do with the structure of the simulation. For a couple hours or more the player endures substantial doses of frustration, tedium, and difficulty. By the time the Willamette or Rogue Valleys come up on the screen we, the simulated trekkers, feel that we deserve the land, that our labors in transit should be "richly rewarded" with the best land we can find.

Data Deception and What to Do About It

In the Beatles' song, all you need is love; in *Oregon Trail*, all you need is data. *Oregon Trail* offers students gobs of information: snake bite remedies, river locations and depths, wagon specifications, ferry costs, daily climate reports. Loaded with facts, it feels comprehensive. Loaded with people voicing contrasting opinions, it feels balanced. Loaded with choices, it feels free. But the simulation begins from no moral or ethical standpoint beyond individual material success. It contains no vision of social/ecological justice, and hence promotes the full litany of sexism, racism, and imperialism, as well as exploitation of the earth. And simultaneously, it hides this bias. The combination is insidious, and makes interactive CD-ROMs like this one more difficult to critique than traditional textbooks or films. The forced identification of player with simulation protagonist leaves the student no option but to follow the ideological map laid out by the programmers.

Nonetheless, my critique is not a call to boycott "edutainment" resources. But we need to remember that these CD-ROMs are not teacher substitutes. The teacher's role in analyzing and presenting these devices in a broader ethical context is absolutely vital. Thus teachers across the country must begin a dialogue toward developing a critical computer literacy. We need to figure out ways to equip students to recognize and evaluate the deep moral/political messages imparted as they maneuver within various computer software programs.

Before choosing to use CD-ROMs that involve people and place, like *The Oregon Trail*—or, for example, its newer siblings *The Yukon Trail*, *The Amazon Trail*, and *Africa Trail*—teachers can consider a series of questions. These include:

- Which social groups are students not invited to identify with in the simulation? For example, Native Americans, African Americans, women, and Latinos are superficially present in *Oregon Trail*, but the stuff of their lives is missing.

- How might these social groups frame problems differently than they are framed in the simulation? As we saw in this critique of *Oregon Trail*, women tended to focus more on maintaining community than on hunting. Native Americans had a profoundly different relationship to the earth than did the Euro-American "tamers of the wilderness."

> *Oregon Trail contains no vision of social/ ecological justice, and hence promotes the full litany of sexism, racism, and imperialism, as well as exploitation of the earth.*

- What decisions do simulation participants make that may have consequences for social groups not highlighted in the simulation? And what are these consequences? Even though the very existence of the Oregon Trail contributed to the decimation of Plains and Northwest Indians, simulation participants are never asked to consider the broader effects of their decision-making. What may be an ethical individual choice may be unethical when multiplied several hundred thousand times. (In this respect, CD-ROM choice-making both reflects and reinforces conventional notions of "freedom" that justify disastrous social and ecological practices.)

- What decisions do simulation participants make that may have consequences for the earth and nonhuman life? Similarly, a simulation participant's choice to cut down trees for firewood may be "rational" for that individual, but may also have deleterious effects on the ecological balance of a particular bio-region.

- If the simulation is time-specific, as in the case of *The Oregon Trail*, what were the social and environmental consequences after the time period covered in the simulation? The wars between Indians and U.S. Cavalry in the latter decades of the 19th century are inexplicable without the Oregon Trail as prologue.

- Can we identify the ideological orientation of a particular CD-ROM? The question is included here simply to remind us that all computer materials— indeed, all curricula—have an ideology. Our first step is becoming aware of the nature of that ideology.

What decisions do simulation participants make that may have consequences for social groups not highlighted in the simulation?

These are hardly exhaustive, but may suggest a useful direction to begin thinking, as CD-ROMs become increasingly available and as they come to cover more and more subjects. Finally, let me use the example of *Oregon Trail* to sketch out a number of ways that teachers can begin to foster a critical computer literacy:

- Once we've identified some of the social groups that are substantially missing in a CD-ROM activity like *Oregon Trail*, we can make an effort to locate excerpts of their diaries, speeches, or other communications (to the extent that these cultures are print-oriented) and read these together.

- We might then engage students in a role play where, as a class, students face a number of Oregon Trail problems. For example, class members could portray women on the Oregon Trail and decide how they will attempt to maintain a community in transit. Or they might role-play a possible discussion among Oglala people as they confront the increasingly disruptive presence of Wasi'chu crossing their lands.

• Students might be asked to list all the ways that African Americans would experience the Oregon Trail differently than Euro-Americans would—from planning to the trip itself. (It's unlikely, for example, that every white person on the streets of Independence, Missouri said a friendly "Howdy," to blacks encountered, as each of them does to the implied but unacknowledged white male *Oregon Trail* simulation player.)

• In playing the *Oregon Trail* simulation, students could assume a particular racial, cultural, or gender identity, and note whether the choices or experiences described in the simulation make sense from the standpoint of a member of their group. For example, would a typical African American in Missouri in 1850 be allowed to choose from which city to begin the trek west?

• As we share with students the social and ecological costs of the Oregon Trail, we could ask them to write critical letters to each of the "pioneers" they portrayed in the simulation. Some could represent Rogue Valley Indians, Shoshoni people, or even Mother Earth. For instance, how does "Mother Earth" respond to the casual felling of every cottonwood tree along the Platte River?

• A Native American elder or activist could be invited into the classroom to speak about the concerns that are important to his or her people and about the history of white-Indian relations.

• We could encourage students to think about the politics of naming in the simulation. They could suggest alternative names for the Oregon Trail itself. For example, one historian of the American West, Frederick Merk, aptly calls the Oregon Trail a "path of empire." (1978) Writer Dan Georgakas names it a "march of death." (1973) Other names might be "invasion of the West," or "the 20-year trespass." Just as with Columbus' "discovery" of America, naming shapes understanding, and we need classroom activities to uncover this process.

• Students could write and illustrate alternative children's books describing the Oregon Trail from the standpoint of women, African Americans, Native Americans, or the earth.

- Now have them "play" *The Oregon Trail* again. What do they see this time that they didn't see before? Whose world view is highlighted and whose is hidden? If they choose, students might present their findings to other classes or to teachers who may be considering the use of CD-ROMs.

The Oregon Trail is not necessarily more morally obnoxious than other CD-ROMs or curricular materials with similar ideological biases. My aim here is broader than to merely shake a scolding finger at MECC, producer of the *Oregon Trail* series. I've tried to demonstrate why teachers and students must develop a critical computer literacy. Some of the new CD-ROMs seem more socially aware than the blatantly culturally insensitive materials that still fill school libraries and bookrooms. And the flashy new computer packages also invoke terms long sacred to educators: student empowerment, individual choice, creativity, high interest. It's vital that we remember that coincident with the arrival of these new educational toys is a deepening social and ecological crisis. Global and national inequality between "haves" and "have-nots" is increasing. Violence of all kinds is endemic. And the earth is being consumed at a ferocious pace. Computer programs are not politically neutral in the big moral contests of our time. Inevitably, they take sides. Thus, a critical computer literacy, one with a social/ecological conscience, is more than just a good idea—it's a basic skill.

It's vital that we remember that coincident with the arrival of these new educational toys is a deepening social and ecological crisis.

References

Applegate, S. & O'Donnell, T. (1994). *Talking on paper: An anthology of Oregon letters and diaries.* Corvallis, OR: Oregon State University Press.

Armstrong, D. (February 23, 1996). Lucas getting into education via CD-ROM. *The San Francisco Examiner.*

Beckham, S.D. (1991). Federal-Indian Relations. *The first Oregonians.* Portland, OR: Oregon Council for the Humanities.

Bowers, C.A. (1988). *The cultural dimensions of educational computing: Understanding the non-neutrality of technology.* New York: Teachers College Press.

Davidson, J.W. & Lytle, M.H. (1992). *After the fact: The art of historical detection.* New York: McGraw-Hill.

Deloria Jr., V. (1977). *Indians of the Pacific Northwest.* Garden City, NY: Doubleday.

Faragher, J., & Stansell, C. (1975). Women and Their Families on the Overland Trail to California and Oregon, 1842-1867. *Feminist Studies 2.* 150-166.

Georgakas, D. (1973). *Red Shadows: The History of Native Americans from 1600 to 1900, From the Desert to the Pacific Coast.* Garden City, NY: Zenith.

Hill,W.E. (1989). *The Oregon Trail: Yesterday and today.* Caldwell, ID: Caxton. (p. 58).

Johansen, B. & Maestas, R. (1979). *Wasi'chu: The continuing Indian wars.* New York: Monthly Review.

Kesselman, A. (1976). Diaries and Reminiscences of Women on the Oregon Trail: A Study in Consciousness. In R. Baxandall, L. Gordon, S. Reverby (eds.), *America's working women: A documentary history—1600 to the present.* New York: Vintage.

Lazarus, E. (1991). *Black Hills/White justice: The Sioux Nation versus the United States—1775 to the present.* New York: HarperCollins.

Limerick, P.N. (1987). *The legacy of conquest: The unbroken past of the American West.* New York: W.W. Norton.

McLagan, E. (1980). *A peculiar paradise: A history of blacks in Oregon, 1788-1940.* Portland, OR: The Georgian Press.

MECC (1994). *The Oregon Trail II.* Minneapolis, MN.

Merk, F. (1978). *History of the westward movement.* New York: Knopf.

Pride, B. & Pride, M. (1992). *Prides' guide to educational software.* Wheaton, IL: Crossway Books.

Provenzo Jr., E.F. (1991). *Video kids: Making sense of Nintendo.* Cambridge, MA: Harvard University Press.

Schlissel, L. (1992). *Women's diaries of the westward journey.* New York: Schocken.

Unruh Jr., J.D. (1993). *The plains across: The overland emigrants and the trans-Mississippi West, 1840-1860.* Urbana and Chicago, IL: University of Illinois Press.

CHAPTER THIRTY-SIX

For My People

Using Margaret Walker's poem to
help students 'talk-back' to stereotypes and to affirm their self worth

Linda Christensen

"I don't understand how you could walk into that building day after day for 22 years," the older woman at the
copier told me. "I have to go in there once a week, and
I fear for my life every time I walk up those stairs. All of those black
boys with their hoodlum clothes—sweatshirt hoods pulled up over
their heads, baggy pants—I'm afraid they're going to knock me
down the steps and steal my purse."

I looked at her and remembered Damon and Sekou, young
black men I taught at "that building": Jefferson High School, Portland, Ore. I remembered their brilliance, imagine their faces—one
was at law school, one was at NASA. I thought of Kanaan's huge

heart, of Frank's humor. I thought of Aaron Wheeler-Kay's poem written after we visited an art museum exhibit of Carrie Mae Weems' work:

> I Went Looking For Jefferson
>   and I found...
> all the nations of the world
>   wrapped in baggy jeans
>   sweatshirts
>   braids.
> Closed minds slowly opening
>   like doors under water.
> Jefferson is our whetstone
>   the blade is our mind.

There was no blade to open the mind of the woman at the copy machine. I'd met her before in countless other closed minds through the years: people—teachers, parents, reporters, students from other schools—who sized up those who attended or worked at Jefferson based on stereotypical images, usually without ever venturing inside our classrooms.

Students and Stereotypes

Students, particularly students who don't fit the social norm because of their race, language, sexual orientation, weight, or ability to purchase the latest fashions, bear the brunt of such stereotypes. They sometimes share their anger and frustration at inappropriate times and in inappropriate ways. But the classroom can be a safe place for students to not only talk back, but to affirm their right to a place in the world.

The classroom can be a safe place for students to not only talk back, but to affirm their right to a place in the world.

During the years I worked at Jefferson, I found it necessary to help students "talk back" to disrespectful and untrue stereotypes of our school. In one particularly helpful assignment, they write a poem as their way of "talking back."

I began by reading Margaret Walker's powerful poem "For My People." Walker's poem teaches about the hardship that African Americans endured, but also celebrates the triumphs of her people. She ends the poem with an exhortation: "Let a new earth rise. Let another world be born. ... Let a race of men now rise and take control!"

We looked at how Walker constructs her poem with the repeating phrase "For my people." She uses the phrase as an introduction to her theme for that stanza and follows it with a list. For example:

For my people everywhere singing their slave songs
repeatedly: their dirges and   their ditties and their
blues and jubilees, praying their prayers nightly to an
unknown god, bending their knees humbly to an unseen
power;

Walker's poem teaches the strength of using repetition and
lists in poetry. I also pointed out the rhythm of the line—
"their dirges and their ditties and their blues and jubilees," and
the repetition of sounds—singing slave songs, dirges and ditties, and praying prayers.

Then I asked students to create a list of their "people." I
told them to think of all of the communities they belonged to.
I list mine on the board as a way to stimulate them to think
beyond their immediate categories. My list consisted of Jefferson, poor whites, working class, Norwegians, Germans, teachers, feminists, social activists, women, mothers, overweight
people, environmentalists.

I often used Jefferson as a model because it's the one community we all shared. We catalogued reasons to celebrate our
school: the diverse student body, the many languages heard in
the halls, the Jefferson dancers and the gospel singers, Michele
Stemler's Spanish classes, the powerful student-created murals
on the walls. Then I asked them to pick one of their communities and list what they could praise about it. I also asked
them to think about any common misconceptions people have
about any of their "people" and suggested that they might "talk
back" to those judgments in the poem I asked them to write.

My student Cang Dao wrote in his poem "Race":

> People don't know how I feel "You
>   can't talk like us."
> The words hurt me more than
> It hurts them to say.
> I'm getting an attitude.
> Too many jokes,
>   I can't accept it.
> What's wrong about me
> That may not be accepted by them?
> Is it the way I look or
> The way I talk?
> How many languages can you speak?
> I speak four.
> Is there something from

Me that you want?
My beautiful brown eyes or
My lovely skin?
Don't get jealous.

When Cang wrote this poem, we discussed how kids made fun of his newcomer English, but we also discussed how he can speak more languages than most of the student body. He embedded pieces of that talk in his poem.

Lori Ann Durbin, then a senior in my Writing for Publication class, was a transplanted cowgirl who ended up at Jefferson High School. Her poem "Country Folk" celebrates that heritage:

For my folk, two-steppin', shit-
    kickin' pioneers.
Blue collar, redneck, bowlegged
    horsemen …
This is my song to you.
Moonshiners, horse ranchers, hill
    billy roots,
wild women, bare feet, it's nothin'
    or it's boots,
twangy sweet fiddle, songs about
    our lives,
maybe sappy to everyone else, but
    that's how we survive.
Fishin', singin', ridin' bareback in
    the field,
tight cowboy butts and Wranglers.
I love the way they feel.
Tailgate parties, couples in the
    barn, hay in our hair.
It's not just music.
It's a way of life.

Justin Morris, another senior, took the stereotypes about black people and used them in his celebration. His poem demonstrated an in-your-face love for all aspects of his heritage. (One night I was at a local copy store making huge posters of these poems to hang around the school. Several African American men from the community were copying on a machine close to my oversize machine. They laughed when they read Justin's poem and took one of the copies to hang in their office.) This is Justin's poem:

For My People
This is for my people
who are "colored"
who are proud.

For my people
who cause white women to clutch

    their purses
who white men look down on
who drank from different
      fountains
who fought prejudice.

For my people
with kinky afros
and gheri curls.

For my people
with big lips
and wide noses.

For my people
with black power
fingertips drenched with barbecue

    sauce.

the people
with pink hearts
and brown/black skins.
For my people:
Stay strong.

The woman who feared for her life each time she walked Jefferson's halls "confessed" her racism—which is perhaps the first step toward change. I will bring her my students' poems. I want her to see beyond the baggy pants and sweatshirts to the whetstone that sharpened their minds. I hope that by reading their words, she'll see the "pink hearts" inside the "brown/black" skin, she'll hear the intelligence that ricochets off Jefferson's walls and know she doesn't have to be afraid.

RESOURCES

Giovanni, N. (2001). Legacies. In B. Rochelle (ed.) *Words with wings: A treasury of African-American poetry and art*. Singapore: HarperCollins.

Hughes, L. (2001). My people. In B. Rochelle (ed.) *Words with wings: A treasury of African-American poetry and art.* Singapore: HarperCollins.

Walker, A. (2001). Women. In B. Rochelle (ed.) *Words with wings: A treasury of African-American poetry and art.* Singapore: HarperCollins.

Walker, M. (1989). For my people. *This Is My Century: New and Collected Poems.* Athens: University of Ga. Press.

CHAPTER THIRTY-SEVEN

Math, SATs, and Racial Profiling

By Eric Gutstein

In our classrooms, we may not often think of technology as a tool for teaching for social justice. But in my experience of teaching middle school mathematics, I've found that technology can be a powerful asset.

Although I am a university-based mathematics educator, I regularly teach at Rivera school, located in a Mexican immigrant community in Chicago. The following are examples of how my students and I have used technology to investigate racial profiling and to analyze the relationship of family income level to scores on standardized tests.

Jean-Claude Lejeune

In particular, I want to show the potential of using graphing calculators with students. (A graphing calculator is basically a hand-held computer that can do sophisticated mathematics, display various types of graphs and create tables from data, and perform various types of statistical analyses. While they are still too expensive for many students, many high school and middle school math departments have them.)

Mathematics plays a central role in understanding racial profiling. The essence of profiling is proportion and expected value: A higher proportion of African Americans (or Arabs/Arab Americans today) are stopped and searched than would be expected given their percentage in the population—assuming random (i.e., fair) searches or stops.

Mathematics plays a central role in understanding racial profiling.

Driving While Black

In 2001, I did a project with my 7th-grade class called, "Driving While Black/Driving While Brown: A Mathematics Project About Racial Profiling." I gave students data about percentages of stops of Latino drivers and the percent of Latino drivers in Illinois. This was a difficult project conceptually because students had little experience with the mathematical ideas of expectation. Also, there is plenty of research documenting confusion about basic probability, in both children and adults. Children often believe results based on a few events and tend to overgeneralize. For example, if one tosses an unbiased coin three times and it comes up heads each time, children may wrongly believe that the odds are better (or worse!) than 50 percent that the next toss will be tails.

In mathematics, expected value is based on theoretical probability. If 30 percent of drivers are Latino, we would expect that 30 percent of random stops would be of Latinos—but only in the long run. This does not mean that if police made 10 stops and five were of Latinos that something is necessarily out of line, but it does mean that if they made 10,000 stops and 5,000 were of Latinos, something is definitely wrong.

Technology comes in handy to show how actual results tend to converge with theoretical probability as the number of events increases. I used a graphing calculator in class to demonstrate this on a graph called a histogram, which can visually display the results of probability events. I used a simple computer program (written for the calculator) which simulates a dice-tossing situation. If you throw two dice, the probability of throwing a seven is 1/6, while the probability of throwing a two is 1/36. However, if you toss two dice and do this just six times, there is good chance (about 1 in 3) that you won't even get one seven!

With the calculator and program, I simulated 10 tosses, then 100, 1,000, and finally 10,000, and we looked at each resulting histogram (shown on an overhead projector that displays the calculator screen). As the number of tosses increased, the histogram began to take on the "ideal" shape as predicted by the theoretical probability (for example, 1/6 of 10,000 is about 1,667, and we had quite close to that number of sevens). These gradually converging "shapes" helped students realize that the greater the number of "trials," the closer to the theoretical probability the results should be.

Students learned important mathematical ideas about probability through considering actual data about "random" traffic stops and compared these to the theoretical probability (what we should "expect"). Graphing calculators can easily simulate large numbers of random "traffic stops" (since they have a built-in "random" number generator).

Without calculators, one can still do the simulation, albeit with fewer repetitions and more effort. I had students pick cubes from a bag (without looking) where three of 100 were brown (Latino), and the rest white (because in that part of Illinois, 3 percent of the drivers were Latino). Each group's record of 100 picks simulated how many Latinos should have been stopped out of 100 random stops. We then combined all the groups' data and had a larger number which came fairly close to 3 percent, although individual groups' data ranged from 2 percent to 7 percent. But in real life, the percentage of Latinos actually stopped was about 21 percent. Students saw through their own simulations that what they "expected" was not what the Illinois State Police actually did.

At the end of the project, students reflected on what they had learned through using mathematics and technology. They had a range of responses, but most reached the conclusion that the disproportionate number of traffic stops for Latinos was related to racial discrimination. A fairly typical response was:

> I learned that police are probably really being racial because there should be Latino people between a range of 1-5 percent, and no, their range is 21 percent Latino people and also I learned that mathematics is useful for many things in life, math is not just something you do, it's something you should use in life.

But not everyone saw it that way. One student commented:

> Police are maybe just stopping people because they might look suspicious, drunk, or something. They don't just stop you for anything. I think that this project was not accurate

Students learned important mathematical ideas about probability through considering actual data about 'random' traffic stops and compared these to the theoretical probability.

to prove anything. I mean what is it proving, it is not accurate in the cubes.

In hindsight, a weakness in the project was that although students understood that the data showed something was amiss, we spent insufficient time discussing and analyzing the complexities of racism. What did emerge was students' sense of justice ("Why do they make random stops? … Just because of their race and their color?") and sense of agency, as well as perhaps a sense of naïveté ("And Latinos shouldn't let them [police], they should go to a police department and tell how that person was harassed just because of a racial color.").

What did emerge was students' sense of justice and sense of agency.

Bias in SAT scores

This issue of the complexity of the social issues also surfaced in an earlier project I did with an 8th-grade class in 1998-99. In this project, students investigated the relationship between race, gender, and family income and ACT and SAT scores. We were studying data analysis and creating scatterplots, a type of graph one can use to visually inspect the correlation of two variables (e.g.,

1997 SAT Scores

SAT: Total Test-takers (1.1 million)

	Verbal	Math	Total
American Indian or Alaskan Native	475	475	950
Asian, Asian Amer,. or Pacific Is.	496	560	1056
Black or African American	434	423	857
Mexican American	451	458	909
Puerto Rican	454	447	901
Hispanic/Latino	466	468	934
White	536	526	1052
Other	512	514	1026
Males	507	530	1037
Females	503	494	997
ALL TEST TAKERS	505	511	1016
less that $10,000/year	428	448	873
$10,000 – $20,000/year	454	464	918
$20,000 – $30,000/year	480	492	972
$30,000 – $40,000/year	496	497	993
$40,000 – $50,000/year	507	508	1015
$50,000 – $60,000/year	515	518	1033
$70,000 – $80,000/year	522	526	1048
$80,000 – $100,000/year	540	544	1084
more than $100,000/year	559	571	1130

test scores and family income). Students had to create a scatter-plot from data that I downloaded from FairTest's web site (www.fairtest.org). We did not use graphing calculators for two reasons—individual scores and income levels were not available (the FairTest data aggregated the 1,127,021 students who took the test in 1997 by income level ranges of $10,000 or $20,000) and at the time, Rivera had no graphing calculators (they have since bought a classroom set).

But if individual data were available and we had calculators, I would have had groups of students input 500 pairs of data and inspect the graphs. In fact, I have had university math methods classes do similar work with graphing calculators, where they examined correlations of test scores of individual Chicago public schools with the percentage of low-income students in each school. At Rivera, due to circumstances, students made hand plots.

For the SAT, the raw data themselves make the correlation pretty clear (since the data set is so small), but the graphs students created made it even clearer to them. SAT scores go up in an almost lockstep correlation with family income. Students, who also saw Mexican Americans near the bottom of the listed racial groups and males above females, had plenty of questions.

In Part 2 of the project, I had students write letters to Educational Testing Service (ETS) about the data, asking any questions and making any points they wanted to. Their responses ranged, but many asked pointed (and sometimes confused) questions about inequality and about the interrelationships of race and class; some even expressed hope and trust in ETS to change what was obviously an unjust situation. Samples from two letters follow:

> Both the SAT's and the ACT's had a low score if their income was low. I think this really isn't giving anyone a chance. You see, what if you have a really smart student that only [has] an income of $9,000, would he/she not get much of an education? Is it just a stereotype or do you give a better education to people that pay more? If this is true, I hope you can make a change.
>
> I have noticed that the people and genders who have been "oppressed" are doing worse than the "whites." I have noticed that many books used at my curriculum (8th grade) have not been related to me in any way because I'm a Mexican American. I don't believe that they relate to anyone except "whites." For some reason I believe that's the reason, but not the whole reason ... Minorities—when you hear that word, what does it mean? It means poor African

SAT scores go up in an almost lockstep correlation with family income.

Americans, Mexican Americans, Puerto Ricans and other poor non-white people. You don't hear a lot about poor whites and minorities! You hear about rich whites. So who do you think has the high scores with the high salaries? Who? Why?

This story would not be complete without raising a few other issues. For three full class periods, we sat in a circle, and students read and discussed their letters with each other. This was difficult and emotional, since students saw themselves at the bottom of the data. But this was an honors class, and students were strongly college oriented. They wanted an answer to their key question: Why are we on the bottom?

I tried to help them understand that there were multiple, interconnected reasons: that schools in general and the tests in particular did not value (nor assess) their "cultural capital"— their home language, culture, ways of communicating, and experiences—but were instead geared to that of white, middle-class families. We talked about how schools in wealthier areas usually had more resources, smaller classes, more experienced teachers, and more challenging curricula, and that in the United States, the overall educational opportunities for urban students of color tended to be inferior compared to those of white students.

But some of these ideas were abstract to students who rarely experienced other communities or cultures, and we did not end the discussion with a definitive answer—nor was that my intent. While they understood that both race and class played a role—the data speak clearly to this—they continued to search and think, throughout the year, about the meaning of what they were learning.

And different students reached various levels of awareness, including some who tended to explain away what appeared to other students to be unjust situations (e.g., espousing the view that immigrants expected to be at the bottom in a new country to justify why Mexicans so often wound up with the jobs no one else wanted.)

Read the World

Paulo Freire, the noted Brazilian educator, stressed the idea of teaching students not only to read but to "read the world." In my lessons, I did not try to answer their questions about the world (nor could I always do so), because my focus was more on helping them develop the orientation to raise questions and critique rather than satisfying them with answers. But in this case, their reading of the world had the real potential to paralyze and demoralize them.

For three full class periods, we sat in a circle, and students read and discussed their letters with each other. This was difficult and emotional, since students saw themselves at the bottom of the data.?

This raises a question about the relationship of students reading the world to their self-perceptions and points out our responsibilities when we attempt to teach for social justice. That is, how do we help students develop a sense of agency, confidence, and determination while at the same time helping them learn about concrete examples of racism, classism, and injustice that may be outside their immediate experience? There is no room to address this here, but I leave readers with a comment from a student I taught for close to two years as she reflected on what she had learned at the end of our time together:

> With every single thing about math that I learned came something else. Sometimes I learned more of other things instead of math. I learned to think of fairness, injustices and so forth everywhere I see numbers distorted in the world. Now my mind is opened to so many new things. I'm more independent and aware. I have learned to be strong in every way you can think of it.

These examples may serve as food for thought as we consider how technology and mathematics—neither of which many of us immediately link to social justice—can be used to help students read the world and begin to make sense of things like racism and classism. Clearly, initial explorations should not serve as final explanations, as these are complex issues that even adults are often trying to make sense of and connect to other aspects of society. They cry out for further and ongoing investigations, to be returned to again and again. But the possibilities exist to help young people develop the orientation to seek ever-deeper answers to these types of questions, and we can take advantage of available technology and turn it to uses for social justice. Students, as young people and as they become adults, can and will raise their own voices in the world. Ultimately, it is how we structure society—for what purposes and in whose interests—that determines how science and technology are used.

How do we help students develop a sense of agency, confidence, and determination while at the same time helping them learn about concrete examples of racism, classism, and injustice that may be outside their immediate experience?

Bringing the Civil Rights Movement into the Classroom

By Larry Miller

When I taught a freshman citizenship class to all entering students at Metropolitan High School, a predominantly African American high school in Milwaukee, I included a five-week introduction to the history of the Civil Rights Movement. I felt strongly that students of every race should have an understanding of the rich history of struggle for equality in this country. We examined the tactics of the Southern Civil Rights movement, the Black Power movement as exemplified by the Black Panthers, and government repression against African Americans. We concluded the unit with a debate that represents the spectrum of opinion of 20th century African American leaders.

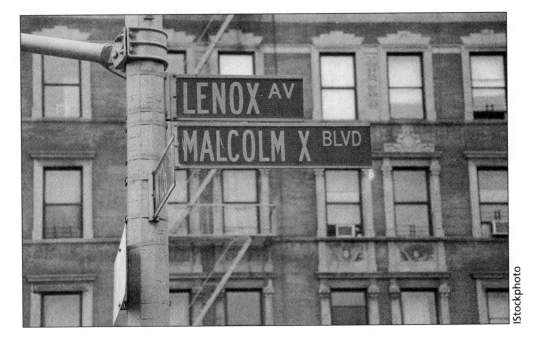

iStockphoto

Southern Struggles

I started by introducing students to some of the key battles in the South in the 1950s and 1960s. An invaluable resource throughout the unit was the *Eyes on the Prize* series, a two-part film documentary that begins with the Emmett Till murder in 1955 (see below) and goes through 1985. The first, *Eyes on the Prize: America's Civil Rights Years 1954-1965*, is a six-segment documentary that first aired on PBS. Eyes on the *Prize II: America at the Racial Crossroads, 1965-1985* is broken into eight parts of roughly one hour each. Both documentaries have extensive accompanying material in print.

I also used *Free at Last: A History of the Civil Rights Movement and Those Who Died in the Struggle*, a 104-page magazine-sized booklet that begins with a section on slavery and ends in the 1960s. It tells the history of the movement by focusing on individuals who gave their lives to the struggles in the 1950s and 1960s.

I edited selections from *Eyes on the Prize*, and kept the length of each segment between 10 and 20 minutes. I then followed with a reading from the booklet *Free at Last* that has a short description of each of the events just covered in the documentary.

Each day after showing the video segment and doing the reading, I held a discussion where I asked for students' impressions and thoughts. Then I had students write in their journals, giving their thoughts about what they just viewed, read, and discussed. I repeated my instructions for writing in journals each day, and I also wrote them on the board: "Don't just describe what you see or hear. Include your reactions and emotional responses, the questions the video and reading raise for you, and your thoughts on how you might have responded if you were there at the time." While students did this I walked around class and read their reactions as they finished.

Then at the beginning of class the next day I read from three or four of the journals, both to sum up discussions and spark new lines of inquiry. Here I talked to students about the tactics used in the particular struggles we are observing and studying.

One student, after seeing the brutality toward students sitting in at a lunch counter in Nashville, said, "I could never be nonviolent, turn the other cheek, and not hit back. It makes me mad just to hear about this. No way would I put up with it." This comment gave us a chance to discuss the philosophies of nonviolence of Gandhi and Martin Luther King Jr., and the role of nonviolent civil disobedience in the Civil Rights Movement. It also led to a discussion on anger. One Latina student said she felt angry when she heard about what happened to African Americans during that era. We talked about how all of us, no matter what our race, should be angry about injustices in our history.

The historical events we have studied in this unit so far are:

- The murder of 14-year-old Emmett Till in 1955 in Money, Miss. Till, who was from Chicago, violated the white supremacist codes of the time by—acting on a dare from another teenager—flippantly saying "Bye Baby" to a white store clerk as he left a country store. That weekend he was beaten, shot in the head, and dumped into the Tallahatchie River because, as the clerk's husband later said, "He thought he was as good as any white man." An all-white jury found the murderers "not guilty." (Shown in the "Awakenings 1954-1956" segment of *Eyes on the Prize* and on pages 40-41 of *Free at Last.*)

- The Montgomery bus boycott in 1955, in which Rosa Parks, the young Martin Luther King Jr., and many others joined a growing movement to end the Southern Jim Crow rule that blacks had to sit at the back of the bus. I use this section in particular to highlight the courage and resourcefulness of black communities. (Shown in the "Awakenings 1954-1956" segment of *Eyes on the Prize* and on pages 14-15 of *Free at Last.*)

- The lunch counter sit-ins in Nashville, Tenn., to demand that public accommodations such as restaurants and restrooms be open to African Americans. In one year alone, 70,000 people—mostly young people and college students—participated in sit-ins at public accommodations, and 3,600 were arrested. This section is especially useful to talk about the bravery of young activists and to explain the philosophy of nonviolence that was characteristic of many in the Civil Rights Movement. (Shown in the "Ain't Scared of Your Jails 1960-1961" segment of *Eyes on the Prize* and on pages 18-19 of *Free at Last.*)

- The Freedom Rides in 1961, in which journalists reported on the bus rides of whites and blacks who set off from Washington in a heroic action to test compliance with a court ruling outlawing the segregation of buses and terminals. Angry white mobs attacked the Freedom Riders as they disembarked from buses. The Freedom Rides, organized primarily by the Congress on Racial Equality (CORE), were one of the

One Latina student said she felt angry when she heard about what happened to African Americans during that era.

first times in which the Civil Rights Movement consciously used the power of the media, in this case mostly print journalists, to win people over to their cause. (Shown in the "Ain't Scared of Your Jails 1960-1961" segment of *Eyes on the Prize* and on pages 20-21 of *Free at Last.*)

- The Birmingham struggle in 1963 demanding jobs for blacks and an end to segregation in this key southern city. Protesters led by the Rev. Martin Luther King Jr. and the Southern Christian Leadership Conference were attacked by dogs and fire hoses under the orders of Police Chief Bull Connor. I note the movement's use of the television media, which brought the reality of southern bigotry directly into the living rooms of households across America. (Shown in the "No Easy Walk 1961-1963" segment of *Eyes on the Prize* and on pages 22-23 of *Free at Last.*)

- "Freedom Summer" in 1964, which highlights the work of the Student Nonviolent Coordinating Committee (SNCC) in Mississippi, pointing out the blatant and widespread violation of the voting rights of African Americans. The section brings us into the issue of voting rights and also focuses on the role of young organizers. (Shown in the "Mississippi: Is This America? 1962-1964" segment of *Eyes on the Prize* and on pages 26-30 of *Free at Last.*)

- The Selma march in 1965 that united SNCC, CORE, and the SCLC in the demand for voting rights and was instrumental in the passage of the Federal Voting Rights Act of that year. (Shown in the "Bridge to Freedom 1965" segment of *Eyes on the Prize* and on pages 30-31 of *Free at Last.*)

More on Southern Battles

I then showed the movie *Murder in Mississippi*, a made-for-TV movie that re-enacts the 1964 murders of three civil rights organizers who were preparing for Freedom Summer. (This movie should not be confused with the Hollywood version of these murders, *Mississippi Burning*, which glorifies and distorts the role of the FBI in the Civil Rights Movement, transforming it from a tool of government repression into the "white saviors" of embattled blacks.)

In this section, because it highlights voting rights and "Freedom Summer," I also had students take the 10-minute Louisiana Literacy Test, used to prevent African Americans from voting. I write on the chalkboard, "Spell backwards, forwards" and "Print the word vote upside down, but in the correct order." Students always respond with dismay, asking, "Why?" I explained that these are the types of questions African Americans were asked in Louisiana on literacy tests as they attempted to vote. By actually taking the test, the students were able to see how hard the state of Louisiana worked to stop the black community from voting.

The Black Panthers and Government Repression

Here I focused on the Black Panther Party. The Panthers were the target of a coordinated attack from police departments and the FBI. By looking at the Black Panther Party experience, students saw the extent to which local and federal government agencies were willing to go to suppress a militant urban movement of African Americans.

We started with a discussion of the Panther Ten Point Program (See *Rethinking Schools* Vol. 16, No. 1 or www.blackpanther.org.). Students then wrote reflections on each of the 10 points. I asked students to do this as homework because of the length of the 10 points. The following day students discussed their reflections and answer for each of the 10 points, "Does it have meaning today?"

Students generally agreed with the 10 points. But in one class, Naquandra expressed reservations about Panther point number 9, which calls for the release of all black men from jail because of the racist justice system. She stated, "The 10 points have a lot of meaning, even today. All black men have faced racism, but some are in jail for murder and rape. Some of them I don't want on the streets."

We then watched the section on the Panthers from *Eyes on the Prize*, which explains the origins of the Black Panther Party in Oakland and its focus on issues of police brutality and the creation of community programs to "serve the people." (Shown in "Power! 1966-1968" of *Eyes on the Prize II*.)

From here we watched the *Eyes on the Prize* section on the Chicago Panthers and the assassination of Fred Hampton by the FBI and Chicago police in 1969. The fact that the FBI played an open and direct role in Fred Hampton's death startled a number of students. This sets the stage to study the activity of the FBI and U.S. government toward black liberation leaders and organizations. (Shown in "A Nation of Law? 1968-1971" of *Eyes on the Prize II*.)

By looking at the Black Panther Party experience, students saw the extent to which local and federal government agencies were willing to go to suppress a militant urban movement of African Americans.

We looked at the FBI's infiltration, surveillance, and disruption of black leaders and organizations. Students read the article "J. Edgar Hoover and the Infiltration of Black Activists: a Comparison of FBI Surveillance of Marcus Garvey, Paul Robeson, and Martin Luther King," (See *Rethinking Schools'* website for details) which shows how the FBI paid people to disrupt organizations and spread derogatory information about peoples' personal lives to try to destroy the freedom struggle of African Americans. Included with it are biographies of the three leaders and primary documents from FBI records. Students, in groups, gave biographies of the three men discussed in the articles and the ways in which the FBI harassed them.

I then had students brainstorm responses to the question, "What are the ways that enemies of freedom movements can try to undermine them?" The list of responses always included buying people off, brutality, murdering leaders, jailing people, sabotage, subversion, lies, cowardice, denigration, complacency, eroding the base of support through the introduction of drugs, and the spreading of propaganda. I then went through the brainstorm list and asked students to give examples from our study.

Finally, I had students study the perspectives of a selection of African American leaders representing a spectrum of those who organized from as early as the turn of century through the 1960s. They debated each other representing those historical figures.

As the unit concluded, my students felt they had a more realistic picture of the history of this country.

As the unit concluded, my students felt they had a more realistic picture of the history of this country. One white student stated, "I was surprised to see that this country was not completely built on the Constitution. I realized that there is a lot of U.S. history to be angry about."

"This knowledge will help me with perseverance," wrote Shawanda. "I know I will have to overcome racism and prejudice. But instead of focusing on people's negatives I am going to focus on what I am going to be as a black woman. Right now I am using my education and hopefully someday I will be able to speak out for freedom as someone who is respected and strong. I don't think anybody can take that away from me."

'We Need to Know This!'

Student power and curriculum

By Jody Sokolower

Five minutes into the period, as I was explaining the industrialization project to my 10th-grade World History class, Tiffany had her hand in the air.

"It's almost the end of February and we haven't done anything about black history! Why don't we ever do anything about black people?" she demanded. A chorus of voices, all African American, backed her up.

"But we just finished studying Haiti," I protested. "Doesn't that count?"

"No!" they shouted. "This class is racist!"

IStockphoto

My mind was a jumble. On one hand, I could see my plans for the next months and my relationship with my history teaching partner shattering before my eyes. On the other hand, I knew they were getting at something really important.

As a white teacher, this accusation always hits me in the gut. My initial reaction was defensive—hadn't I started the year with a section on medieval Africa? Didn't I expand the curriculum to include more on the transatlantic slave trade and the Haitian revolution?

My mind was a jumble. On one hand, I could see my plans for the next months and my relationship with my history teaching partner shattering before my eyes. On the other hand, I knew they were getting at something really important—and that I needed to acknowledge the justice of their demand. I took a deep breath and promised to come back with a plan for discussing the issue.

"I can see three different approaches to adding more black content to the curriculum," I explained to both World History classes the next day. "We can look at what was happening to African Americans at each point in world history; we can focus more on African history; or we can look at what African American and African leaders were saying about world events. What do you think would be best?"

I was amazed at the discussions that resulted. No one asked which alternative would be less work, or more points. Students took the question seriously, listened to each other, and shared their frustration at their previous experiences with African history.

"I don't want to learn about slavery any more," said Rachelle, a conscientious and high-achieving African American student. "Every time we learn about black people, it's just about us being victims and it makes me feel terrible."

"What about Haiti?" I asked. "We learned about how Toussaint L'Ouverture led a successful revolution that created an independent country."

"I only remember the part about slavery," she responded.

"Every year we learn the same stuff about Rosa Parks and Martin Luther King—that's it," added another student.

After much discussion, the classes agreed that they wanted to focus on African history.

"We know less about Africa than anywhere else in the world," Emily, a white student, explained.

"OK," I agreed. "The next unit is on imperialism—that's the fight over land and resources before World War I. I'll look for information on the fight over Africa from an African perspective."

"I don't want to read a bunch of stuff that's just going to make me feel worse," Rachelle warned as the bell rang.

Rethinking History Teaching

As a college student in the late 1960s, discovering the historical truth behind the lies in my history books was a liberating and empowering experience. But most of my students see things differently. In the 1960s and '70s, revolutions around the world and boundless activism in the United States reinforced the connection between real history and social change. In the absence of that exciting tumult, many youth today experience the bitter truths of U.S. history as depressing—it only feeds their feelings of powerlessness and alienation. My African American students often express anger at a history where their ancestors are overwhelmingly portrayed as victims, relieved by a few pasteboard heroes.

I hoped that this unit, demanded by my students, would have a different effect. Their energy helped soothe my anxiety about falling even further behind in our race to finish all of world history by June. I revised my goals for the unit. To my original goal:

Students will demonstrate understanding of the Era of Imperialism in Africa, I added the following:

Students will begin to explore their stereotypes, thoughts, and feelings about Africa. (I hoped this would free students like Rachelle to look at the positive and negative aspects of African history.)

Students will analyze historical sources for point of view, including "bias by omission." (I wanted them to see that no historical source is neutral—textbook authors, like all historians, express a point of view.)

Students will recognize the power of articulating their own questions about history. (All students have "enduring questions" about the world and how it got to be this way— I hoped to validate those questions and bring them into the classroom.)

I started my research by looking for something to read that would enable us to talk about Africa—about the images of Africa in the media, and about the complicated relationship between African Americans and Africa. I chose the first chapter of *Mandela, Mobutu and Me*, by Lynne Duke, a young African American journalist covering Africa in the 1990s. In the first chapter, she talks about her feelings of connection and pride at Africa's beauty and strength, her angst about the level of brutality and corruption, her hope for the future.

As we read the chapter aloud, I asked students to keep a dialogue journal—noting quotes and images on one side of the

My African American students often express anger at a history where their ancestors are overwhelmingly portrayed as victims, relieved by a few pasteboard heroes.

paper, their reflections on the other. Almost every student in both classes completed the dialogue journal, including Ida, an English language learner from Brazil, who hadn't turned in a piece of written work all year, and Kyla, an African American student who had just transferred into my class and up to that point had kept her head buried in a book. Here are a few excerpts from Kyla's reflections:

> Lynne Duke and her co-workers were hecka brave to go to Africa. It was sad to read about the chaos that was going on there. I could tell how frustrated Lynne was getting from the blackouts, the food shortages, the violence that went on in the streets and just to see how Africa was in ruins. ... I didn't think that Africa was still in wars and stuff. I thought that Africa was like peaceful and full of fun and beauty. I didn't know about all the struggle and violence. ... I think she finished the chapters with the drummers on the boat because it was like symbolism. She said with each beat she was further away from despair and she called it her rhythm of salvation.

Maria, a white student, quoted Duke: "I thought of all the people, so many, many people, who had every reason, every right, to lose hope in Africa but did not" and then reflected: "These kinds of people amaze me. To some degree, I strive to be one of these people. Believing in something is what gets people through things. I want that."

Through African Eyes

Meanwhile, I began a search for Afrocentric (written from an African perspective) histories of African conflict with Europe from 1880 to 1918. I was appalled at how difficult it was to find anything at all. There were lots of histories of Africa, many of them anticolonial, but all of them quoted European historians and discussed the period from a European perspective. Eventually I found a brief section in Pan-African scholar John Henrik Clarke's *African People at the Crossroads: Notes for an African World Revolution* that described the fierce resistance mounted by dozens of African cultures against European intrusions.

Before we read the Clarke, I had my students read the section on "The Age of Imperialism" in their McDougal Littell textbook, *Modern World History, Patterns of Interaction.* "Make a list of what you consider the most important facts," I told them. They compared their lists in small groups and we came up with a class list of main events and concepts.

There were lots of histories of Africa, many of them anticolonial, but all of them quoted European historians and discussed the period from a European perspective.

Then we turned to the Clarke reading. I had the students keep three running lists as we read the chapter aloud: important facts, personal reflections, and questions generated by the text.

I put the students into small groups and had them compare the two texts by answering the following questions:

What differences do you see between the two texts?

What are the strengths and weaknesses of the textbook?

What are the strengths and weaknesses of the Clarke?

What examples of point of view do you see in each text?

What questions do you have now?

"Look at this," a usually alienated white student named Eric shouted. "Clarke says Europeans always called African leaders chiefs instead of kings because they didn't want them compared to European kings. Right here in our textbook they call Shaka a Zulu chief!"

"I don't know," Molly, also white, said. "The Clarke seems awfully biased. How do we know what he says is true?"

"Clarke has so many examples of resistance movements and Europe didn't really control African land for that long," reasoned Elijah, one of the African American students who was angriest with me that first day. "But in the textbook it subtitles that whole section, 'Unsuccessful Movements.' That's cold."

Our discussion comparing the two texts was one of the most engaged and thoughtful of the whole year, and the quality and quantity of work I received was exceptional. It was the high point of the year for most of us.

Same Curriculum, Different Results

This year I taught World History again. At the appropriate point in the curriculum, I explained what happened in my class last year, and we studied the same texts in the same way. But the results were very different. Some students were interested in the readings, and students who were good at critical analysis wrote thoughtfully about the differences in perspectives and information. But the excitement was gone. It was an educational experience, but not an empowering one. Most importantly, it did nothing to support African American leadership in the class. The student demand to learn something that they needed to know was an essential part of the equation.

I have realized more and more as I teach history that progressive content is not enough. Teaching accurate, multicultural

The student demand to learn something that they needed to know was an essential part of the equation.

history doesn't necessarily have the impact on students that we, as progressive teachers, hope it will. If it's disconnected from students experiencing themselves as architects of their own education and makers of history, it often reinforces their feelings of cynicism and hopelessness about social change.

Being receptive to student need and allowing space for students to think about and express what they want to learn is critical to education as a liberating experience, as a component of social justice. It's more than offering a choice—would you rather create a diary or a graphic novel? It's creating an environment in the classroom where students will make demands. And it's listening, really listening, so we hear the demands and separate them out from the idle complaints.

The more substantive the choices we offer students, the more likely they are to articulate their ideas. (For example, "What should we do with the information we've learned about immigration—take a field trip to the capitol to lobby legislators or write letters to the editor? What ideas do you have?" And then, "What else do we need to learn before we do that?") But some of it I experience as a kind of letting go, of being open to what they have to say, being open to messing up my plans for something exciting and unscripted.

This is not an argument for spontaneity or against the importance of planning and perfecting curriculum over time. Developing strong curriculum takes an enormous amount of time and energy. The first few times I teach material, I realize the problems, try to fill the holes and inject more scaffolding. Carefully constructed units that have been honed through trial and error remain the backbone of effective teaching.

Finally, there are clear tradeoffs to this approach. We never did get past Vietnam that year, and student demands probably won't dovetail with state standards or the upcoming standardized test. But we each have to ask ourselves—in the final analysis, who are we answerable to? If we can help our students see that knowledge is power and that they have the right and the responsibility to demand the knowledge they need, it's a good day at school.

Being receptive to student need and allowing space for students to think about and express what they want to learn is critical to education as a liberating experience, as a component of social justice.

Resources

Clarke, John Henrik. *Africans at the Crossroads: Notes for an African World Revolution.* Trenton, New Jersey: Africa World Press, 1991.

Duke, Lynne. *Mandela, Mobutu and Me: A Newswoman's African Journey.* New York: Doubleday, 2003.

CHAPTER FORTY

Bias and CD-ROM Encyclopedias

By Bob Peterson

When our elementary school library got its CD-ROM encyclopedias, I hoped my 5th graders would use them for social studies research projects. Little did I know that they would become the basis of a broader project using math to explore racial and gender bias in educational materials.

As in many 5th grades, my students do a major research project on a famous American. Perhaps less typically, it has to be an American who has fought for justice, and "American" is defined to include people from Mexico and Puerto Rico (as many of my students are from those two places). I told my students

Bettmann/Corbis

Hulton-Deutsch Collection/Corbis

I feared that the new technology would add just one more source of information to be copied and plagiarized by uncritical and inexperienced researchers.

that in addition to biographies and encyclopedias, they'd be able to use the library's CD-ROM encyclopedia. They were excited. I was skeptical. I feared that the new technology would add just one more source of information to be copied and plagiarized by uncritical and inexperienced researchers.

During writing workshop, the students went in pairs to the library to look up information on their famous person, and to get a printout of the CD-ROM entry to be used as one of the sources for their report.

When the first two girls, Jade and Lafayette, returned from the library, they raised an issue that I hadn't thought about. Jade, who had chosen to write about Harriet Tubman, was upset that Lafayette's printout on Thomas Edison was four or five times longer than hers. (My immediate reaction was to question how Lafayette had concluded that Thomas Edison fit the criterion of a famous person who fought for justice, but she was determined to report on him so I let that matter drop.) When I asked Jade why she thought there was this difference her response was, "I don't know."

I asked Jade and Lafayette to quantify the difference somehow and to tell the rest of the class about their research during sharing time at the end of writing workshop. They reported that while there was less than 2 inches of information on Harriet Tubman, there was more than 10 inches on Thomas Edison. Some students thought this wasn't fair, but there were no profound insights as to the cause of the inequity. When I asked the class how we might find out why there was this disparity, a popular response was to ask the librarian. So we postponed further discussion until our next library visit a few days later.

During the next library visit, the librarian, Maggie Melvin, and I led a discussion that tried to get students to think more deeply about the nature of the information in the CD-ROM encyclopedia and other educational materials. We used Jade's concern as a jumping-off point. We taped to the wall the printouts on Harriet Tubman and Thomas Edison and asked the kids what they noticed and what they knew about the two individuals. The students agreed that both Edison and Tubman were dead and famous; that Edison was a white man who invented things, while Tubman was an African American woman abolitionist who fought for freedom.

Children came up with a variety of hypotheses to explain the length difference. Some thought that the CD-ROM makers "didn't know much about Harriet Tubman;" "didn't get much information about Harriet Tubman when they were little;" "had to meet a deadline and didn't have time to put Harriet Tubman in;" or that "maybe they were racist, so first they put in white inventors and then they added a little extra." Another student disagreed that the disparity was due to racism and suggested that it was because "Thomas Edison was a man and Harriet Tubman was a woman and maybe it was men who did the CD-ROM."

When one student suggested that perhaps inventors were more important than other people, a Puerto Rican girl disagreed. She argued that abolishing slavery "was more important than the light bulb." Another boy said that the disparity wasn't fair because "Harriet Tubman had to risk her life and did work that was more dangerous" than Edison's.

We then began a conversation about what criteria one should use to put people into the encyclopedia and how much should be written about them. Some kids thought "everybody should get treated the same," while others argued that those who helped people should get more space.

To broaden the discussion we taped on the wall two additional print-outs—bibliographies of books in our library on Thomas Edison and Harriet Tubman. Our school library had three or four times more books on Tubman than Edison. One student concluded from this that "the CD-ROM people are just making up for the difference in the amount of books we have at our school." This in turn led to a lengthy conversation about who makes decisions about educational resources. At our school, I told the kids, teachers have tried to make up for the lack of information about women and people of color in the mainstream libraries and encyclopedias by buying more books about those people. In fact, the availability of such biographies in the the school library was the way many of the kids came to choose their famous person in the first place.

We ended our conversation by asking students how we might find out if the accusations of racism or sexism were accurate. One student thought we should write to the CD-ROM makers and ask them, but most thought the company wouldn't be honest. Finally, it was agreed that two examples weren't enough, and that as a class we would chart the length of the printouts on all the famous people that we were studying, as well as the person's race and gender.

Over the next two weeks students recorded the length of entries for 30 different individuals on large chart paper on the classroom wall. Students were surprised to find that Felisa

At our school, teachers have tried to make up for the lack of information about women and people of color in the mainstream libraries and encyclopedias by buying more books about those people.

Rincón de Gautir, the first woman mayor of San Juan and a famous Puerto Rican leader, was not listed, nor were the 19th century African American journalist Ida B. Wells, Mexican American farmworker organizer Dolores Huerta, the first female chief of the Cherokee Nation Wilma P. Mankiller, or Puerto Rican scientist Maria Cordero Hardy. Two presidents, Abraham Lincoln and George Washington, had the longest entries, and others varied from 2 to 13 inches. (A complete list of people studied is at the end of the article.)

Analyzing the Data

I realized that a key tool in analyzing the data would be the concept of averages. So I worked with my student teacher Susan Hersh and math teacher Celín Perez to develop a mini-unit on averages. We built on the students' existing knowledge of averages—mainly involving sports and grades—and deepened their understanding by having them use counters and other physical objects. We also discussed and practiced using the formula for figuring out an average.

The students were ready to analyze the data. We prepared a sheet that helped students organize their work, then pairs of students chose different categories of people (white females, Mexican females, etc.) and found the average length of the entries in inches. They each calculated a number of groups and recorded their answers on chart paper in the front of the room. When pairs came up with different averages, they rechecked their work until they agreed.

After all the conceivable categories were calculated, we gathered as a group. I asked for observations. The students saw that the "white males got the most information" and "Puerto Rican females got nothing." Other observations included more specific comparisons: for example, that the information for males was "three times as long as information for females" and that "information for whites was three times as long as information for nonwhites."

We asked the children how they felt about what they had discovered. Some of the comments: "I feel very bad because the Puerto Ricans don't have much information;" "I hate it because it's not fair;" "Other kids might think that women don't do very many important things."

Other students weren't as upset and said: "We should not blame them [CD-ROM makers] for what they did. If we don't like it, just don't buy it and get a book." Others countered that the

The students saw that the 'white males got the most information' and 'Puerto Rican females got nothing.'

disparities were important because younger students would use the CD-ROM and not get sufficient information.

I asked how the students might present the information to other children in the school. They decided to make large wall graphs using sticky tape, which the children did in groups of four. The construction of the large graphs was difficult, as the average lengths ranged from 0 inches for Puerto Rican females to 28 inches for white males. The vibrant colors of the sticky tape made the finished products show quite clearly the bias that we had discovered in the CD-ROM.

Some students wanted to do more than just show other kids the results of their research. A couple suggested we visit the CD-ROM makers and tell them to change their encyclopedia. When the kids found that the company was based in California, that put a damper on that idea. Instead students role-played what they would have said and wrote letters to the company. The students wrote from the heart: "My name is Alfonso and you made me and kids in my classroom mad. You discriminated against people that are ladies and nonwhites;" "I am a Puerto Rican student at Fratney Street School and I did not like what you gave Puerto Rican people on the CD-ROM encyclopedia." Some wrote in Spanish: "No es justo que haiga más información sobre hombres que mujeres." [It is not just that you had more on men than on women]; "Women and men of all cultures should be treated fairly!" wrote another. One student threatened, "You better do something about it before I take you to court."

One student who didn't think writing to the company would do much good wrote to the superintendent of the school district instead, informing him of our investigation. He wrote: "The purpose of this letter is to try to get the people who buy or make this program to either stop making it or to change the information. This might not matter to me cause I'm going to 6th grade next year and my new school doesn't have a CD-ROM system in their computers. But this matters to the kids who are going to get the information from this encyclopedia in the future." He went on to suggest that "the school system not buy any more CD-ROM encyclopedias from this company."

'My name is Alfonso and you made me and kids in my classroom mad. You discriminated against people that are ladies and nonwhites.'

Problems and Lessons

The whole project took several weeks and involved a great deal of discussion. It was not part of my preplanned curriculum. The fact that the project was initiated by students' concerns about the learning materials in the school was positive and provided important motivation. It fit well into our school district's K-12 Learning Goal #1, that "students will project anti-racist, anti-biased attitudes" and "analyze, critique, and assess bias in all forms of communication." It also gave the students a chance to act on their concerns.

In retrospect the project had some serious shortcomings. First, while we were looking at one aspect of bias in the CD-ROM encyclopedia, we barely approached the larger, more important issue: the content of the information itself. While I encouraged children to look out for stereotypes or misinformation in the text, with a limited knowledge base this type of critique is difficult at the elementary school level. Students found some incongruities with other sources of information—for example, with the dates given for the births of Nat Turner and Harriet Tubman. But it was usually only when I pointed out that the encyclopedia selection omitted something that the students became aware of potential content problems.

Earlier in the year we had spent time analyzing children's books that dealt with Christopher Columbus—whose voice was being heard and whose was being silenced, what was being omitted in books, etc. While that experience might have helped spur Jade and Lafayette into questioning the new learning materials they encountered, it did little to prepare kids to critique encyclopedia sections, or even come up with ways of thinking about the issue beyond the question of omission and voice.

Another problem was that our statistical approach was far from accurate. Our sampling was limited, and the inclusion of the two presidents weighted the statistics in favor of white men. Nonetheless, the students gained experience in collecting data, manipulating it, and looking at it through the lens of race and gender, something that isn't readily encouraged in most texts and curricula. Similar projects could be done by looking at traditional encyclopedias, or by analyzing the racial and gender composition of the biographical books in a school library.

Finally, the project raised several questions that we didn't fully answer: Who makes the decisions for CD-ROM encyclopedias? What criteria are used for the inclusion or exclusion of people? What criteria should be used?

Because this project was started near the end of the school year, such questions were raised, but left unanswered. With more time I could have had students develop their own criteria for inclusion in encyclopedias. Then they might have tried to use such criteria to rank the famous people they had studied. We

> *While I encouraged children to look out for stereotypes or misinformation in the text, with a limited knowledge base this type of critique is difficult at the elementary school level.*

might have organized a debate or role play, with students representing different groups of people arguing for their inclusion.

But even with these shortcomings, lessons were learned. One was that even something as sophisticated and flashy as a CD-ROM encyclopedia cannot always be trusted as an "objective" source of information. Students need to find multiple sources of information, and read everything with a healthy dose of skepticism.

A second important lesson was that mathematics can be an effective tool, like written and oral language, in the fight against injustice and discrimination. Knowing how to figure out things like averages and percentages, being able to use mathematical data in arguments, and making clear graphs became more than just preparation for next year's math class, but a means by which one can help figure out and change the world.

Author's Note:

The famous people chosen for study by the students included: Harriet Tubman, Thomas Edison, Felisa Rincón de Gautir, Abraham Lincoln, Langston Hughes, César Chávez, George Washington, Jackie Robinson, Roberto Clemente, Nat Turner, Helen Keller, Wilma Mankiller, Ida B. Wells, Emiliano Zapata, the Wright Brothers, Martin Luther King Jr., Malcolm X, Sitting Bull, General Custer, Frederick Douglass, Juana Ines de la Cruz, Susan B. Anthony, Amelia Earhart, John Brown, María Cordero Hardy, Dolores Huerta, Benito Juarez, Marie Curie, Sojourner Truth, Diego Rivera, and Miguel Hidalgo.

The CD-ROM encyclopedia analyzed by my class is the Multimedia Encyclopedia, published by Software Toolworks, of Novato, Calif. Since my students looked at this encyclopedia, I have looked at the even-flashier Grolier's Multimedia Encyclopedia and Microsoft's Encarta. While I have not had time to review these encyclopedias, I did repeat the original activity that led to the classroom project described above. In both cases Edison has about five times more text than Tubman, and neither encyclopedia had articles on Ida B. Wells, Felisa Rincón de Gautir, Dolores Huerta, or Maria Cordero Hardy.

Author Bios

Wayne Au, a former high school social studies and language arts teacher, is a *Rethinking Schools* editor and an Assistant Professor in the Department of Secondary Education at California State University, Fullerton. Most recently he is author of *Unequal By Design: High-Stakes Testing and the Standardization of Inequality* (Routledge, 2009) and co-editor of *The Routledge International Handbook of Critical Education* (Routledge, 2009).

Harold Berlak is an educational researcher and writer residing in Oakland, Calif. He holds a master of arts in teaching and doctorate in educational research from the Harvard Graduate School of Education. He is a former teacher, teacher of teachers, and professor at Washington University in St. Louis. He writes about curriculum, learning, and assessment policy. He edited and coauthored *Toward a New Science of Educational Testing and Assessment* (SUNY Press, 1992).

Berta Rosa Berriz, Ed.D., was born in Cuba. She is a National Board Certified (2006) bilingual teacher, National Faculty at Lesley University, a dancer, a writer, and storyteller. Her doctoral research at Harvard Graduate School of Education (2005) investigated the relationship between the cultural identity of Puerto Rican and Dominican second-generation students and their teachers' assessment of their academic performance. Her current work within Boston Public Schools is 5th Grade Sheltered English Immersion Teacher at the Sumner Elementary School in Roslindale, Mass.

Bill Bigelow is curriculum editor of *Rethinking Schools* magazine. He began teaching high school social studies in Portland, Ore. in 1978 and is author of *A People's History for the Classroom*.

Patty Bode is Director of Art Education for Tufts University in affiliation with The School of the Museum of Fine Arts, Boston. Before Patty became a teacher educator for Tufts/SMFA, she was an art teacher in public schools for 16 years, and in summers she directed an arts camp for teens for nine years. She holds an Ed.D. from University of Massachusetts Amherst with a concentration in Language, Literacy and Culture. She is co-author with Sonia Nieto of the 5th edition of *Affirming Diversity: The Sociopolitical Context of Multicultural Education*.

Benji Chang is a former teacher in the Los Angeles Unified School District, current doctoral candidate in the Graduate School of Education at the University of California, Los Angeles, and is involved in community organizing work in Los Angeles' Chinatown.

Linda Christensen is director of the Oregon Writing Project at Lewis and Clark College in Portland, Ore. She is an editor of *Rethinking Schools* and author of *Reading, Writing, and Rising Up.*

Lisa D. Delpit, an award-winning author, scholar, and teacher, is currently the Executive Director/Eminent Scholar for the Center for Urban Education & Innovation at Florida International University, Miami, Florida.

Lisa Espinosa is a teacher, healer and writer. She has taught on the South Side of Chicago for nine years.

Salvador Galbadon is a Language Acquisition Specialist with the Language Acquisition Department for Tuscon Unified School District in Arizona.

Eric (Rico) Gutstein teaches mathematics education at the University of Illinois-Chicago. He has taught middle and high school mathematics, is a founding member of Teachers for Social Justice (Chicago), is the author of *Reading and Writing the World with Mathematics: Toward a Pedagogy for Social Justice* (Routledge, 2006) and the co-editor of *Rethinking Mathematics: Teaching Social Justice by the Numbers* (Rethinking Schools, 2005).

Denise Hanson-Rautiainen teaches at West High School in Madison, Wis.

Asa Hilliard, now deceased, was the author of numerous books and articles on education, particularly the education of African American children.

Stan Karp taught English and Journalism to high school students in Paterson, N.J. for 30 years. He is currently Director of the Secondary Reform Project for New Jersey's Education Law Center and an editor for Rethinking Schools. He is a co-editor of several books, including *Rethinking Our Classrooms: Teaching for Equity and Justice*, and *Rethinking School Reform: Views from the Classroom.*

Stephen Krashen is best known for developing the first comprehensive theory of second language acquisition, introducing the concept of sheltered subject matter teaching, and as the co-inventor of the Natural Approach. He has contributed to theory and application in the areas of bilingual education and reading. His current books are *Summer Reading: Program and Evidence* (with Fay Shin, published by Allyn and Bacon), *English Learners in American Classrooms* (with Jim Crawford, published by Scholastic), and *English Fever* (Crane Publishing Company, Taipei).

Enid Lee is the director of Enidlee Consultants Inc., a Toronto-based consultancy dedicated to anti-racist education and organizational change. She has over 35 years' experience in the classroom and is the former supervisor of race/ethnic relations for the North York Board of Education in metropolitan Toronto. Her publications include *Letters to Marcia: A Teacher's Guide to Anti-racist Education*, and *Beyond Heroes and Holidays: A Practical Guide to K–12, Anti-racist, Multicultural Education and Staff Development*, which she co-edited. She is currently a Visiting Scholar with Teaching for Change in Washington, D.C., and formerly held the same position at The New Teacher Center, University of California at Santa Cruz.

Kate Lyman has been teaching kindergarten through 3rd grade in the Madison, Wisconsin School District for 33 years. She has a master's degree from University of Wisconsin with a focus on multicultural Education and has done further course work on teaching English language learners. She is committed to including social justice issues in her curriculum and enjoys spending time outdoors with her family and her three rescued dogs.

Peter McLaren is Professor of Education, Graduate School of Education and Information Studies, University of California, Los Angeles. An educational activist, he is the author of the award-winning *Life in Schools* and numerous other books in the field of critical pedagogy and multicultural education. His writings have been translated into 20 languages.

Larry Miller taught in Milwaukee Public Schools for 18 years. He is presently an adjunct professor at Marquette University and National Louis University and a candidate for School Board for Milwaukee Public Schools.

Barbara Miner is a Milwaukee-based journalist. She is a columnist for the education magazine *Rethinking Schools* and writes for a variety of publications, from the *Milwaukee Journal Sentinel* to the *Progressive*. She has co-edited a number of books on education, from the award-winning *Rethinking Columbus* in 1991 to, most recently, *Keeping the Promise?: The Debate Over Charter Schools* .

Laura Linda Negri-Pool has worked in the field of early childhood education for more than 30 years. Her work experiences have included Head Start, Early Head Start, private child care, and teaching community college. She is Education Coordinator for Nike Child Development Programs in Beaverton, Ore.

Bob Peterson is a 5th-grade teacher at La Escuela Fratney in Milwaukee, Wis., and a co-founder of *Rethinking Schools.*

Steven Picht-Trujillo is a Spanish teacher at Valencia High School in Placentia, Calif.

Kelley Dawson Salas is a *Rethinking Schools* editor. She is on childbearing leave from her 4th-grade teaching position at La Escuela Fratney in Milwaukee, Wis.

Alejandro Segura-Mora is a facilitator and founder of Mind Growers, a consulting organization dedicated to helping schools close the racial achievement gap and lead all students to excellence. He may be reached at Ale@MindGrowers.com.

Christine Sleeter is is Professor Emerita in the College of Professional Studies at California State University, Monterey Bay. Formerly a high school learning disabilities teacher in Seattle, before moving to California she was a faculty member at Ripon College in Wisconsin and at the University of Wisconsin-Parkside. Her research focuses on anti-racist multicultural education and multicultural teacher education. Her books include *Un-Standardizing Curriculum* (Teachers College Press), Facing Accountability in Education (Teachers College Press) and *Doing Multicultural Education for Achievement and Equity* (with Carl Grant; Routledge).

Nathaniel W. Smith, Ph.D. is a lecturer at the University of Pennsylvania's Graduate School of Education, where he teaches courses in diversity, intercultural communication, and urban teacher certification.

Geneva Smitherman. Dr. Geneva Smitherman (aka "Dr. G.") is University Distinguished Professor of English at Michigan State University (MSU). A linguist and educational activist, she has been at the forefront of the struggle for language rights for over 25 years. Dr. G is author of several books including, *Word from the Mother: Language and African Americans* (Routledge, 2006). *Talkin That Talk* (Routledge, 2000) and *Talkin and Testifyin* (Wayne State University Press, 1986).

Jody Sokolower is an educator and a longtime anti-imperialist activist from Berkeley, Calif. She has many years of experience teaching middle school, high school and adult learners.

Alan Stoskopf is a Senior Fellow for Social Sciences and the Humanities in the School of Education at Northeastern University. He is currently part of an international team of researchers designing a new cross-cultural measure evaluating how students' make meaning of history.

Paola Suchsland is a Spanish teacher at Valencia High School in Placentia, Calif.

Joseph Suina retired from the University of New Mexico faculty in 2006. He now devotes himself entirely to farming, family, and the Cochiti tribal council. His writings have appeared in the journal, *Anthropology & Education Quarterly*, and the book, *Native Heritage*, among others.

Carol A. Tateishi is Director of the Bay Area Writing Project, a University of California at Berkeley program dedicated to improving the teaching of writing in Bay Area schools.

Rita Tenorio, a founding editor of *Rethinking Schools*, is currently the principal at La Escuela Fratney, a two-way bilingual elementary school in Milwaukee, Wis., that she helped start and has taught at since 1988. In 1990, Rita was named the Wisconsin Elementary Teacher of the Year.

Heidi Tolentino lives in Portland, Ore. She teaches English at Cleveland High School, an urban school in the Portland Public School District.

Sören Wuerth lives in Ketchikan, Alaska. An earlier version of his article appeared in the online site insurgent 49.

Index

RETHINKING SCHOOLS
FOUR EASY WAYS TO ORDER

❶ **CALL TOLL-FREE: 1-800-669-4192 8am-9pm (ET) M-F**
❷ **SECURE ONLINE ORDERING: www.rethinkingschools.org**
❸ **FAX ORDER FORM TO: 802-864-7626**
❹ **MAIL ORDER FORM TO: Rethinking Schools, P.O. Box 2222, Williston, VT 05495**

MASTERCARD, VISA AND PURCHASE ORDERS ACCEPTED

Name _____

Organization _____

Address _____

City/State/Zip_____

Phone _____

E-mail _____

METHOD OF PAYMENT

☐ Check or money order made payable to Rethinking Schools
☐ Purchase order   ☐ MasterCard   ☐ Visa

Credit Card No. _____

Exp. Date _____

Authorized Signature_____

QTY	TITLE/ITEM	UNIT PRICE	TOTAL

MAIL: Rethinking Schools, P.O. Box 2222
Williston, VT 05495
FAX: **802-864-7626**
CALL: **1-800-669-4192 FOR A FREE CATALOG
OF ALL OUR MATERIALS**

Subtotal	$
Shipping	$
Donation	$
TOTAL	$

* U.S. shipping and handling costs are 15% of the total
(minimum charge of $4.00). Canadian shipping and handling costs
are 25% of the total (minimum charge of $5.00).
Subscriptions already include shipping costs. Payment in U.S. dollars.

2BREMU

If you liked *Rethinking Multicultural Education,*
then *Rethinking Schools* magazine is for you!

Take advantage of this special discount coupon to receive
the country's leading social justice education magazine.

INTRODUCTORY OFFER!
Subscribe today and save!

"A teacher's close friend –
insightful, intelligent, and
compassionate."
Michele Forman
2001 Teacher of the Year

☐ **$22.95** Two-year subscription *(Save $24.65 off the cover price!)*
☐ **$14.95** One-year subscription *(Save $8.85 off the cover price!)*

☐ Please send me a free catalog of all your materials.
☐ Bill me.
☐ Enclosed is my check payable to Rethinking Schools.

Name _____

Organization _____

Address _____

City/State/Zip _____

Phone _____

E-mail _____

RETHINKING SCHOOLS
P.O. Box 2222, Williston, VT 05495 • toll-free: 800-669-4192 • fax: 802-864-7626

2BREMU

INTRODUCTORY OFFER!
Subscribe today and save!

"Absolutely the best,
most important education
publication in the country."
Jonathan Kozol

☐ **$22.95** Two-year subscription *(Save $24.65 off the cover price!)*
☐ **$14.95** One-year subscription *(Save $8.85 off the cover price!)*

☐ Please send me a free catalog of all your materials.
☐ Bill me.
☐ Enclosed is my check payable to Rethinking Schools.

Name _____

Organization _____

Address _____

City/State/Zip _____

Phone _____

E-mail _____

RETHINKING SCHOOLS
P.O. Box 2222, Williston, VT 05495 • toll-free: 800-669-4192 • fax: 802-864-7626

2BREMU

NO POSTAGE
NECESSARY
IF MAILED
IN THE
UNITED STATES

BUSINESS REPLY MAIL
FIRST-CLASS MAIL   PERMIT NO.2222   WILLISTON VT

POSTAGE WILL BE PAID BY ADDRESSEE

RETHINKING SCHOOLS
PO BOX 2222
WILLISTON VT 05495-9940

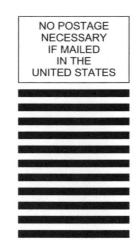

NO POSTAGE
NECESSARY
IF MAILED
IN THE
UNITED STATES

BUSINESS REPLY MAIL
FIRST-CLASS MAIL   PERMIT NO.2222   WILLISTON VT

POSTAGE WILL BE PAID BY ADDRESSEE

RETHINKING SCHOOLS
PO BOX 2222
WILLISTON VT 05495-9940